❖   Abortion Politics, Women's Movements,
and the Democratic State

Juniata College
Beeghly Library

Aaron and Clara Rabinowitz
Memorial Library Fund

Gender and Politics represents the most recent scholarship in the areas of women, gender, and politics, and is explicitly cross-national in its organization. Recognizing the contribution of women's studies to gendered political analysis, the goal of *Gender and Politics* is to develop, and to publish, frontier analysis, the empirical research exemplary of the inter-section between political studies.

The series is edited by Professor Karen Beckwith at the Department of Political Science, College of Wooster and Professor Joni Lovenduski, Department of Politics, University of Southampton.

Other books in the series:

Gender and Welfare State Regimes
Edited by Diane Sainsbury

Theorizing Feminist Policy
Amy Mazur

Women's Access to Political Power in Post-Communist Europe
Edited by Kathleen Montgomery and Richard Matland

❖ Abortion Politics, Women's Movements, and the Democratic State

A Comparative Study of State Feminism

Edited by
DOROTHY MCBRIDE STETSON

OXFORD
UNIVERSITY PRESS

This book has been printed digitally and produced in a standard specification
in order to ensure its continuing availability

OXFORD
UNIVERSITY PRESS

Great Clarendon Street, Oxford OX2 6DP

Oxford University Press is a department of the University of Oxford.
It furthers the University's objective of excellence in research, scholarship,
and education by publishing worldwide in

Oxford New York

Auckland   Cape Town Dar es Salaam Hong Kong Karachi
Kuala Lumpur Madrid Melbourne Mexico City Nairobi
New Delhi Shanghai Taipei Toronto
With offices in
Argentina Austria Brazil Chile Czech Republic France Greece
Guatemala Hungary Italy Japan South Korea Poland Portugal
Singapore Switzerland Thailand Turkey Ukraine Vietnam

Oxford is a registered trade mark of Oxford University Press
in the UK and in certain other countries

Published in the United States
by Oxford University Press Inc., New York

ISBN 0-19-924266-6

❖ Preface

At first glance, this book looks like an edited collection of separate case studies pertaining to abortion politics in different countries. Such an impression would be incorrect. It is true that readers will learn a great deal about current abortion laws and how they have changed since the 1970s. Nevertheless, the publication of *Abortion Politics, Women's Movements, and the Democratic State: A Comparative Study of State Feminism* offers something quite different from the usual anthology: a comprehensive and integrated research project in comparative policy analysis. The introduction presents the research design, the country chapters deliver the data, and the conclusion reports and analyzes the findings. As such, the purpose of the work is to contribute to the development of an empirically vetted theory of state feminism, that is, systematically related generalizations explaining the activities and effectiveness of state agencies established to promote women's status and rights.

The authors in this book are members of the Research Network on Gender, Politics, and the State (RNGS). The publication in 1995 of an earlier work, *Comparative State Feminism*, edited by Dorothy McBride Stetson and Amy G. Mazur, was the stimulus for formation of this network. *Comparative State Feminism* is an edited collection of case studies of women's policy machineries, defined as 'state structures established to advance the status of women'. State feminist machineries referred to 'those agencies that concretely achieve their formal charge in some way' (Stetson and Mazur 1995: 5). In that book, each author wrote her chapter following a common outline. In the final chapter, the editors attempted to reach some conclusions about where state feminist machineries were found and why. The contributing authors were disappointed that the outline did not provide comparable and convincing evidence to determine where women's policy agencies improved the status of women and why.

Thanks to a National Science Foundation International Programs Grant (#9411142), the Joint Workshop on the Comparative Study of State Feminism was held in July, 1995, in Leiden, the Netherlands. The meeting brought together contributors to *Comparative State Feminism* and others interested in finding a way to answer the question: does state feminism exist? RNGS was formed in Leiden, and since that meeting more than 40 scholars from the US, Canada, and Europe have joined what has become a cross-national longitudinal study of policy-making processes in 15 countries plus the European Union. Through a series of collaborative meetings, these scholars developed a research project design intended to produce a comprehensive picture of the activities of women's policy agencies in advanced industrial democracies. The design fuses strands from theories of social movements, especially the little-studied question of movement impact on the state, as well as comparative policy, new institutionalism, and democratic representation.

The study of state feminism focuses on policy activities of the state. In the initial work, *Comparative State Feminism*, comparisons were made in agency activities in only one area: equal opportunity policy (EOP). This turned out to be one of the weaknesses of that work because selecting EOP did not take into account national variations in the mandates of the agencies or salience of that issue. At Leiden the researchers decided to do a more comprehensive study by investigating five different issue areas: job training; abortion; prostitution/traffic in women; political representation; and an issue of national priority we call the 'hot' issue.

Along with the development of the design, RNGS was organized to execute a detailed research plan. At first, experts in women and public policy volunteered to direct the research in each country. Country directors then recruited scholars to take responsibility for studying women's policy agency activities in each of the five issue areas. As we moved from design to data gathering, RNGS organized into issue networks composed of all the scholars working on a particular issue and headed by a network director. The authors in this book are members of the abortion issue network. As network director, I had responsibility for planning the book, setting the deadlines, bringing all chapters into compliance with the RNGS research design, and drafting the analytical conclusion. Although these tasks were necessary to bring the work to completion, I want to emphasize that this book, like all the RNGS activities, would not have been possible without the difficult collaborative work of a wonderful group of authors: Regina Köpl, Karen Celis, Melissa Haussman, Jean Robinson, Lynn Kamenitsa, Evelyn Mahon, Marina Calloni, Joyce Outshoorn, and Celia Valiente.

This book is the second of five envisioned by the RNGS project. The first, *State Feminism, Women's Movements*, and *Job Training Policy in the Global Economy: Making Democracies Work*, published in 2001 under the direction of Amy G. Mazur, reported on the findings of the job training network. Future volumes will cover prostitution and traffic in women with director Joyce Outshoorn, political representation with director Joni Lovenduski, and the 'hot' issue coordinated by Melissa Haussman and Birgit Sauer.

The entire RNGS project is dependent on finding space and place, time, and, of course, resources, to come together to solve problems and share research. In this work, we have benefited from the assistance of a number of organizations. The American Political Science Association annual conference organizers welcomed us to convene workshops; especially significant was the workshop on studying gender in comparative politics held in 1996 in San Francisco. The abortion network presented initial research findings on an APSA panel in Boston in 1998. Since Leiden, RNGS has held full meetings at CREDEP of the University of Paris in 1998 and at Southampton University/Chilworth Centre in 1999. The Southampton meeting was funded by a generous grant from the European Science Foundation.

RNGS has been able to sustain what will be a ten-year collaboration of more than 40 scholars across 15 countries over five issues due to many factors, not the least of which are advances in electronic communication. However, I know that our chances of success and my own capacity to keep the network going would have been nil without the work of my RNGS co-convener, Amy G. Mazur of Washington State University. She shares her energy, commitment, and friendship with all members of our network. I have benefited greatly from our partnership.

Dorothy McBride Stetson

March 2001

❖ Contents

❖ List of Figures

❖ List of Tables

❖ Notes on Contributors

Marina Calloni is Professor of Philosophy of Social Sciences at the University of Milan-Bicocca and coordinator of the International Network for Research on Gender at the Gender Institute of the London School of Economics and Political Science. She is author of *Democrazie e teorie di fronte all'aborto* and *Uno sguardo 'diverso': Reflessioni su filsofia, scienze sociali e studi di genere.*

Karen Celis specialized in Women's Studies as a student at the University of Antwerp. She is completing her Ph.D. at the Department of Political Sciences at the Free University of Brussels where she has received a special doctoral grant from the Fund for Scientific Research–Flanders to complete her dissertation: 'Looking after Women's Issues by the Belgian Parliament, 1880–1980'.

Melissa Haussman is Assistant Professor in the Department of Government at Suffolk University, Boston, Massachusetts. She received her Ph.D. from Duke University specializing in Canadian-US comparative politics and is author of 'The Relationship of Abortion Law to Gender: Canadian Experiences of Reform, 1969–1991' in *International Journal of Canadian Studies.*

Lynn Kamenitsa is Associate Professor of Political Science and Women's Studies at Northern Illinois University. She is author of 'Equality Offices in Eastern Germany: Does Institutionalization Help Marginalized Groups?' in *German Politics and Society* and 'The Process of Political Marginalization: East German Social Movements After the Wall' in *Comparative Politics.*

Regina Köpl is Assistant Professor of Political Science at the University of Vienna. She received her Ph.D. from the University of Vienna and a post-graduate diploma from the Institute of Advanced Studies, Vienna, and is author of articles and research reports on feminism and women's organizations in Austria.

Evelyn Mahon is Senior Lecturer in Sociology at Trinity College Dublin where she is Director of the M.Sc. in Applied Social Research. An active policy-oriented sociologist, she has conducted research and published on gender and work and on social inequalities. She was Research Director (1995–7) of the Women and Crisis Pregnancy in Ireland study commissioned by the Department of Health and coauthor of its final report.

JOYCE OUTSHOORN is Professor of Women's Studies, Director of the Joke Smit Centre for Research in Women's Studies, and a member of the Department of Political Science at Leiden University, the Netherlands. She has written extensively on the women's movement, women's public policy, and abortion politics including *The New Politics of Abortion* (1986) coedited with Joni Lovenduski, and, most recently, 'Abortion in the Netherlands: the Successful Pacification of a Controversial Issue' in *Regulating Morality* (2000).

JEAN C. ROBINSON is Associate Professor of Political Science and dean for Women's Affairs at Indiana University. Originally a China specialist, she has also done comparative research on women's policy machinery in Poland and France and is conducting a comparative study of RU-486.

DOROTHY MCBRIDE STETSON is Professor of Political Science and Associate Dean of the Dorothy F. Schmidt College of Arts and Letters at Florida Atlantic University in Boca Raton. She is author of *Women's Rights in the USA: Policy Conflicts and Gender Roles* (1997) and coeditor of *Abortion Politics: Public Policy in Comparative Perspective* (1996) with Marianne Githens and *Comparative State Feminism* (1995) with Amy G. Mazur.

CELIA VALIENTE is Lecturer in the Department of Political Science and Sociology at the Universidad Carlos III de Madrid. Her main research interests are public policies and social movements in Spain with an analytical focus on gender and is author of 'The Power of Persuasion: The *Instituto de la Mujer* in Spain' is *Comparative State Feminism* (1995) and 'State Feminism and Gender Equality Policies: The Case of Spain 1983–95' in *Sex Equality Policy in Western Europe* (1997).

1 ❖ Introduction: Abortion, Women's Movements, and Democratic Politics

Dorothy McBride Stetson

Is there really such a thing as 'state feminism'? A provocative question, certainly, especially for those who see it as an oxymoron. How can the state, representing the institutional power of a male-dominated social hierarchy, promote goals that will undermine its own power? Yet, for over 30 years, women's movements have sought to influence the state to use that institutional power to reach feminist goals and to open the state to access by women. At the same time, governments in advanced industrial democracies have put institutional machineries in place to improve the status of women. These machineries have taken a variety of forms, and they are ubiquitous and enduring (Stetson and Mazur 1995). The research described in this book addresses the role of these institutional actors inside the state—women's policy agencies—in advancing the goals of women's movements in advanced industrial democracies.[1]

This research enterprise is a cooperative effort of the authors.[2] We have opted to study the issue of abortion in order to understand the role of institutional actors inside the state in advancing the goals of women's movements in eleven countries in Western Europe and North America. Demands for changes in long-standing abortion laws, second-wave women's movements, and new women's-policy agencies all entered the public policy arenas of democratic governments around the same time. Policy actors faced growing discontent with restrictions on access to abortion and looked for solutions to the ensuing conflict. Interest in abortion-policy reform occupied all women's movements; in many, expanding access to abortion was the only goal that could unify disparate wings, from radical feminists in autonomous groups on the one hand to well-established traditional women's organizations on the other. At the time when women's movements were gaining public attention and contests over abortion reform were heating up, women's policy agencies—many newly established—were testing the limits of their mandates to improve the status of women. The convergence of these events makes the abortion issue an especially good subject for the study of state feminism.

Our interest in abortion politics is not limited to these periods of initial reform and legalization which took place in most countries in the 1970s and early 1980s. This project is a *longitudinal* analysis of women's movements' involvement with the state on the abortion issue, covering the life of the issue from its initial appearance on the public agenda to the latest important debates. It is also a *comparative* study of abortion policy debates, presented in twelve chapters in addition to this introduction covering Austria, Belgium, Canada, France, Germany, Great Britain, Ireland, Italy, Netherlands, Spain, the US, and a comparative conclusion.

Readers of this book will find lots of information about the impact of the women's movements on the content of abortion policies and the extent to which the women's policy agencies were their allies, advocates, or adversaries, or ignored their concerns altogether. While the content of the laws is important, it is not the most significant feature of the movements' impacts in the last decades. Their effect on the *policy-making process* is likely to be the most lasting. The authors use the story of abortion politics to gather essential data about the extent to which women's policy agencies have interceded on behalf of movement activists in opening up the policy process to women, in other words contributing to making political systems more democratic and inclusive.

Since this is a comparative project, we expected to find variations in the activities and characteristics of women's policy agencies and the impact of women's movements on making these democracies more democratic. Cases are discrete abortion policy debates, and they vary among themselves as well as cross-nationally and over time. In expectation of this, researchers gathered information about the context of abortion policy debates that may explain these variations, including the policy environments and the characteristics of women's movements.

The main focus of this work is the intervention of women's policy agencies, on behalf of women's movements, in opening up the political process to women. Along the way, however, a number of other intriguing questions about abortion politics will be considered. Why is the abortion issue more contentious in some countries and apparently settled in others? When is abortion a partisan issue? Are socialist parties allies of women's movements on this issue? Is there a feminist position on the abortion issue common across the different countries? Where have anti-abortion groups been most effective in stalling women's movement demands? What was the catalyst for initial liberalization of the abortion law? What happened after that initial liberalization?

❖ Dorothy McBride Stetson

In this introductory chapter, readers will find a discussion of the theoretical underpinnings of this research and information about the methods followed by the authors.

❖ THE ISSUE OF ABORTION AND THE POLICY-MAKING PROCESS

In order to situate the abortion issue in the context of the women's movements and democratic states, it is useful to think about the larger question of *gender conflict*: disputes pertaining to people in their roles as females and males (Dahlerup 1987). In all societies there are many examples of gender conflict; most arise from three major dimensions of gender roles: work and family, sexuality, and reproduction. The reproductive dimension includes the question of induced abortion: actions intended to end pregnancy. Abortion affects females and males differently, and there is a potential gender conflict in every human society over its use, especially over who should have legitimate control over abortion.

When social conflicts over gender roles come to the public agenda they are called *gender issues*, which are questions over public policies that affect people in their gender roles. As gender issues, they assume the status of public problems, each incorporating a *definition* or *frame*, that is, an explicit expression of why the issue deserves government attention and action. Many gender issues are *not* defined explicitly as *gendered issues*; in other words, policy actors do not explicitly describe them in terms that affect men and women differently, despite the fact that they have such different effects. For example, policy actors may debate whether or not doctors should be given more freedom in making decisions about abortion, not even mentioning anything about women's role in that decision.

Over the long view of history, abortion has given rise to gender conflict, but it has come to the status of a public gender issue only rarely: in the nineteenth and early twentieth centuries when many countries criminalized or recriminalized the procedure and again in the late twentieth century when most countries reformed and liberalized their abortion laws.[3] When the issue is before the public, despite the fact that abortions are performed only on women and never on men, policy-makers have often framed it in other terms—doctors' rights, fetal rights, law enforcement, morality, religion, progressivism, family planning, eugenics—rather than discussing women's privacy, choice, health, autonomy, or sexuality.

This situation points to the importance of understanding the way issues are framed in policy debates. The policy-making process is, essentially, a pattern of argument among policy actors over what problems deserve attention, how those problems should be defined, and what should be done about them (Anderson 1994; Kingdon 1995; Stone 1997). In other words, the process is a

4

conflict of ideas. Each issue that arrives on the public agenda forms part of a hierarchy of conflicts that policy-makers have decided warrant their attention. These are privileged conflicts because, of the myriad social controversies that could gain attention, only a few are taken up for action. For social movement advocates who want government to attend to their concerns, gaining access to the agenda for public attention is the first hurdle. The next battle is to ensure that the issue is framed in terms that advance the goals of the movement (Snow and Benford 1992).

The conflict over the meaning of the issue is at the heart of democratic policy-making (Schattschneider 1960; Przeworski 1991). The ideas contained in issue frames comprise the pattern of substantive interests in the policy process, and such definitions may include a narrow or broad range. When a group's frame of the issue is incorporated into the dominant frame of debate, then it also provides a basis for participation of that group: in other words, if the policy debate unfolds in terms that concern them, then they have a basis to claim a place in the policy process (Cobb and Elder 1983; Schneider and Ingram 1993). Further, when policy actors agree on a dominant frame of debate, it is likely to provide the basis for subsequent debates on the issue, setting the course for future policies.

It is no wonder that a political strategy for any social movement is to insert the movement's frame of the issue into the policy debate in the hope of affecting both policy content and access to policy-makers. In most countries, abortion came to the public agenda, not as a women's movement demand, but as a response to demands from doctors and progressive politicians to respond to the increase in abortions outside the law. But it was not gendered. Instead, the debate over reform of abortion laws was presented primarily as a problem for doctors who wanted less outside control over their use of the procedure against moralists and religious groups who considered abortion to be immoral, even murder.

The goals of the women's movements were to gender the dominant frames of the policy debates in terms that would improve the status of women. Once successful, the task would be to maintain these frames so that whenever the question of abortion might rise to public attention it would be as an issue that was central to the rights and status of women: in other words, the debate would be conducted in *feminist* terms.[4] In all countries except Ireland, abortion laws were liberalized (Lovenduski and Outshoorn 1986; Outshoorn 1996a; Rolston and Eggert 1994). But, in general, these laws did not fully incorporate the policy goals of the women's movements.

In this research the impacts of the women's movements are assessed only partially in terms of the content of policies. We also want to examine whether movements have had any effect in changing the *policy processes* to be more inclusive of movement perspectives and women's participation, and this goal

❖ DOROTHY MCBRIDE STETSON

involves more than looking at the content of the laws. There are three further questions to answer in determining movement impact: (1) to what extent have the frames of policy debates on abortion become gendered?; (2) do these frames lead to policies that coincide with women's movement perspectives?; (3) to what extent have policy-making processes expanded to include participation of women and women's movements?

❖ DEMOCRATIC POLITICAL REPRESENTATION

The kind of impacts discussed here pertain to changes in the political representation of women. Democracies are usually assessed in terms of the extent to which they include societal interests. Many authors have questioned whether contemporary free-market democracies with highly developed welfare states, by their failure to represent women, are actually democratic (for example, Phillips 1991; 1995; Pateman 1988; Inglehart 1990; Edelman 1985). Many of these critiques are based on looking at how many women hold positions within political and government institutions or the content of laws enacted by these institutions. Indeed, over the period under study—from the 1960s to the 1990s—the percentage of women in such offices has changed only gradually, with major gains made since the adoption of positive measures in the late 1980s and 1990s (Kelber 1994; United Nations 1992). Attempts to assess the representativeness of policies have sought to characterize the patterns of welfare policy in each state and, if possible, to include it in various classification schemes (Sainsbury 1994; Lewis 1993; Orloff 1993).

In this study, we look at democratic representation of women not by asking 'how many women are in office?' or 'is the state woman friendly?' but rather 'are women being included in the day-to-day process of making decisions?'. In other words, do they have *access*? By asking this question we shift the inquiry away from comparing percentages of women in legislatures and classifying approaches to welfare towards studying the patterns of debates about policy decisions over time. This also constitutes a shift from examining the state and its institutions as a whole to looking at a series of actions taking place in a variety of public arenas. By this approach, we do not abandon the effort to compare and classify according to representativeness. But we do switch the focus from describing and classifying nation-states towards describing and classifying instances of policy-making within states.

Following Pitkin (1967), two aspects of representation are important in this study.[5] *Descriptive representation*, where a person stands in for others based on their similar characteristics, can be used to characterize the inclusion of women's movement actors in the policy-making process. Most social movements seek inclusion of social movement organizations (SMOs) in politics (Gamson 1975). In efforts to open the system, women's movement activists have also been interested in inclusion of *women*—a demographic category—whether or not they are active in the organized women's movement. Thus, to study descriptive representation it is necessary to look for participation by women as individuals, in organizations, and in networks and publics both inside and outside the movement itself. *Substantive representation* occurs when a group's policy preferences—women's movement demands—are incorporated into the policy process. The women's movements' strategies have been to achieve substantive representation by gendering policy debates in ways that coincide with their demands as well as being successful in gaining policies that promote the fortunes of their constituencies.

In characterizing the impact of women's movements on increasing democratic representation of women in abortion policy-making, the authors ask: Has the state itself, through its women's policy agencies, played an active role or are these agencies just symbolic decoration? By examining the role of agencies in the process of abortion policy-making, we first learned whether or not they advocated women's movement goals and were successful in gendering policy debates according to movement desires. Then we investigated whether or not women's policy-agency activities helped to achieve those policies the movements advocated. In anticipation of variations in the role of women's policy agencies as insiders, marginal allies, symbolic decoration, or non-feminist adversaries of movement strategies regarding abortion policy, we gathered information on the characteristics of the women's policy agencies: resources, political clout, and mandate.

❖ VARIATIONS: WHAT AND WHY?

In preparing this research, the authors were well aware that there was likely to be a wide variation in both women's movements' impacts and women's policy-agency activities because of the sensitivity of the abortion issue to cultural, religious, and legal patterns. Although previous research had found some common trends among countries in Western Europe (Lovenduski and Outshoorn 1986; Outshoorn 1996a), there were enough countries in this study—Ireland, Germany, Spain, USA, Canada—that did not fit these trends to reinforce our expectations. Anticipating such variations, researchers looked in advance for possible explanations, consulting literature on social movement impact (for example, Gamson 1975; Rochon and Mazmanian 1993; McCarthy and Zald 1979; Giugni 1995; Tarrow 1989).

Explanations for social movement impact are usually derived from two theories: *resource mobilization theory*, which emphasizes characteristics of movements, and *political opportunity structure theory*, which directs attention to the environment of movement action. Following this conventional approach, authors have gathered information about the characteristics of women's movements at the time of the various policy debates on abortion. In addition, we have paid attention to the policy environment, especially the degree of openness and ideological support for movement goals.

❖ RECAPITULATION WITH DIAGRAM

Before describing the theory and methods involved in this project, a recapitulation of the research question will help pull things together for the reader. Along with this summary, there is a diagram (Fig. 1.1) that sets forth the elements of the research problem.

This book comprises the results of a cross-national research project. Each of the authors has contributed to all aspects of the research design and its elaboration. The problem for inquiry is *state feminism*, that is, the role of institutional actors inside the state—women's policy agencies—in relation to efforts by women's movements to affect state action. The authors have elected to examine policy-making on the abortion issue in political systems of eleven advanced democratic states. The study is longitudinal and comparative.

The chapters describe and classify each policy debate on abortion according to two categories: the impact of the women's movement on the state and women's policy agency activities in achieving that impact. To study impact, the authors are interested in the changes in the policy-making process, specifically the gendering of policy debates on abortion, the content of policy, and the participation of women and women's movement organizations. Information on

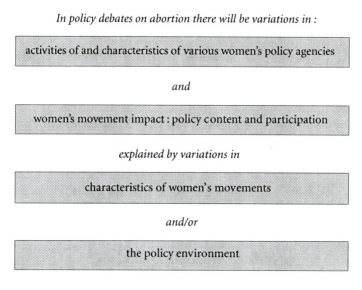

In policy debates on abortion there will be variations in :

activities of and characteristics of various women's policy agencies

and

women's movement impact : policy content and participation

explained by variations in

characteristics of women's movements

and/or

the policy environment

Figure 1.1. The elements of the research problem

these topics provides clues to any changes in the political representation of women by the end of the debate. In short, the study focuses on the role and characteristics of women's policy agencies in movement attempts to increase both substantive and descriptive representation of women. Explanations for variations—cross-debate, cross-national, and longitudinal—are examined according to variations in two clusters of independent variables: women's movement characteristics and policy environments. The results will contribute to the development of empirically tested theory of state feminism.

❖ THEORY OF STATE FEMINISM

As a comparative project, this research, part of the larger project of the Research Network on Gender Politics and the State (RNGS),[6] aims to make a contribution to an empirically tested theory of state feminism. In the scholarly literature, state feminism has had a variety of definitions, referring to the activities of feminists or femocrats in government and administration (Hernes 1987; Sawer 1990); institutionalized feminism in public agencies (Eisenstein 1990; Outshoorn 1994); and, more generally, the capacity of the state to contribute to the fulfilment of a feminist agenda (Sawer 1993; Stetson 1987; Walker 1990). In exploring the state's ability to act on behalf of feminists, the RNGS project, building on the research in *Comparative State Feminism* (Stetson and Mazur 1995), focuses directly on role of women's policy agencies inside the state itself. In this study findings that show that women's policy agencies act as advocates or allies to achieve desired state responses to women's movements' strategies in abortion debates constitute evidence of *state feminism.*

The state feminist conceptual framework (Fig. 1.2) incorporates the topics discussed so far in this chapter as the building blocks of a theory of state feminism. The units of analysis are individual abortion policy debates. The first step in constructing the theory is to establish the extent of variation in the success of women's movements in achieving substantive and descriptive representation in the state at the conclusion of these debates. Therefore the dependent variable is *women's movement impact.* The second step is to examine the patterns of activities of women's policy agencies in effecting changes in the policy-making processes on behalf of women's movements. At this point the *women's policy agency characteristics and activities* can be considered as independent variables explaining variations in movement impact, that is, the state feminism explanation.

The final, and most important, step in building the theory is to assess the state feminism explanation in terms of alternative explanations for movement success in abortion policy debates. As discussed earlier, these explanations are derived from resource mobilization and political opportunity theories in the social movement literature. Specifically, the framework

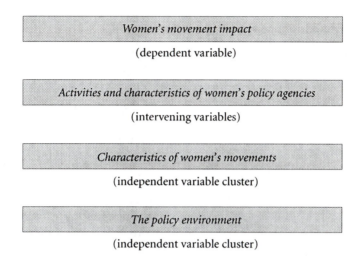

Figure 1.2. The conceptual framework of state feminism

includes as independent variables women's movement characteristics and features of the policy environments for each debate. When the association between these variables on the one hand and the women's policy agency activities and movement impacts variables on the other is examined, women's policy agency activities becomes an intervening variable. The most compelling evidence for state feminism would be those instances where movements could not have achieved a successful response from the state without the intervention of the agencies: in other words, where the agencies were not only *effective* but also *necessary.*

The following propositions or hypotheses structure and clarify the steps in exploring the theory of state feminism in this comparative study of abortion policy debates:

1. Women's movements in democratic states have tended to be successful in increasing both substantive representation, as demonstrated by policy content, and descriptive representation, as demonstrated by women's participation in policy-making processes, that is, dual response.

2. Women's movements in democratic states have tended to be more successful where women's policy agencies have acted as insiders in the policy-making process, that is, have gendered policy debates in ways that coincide with women's movement goals.

3. Women's policy agencies with greater resources and institutional capacity defined by type, proximity, and mandate have been more effective than

agencies with fewer resources and less capacity in providing linkages between women's movements and policy-makers.

4. Variations in women's movement characteristics and/or policy environments explain variations in both women's policy-agency effectiveness and movement success in increasing women's representation.

5. If women's policy agencies are necessary and effective linkages between movements and state responses, then variations in movement resources and policy environments will have no independent relationship to state responses.

With the ambitious goal of contributing to the development of empirically tested theory in comparative politics, the authors and other members of the RNGS project have paid special attention to the methods that guide the collection of data. The following sections describe the methodological approach and specific steps taken by each researcher in studying abortion debates in each country.

✧ THE COMPARATIVE METHOD: A PRIMER

When a research question requires in-depth analysis of a number of cases, the *comparative method* is the appropriate approach (Lijphart 1971; Collier 1991). It is considered a qualitative approach in contrast to quantitative comparative approaches which use large numbers of cases and statistical methods to test general hypotheses. The strength of the detail-rich comparative method is that it permits the study of complex phenomena with adequate attention to diverse cultural contexts where political action takes place. This strength usually undermines the contributions studies using the comparative method can make to scientific inquiry and the development of theory. Yet, by careful attention to design and increasing the number of observations, such qualitative approaches can make contributions to theory building (King, Keohane, and Verba 1994). Individual scholars, however, do not have the resources or needed expertise in language and culture to study a research question in more than a few cases, especially across more than two or three political systems.

Expanding the number of observations or cases—each studied in detail—means increasing the number of researchers. But then a new problem arises: *conceptual stretching*, which is the over-extension of concepts to many cultural contexts where they have different meanings. There is a danger that conceptual stretching will undermine the explanatory efforts of the comparative method (Sartori 1970; Collier and Mahon 1993). Both the nominal and the operational definitions of each concept included in a research question must be appropriate to every case. The only way to avoid these problems is through close collaboration among the researchers at each stage of the project: development of the question, elaboration and operationalization of key concepts, analysis of the cases, and final comparative analysis. The authors in this project have worked closely together on all these steps.[7] What follows is a summary of the specific methods in the project developed by the authors through this collaboration. Each chapter in the book reports the results of the study using these definitions and operational steps. The reliability and validity of these procedures provide confidence in the contributions to the theories of state feminism and social movement impact found in the concluding chapter.

❖ SPECIFIC METHODS

This description of the definitions and operational steps used by each researcher sets forth the topics covered in each of the chapters in the book. Although the book is organized according to political systems, it is important to recognize from the outset that the *unit of analysis* for this comparative study is not the nation-state but the discrete policy debate about abortion taking place within a political system. Thus, all the measures pertain to the features of each debate.

A *policy debate* is the active consideration of proposals regarding abortion policy. The first step for each researcher is to present the policy debates selected for study. The criteria for selection are (1) that the debate takes place in public arenas such as the legislature, bureaucracy, courts, or political parties, and (2) that the debate ends with an official decision, including, for instance, legislation, an executive order, a court ruling, or a government or party policy proposal. The time frames for the debates may vary.[8]

The authors agreed that, if possible, they would each select three debates that were representative of the abortion issue in their country. This involved a three step process:

1. Determine which decisional systems—institutions—in the political system make the most important laws on abortion, that is, the major, defining decisions to regulate abortion decisions, access, and services.

2. Develop a list of policy debates that have come up in these institutions since the 1960s.

3. Select debates that satisfy three criteria of representativeness; authors are to make these criteria explicit in their chapters. These are (a) decisional system importance: a policy debate from each major decisional system that makes abortion laws; (b) life cycle of the issue: that is, the debates that cover the time frame of active consideration of abortion policy; and (c) issue area salience: that is, the debates that include the most important decisions on the topic.

By following these steps we have confidence that the 32 debates described in the following chapters are of comparable significance in representing policy-making in the eleven countries.

In studying each debate, the goal has been to describe how the debate came to the public agenda and to determine the dominant frame of the issue—how the problem relating to abortion is defined as a public concern—at the beginning of the debate period and through the debate cycle. At this point, the researchers reported the extent to which the debate was gendered, that is, whether policy actors explicitly defined the problem using ideas about women as a separate group or in relation to men.

To assess women's movement impact, the authors examined the content of the decision that ended the debate to see whether or not it coincided with women's movement demands. At this stage information about the participation of women—as individuals, in organizations, networks, and women's publics—is presented. This information provides the basis for classifying the debate in one of four categories of movement impact: *dual response*, where the state accepts women into the process and effects policy which coincides with movement goals; *co-optation*, where the policy-makers bring women participants into the process but do not render policy the movement desires; *pre-emption*, where the state gives policy satisfaction to the movement but does not include women into the policy process on the issue; and finally *no response*, where the movement achieves neither access for women nor policy success. Any existing women's policy agency was described, giving information about its involvement in the debate and its structural and resource characteristics. Judgements were made as to whether any women's policy agencies advocated gendered frames and whether these gendered terms coincided with the frame advocated by women's movement leaders. With this information the debate was then classified according to four types of women's policy agency activities (WPAA): successful *insider*: both pleading the case for the women's movement and effectively gendering the policy debate in these terms; *marginal* ally: asserting movement goals, but not succeeding in gendering the policy debate; *non-feminist* adversary: succeeding in gendering the policy debate but in terms not supported by the movement; and *symbolic*, in existence, but neither articulating movement goals nor active in the process. Authors also compared the structure and resources of agencies whether or not the agencies were active in the debate. This information on women's policy agency characteristics was used to draw conclusions about whether certain resources, policy scope, leadership, type of structure, or proximity to power explain differences in agency activities on behalf of women's movements in the abortion debates.

In analyzing the debates, the authors have been diligent in providing compelling evidence for their decisions regarding these essential dependent variables: women's movement impact and women's policy agency activities. Further, the editor has reviewed each author's classifications. With confidence in the measurement of the dependent variables, we move to the measurement

✧ DOROTHY McBRIDE STETSON

Table 1.1. Indicators for women's movement and policy environment independent variables

Women's movement variables	Policy environment variables
STAGE	POLICY SUB-SYSTEM
(1) Abeyance/emergence: low public support, few organizations, few women's movement events.	(1) Open: organization is amorphous, no common rules or conventions; participation is wide and changing with a variety of interest-group representatives and free agents. Power balance shows no clear chain of command.
(2) Growth: moderate public support, moderate number of organizations, moderate number of movement events.	
(3) Consolidation/decline: increasing public support, fluctuating number of organizations, low number of events.	(2) Moderately closed: organization is more clearly defined but changing over time. Participation shows some regular actors but some free agents around. Power balance shows several actors trying to dominate the group but no single line of command.
CLOSENESS TO LEFT	
(1) Very close: feminist groups formally ally with or work with political parties and/or trade unions of the left. Ideas from the feminist movement are taken up by left-wing parties in party platforms. Feminists have internal power positions in the left-wing parties.	(3) Closed: codification of system through regular meetings and rules. Participation is limited with few free agents. Power balance shows one major set of actors controls policy space and parameters of the arena.
(2) Close: feminist groups formally ally with or work with political parties and/or trade unions of the left. They do not have internal power positions in the parties or unions and if the left takes up the ideas of feminist movements they do so without stating so and bring these ideas to fit the party line.	PARTY OR COALITION IN POWER
	(1) Left in power: majority in legislature and executive.
	(2) Moderate left-wing control: left-wing parties may have one of the popularly elected chambers only and not the executive.
(3) Not close: feminist movement and the left are remote or hostile to each other.	
PRIORITY OF ISSUE	
(1) High: issue is one of the top priorities of the women's movement and serves to forge alliances among the various wings and tendencies.	
(2) Moderate: not a uniting issue, but is a priority for some activists and organizations.	
(3) Low: not a priority for any organization, but mentioned by some. Not on the agenda. Not present at all on agendas of individuals and organizations in the movement.	
STRENGTH OF COUNTER-MOVEMENT	
(1) Strong: prevalent and proactive movement aimed at issue or issues taken up by different parts of the women's movement.	
(2) Moderate: counter-movement less active against women's movement issues.	
(3) Weak: nearly moribund or non existent.	

of the explanatory concepts (see Table 1.1 for a summary of indicators of the independent variables).

With respect to *women's movement characteristics* that may affect state responses and the role of women's policy agencies, the authors gathered information on the stage, closeness to the left, issue priority, counter-movements, and cohesion of the movement during the time of each policy debate studied. With this information, the following questions are among those to be addressed:

- Are movements more successful when emerging, growing or mature?
- Are women's policy agencies more likely to intervene when the movement is close to the left-wing parties?
- Does high priority of the abortion issue to the movement's agenda lead to greater success?
- Can women's policy agencies that are successful movement advocates inside the state overcome the effect of strong anti-abortion counter-movements?
- Does cohesiveness of the movement make a dual state response to movement goals more likely?

The *policy environment* is an important variable. Both women's policy agencies and women's movement activists may be effective in influencing the policy process towards feminist goals in some cases and frustrated in others. Before concluding that state feminist activity has been uncovered in the former situation, it is important to ask whether the successful cases are also those with a more inviting policy environment. Two indicators stand for such an environment: when the policy sub-system on abortion policy is open as opposed to closed and when the political executive and legislatures are in the hands of left-wing parties, that is, those parties that are more receptive to social movements that tend to promote greater political, social, and economic equality. The relationship among the policy environments and various characteristics of the movements forms the basis for explaining variations in the extent to which state institutions and processes have furthered women's movement goals in abortion politics and policy-making in advanced industrial democracies.

❖ ORGANIZATION OF THE BOOK

The following chapters present the results of authors' research using the concepts and methods of state feminism. Chapters are in alphabetical order by country and each chapter follows the same outline. The introduction reviews the background of the abortion issue in the country and provides important historical context for understanding the ensuing policy debates. This is followed by a careful review of the universe of abortion policy debates and

❖ DOROTHY McBRIDE STETSON

justification for the selection of the particular debates explored in the chapter. In writing this section, each author was aware of the importance of demonstrating the representativeness of the sample of debates. Most of the chapter describes the findings for each debate on the following topics: how the debate came to the public agenda; the dominant frame of the debate; gendering the policy debate; and the policy outcome. After this review, the author classifies the debate according to the variables in the framework: movement impact, women's policy agency activities and characteristics, women's movement characteristics, and policy environments. Readers should keep in mind that because authors have agreed to contribute data to the larger comparative analysis, they were not able to include all the descriptive information about politics, women's movements, or abortion politics that might be found in stand-alone case studies of their countries. Nevertheless, each has done a remarkable job in adhering to the framework without sacrificing the detail. The following chapters comprise a comprehensive story of abortion politics, women's movements, and democracy in the last third of the twentieth century.

❖ NOTES

1 This term is based on World Bank's classification of democracies with 'industrial market economies'. They are similar, being stable nation states with high levels of economic wealth and large service sectors, and either have traditions of well-established representative democratic institutions or have emerged as stable democracies since World War II (Wiarda 1993: 9).

2 All are members of the Research Network on Gender, Politics, and the State (RNGS) studying the impact of women's policy agencies on a range of issues and countries (Stetson and Mazur 2000; Mazur and Parry 1998). The research design used in this study has been developed through intense collaboration by the RNGS members: more than 40 scholars from 15 advanced industrial democracies and the European Union. The design envisions the completion of research on the relation between women's policy agencies and women's movements in policy-making relating to four issues in addition to abortion: job training, political representation, prostitution/traffic in women, and an issue of national priority in each country. Amy Mazur has edited and analyzed the RNGS research findings about job training in her recent book *State Feminism, Women's Movements and Training Policy in the Global Economy: Making Democracies Work* (2001).

3 There are some exceptions: Fascist regimes in Austria, Spain, and Germany adapted abortion restrictions to eugenics and pro-natalist goals. Catalonia in Spain briefly liberalized its abortion laws in the 1930s. There was debate in Great Britain over the apparent extension of doctors' discretion as a result of the *Bourne* defence in 1938 (see Ch. 7).

4 The use of the term 'feminism' here refers to an ideology that seeks to further the interests of women within a gender hierarchy and to undermine that hierarchy. We

offer no universal definition beyond this general one. The authors are fully aware that there is great disagreement among advocates for women over exactly what actions will accomplish these ends. In fact, there is great disagreement over the use of the term 'feminism' itself (Harding 1986; Kaplan 1992).

5 Pitkin also mentions *symbolic* representation, where a leader stands for national ideas, and *authorized* representation, where a representative is legally empowered to act for another.

6 See note 2 above.

7 Intensive collaborative sessions were held at several venues: the University of Leiden in 1995 supported by an NSF International Programs Grant #1116345; a Short Course/workshop at the American Political Science Association in 1996; a two-day conference in Paris/CREDEP, 1998; an APSA panel in 1998; and a three-day conference at the University of Southampton/Chilworth Centre in 1999, sponsored by the European Science Foundation.

8 A third criterion, namely, that the debate take place at a time when a women's policy agency was in existence, guided most of the researchers. In the Netherlands, Germany, and Italy, major abortion debates took place before any agency was in place. The group agreed that the criterion of salience was more important to give a clear picture of the life of the issue over time. Therefore four such debates—the first ones in Netherlands and Germany and debates one and two in Italy—were included.

2 ❖ State Feminism and Policy Debates on Abortion in Austria

Regina Köpl

❖ INTRODUCTION

For more than 100 years, Austrian abortion policy was more or less ruled by the 1852 law which banned abortion as a crime. Both the woman willingly trying to terminate pregnancy and the person performing the abortion were liable for punishment of up to five years in prison. But there were some legal exceptions. There was no punishment if the pregnant woman's life was in immediate danger or her physical and mental health would be greatly impaired by continuing the pregnancy, or if the pregnancy was due to rape and use of force. In these exceptional cases, only a medical doctor was allowed to perform the abortion.

The Austrian Social Democratic Party, a party with a long tradition of women's movement activism, took the lead in demanding the liberalization of the nineteenth-century abortion law. In 1920, female Social Democratic MPs advocated legalizing abortion within the first trimester of pregnancy. In 1924, party leaders brought forward a new proposal to permit abortion for medical, social, or eugenic reasons along with proposals for better sex education and the establishment of information centres. The party programme of 1926 devoted a whole paragraph to the abortion question. Some of the arguments seem quite modern: for example, that abortion done by a medical doctor in a public clinic on medical and social grounds should be legal and paid for by public funds. Among the social grounds proposed were the effect of pregnancy on women's professional careers. Social Democratic Party leader Otto Bauer placed the demand for abortion reform within the broader context of sex education and also the party's goal of providing more rational, more hygienic, and more humane methods of birth control (Köpl 1983).

Social Democrats had no chance to realize or even promote their demands in the inter-war period. They were confronted by stalwart Catholic opposition in the society and the traditional conservatism of the Catholic conservative majority in Parliament, and finally overwhelmed by economic crises and unemployment, civil war, and the rise of fascism. During 1934–8, the authoritarian Christian conservative government moved to tighten up the existing abortion law by eliminating exemptions on grounds of rape or use of force. During 1938–45, Austria was part of the German empire and abortion practices were governed by Nazi law. Under the Nazis, abortion was legal if the life of the mother was endangered but also on eugenic grounds relating to the *Volksgesundheit*, the health of the German race. Special administrative bodies dealing with eugenic and racial issues were established to decide whether an abortion was permitted in specific cases.

After World War II, during the first decades of the Second Republic, the abortion law in practice reverted back to the law before 1934: no legal abortions other than those for medical and eugenic reasons or for pregnancies arising from rape and the use of force. Social democrats campaigned to include social conditions as a basis for qualifying for an abortion. They argued for social justice, claiming that access to abortion reflected social influence and income and that well-off and well-educated women had access to abortion by using the rape and use of force paragraph and by paying doctors to certify medical conditions. Others went to Bratislava in Czechoslovakia, Hungary, or the former Yugoslavia, where abortion was available in medical centres. These reform efforts aimed to help the majority of women—especially lower middle class and poor women—who were forced to try to terminate pregnancy illegally or by themselves under poor medical conditions.

❖ The Women's Movement and Abortion Politics in Austria

Austrian feminists have historically been organized and influential as pressure groups within established institutions like the Austrian Social Democratic Party and the trade unions. Despite concern about cooptation and ideological dilution by male-dominated structures, second-wave feminists, too, have sought to develop alliances with these institutions to further political goals. Activism on behalf of women's rights dates back to the last decades of the nineteenth century. Most important was the Austrian working-class women's movement fighting for better standards of industrial health and safety and reductions in working hours as well as for women's rights. Political participation of women was the main demand of the social democratic women's movement. After World War I the Austrian socialist women's movement came into its own. 'The women were able to obtain party support on a range of issues including contraception and abortion and were by every measure a successful feminist political group' (Lovenduski 1986*a*: 52–3).

From 1945 until the 1970s, most of the women's rights activities again took place on the left, especially in the women's organizations of the Social

Democratic Party. When the second-wave women's movement emerged in Europe, Austrian feminists soon followed suit and formed autonomous groups outside the institutional channels of the party. This led the feminist organization to split into two wings. One wing, the more radical branch favouring spontaneous, sometime illegal, activities, organized itself in autonomous feminist groups. In 1972, the Aktion unabhängiger Frauen (AUF, Platform of Independent Women) was founded. These groups were more concerned with creating self-help projects than with exerting political influence. The older wing of the movement was more reform-oriented, emphasizing rights and legal change. It operated within the decision-making process through the Austrian Social Democratic Party. Both wings were close to the political left, favouring an extension of welfare-state policies. And, despite differences in strategy, both wings are linked together and, in a way, in constant need of each other.

In Austria there is a rather weak tradition of private sponsorship; and feminist projects are financed mainly by public authorities such as government, federal States, and communities. Autonomous feminists therefore need advocates within the political system to obtain resources for their projects, such as houses for battered women, counselling centres for women, as well as feminist bookshops and communication centres. Women working within the decision-making process also provided support for autonomous feminist projects. On the other hand, feminists organized within the Social Democratic Party were, and are, dependent on the political ideas and inputs coming from the autonomous wing.

In the early 1970s the abortion issue was the top priority of both wings. For the older wing, access to abortion was a question of social justice. They argued that illegal abortion would force poor and working class women to terminate unwanted pregnancies under the worst hygienic conditions, resulting in legal action being taken against them. Autonomous feminists focused more on self-determination, linking abortion to men's responsibility for controlling women's sexuality and reproduction.

❖ SELECTION OF DEBATES

Because abortion law is part of the criminal code, the Parliament is the primary decision-making site for abortion policy. The Austrian Parliament consists of two chambers, which have different powers and different ways of selecting their members. The first chamber, the National Council (*Nationalrat*) is elected directly by the population under a proportional-representation electoral system. This chamber performs the main functions of legislation and political control. The second chamber, the Federal Council (*Bundesrat*), based on the number of seats each of the parties holds in the regional parliaments, has only a suspensive veto power and performs primarily a limiting and delaying role within the legislative process (Pelinka 1998).

Cabinets are obliged to resign after a National Council election and a new cabinet is chosen from party members or a coalition of two or more parties which hold the majority. As in most parliamentary systems, the government depends on majority support to remain in office as well as to govern effectively. The parties represented in Parliament are highly disciplined and operate under the control of their leaders. The MPs vote along party lines, meaning that the party or the coalition of parties representing the government is able to get a majority of votes in final decision-making. Thus, a party or coalition of parties that is in control of the legislature and the executive is able to pass and implement policies. Parties in opposition are relatively powerless as far as the legislative process is concerned, and use the assembly as a deliberating forum.

A distinctive feature of the Austrian parliamentary system is its consociational character, emphasizing representation by all major groups in policy-making (Lijphart 1989).[1] In this system, political decision-making is synchronized through a combination of structural and personal links. All major interest groups, especially economic ones, participate in the pre-parliamentary legislative process. In addition, Austria is a 'party state, with all elections . . . being structured by parties and all office holders in the representative institutions being party nominees and, in almost all cases, also party members and functionaries' (Müller 1996a: 59).

Until the mid-1980s there were two major parties reflecting the socio-economic and religious cleavages in society: the Social Democratic Party and the Austrian Peoples Party.[2] They controlled not only policy-making but also the civil society through a network of affiliated organizations, such as youth organizations, sport clubs, and organizations for women and retirees. The *Lager*—that is, camps, or groups advocating a theory or doctrine—can be thought of as social sub-systems that transform their clientele's demands and interests into the political agendas transmitted by the two major parties.[3] Interest aggregation takes place primarily within the parties and at party conventions, and as party leaders hear the demands of different groups linked to the party. The parties continue to perform the function of interest aggregation in the legislature and executive.

The parties, especially the Austrian Social Democratic Party, have been so central to the policy-making process that they must be included, along with the Parliament, among the decision-making arenas where most important policy on abortion is adopted. From 1971 to 1983 the Social Democratic Party held an absolute majority of votes and seats and was the sole governing party. As *the* governing party, it was able to control political decisions on all policy issues. Although the Social Democratic Party lost its absolute majority in 1983, it remained the strongest party in Parliament and played a dominant role within several coalition governments until 1999. Thus, the Austrian Social Democratic

Party dominated government and Parliament for almost 30 years, a period of rule which was unique for a western European party.

The universe of abortion debates in Austria between the 1970 and the present has therefore been drawn not only from decisions that took place in Parliament but also from those in the Austrian Social Democratic party and its *Lager*. The universe of debates includes (1) the Party's 1972 conference proposal to decriminalize abortion within the first trimester of pregnancy; (2) the National Council's decision to liberalize abortion in 1974; (3) the anti-abortion People's Initiative and the National Council's reaffirmation of the 1974 law in 1978; and (4) the anti-abortion movement's effort to criminalize abortion during the formal application for official permission to use the abortion pill. Between 1978 and 1999 none of the abortion debates resulted in a state or party decision, a court ruling or a government proposal. Although pro-choice activists advocated better access to abortion clinics, and doctors and anti-abortionists protested, neither defenders nor challengers successfully entered the official decision-making arena.

This chapter focuses on three of the four debates: the Social Democratic Party draft liberalization of 1970–2; the People's Initiative and National Council reaffirmation of this liberalization in 1975–8; and the abortion pill debate in 1998–9. These three debates represent the major policy decisions affecting abortion rights in Austria: the proposal for abortion on demand in the first trimester, the reaffirmation of this decision in 1978, and the expansion of choice through approval of RU-486, an alternative to surgical procedures. They also cover the life cycle of the abortion issue in Austria from the early 1970s to the late 1990s. By including one party decision, one parliamentary decision, and one debate where the final decision was a bureaucratic one, these debates also represent the major decisional arenas on the issue.

❖ DEBATE 1: SOCIAL DEMOCRATIC PARTY POLICY, 1970–1972

❖ *How the debate came to the public agenda*

In the 1950s, newspapers reported on abortion cases which had been brought to court (Mesner 1993), and these reports were the only means of keeping the abortion issue before the public. During the 1960s, as part of a general investigation of criminal law codes, an official government commission took up the question. Experts proposed to extend the conditions under which abortion could be performed to include social and economic factors. The commission's proposals did not achieve the status of a bill because the coalition government that established it ended in 1966. From 1966 to 1970 the Austrian People's Party held a majority of seats in Parliament and fashioned a single-party cabinet. During this administration, the government proposed a draft that framed abortion as a moral issue and would restrict it even further. In opposition, the Social Democrats presented themselves as a political party or *Lager* interested in the reform and modernization of society. The Social Democratic women's and youth organizations started campaigning once again for liberalizing the abortion law, and by 1969 the party programme included this demand.

The Austrian Social Democratic party won the 1970 national elections and formed a single-party government. The new government brought forward a proposal on abortion law reform prompting another policy debate. The government's draft provided for abortion without prosecution and punishment not only on certain medical and eugenic grounds but on social grounds as well. The law would empower physicians to decide whether a woman qualified on a case-by-case basis. The Austrian People's Party and the Austrian Freedom Party, which were in opposition, brought forward their own proposals for expanding the grounds for legal abortion. With surveys illustrating that Austrian society would support a moderate abortion law, the Austrian People's Party, recognizing that abortion law reform would bring votes, changed its official party line. Although all parties by then agreed that there should be some liberalization of the law, they disagreed over whether the legal grounds should be medical only or medical and social , and over who should decide whether a woman was entitled to have a legal abortion. For the Social Democratic Party's elite only the medical doctor could weigh the possibilities and decide on the termination of a pregnancy. For the opposition parties, abortion needed to be under the control of authorities representing society, such as committees or courts.

❖ Dominant frame of the debate

Social Democrats believed that the purpose of abortion law reform was to promote social justice. They argued that restrictive criminal abortion laws did not reduce the number of abortions, whether legal or illegal. Rich and better educated women had always had access to abortion by making use of the loopholes in the existing law or by travelling to European countries where abortion was legal. Poor and uneducated women, who were not trained to argue with the authorities and/or could not pay for a doctor's (illegal) help, were the ones who risked their health and punishment to find help in ending their unwanted pregnancies.

Left-wing promotion groups inside and outside the Social Democratic Party went further than the party leaders and asked for decriminalization of abortion without limitation. In the winter of 1971–2 the 'Aktionskomitee für die Abschaffung des §144' (action committee for the repeal of §144), an umbrella organization, was founded. Most members of this committee were younger women mainly organized in Social Democratic youth or student organizations, which were part of the 1968 student movement in Austria. Judged by the ideals of the student movement, especially on moral matters, the government's proposal still seemed too restrictive. Left-wing promotion groups also demanded better education and information on sexual matters as well as universal access to contraception.

❖ Gendering the debate

Along with their interest in social justice and access, the Aktionskomittee sought liberalized abortion laws to promote women's rights to free choice and self-determination. In the early 1970s the scope of the conflict expanded as this new perspective increasingly took hold in the public debate. It was the more intellectual second-wave feminist women of the Aktionskomitee, not the 'old guard' social democrats, who linked the abortion question to the issues of women's individual rights and emancipation.

The Social Democratic women's organization soon incorporated these feminist ideals and advocated feminist goals. Focusing on women's rights of self-determination, the emerging feminist movement within the Social Democratic Party not only gendered the debate but also was able to change the dominant frame. Instead of emphasizing old class-struggle arguments, women's issues themselves were at the centre. Social Democratic Party officials themselves publicly recognized the dominant shift: the battle for abortion law reform more and more had become a battle for women's emancipation (Gößler-Leirer and Edlinger 1982).

The mobilization of the Social Democratic Party's grass-roots movement, together with the activities of the Aktionskomitee, launched a conflict within the party and forced the party elite to reopen the debate on the abortion issue. At the 1972 Social Democratic Party Conference many petitions for liberalization were brought forward. Some asked for legalization without limitation, but most prominent was the request of the women's organization calling for the decriminalization of abortion within *Fristenlösung* (the first three months of pregnancy). The party elite, including the chairwoman of the women's organization, who was the only female minister at the time, merely wanted a reform that would expand the grounds for legal abortion, not remove the prohibition altogether. The party elite was reluctant to back abortion on demand without limitation and risk an open conflict with the Catholic Church that could result in a loss of votes.

❖ Policy outcome

Confronted with an unexpectedly fierce conflict, the party leaders finally supported the proposal of the women's organization for abortion without limits in the first trimester, which was considered a compromise between those who wanted complete decriminalization and those who sought to keep many restrictions. In the end, a majority voted for the so-called *Fristenlösung*. Social Democratic MPs were instructed to start a parliamentary initiative reflecting the women's organization's proposal, which from then on was the official party line. The Social Democratic majority in Parliament supported the party's bill and settled the debate at the legislative level in 1974. The new law legalizes abortion on demand within the first trimester of pregnancy. It is up to the woman to decide, after consulting a trained counsellor or medical doctor, whether or not to interrupt a pregnancy. After the first trimester there is only limited access to abortion. Legal abortion is available only where there is a physical or mental risk to the pregnant woman, where the child is expected to suffer from a mental disease, and where the pregnant woman is a minor.

❖ Women's movement impact

The impact of the women's movement on the state in this first debate was 'dual response'. The Social Democratic Party's reform bill reflected the goals of the women's movement on the question of self-determination for women in deciding whether and when to seek an abortion. Women's movement activists were accepted as participants in the policy-making process in the Social Democratic Party. The emerging feminist movement was at first linked to Social Democratic peripheral organizations. The Aktionskomitee was also connected to the younger generation within the Social Democratic women's organization. The more intellectual, second-wave feminist women of the Aktionskomitee brought a new concept of feminism to the Social Democratic women's organization, which had been feminist in a more traditional way. Johanna Dohnal, who has served as Minister of Women's Affairs and was a veteran of the traditional Social Democratic women's movement, recalled in an interview that she was politically socialized a second time when she came in contact with these groups (Köpl 1983).

❖ Women policy agency activities

There was no formal state women's policy agency in Austria at the time of the first debate. Women bureaus and councils were established, instead, as a consequence of the debate over liberalization of the abortion law. A state secretary for women's affairs was appointed in 1979 with a brief to coordinate and promote emancipation policy. Women's bureaus at regional, municipal, and departmental levels came into being in the mid-1980s. Finally, in 1992 the former under-secretary of state for women's affairs was granted the status of a minister, which remained until the right-wing government abolished it in spring 2000.

However, there was a considerable involvement in the debate by the women's organization of the Social Democratic Party; and it played a major role in the process of developing the abortion reform of 1974, supporting and transmitting feminist demands within the Social Democratic Party as well as in parliamentary decision-making. Given the fact that in Austria the political parties are major institutional arenas for public policy-making, these standing women's party organizations perform the same functions for the party as state women's policy agencies could perform for the formal government: seeking to influence policy to advance women's interests. Considering the prominent role of the Social Democratic women's organizations in the policy-making process during the debate, we can treat the Social Democratic women's organization as a quasi-women's policy agency, having the function of a women's policy agency without the formal governmental role. By advocating feminist demands and gendering the debate this quasi-women's policy agency can be classified as an *insider*.

Like the youth organization and the organization for senior citizens, the Social Democratic women's organization is one of the political affiliated organizations of the Social Democratic Party. It is concerned with a cross-sectional policy mandate. The organization holds annual meetings and passes resolutions forwarded to the party's national conferences, where they have direct representation. The chairwoman of the women's organization is a permanent member of the party's highest decision-making bodies. It has its own staff and budget. It faces a continuing struggle to be accepted as an equal partner by the male-dominated party hierarchy. There are efforts to subordinate and discipline the women's organization representatives, especially at regional and local levels. Women's organization representatives always have to fight for resources, budget, and autonomy. At times they are forced to subordinate their demands to the general interest of the Social Democratic Party.[4] At the time of the first debate the leader, who was politically socialized in the inter-war-period, was a feminist in the traditional social democratic way, which means linking emancipatory ideals to class-struggle arguments. Focusing on gender was a new concept to the older generation of Social Democratic women, and by the 1970s a generation gap had developed within the women's organization.

❖ Women's movement characteristics

The second wave of the women's movement in Austria evolved out of the political left, mostly from organizations within the existing Social Democratic and Communist party structures, in response to the 1970–2 debate on abortion. Abortion was the unifying question and a high priority for the emerging women's movement. Other than the more pragmatic and consensus-oriented party elite, there was no real counter-movement against the women's movement's demands within the Social Democratic Party. Outside the party the Catholic lay organizations played a major role in organizing opposition to abortion law liberalization. In the general public debate, opinion became more and more polarized. Newspapers reported on court cases, and there were discussions on television and radio. A counter-movement umbrella organization named Aktion Leben (Action for Life) was founded in 1971. Anti-abortionist organizations soon emerged and anti-abortion propaganda started to spread.

❖ Policy environment

This first debate provides evidence to the important role political parties had, and still have, in the power structure of Austrian policy-making processes. Political parties are particularly important in interest aggregation. The process of interest aggregation continues through the parties in the legislature and the executive. During 1971–83 the Social Democratic Party held absolute power over the executive and the legislature. Its decision to promote the legalization of abortion on demand within the first three months of pregnancy was already akin to a state decision. The political culture of the sub-system in which the first decision took place was very closed due to the hierarchical structure of the Austrian Social Democratic Party. Only functionaries and elected representatives of forefield organizations that are accepted within the party statute get involved in decision-making. There is no access for outside actors to the official decision-making bodies or their regular meetings. Only women who were delegated by the women's organization or other peripheral organizations were able to participate in decision-making. Thus, what we have is a policy sub-system closed to direct participation by outside autonomous women's movement organizations. They gained access by means of an insider women's policy agency, however, and movement goals were incorporated into policy content.

❖ DEBATE 2: THE PEOPLE'S INITIATIVE, 1975–1978

❖ How debate came to the public agenda

Almost immediately after the Social Democratic majority in Parliament decided to legalize abortion within the first trimester of pregnancy, the counter-movement's umbrella organization Aktion Leben moved to reopen the debate. It used a special political instrument related to direct democracy: the people's initiative. The people's initiative is a means for ordinary citizens to place a bill on Parliament's agenda. At least 100,000 voters must sign the initiative in the presence of authorities, and all signatures must be collected within one week.

Action Leben's initiative included three demands: (1) to add a paragraph to the Austrian constitution on the protection of human life; (2) to extend help for pregnant women in need to find alternatives to abortion; and (3) to re-criminalize abortion for other than medical reasons. If the initiative were successful, the National Council would then be obliged to consider the bill, although there is no legal requirement beyond this. The initiative served as a mechanism for anti-abortion groups to mobilize resources outside the institutionalized political system to generate a new debate on abortion. They hoped by this means to reframe the abortion issue in public debate.

❖ Dominant frame of the debate

After the 1970–2 debate, the dominant frame of debate on the abortion issue privileged women's emancipation and self-determination. Social Democrat leaders continued first and foremost to frame the need for legalized abortion as a class problem. But the Social Democratic Party's women's organization, as well as younger functionaries and members, dominated party discussion by emphasizing that the right of a woman to terminate an unwanted pregnancy is a central part of women's liberation. The Austrian Lawyers' Association officially recommended abortion on demand in terms of furthering social justice. The Medical Doctors' Association took a conservative stand, but prominent individual doctors became active proponents of the pro-abortion movement, arguing that interrupting pregnancy was less dangerous than giving birth to a child.

With the people's initiative, the Catholic Church moved to take charge of the issue and bring the debate back to focus on the right to life of the unborn. The Church had always officially opposed abortion. But in 1973, the Austrian Catholic Church hierarchy for the first time took an official position in support of the counter-movement (Weinzierl 1986). Kardinal König, the chairman of the Austrian Bishops' Conference, which is the most important decision-making body within the Catholic Church, wrote an open letter to Chancellor Bruno Kreisky. In it, he emphasized the moral dimension, opposing free-choice abortion as a renunciation of society's responsibility to protect life, including unborn life (Weinziel 1986, Gößler and Edlinger 1982). Interestingly enough, the letter used only gender-neutral phrases.

In 1975, the Austrian Catholic Church played an important role in mobilizing people to give their signatures to the people's initiative. The Bishops' conference instructed priests to read an official note on the matter during Sunday mass. The pressure on people to sign the initiative was high, especially in rural areas where most people are active Catholics and know each other well. This was the first time in the Second Republic—this term refers to the democratic political system set up after World War II—that the Catholic Church got involved in such a direct way in policy-making.

❖ Gendering the debate

The growing women's movement responded to the Aktion Leben and the people's initiative by mobilizing members to defend abortion on demand. The autonomous women's movement used street activism as a strategy and extended its demands to the funding of women's counselling and health centres. Increasingly, the autonomous women's groups brought up new issues which were not on the agenda of the Social Democratic women's organization at that time. For example, they started to question men's control over sexuality, embedding the abortion issue in the broader frame of challenges to patriarchy. It would be some years before these perspectives found their way into the Social Democratic Party's feminist policy-making. At the time of the second debate Social Democratic women's representatives focused on the more traditional gendering stressing self-determination and equality.

Gendering, especially of questions of sexuality, was also central to most Catholic challengers. They emphasized the effect of liberalizing abortion on women's morality. Their main argument was that fear of unwanted pregnancy restricted women's sexual behaviour. Thus, women were portrayed as having little control over their sexual desire and using abortion on demand as a means of birth control. Despite the efforts of the Catholic hierarchy, the dominant frame for this second policy debate remained one of social justice linked to the women's right to choose versus protecting the right to life of the fetus.

❖ Policy outcome

Almost 900,000 people—that is, 18 per cent of Austrian voters—signed the demands of the people's initiative. While the initiative's supporters were still campaigning for signatures, new elections extended the Social Democrats' dominance as the ruling party. Finally, a sub-committee in Parliament was established to discuss the legitimacy of the demands of the public referendum. As in Debate 1, Social Democratic female MPs were actively involved in this process. The sub-committee came up with a final report reflecting the opinions of the various political parties represented. This report, however, lacked a common recommendation, leaving the final decision to the Parliament, specifically the National Council, where the Social Democrats had control over the majority of MPs. As expected, the majority decided to reject the demands of the people's initiative in favour of maintaining abortion on demand within the first trimester of pregnancy.

❖ Movement impact

The policy furthered the women's movement's central demand for abortion rights. Women played a prominent role in networks that developed within the growing feminist movement around the key issue of self-determination as well as within the growing counter-movement of anti-abortionists. And, in their role as Social Democratic MPs and party officials, women and pro-choice activists had direct access to the decision-making. By defending the liberalization of the abortion law and maintaining women's right to choose, the state provided a dual response to the women's movement's demands for self-determination.

❖ Women's policy agency activities

At the time of this second debate there still was no formal state women's policy agency, but the Social Democratic women's organization, as a quasi-women's policy agency, continued to play a significant role by inserting feminist demands for abortion on request in the parliamentary debate as well as in Social Democratic and more left-wing public opinion. Thus, the party women's policy agency can be classified as an *insider* in the second debate. With its own staff and limited budget it was concerned with a cross-sectional policy mandate. It was political and linked to the party's highest decision-making bodies. The chairwomen of the women's organization was a member of these bodies. At the time of the second debate the leader was moderate first-wave feminist. As in the first debate, reform of abortion law was a central demand of the Social Democratic women's organization. In the late 1970s second-wave feminist arguments brought forward by younger, better-educated members, became more and more popular within the Social Democratic women's organization.

❖ Women's movement characteristics

At the time of this debate, the women's movement was in the growth stage. Activists in the Social Democratic Party continued to thrive and autonomous groups were increasing in number. Movement activists devoted a great deal of attention to maintaining laws that permitted abortion on demand. However, this increased activism by feminists organized around the abortion issue led to a split between the two wings of the feminist organization over tactics: the more radical branch favoured more spontaneous, sometimes also illegal, activities organized through autonomous feminist groups, while the moderate wing sought to work through conventional channels. There was also a division of labour between the two feminist wings. Autonomous feminists became more engaged in organizing spectacular events on the streets and got involved in what was sometimes a physical struggle with anti-abortionists. Reformist feminists favoured more conventional forms of political activism and were also responsible for bringing forward the feminist plea for abortion on demand in parliamentary debates. The counter-movement was at its peak and had remarkable organizing capabilities. The propaganda machinery started by setting up press conferences, public discussion, and street activities in order to persuade people to sign the people's initiative. Thus, during the second debate both the Austrian feminist movement and the anti-abortion movement were growing in strength and support.

❖ Policy environment

The policy sub-system and leadership had not changed. The Austrian Social Democratic Party was still in power, having the majority of MPs, and able to exercise strong left-wing control. Therefore the party could reject any parliamentary initiatives aimed at reopening the abortion question brought forward by the opposition parties. Given the power structure at the time, the political opposition had no access to the political agenda. The only political means to reopen the debate and move towards a new policy on abortion was through the people's initiative, which directly involves the Austrian citizens in policymaking. But with final decision-making still in the hands of Parliament, dominated as it was by the left, bringing the proposals to public attention was as far as the anti-abortion activists could go. At the end of the second debate, abortion in the first trimester was legal and a matter of woman's choice; and the issue was framed in gendered terms as an issue of women's self determination and social justice.

❖ DEBATE 3: AUTHORIZATION OF MIFEGYNE, 1998–1999

❖ How the debate came to the public agenda

Debate 3 entered the public agenda nearly 25 years after the enactment of the law providing for abortion on demand within the first trimester of pregnancy. During the 1980s and 1990s efforts by anti-abortionists to restrict the existing law did not succeed in placing the issue on the Parliament's agenda. The Austrian people widely accepted the 1975 legislation, and the existing framework on abortion remained for the most part unchallenged.

A new debate started when, in 1998, the pharmaceutical industry wanted the Austrian state to authorize the use of mifegyne, also known as RU 486 or the 'abortion pill'. Mifegyne offers an alternative to surgery for women seeking an abortion. The use of mifegyne to terminate pregnancies had already been authorized in several countries of the European Union. Reports from France, where the pill had been in use for some years under medically supervised conditions, showed a number of women choosing this new method.

❖ Dominant frame of the debate

Initially, the dominant framework of the debate was a medical one focusing on the pros and cons of mifegyne as a medication and an abortion technique and on the conditions under which this pill would be used. Some medical experts argued that mifegyne would decrease health risks for women because they could now avoid surgical abortion methods. Most of this discussion occurred in

31

the media, especially the state-run television channels. Before long, however, the initial medical discourse on mifegyne switched into a debate on principles relating to the question whether existing legislation should be changed.

This effort can be traced to conflicts within the Austrian Catholic Church. Fundamentalists clashed with more liberal Catholics, contributing to an on-going power struggle within the Catholic Church. Lay associations organized a campaign for more democracy and participation in the Church. They questioned the traditional roles of women and pressed for modernization on matters of sexuality and contraception. Fundamentalists opposed these demands and used the medical debate on mifegyne to advance fundamentalist moral positions.

Anti-abortionists sought to shape the discourse on mifegyne to force, once again, a debate on the morality of abortion itself. At first they were successful in turning public attention away from the medical to the ethical questions. A great deal of attention was paid to the question of the right of the fetus to life. Anti-abortionists portrayed abortion as killing, murder, even virtual euthanasia: in other words, as morally and ethically wrong. Of course, they realized that the public consensus in support of the existing law would likely prevent any effort to change the law. Instead their goal was to change the dominant frame of debate on abortion from a focus on the woman, her choices, and the methods she might prefer to a discourse on values and a new moral order symbolized by the right to life of the unborn. Catholics expanded their discussion to the moral aspects of sexuality. The Catholic Church generally is against the use of contraception because, for it, sexuality is deeply connected with procreation.

Moderates in the anti-abortion movement whose slogan was 'help instead of punishment' generally accepted that they could not secure more restrictive abortion laws. Many, such as the liberal branch of the Catholic Church in Austria, some bishops, and most lay organizations argued against the use of mifegyne because they feared that this pill would ease the moral dilemma of choosing abortion. They sought an executive order to restrict access to abortion. But, in contrast to the fundamentalists, the liberal branch focused on ways of helping women who had problem pregnancies. They demanded more counselling and argued that the counsellor should not be the same person as the doctor who performs the abortion, as is possible under to the existing law. They also sought to introduce an obligatory time span of one week or more for thought between the counselling and performing the abortion.[5] Despite all these efforts, however, anti-abortionists did not succeed in changing the dominant frame of the debate relating to the authorization of mifegyne, which remained one of medical progress and health.

❖ *Gendering the debate*

Most Austrian parties were pro-choice and pro-mifegyne. They responded to the anti-abortion movement's efforts to control the discourse by reasserting the conceptual framework that has guided the treatment of the abortion issue in Austria since the 1970s. The Social Democrats, the members of the Green Alternative, and the Liberal Party's representatives agreed that women have the right to decide about their own pregnancies and that mifegyne would extend women's choices. The left-wing parties' views coincided with the goals of women's movement advocates, and both countered the anti-abortionist rhetoric by focusing on women's right to choose the abortion method appropriate for them. In addition, Social Democratic women brought male gender roles into the discussion, specifically men's responsibility for reproduction, including family work. Based on this argument, they used the debate on the abortion issue to demand more public funding of day-care facilities. Catholics, but also some feminists, sought to introduce gender into the debate by focusing on men's responsibility in reproduction. Anti-abortionists argued that mifegyne would shift the burden to women and that men will force women to use mifegyne. Feminists counter that it is up to society to invoke its moral standards to urge men to fulfil their duties.

❖ *Policy outcome*

No political party, whether in the government or in the opposition, supported radical anti-abortionist demands to make abortion a crime again. Spokespersons from all parties argued for maintaining the existing abortion law. In the case of the Austrian People's Party, the new debate marked a political turning point. In the 1970s, the Austrian People's Party had opposed abortion law reform, especially the right of women to choose. The party was explicitly Christian and traditionally deeply connected with Catholicism, and for them abortions were against Christian moral standards. However, because the traditional political base has splintered since the 1970s, Austrian political parties have entered into greater competition with each other. The proportion of voters who change their voting behaviour in each election has increased. The Austrian People's Party now has to compete for votes beyond the traditional Christian community due to the change in political culture and political behaviour. For these reasons, and in response to the fact that according to opinion polls nearly 70 per cent of Austrians approve of the *Fristenlösung*—abortion on demand within the first trimester of pregnancy—Austrian People's Party officials decided to accept the existing abortion laws and to say 'yes' to mifegyne.

In the middle of March 1999, the application for mifegyne was submitted directly to the European Agency for the Evaluation of Medicinal Products

(EMEA) in London. According to European Union legislation on medicinal products, EU Member States must gather written expert opinions to gain authorization. The national experts' reports were submitted to the EMEA, which authorized the new product based on their conclusion that there was no medical or juridical objection to it, such as conflict with the national legislature. In Austria, as in France, mifegyne is to be used only in public or private clinics and hospitals. Debate on retaining the existing law was not reopened in Parliament, despite the highly emotional debate in the media over abortion on demand, so there was no further policy action.

❖ Women's movement impact

The women's movement's impact was a dual response on the question of authorizing mifegyne and reopening the legislative debate. Mifegyne became available to Austrian women in clinics and hospitals as an alternative to surgical abortion. Furthermore, the official framework for discussions of abortion policy in the Austrian Parliament remained founded on discourse that emphasized women's right to choose abortion in the first trimester as it had been established in the 1970s. Women representing the movement both inside and outside the political parties participated in the debate over mifegyne; in fact, women in the Social Democratic Party retained their central role in policy-making process relating to legalized abortion.

❖ Women's policy agency activities

During Debate 3 there was an official state women's policy agency, the Ministry of Women's Affairs (MWA), established in 1979. The Minister was a feminist Social Democrat who advocated moderate feminist goals. This women's policy agency had a broad mandate and its policy was cross-sectional. The Ministry helped to provide resources for a variety of women's organizations and was a forum for a variety of women's concerns. The MWA was located at the top level of the government hierarchy and operated as a complete insider in the policy debate over mifegyne. From the beginning of the public debate, the Ministry was against reopening the legislative debate, and in favour of mifegyne. The Minister was not officially involved in decision-making on the authorization of mifegyne, because the Ministry of Health alone was responsible for the registration procedure. Registration is a highly formalized procedure, based on reports of autonomous medical and juridical experts. In terms of public debate as well as of the defence of the existing law, the MWA played an important role. At the climax of the public debate on abortion policy, the Ministry published a brochure about abortion in Austria, which included new information such as the addresses of abortion clinics. The MWA also demanded easier access to abortion in the western parts of Austria, where abortion has not been available in public hospitals. Thus, the Ministry's position on the issue coincided with the women's movement's goals and the Ministry aided in maintaining the gendered pro-woman official definition of the issue in the Austrian Parliament.

❖ Women's movement characteristics

In the third debate, the women's movement has been characterized by shifts in organizational practice and political strategies. During the 1980s, the institutionalization of the more moderate part of the women's movement grew rapidly. Also, women's policy agencies were established at the regional and the local levels. It was not the autonomous wing but, rather, feminist women organized within the official parties, especially within the Social Democratic Party, the Liberal Party, and the Green Alternative that got involved in the debate. In the 1990s, agenda setting in terms of women's policies was on the side of women working at an institutional level. Women's movement policies became pragmatic. Feminists worked on women's economic issues, such as pay equity, job discrimination, and training for non-traditional jobs, as a top priority. There were also campaigns for the promotion of women and debates on how to achieve gender parity in political representation. Meanwhile, radical feminists set up alternative non-government institutions such as battered women's houses, rape crisis centres, and feminist health centres. When the abortion debate came on to the public agenda, the autonomous groups lacked leadership and took part in few actions on the issue. In contrast with the early 1970s, abortion was not the main feminist issue preoccupying movement activists, but it still was a high priority to the consolidated women's movement.

The counter-movement had lost some of its strength; the anti-abortionists of the 1990s were not the same as those of the 1970s. There were shifts in strategies and the coalition disintegrated. Radical anti-abortionists built up a new coalition with the extreme right and fundamentalist Catholics. This wing is ideologically and personally linked to the pro-life movement in the United States, which supplied strategies and propaganda material as well as the name of the group Ja zum Leben (I Choose Life). Radical anti-abortionists demonstrate on the pavements in front of abortion clinics, partly praying, partly agitating, and they also use intimidating strategies against doctors, abortion clinic personnel, and women who have decided to terminate their pregnancies. The more fundamentalist bishops within the Catholic Church supported these small but energetic radical groups. There was and still is a split within the Catholic Church. The official Church hierarchy is mostly conservative. However, there is a strong lay movement in Austria that supports more democracy within the Catholic Church, access for women to the priesthood, marriage for priests, and sexual intercourse before marriage. These groups accept abortion as a matter of fact and recommend liberal and feminist counselling for women seeking help.

❖ REGINA KÖPL

❖ *Policy environment*

Since Austria is a member of the European Union, authorization of pharmaceutical products at the national level is governed by the European system. Applications are submitted directly to the European Agency for the Evaluation of Medicinal Products in London. If a product is authorized in one EU Member State, authorization in other Member States proceeds according to the principle of mutual recognition. National health authorities have the right to come forward with experts' reports. If the pharmaceutical product does not conflict with national legislation and there are no medical objections to it, authorization at the national level is only a question of time. In case of disagreement between Member States, the final decision is made by the European Commission or by the Council of the European Union.

At the national level, the Ministry of Health takes responsibility for the authorization procedure. The policy sub-system is a closed one. Only medical experts and bureaucrats have access to decision-making at the national level. In principle, the authorization of pharmaceutical products is thus only a formal administrative procedure. On the side of the public debate as well as the efforts to recriminalize abortion, the political parties agreed that there would not be any treatment of the abortion issue at the parliamentary level. Neither the government nor any of the parties in opposition brought forward a bill on the abortion issue.

At the time of the third debate, a coalition government was in power. The social democrats still held a relative majority in Parliament and executive. The Minister of Women's Affairs and the Minister of Health, both women, were prominent members of the Social Democratic Party. In writing reports and organizing experts' networks, femocrats played an important role within the authorization procedure at the national level. Thus, looking at the sub-system culture, we can see that, due to equal opportunity programmes women not only got better access to political decision-making bodies but also successfully entered the bureaucracy.

❖ CONCLUSION

Looking at Austria, we can conclude that the women's movement has been very successful on the abortion issue. In the three major public debates, the substantive and procedural representation of the women in the state was supported by a leftist party in government, a women's movement that was very close to the left, and a women's policy agency or a quasi-women's policy agency with feminist leaders in close proximity to the decision-making hierarchy. Key to this outcome has been the long-term commitment of the Social Democratic Party to liberalization of the restrictive abortion law. For Social Democrats access to abortion, performed by doctors, and without fear of punishment, was a question of social justice.

In the early 1970s, Social Democrats came to power and introduced a proposal for a bill on abortion law that would make abortion available on demand on medical, social, or eugenic grounds. Discussions were based on whether it should be the woman or some authority who chooses to terminate a pregnancy. Although there was no official state women's policy agency during the first two debates, the Social Democratic women's organization played a similar role as a quasi-agency and took an important part in changing the dominant frame of abortion issues in Austria to include access to abortion not only as a question of social justice but also as an essential part of women's right to self-determination in reproduction. This definition of the issue, once established, has remained the dominant approach despite efforts by the anti-abortion movement to insert official support for the rights of the unborn into the discourse.

The second debate started with the formation of a strong counter-movement, which used the instrument of direct democracy to contest the new law. The strategy of the counter-movement was to moralize the debate by opposing the woman's right to choose against the fetus's right to life. Further, anti-abortionists focused on the responsibility of the state to protect all human life, including that of unborn children. Women's movement activists, defending the right of women to choose an abortion, gained access to media but also to a female public. The women's movement was growing at the time and the abortion issue was a top priority to the emerging movement. The Social Democratic Party still held a majority in Parliament and rebuffed the demands of the counter-movement. Female Social Democratic MPs who held top positions within the Social Democratic Women's Organization participated in decision-making. Finally, the dominant framework of this debate remained a gendered one, focusing on women's rights and self-determination.

Women's rights to reproductive control was also at the centre of the third debate that became public almost 25 years after the parliamentary decision to legalize abortion on demand within the first trimester of pregnancy. The initial framework of this debate was medical: whether a new pharmaceutical product offered an appropriate alternative to conventional abortion methods. A weak and splintered anti-abortionist movement, importing pro-life strategies from the US, tried to use medical discourse to recast the debate in moral and ethical terms. The Women's Policy Agency and the women's movement successfully rose to the challenge and widened women's right to choose an abortion method. In this the Ministry of Women's Affairs was an ally, advocating feminist goals inside the top levels of the Social Democratic government. Also, the women's movement gained access to the policy-making arena using strategies of promoting women to top positions within administrative and political structures

❖ Regina Köpl

including those that were engaged in the authorization of myfegyne at the national level.

Longitudinal comparative analysis of debates on the abortion issue in Austria confirms some of the propositions relating to state feminism set out in Chapter 1.

1. All debates ended with dual response from the state to women's movement demands. This achievement, with the help of insider women's policy agencies, supports assertions that state feminism, or at least quasi-state feminism, exists.

2. Success occurred in three different stages of the women's movement: emergence, growth, and consolidation, magnifying the critical role of the women's policy agencies.

3. The Austrian pattern of insider/dual response state feminism is due primarily to the policy environment dominated by the left, with a feminist women's organization as a significant actor in the sub-system but closed to countermovements no matter how strong.

❖ NOTES

1 Austrian-style consociational democracy was a result of the experience of deep fragmentation and civil war in the First Republic (1918-38) when Austrian society and its political system were deeply divided into the socialist and the Christian-conservative camps. After 1945, the fragmentation and the 'Lager Mentalität' were still at work in society. But the political leaders changed their attitudes to one another and installed a new alliance at two levels. First, there was cooperation between the two major parties representing the camps: the Austrian Peoples party (ÖVP) and the Social Democratic Party (SPÖ) cooperated at the government level. Second, a corporatist model of economic interest representation and intermediation (social partnership) was established (Talos 1996: 103ff.).

2 The German-national-liberal camp represented by the Freedom Party of Austria (Freiheitliche Partei Österreichs) did not catch more than 5% of the votes till 1986. The Communist Party lost its representation in parliament in 1955 and never played an important part in policy-making.

3 Social, cultural, ideological, and sometimes also geographical indicators differentiated the *Lager*. Catholic conservatives living in the more rural parts of Austria, entrepreneurs, farmers, and also state employees were organized within the Austrian Peoples Party. Working-class people traditionally were organized within the Austrian Socialist Party (Pelinka 1998).

4 For example, in 1906 the women's organization more or less was forced by the party elite to refrain from demanding the female suffrage. Party officials argued that it was not the time to fight for it because such a demand would endanger achieving universal suffrage for men, which was quite near. So Austrian women had to wait until after World War I in 1918 to participate in national elections.

5 These moral arguments on abortion overlapped with some aspects of the medical and biological discourse. Modern medicine and new technologies speak of fetuses becoming human when the central nervous system and brain are functioning. Therefore, some medical experts agreed with the moralists to reduce the time span in which abortion was legally permitted from twelve to eight weeks.

3 ❖ The Abortion Debates in Belgium 1974–1990

Karen Celis

❖ INTRODUCTION

Abortion was legally prohibited in Belgium until 1990, first banned by the Napoleonic Penal Code of 1810 and later by the law of 1867. This 1867 reform redefined the abortion issue from being a 'crime against the person' to a 'crime against family order and public morality'. The law punished both the woman who underwent the abortion and the doctors and midwives performing it, as well as other 'accomplices' like pharmacists. The parties involved could be sentenced to prison or given a fine (De Keyser and De Meuter 1993: 179). In 1923, the law was reinforced to ban publicity for abortion, abortive drugs, and persons performing abortions. Despite the strict language of the law, very few prosecutions took place. On the contrary, the practice of abortion in Belgium prospered (Celis 1996: 218).

It is therefore not surprising that the arrest of Dr Willy Peers in 1973 for performing abortions produced a strong public reaction. The first (socialist) proposal for liberalizing the abortion law had already been submitted in the Belgian Senate in 1971. But it was the Peers issue that mobilized both opponents and supporters. Abortion demonstrators marched through the Belgian streets, petition drives demanded the release of Dr Peers, and the political parties concerned formulated their opinions very meticulously. Positions polarized, and it looked as if the gap between advocates and opponents of liberalization would be unbridgeable.

It would take the political actors nearly 20 years to reach a political agreement. The 20 years between the emergence of the abortion issue and the amendment of the law, which would only come about in April 1990, were marked by diligent activity in Parliament and an increasingly strong profiling of the pro-legalization front, of which the women's movement was an important part. Abortion became safer during the period with safer and more open execution of abortions in Belgium[1] and the possibility for Belgian women to legally terminate their pregnancies in neighbouring countries. The loud protests of the advocates of liberalization and the silent but growing gap between abortion law and practice made the status quo untenable and ultimately compelled a partial liberalization of abortion. Reading about the reform of the Belgian abortion law of 1990 is all the more interesting because the process leading to it, on many occasions, was a break with conventional Belgian political practice. The final phase of the law was especially unusual: the king refused to ratify the law, so obliging the ministers in the Cabinet to step in and perform that function.

❖ SELECTION OF DEBATES

Belgium has a constitutional monarchy and a recently federated state. Beginning in the 1970s, a number of constitutional reforms, in 1970, 1980, 1988, and 1993, have moved Belgium from a unitary state to a complicated form which is sometimes called 'asymmetrical federalism'.[2] The federation resulted in several layers of political institutions representing linguistic/cultural divisions and territorially based economic differences. The national level has a bicameral legislature—Chamber and Senate—elected proportionally and a parliamentary government composed of a maximum of 15 ministers evenly balanced between the Dutch and French linguistic groups.

Since abortion reform involves a revision of the penal code, the institutions that make abortion policy must according to the Constitution be the national Parliament and Government (Prime Minister and Cabinet). The media also play an important role as mouthpieces of various opinions, together with the court of justice, whose prosecutions often give rise to political activity. The government controls the legislative process and introduces the vast majority of bills approved by the Belgian Parliament.[3] Governments are coalitions across party and linguistic lines and tend to be centre-left. The Christian Democratic parties have almost always been in the ruling coalition in the post-war period together with Socialist or Liberal parties (van de Lanotte, Bracke, and Goedertier 1998). The coalition agreements to a large extent establish the legislation to be initiated by the government, and even the MPs of the majority parties have little freedom to amend these bills (de Winter 1992: 7). Belgium is, above all, a 'partyocracy', a country ruled by the political parties. The behaviour of the individual MPs and the ministers is usually determined by strict party discipline, the governmental status of the party they belong to, and political agreements with other political parties (de Winter 1992: 22).

Very early in the life cycle of the abortion issue, the Belgian Government concluded that it would be impossible to establish an amendment on its own because of fundamental conflicts within the centre-left coalition. First, it tried to postpone the problem by referring it to a special commission, a well–tried method of stalling. As the results of this approach were not satisfactory, the government passed the matter over to Parliament because, it argued, by reflecting the composition of society, it was in the best possible position to reach a consensus that would endure.

The universe of policy debates on abortion includes government decisions, government proposals, and, above all, the dozens of bills that were submitted in Parliament by representatives of several political parties, whose common purpose was the revision of the abortion law. The various bills offered in Parliament sought a solution in several ways: a liberalization of abortion for medical reasons, including socio-psychological ones, and even the permanent or temporary withdrawal of abortion from the penal statute.

The debates selected for study in this chapter come from this long list of attempts to settle the abortion issue in Belgium. The first debate took place in 1974–6 in the State Commission for Ethical Problems (SEP), which was set up by the government to advise on the liberalization of abortion as well as other issues. The reports that were submitted by this so-called 'neutral' commission set forth the terms of the conflict between advocates and opponents of liberalization that would last for years. The second debate, over the bill submitted by Socialist MP Detiège in 1981–2, was the first debate to take place on the floor of the Chamber of Deputies. The goal of the Detiège bill was the temporary suspension of abortion prosecutions, facilitating final legislation. The third debate, between 1986 and 1990, which took place in both the Senate and the Chamber, led, finally, to the reform of the 1867 Abortion law.

These three debates are a cross-section of the major approaches that were followed in the course of the debate and represent the most salient and important debates on the abortion issue in Belgium. The reports of the SEP (Debate 1) had a major effect on the following debates; in fact, it was the compromise between the SEP majority and minority report that would lead to the final law (Debate 3). Debate 2—the suspension proposal—was selected because it represents an interim track followed by several parliamentarians in making a (futile) attempt to overcome the political discord spread by the SEP reports. The selection represents the decision-making system by showing the different locations of the abortion debate, as well as initiatives of different political persuasions. Debate 1 took place in a 'neutral' environment of experts created by the government as a solution for its own inability to reach a compromise. The second debate was situated in the Chamber and was initiated by a socialist parliamentarian. The final debate, leading to the law of 1990, occurred in the Senate—and consequently in the Chamber—and was marked by an agreement between Liberals and Socialists.

❖ DEBATE 1: STATE COMMISSION FOR ETHICAL PROBLEMS, 1974–1976

❖ How the debate came to the public agenda

In 1973, Dr Willy Peers was imprisoned after admitting that he had performed abortions in defiance of the 1867 law. While the Belgian Family Planning Association had been speaking out against the restrictive laws since 1955, it was not until the Peers affair that a large-scale mobilization took place. This co-incided with the formation of a new government coalition between Christian Democrats and Liberals. Abortion, together with birth control, was one of the main issues during the negotiations around the formation of the new government. Because of other urgent political problems between the two language communities, the three traditional parties—Liberals, Socialists, and Christian Democrats—were keen to come to an agreement with regard to abortion. The liberalization of contraception was explicitly mentioned in the coalition agreement. The liberal Minister of Justice Vanderpoorten was put in charge of preparing a proposal for the revision of the abortion law, which turned out to be unacceptable to the Christian Democrats and the Socialists. In 1974 the government fell and in the same year a new coalition without the Socialists decided to found a State Commission for Ethical Problems (SEP), composed of 'experts' (Witte 1990: 444–7). The mission of the SEP was to provide the government with advice concerning birth control, the anonymity of the mother when giving birth, and abortion. Simultaneously, an agreement was reached with the magistracy in order to establish a serene political climate: there were to be no more prosecutions of abortion violations during 1974–7.

❖ DOMINANT FRAME OF DEBATE

The SEP established a political agreement about the liberalization of contraception and the anonymity of the mother. With regard to abortion, however, no consensus was reached. The non-Catholic members of the SEP, supported by two Christian Democratic women, submitted a majority report, the so-called 'report of the thirteen'. The Catholics, on the other hand, submitted a restrictive minority report, the 'report of the twelve'. In the general introduction, President Dr Portray-Kirschen emphasised that neither of the reports included a very precise list of specific indications that would allow abortion, and that both stressed the broad evaluation of the woman's situation. Both reports recommended assistance services that would provide guidance and information to the woman and both placed the right to make a decision in the hands of the woman and the physician (Senaat 1976–7: *Parl. Stuk.* 954). Some important differences could be found, however. The breaking point was the extent to which social circumstances could justify an abortion.

❖ KAREN CELIS

Both reports defined the abortion issue as a fundamental matter of ethics. According to the majority report, the complete juridical ban on abortion and the abortion taboo caused abortions to take place away from a sphere of responsible and conscious ethical reasoning and conduct. First of all, the problem of the failure or unavailability of contraceptives needed to be tackled in order to reduce the number of abortion cases to a 'residue'. Second, the existing law was unjust. Abortions must be made legal not only to reduce the medical risks for women, but also to reduce inequality between those who have the financial means to obtain safe abortions on the one hand and those who are in a less 'fortunate' situation on the other. The minority report was based on the notion that the abortion problem reflected a conflict of values and interests between respect for human life on one side and the health and happiness of women, family well-being, and the survival of society on the other.

The majority proposal stipulated that abortion should not be considered a crime as long as circumstances posed a severe and long-term threat to the physical, psychological, and social well-being of women. Decision making about abortion should be the responsibility of 'the woman together with the physician, after consulting the support team'. The woman had to decide herself whether her husband or partner had a say in the matter. The majority report emphasized the need to provide support and assistance, in the form of information, comfort, and encouragement, to the woman who wanted to terminate a pregnancy. Although the report called for a one-week waiting period before obtaining an abortion, and the support team could discuss 'alternative solutions'—code for 'hand over for adoption'—as well as contraceptive methods, the intent of the majority was that this service should be 'neutral', not act as a would-be court. The majority saw that the abortion issue needed to be integrated into a consistent and broad policy on responsible parenthood and education, a child-focused culture policy, and a birth-control policy. It was these stipulations concerning the assistance service that encouraged the two Christian Democratic women on the committee to sign the majority report (Witte 1990: 448).

The recommendation of the minority report was to maintain criminalized abortion, except when (1) the continuation of the pregnancy would jeopardise the life of the woman, (2) it was known for certain that the pregnancy may cause serious, lasting harm to the physical and mental health of the woman, and (3) an abortion could not be avoided insofar as all the conditions required by law were taken into account. Although the report of the twelve stated that the final decision should be made by the woman herself, in fact the proposal gave the power to decide to the physician, with few exceptions. Since, according to this proposal, abortion would be legal only in cases where there were medical grounds, the woman's decision came down to following her doctor's advice or continuing the pregnancy to full term in spite of the medical risks. Like the majority report, the report of the twelve also emphasized providing relief and aid, as well as advice against abortion. It judged that the legislator was not capable of dealing with the matter of illegal abortions because this would imply that illegal abortions were simply transferred to the category of legal abortions: which, according to the signers, did not resolve the fundamental problem as such.

To sum up, we can state that the different interpretations of the ethical problem of the abortion situation, as a result of the 1867 law, also gave rise to different solutions: the majority report wanted to adjust the law both to facilitate birth control/family planning and to reduce illegal abortions; the minority report wanted to establish the ethical principle of the right to life of the fetus as paramount except where the woman's right to life was endangered.

❖ Gendering the debate

Gender ideas were strongly present in the report of the thirteen and almost absent in the report of the twelve, but in both reports they assumed, at least at certain points, the shape of a paternalistic approach towards women. By taking the overall living conditions of women into account and attributing autonomy to women, the majority report considered the abortion issue to be primarily a female problem. In addition, it considered psychological and sociological as well as medical reasons acceptable as grounds for abortion. According to this approach, the woman, admittedly in close consultation with her physician, had the right to self-assess her state and to decide whether to have an abortion. It was recognized, however, that this right to decide might frequently be curtailed because of external pressure—moral, economic, and cultural dependence on the partner, employer, or family—that forced her to end the pregnancy. The assumption that the abortion issue was a matter of specific importance to women was also made clear in the recommendation that assistance services had to be offered by a committee composed by an equal number of men and women.

The image of women presented by policy actors was rather paternalistic. For example, despite assurances about a woman's autonomy, the majority report allowed her decision to have an abortion only with the physician and after consulting the support team. The minority report went even further down this road by stating that the physician should have the last word (de Clercq 1977: 315) and that those providing assistance must play a role in discouraging abortions. Hence, neither of the reports gave the woman an absolute right to an independent decision. Her role in the decision was on the same level as the physician's in the majority report and on an even lower level in the minority report. Both reports would give her the right to visit another physician if the first rejected her request. Finally, all SEP members agreed that 'abortion according to one's needs is not a sign of the emancipation of women', reinforcing their paternalistic construction of the woman in the debate.

❖ KAREN CELIS

❖ Policy outcomes

The SEP published these two conflicting reports with regard to abortion reform; the policy outcome was, however, no change in the 1867 law. The dominant frame of debate had changed little from the beginning; that is, abortion was defined in terms of the ethics, the values, and the interests involved in making the abortion decision, and, as a result of that, the degree to which abortion could be legalized. It was clear, however, that all parties were in favour of some sort of amendment of the law, and the majority and minority reports presented two alternatives: either a partial decriminalization on socio-psychological grounds or a legalization of therapeutic abortion on medical grounds (Witte 1990: 447). In 1977 the government decided to postpone its own decision and handed the reports over to the United Commission of Justice and National Health of the Senate, a temporary combination of two standing committees, to decide the question. This played into the hands of the advocates of delay: the discussions in the Senate commission would take 14 years, and during this period the 1867 law remained on the books undisturbed (Witte 1990: 488). The government's decision to pass the discussion over to Parliament was, in fact, a non-decision.

❖ Women's movement impact

In order to evaluate the impact of the women's movement on the political process in this debate we need to ask two major questions: 'Were women involved in the policy process?' and 'Does the policy content coincide with the women's movement goals?' The first question can be answered in the affirmative. Of 25 members of the SEP, twelve were women. However women were appointed as lawyers or physicians, not as representatives of the women's movement. Out of the twelve women, six—including two Christian Democrats—signed the majority report and six signed the minority report.

Whether the final policy content coincides with the women's movement goals is not immediately evident. During the negotiations within the SEP, women's movement activists were quiet, reassured by the suspension of the prosecutions and awaiting the SEP report. The arrest and imprisonment of Peers had led to a large-scale mobilization of the women's movement. Immediately, a division appeared between the women's movement of Catholic conviction, which was in favour of keeping the criminal abortion law, and the leftist women's movement and the 'second wave', which were pro-liberalization. In addition, although all advocates of liberalization demanded the right of self-determination, they disagreed among themselves over the extent to which abortion should be legalized. The SEP majority report was more or less consistent with the goals of the leftist and second-wave women's movements, although it did not go so far as to confirm women's right of self-determination. The final government action, however, to postpone reform and direct the matter to Parliament was not at all consistent with the desire of a large part of the women's movement to liberalize the law. By leaving the criminal abortion law on the books, the policy outcome did not concur with the goals of a large part of the women's movement. Thus, this debate is a case of cooptation: that is, women were present in the decision-making process but the policy outcome did not coincide with the women's movement goals.

❖ Women's policy agency activities

In 1974–6 there were two national women's policy agencies active: The Commission on Women's Employment founded in 1974 within the Ministry of Labour and Employment, and the Consultative Commission for the Status of Women founded in 1975 within the Ministry of Foreign Affairs. Both commissions held low positions within their respective ministries in terms of their authority, financial means, and access to the decision-making centres. The policy mandate of the Commission on Women's Employment, whose responsibility was to inform the Ministry of Labour and Employment and the National Labour Council, kept it out of any role on abortion policy.

The Consultative Commission consisted of representatives of a cross-section of political, social, and women's organizations, together with delegates of the departments concerned: justice, labour and employment, social security, national health and family, foreign affairs, and foreign aid (Consultatieve Commissie voor de Status van de Vrouw n.d.: 1). The main tasks of Consultative Commission for the Status of Women were the preparation of the International Women Conferences, making sure that international guidelines would be applied in Belgium, and assisting the Minister of Foreign Affairs in determining the Belgian attitude towards problems concerning the status of women. The commission had the right to take the initiative to give advice when problems concerning the status of women were present on the international agenda. The first chairs—Mieke Coene, Marijke Van Hemeldonck, and Emilienne Brunfaut—were femocrats (Consultatieve Commissie voor de Status van de Vrouw n.d.: 1).

One of the 14 main points of the World Action Plan (1975–1980) which was drawn up as a result of the World Conference for Women in Mexico during the Year of the Woman (1975) was the reminder that there needed to be taken a whole set of measures with regard to 'family education, family planning' and 'other social problems'. In other words, there existed an opening for the Consultative Commission for the Status of Women to formulate advice with respect to these subjects. The Belgian version of this world action plan did not adopt this measure; Belgium would focus instead on the creation of new jobs, equal pay for equal work, and a larger political involvement of women (van Mechelen 1979: 107–8). The subject of birth control and abortion was not touched, probably because another government commission, the SEP, was already investigating these subjects (van Mechelen 1996: 112). With its authority restricted to informing and advising the Minister of Foreign Affairs, the Consultative Commission for the Status of Women was not authorized to give advice to other commissions (Consultatieve Commissie voor de Status van de Vrouw n.d.: 2). The activities and scope of this agency might have permitted it to get involved in the abortion debate that took place over the same time span, but there was no interaction whatsoever. With regard to the women's policy agency activities in the first debate, we conclude that they did not advocate women's movement goals, nor did they gender the policy debate. The agency can thus be characterized as a symbolic actor in the abortion debate at that time.

❖ Women's movement characteristics

The most eye-catching feature of the Belgian women's movement is without a doubt its fragmented nature. Throughout the landscape of the women's movement there are several divisions: confessional versus non-confessional, older versus younger generation, party versus non-party, traditional versus new. Here the focus is on the division between the integrated women's movement organizations and the autonomous groups.[4] Many autonomous women's organizations had their origin in the so-called Second Feminist Wave during the 1970s. The best-known ones were Dolle Mina and the Pluralistic Action Groups Equal Opportunities for Men and Women (PAG.) on the Flemish side and Marie Mineur on the Francophone side. Many integrated organizations were founded as well. The most important ones were the political women's organizations like 'Woman and Society', founded in 1974 within the Flemish Christian Democratic Party, which was the first of its kind. Many autonomous women's organizations were affiliated with the National Women's Council, which had existed since 1905. Another important 'umbrella' in the landscape of the Belgian women's movement is the Vrouwen Overleg Komitee (Women's Consultation Committee), founded as a result of the first national women's day in 1972.

In this diversified scenery, it is very difficult to determine to what extent the Belgian women's movement can be seen as a part of the leftist struggle. It is however possible, especially in an comparative context, to conclude that the Belgian movement was rather close to the left. The socialist women's movement had formal contacts with socialist political parties and trade unions. The non-socialist women's organizations did not have this formal connection, but could through their progressive positions possibly be called leftist. Of course, this categorization is problematic for the women's organizations that were formally allied with the Christian Democratic Party.

During the debates of the SEP, the Second Feminist Wave was in full expansion in Belgium, not least because the abortion debate was one of its priorities. At the same time it was also the subject that caused the greatest amount of discord (Hooghe 1994: 152). The progressive, new, and left autonomous women organizations such as Dolle Mina attained a great deal of media coverage with its frivolous demonstrations. Its slogan Baas in eigen buik (master of one's womb) started to lead a life of its own. The women's organizations tied to the traditional parties on the left such as the SVV-FPS (the socialist mutuality for women) joined the pro-legalization front (Celis 1997). Women's organizations in the Christian Democratic Party, on the other hand, opposed permitting abortions on social and economic grounds.

In this phase of the abortion debate there was no active counter-movement. Pro Vita had formed as a result of the first reform proposal of the socialist Calewaert in 1971. This organization opposed all forms of abortion, but during the 1974–6 debate its activities were still simmering (Vinckx 1991: 180–6).

❖ Policy environment

As a result of the effects of its Vanderpoorten proposal it turned out to be very difficult for the Liberal Party to come to terms with the opposition of its Christian Democratic coalition partner—the socialists did not take part in the government coalition. Just when the mass mobilization around the Peers affair had brought abortion to the public agenda, embedding the abortion debate in the SEP was generally seen as an attempt to shelve the problem and to 'depoliticize' it (Marques-Pereira 1989: 93). The incarceration of this tricky question in a closed structure like the SEP made a public debate impossible, even superfluous.

The composition of this commission was not seen as neutral but rather elitist, which gave rise to the suspicion that it was not intended to provide a quick resolution of the issue. The commission consisted of eleven physicians, eleven lawyers, one pharmacist, and one sociologist. The traditional cleavages dividing Belgian society were present: 13 Flemish and 12 Francophone members; 14 Catholics and 11 non-Catholics (free thinkers). There were many women present as well: 12 women and 13 men (Claeys 1985: 25). Not surprisingly, the dominant line of reasoning turned out to be of an objective scientific and medical nature. Seeking refuge in the company of experts was seen as a sign that the law was no longer capable of guaranteeing social and political cohesion (Marques-Pereira 1989: 92) and that the Catholic-Liberal coalition in power was incapable of handling the problem.

❖ Debate 2: The Suspension Proposals, 1981–1982

❖ How the debate came to the public agenda

After the expiration of the 1974–7 'judicial cease-fire', the public prosecutor resumed prosecutions in 1978 and trials in 1981 (Claeys 1985: 27). The conflict over reform of the law increased, as, in reaction to this renewed judicial activity, individual Members of Parliament submitted suspension bills in the Parliament trying to breach the political impasse. By June 1982 the Parliamentary Commission of Justice, a standing committee, had four bills on its agenda. The first three bills provided for suspension of the law authorizing the prosecution of abortion; the fourth one, submitted by socialist MP Detiège, sought to recognize induced abortion as a medical treatment rather than a criminal offence. The Detiège bill was the most far-reaching proposal to date concerning the self-determination of women.

In order to pool support, MPs supporting reform sided with the bill for a three-year suspension of the law put forth by MP Risopoulus, a member of the Francophone Communal Party (FDF). For the first time, success in reform of the criminal abortion law seemed possible. However, the Liberal Party was divided over strategy. Some thought that if a temporary suspension were accepted in the Chamber, a parallel liberal bill would not stand a chance in the Senate. The Risopoulus bill was defeated by a slight margin in the Parliamentary Commission (Socialistische Vrouwen n.d.: 27–8). Later, in 1981 and 1982, Detiège submitted a suspension bill. Subsequent parliamentary deliberations were aimed at overcoming the political deadlock.

❖ Dominant frame of the debate

With abortion trials under way again, the initial frame of the debate pertained to the uncertainty facing doctors with respect to their practice. During the commission meetings and the plenary assembly covering these bills, the meaning of the suspension issue expanded. Thus, although the Detiège bill provided only for suspension of abortion prosecution, the discussion came to focus more on legalization, the problems of illegal abortion, and the need for a revision of the 1867 law. One of the major concerns expressed was to avoid the health risks linked to illegal abortions. Others commented on the inequality between well-off women who had the means to travel abroad for an abortion and poorer women who had to resort to illegal means to terminate their pregnancy. Advocates for legalization of abortion considered the problem to be a matter of self-determination of women over their own bodies. A final argument for legalization was the large gap between the law and social reality.

The opponents of the suspension proposals were also opponents of legalization; they feared that after a two-year hiatus in prosecutions a more restrictive

50

law would no longer be accepted (Kamer van Volksvertegenwoordigers 1981–2, *Parl. Hand.*, 3 March 1982). The opponents pointed out that by taking the life of the pregnant women into account and ignoring the life of the unborn child, the bill represented the feminist movement point of view and not overall public opinion. To them, the fetus's right to life was fundamental, and they were convinced that abortions should be avoided by, for example, improvement of adoption facilities and better guidance of women, but not legalized. In this reasoning, women were conspicuously absent. Finally, right-wing extremists joined their side using the argument that abortion should always remain illegal because the community has an inviolable right to produce offspring.

❖ *Gendering the debate*

For the advocates of legalization, the problem of criminal abortion was essentially a female one. Female Members of Parliament who participated in the debate spoke as 'women' and asked the listeners to imagine themselves in the position of the women concerned. They tried to break the stereotype that only irresponsible women chose to terminate their pregnancies and drew a more refined image: the 'women in distress' who underwent an abortion were also married, Catholic women who had already given birth to other children. Through this portrayal, they emphasized the relationship between a lack of contraceptives, socio-economic conditions, and the desire for abortion.

Some deputies went further to make a clear link between abortion and the overall emancipation of women. These advocates resisted the idea of installing assistance services for women because this did not respect their right to self-determination, arguing that women should be trusted to make sound decisions. Supporters of women's autonomy found allies in socialist and communist circles, in the Francophone communal parties, and in Flemish liberal circles—more so than among the Francophone liberals. Resistance to the self-determination of women was chiefly found amongst the Christian Democrats (Marques-Pereira 1989: 104).

In comparing women with men, some pointed out that while abortion is a problem that principally concerns women, it is dealt with by men. MPs noted on several occasions that a women's case was being decided by a 'male meeting' without acknowledging women as partners in the debate (Kamer van Volksvertegenwoordigers 1981–2, *Parl. Hand.*, 3 March 1982).

❖ *Policy outcome*

The debate in Parliament concerning the Detiège suspension proposals resulted in an anticlimax. For the first time a compromise, reached in a parliamentary commission, made it to the plenary session. The bill was, however, turned down at the last moment because of a division in the Liberal Party parliamentary

❖ KAREN CELIS

fraction. When compared with the stands expressed in the double report of the SEP, the dominant frame of this second debate was similar except for two points: in the second debate the question of the judicial insecurity of physicians was central and members of the Chamber gave more attention to the right of women's self-determination.

❖ Women's movement impact

What impact did the women's movement have on this abortion debate? As in the first debate the answer is that there was cooptation, which means that women, more explicitly feminist women, were involved in the decision making process,[5] but the women's movement was not satisfied with the outcome of the debate. Members of Parliament like Leona Detiège made sure there was a flow of feminist demands to Parliament (Witte 1993: 50). Most significant was a memorandum from the Committee for the Suspension of Prosecution of Abortion Cases,[6] supported by the feminist movement; many feminists were also members of this Committee. Detiège informed the MPs about the content of the memorandum. Thus both women and feminist ideas were directly and indirectly present in the parliamentary debates. It should be stressed, however, that male Members of Parliament also voiced the feminist point of view, particularly on the right of self-determination. This representation is nevertheless incomplete: those women who took part in the decision-making process were MPs. Fuller representation would have meant, for instance, a committee with formal representatives of the women's movement, or parliamentary procedures—for example, hearings—involving women, individually and in groups, in the decision-making process.

We cannot state, however, that the outcome of the debate was satisfactory for the women's movement. The proposal to suspend prosecutions failed to pass without even provisional legalization. Even a suspension with a period of leniency would have been better than the status quo—continued criminalization of abortion—which was the outcome of this debate.

❖ Women's policy agency activities

Neither existing women's policy agencies, their characteristics, nor their symbolic role in the abortion issue had changed since the previous debate. This was so despite the fact that the 1980 United Nations World Conference for Women in Copenhagen encouraged member states to ban dangerous and illegal abortions as a measure for family planning. When the Belgian section established the agenda for internal legislation, abortion was not mentioned (Ministerie van Buitenlandse Zaken, Buitenlandse Handel en Ontwikkelingssamenwerking 1981: 30, 34–5). In September 1981, Françoise Lavry, a feminist, assumed the presidency of the Consultative Commission (Consultatieve Commissie voor de

Status van de Vrouw n.d.: 1). Nevertheless, agencies did not advocate women's movement goals and did not gender the policy debate. With regard to this phase of the abortion debate they remain symbolic.

❖ Women's movement characteristics

Both the autonomous and integrated parts of the women's movement were in full expansion during the early 1980s (Hooghe 1994: 150). Although it was still characterized by its diverse and rainbow-like character, the movement was more cohesive on the abortion issue than before. The radical leftist groups of the Second Feminist Wave were united in the Fem-Soc movements, formed in 1977. In 1976 National Women's Day events were entirely devoted to the abortion question. It was decided to hold an abortion demonstration in March of every following year (Vander Stichele 1983: 18; Vanmeenen 1991: 30). Many local women's houses and discussion and awareness groups were founded (Van Mechelen 1996). New also was the strong devotion of women organizations in political parties towards influencing their party and 'their' Members of Parliament in favour of a legalization of abortion (4-maart Comité 1977: 1–4). As seen in the first debate, the women's movement remained rather close to the left.

At the same time, the counter-movement also underwent some important changes. On the one hand, tolerance for abortion was growing in Catholic circles (Witte 1990: 454; Marques-Pereira 1989: 65). On the other hand, Pro Vita's campaign became stronger and more clear-cut. During the debate in Parliament many members testified that Pro Vita militants personally approached them.

❖ Policy environment

Contrary to the first debate that took place in the SEP behind closed doors, the debate on the Detiège bill was situated in Parliament, more specifically in the Chamber, which we might consider to be a moderately closed rather than a closed structure. The government explicitly wanted Parliament to debate this matter, permitting persons representing different groups and opinions in Belgian society to take part. Moreover, Members of Parliament were approachable and the women's movement did not hesitate to take advantage of this.

In the end, resolution of the abortion issue was blocked due to party relations. Socialists, who were radicalized by the Socialist Women, were in the opposition and could deal with the issue in Parliament without reservation. The Liberals were divided and tied to their coalition partners, the Christian Democrats, who were adamantly opposed. The Christian Democrats were thus able to force their Liberal coalition partner to accept a non-decision (Witte 1990: 460–4).

❖ KAREN CELIS

❖ Debate 3: Lallemand-Herman-Michielsens Bill, 1986–1990

❖ How the debate came to the public agenda

The socialists learned two things from the prior debate: first, in order to liberalize the abortion law, they had to get the Liberals on their side; and second, the 'suspension strategy' would not work (Witte 1990: 465). The proponents of reform—the parties and Members of Parliament, the women's movement, and lobbies—began to develop a compromise to bridge the gap between Liberals who opposed complete decriminalization and Socialists who strongly advocated the liberalization of abortion. Roger Lallemand, a Socialist senator, and Lucienne Herman-Michielsens, a Liberal senator, came up with a plan to divide the period of the pregnancy into two parts: before twelve weeks and after. In that way the goals of both majority and minority reports of the SEP could be accommodated in the law: a more generous liberalization of abortion during the first period of pregnancy and a more restrictive approach during the second (Hooghe 1990: 15). At the same time, by including the principle that the woman decides and by taking into account the existing abortion centres they could guarantee the support of the lobbies and of the women's movement.

The Socialist-Liberal abortion reform bill did not propose to repeal criminal abortion in the 1867 law. Instead, it set forth circumstances under which abortion would be legal: abortion during the first twelve weeks of pregnancy performed

> under sound medical conditions by a physician in a health care institute, with a connected information service, that supports the pregnant woman and informs her in detail, especially of the rights, social security and advantages, that are guaranteed to families, to unmarried mothers and their children, as well as on the possibility of giving birth to the child and giving it up for adoption. A service that also, when asked for by the physician or the woman, helps her and gives advice about the means that are available to her for solving her psychological and social problems resulting from her condition. (Art. 1, author's translation) (*Belgisch Staatsblad* 1990: 6379–80)

The duty of the consulted physician would be to inform the woman about the medical risks of an abortion as well as about the support services for the child. The law would empower the physician to determine whether the woman had a 'firm will' to end the pregnancy and whether her circumstances constituted a crisis. Based on this judgement of the woman's situation, the physician would have to decide whether to perform the abortion or not. Once made, this decision was to be indisputable. Finally, the physician must wait six days before actually terminating the pregnancy after receiving a written declaration from the woman. The physician or other authorized personnel could not be forced to assist an abortion (Art. 2). After the twelve-week term, abortion could be terminated only when a full-term pregnancy would seriously jeopardize the health of the woman or when it was clear that the child suffered a very serious condition considered to be incurable at the time of diagnosis. Before as well as after the twelfth week of pregnancy, the woman would be given the right to decide if she was in need of an abortion, even on medical grounds.

The Lallemand-Herman-Michielsens bill was first submitted to Parliament in 1985. Between 1986 and 1987, the bill was discussed on 17 different occasions in the United Commission of Justice and National Health. When the government fell in 1987, a great deal of pressure to continue the debate on abortion in Parliament was exerted during the subsequent negotiations, resulting in a mention of the issue in the government policy statement of 1988 (Witte 1990: 469; Socialistische Vrouwen n.d.: 33–4). The proposal was resubmitted in 1989 and would lead to the final (partial) legalization of abortion. Dozens of animated commission and plenary meetings were dedicated to the Lallemand-Herman-Michielsens bill.[7]

❖ Dominant frame of the debate

Many deputies understood the demand for reform as the consequence of social changes that had led to emancipation from traditional controls. The MPs who submitted the reform proposal emphasized that they wanted to safeguard life while guaranteeing the woman's right to independence, to self-realization, and to a useful life. They claimed as well that the new law would address both the ineffectiveness of the 1867 law and the uncertainty it produced in the legal system that compromised the integrity of the constitutional state. Also mentioned, but to a lesser extent, were concerns about the increases in the rate of illegal abortions and the social inequality concerning access to the procedure (Senaat 1988: *Parl. Stuk:* 247–2).

The opponents of a legalization of abortion, chiefly the Christian Democrats and the Volksunie, the Flemish communal party, rejected the proposal because of the image of society it projected: a sick, egocentric society in which there is no place for children. This group's answer to the issue of demand for abortion was to render society kinder towards children. To them, any limit on the right to life would mean the end of democracy (Senaat 1989–90, *Parl. Hand.*, 24 October 1989). The Christian Democrats' negotiating position had been considerably weakened, however, due to a decline in electoral support that had begun in 1981 (Witte 1990: 465–6).

Three specific topics arose in the debate: the concept of 'crisis situation', the question 'who decides?', and the status of the assistance service. In her speech introducing the bill, Deputy Herman-Michielsens admitted that the term 'crisis situation' was difficult to define, but she stated that 'everybody could sense what it means': the 'strength' to withstand an unwanted pregnancy, which is different for every woman (Senaat 1988, *Parl. Stuk.* 247–2). The opponents of the proposal rejected this notion because it lacked any objective foundation for judgement, which would lead, inevitably in their view, to 'abortion à la carte'. To respond, several Members of Parliament filed a variety of amendments intended to define the notion 'crisis situation' (Senaat 1988, *Parl. Stuk.*, 247–6; Kamer van Volksvertegenwoordigers 1989–90, *Parl. Stuk.* 1025–1). They were all rejected because the majority agreed that only the individual woman could determine whether she was in a crisis situation.

This led to the discussion of the second theme: 'Who decides?'. For both the bill's sponsors and its supporters, it must be the woman who decides, with the physician assessing the existence of the crisis situation and her firm will. During the parliamentary debates opponents resisted giving a woman's exclusive decisional power which also excluded her partner.[8] Supporters of the reform bill rejected the idea that only a physician could 'determine' and thus de facto legalize an abortion. They were supported by an advisory opinion from the Supreme Court (Senaat 1988, *Parl. Stuk.*, 247–8), which concluded that this would make the physician both a concerned party and the judge. Finally it was argued that justice should have the power to decide, and an amendment in that sense was submitted (Senaat 1988, *Parl. Stuk.*, 246–6). The amendment was rejected, however, because many believed it would give rise to a new inquisition and would not reduce the risk of prosecution for physicians executing abortions.

The final question addressed the obligation of installing assistant services to advise and support the woman in her demand. The advocates of these support services argued that they would help avoid a large number of abortions because women in distress are often emotional and acted in a frenzy. The opponents of the obligation stated that, in the first place, this wouldn't deter abortions because information would not have an effect on women who didn't ask for it, and, in the second place, the idea did not show a lot of respect for women.

❖ Gendering the debate

Constructions of women were central to the debate, but those of the proponents and the opponents of reform were distinctly different from one another. Proponents, including female Members of Parliament, portrayed the woman who wants an abortion as an individual capable of assessing her situation and considering both her own situation and the unborn child's right to live in a correct way. Although the bill situated this right within provisions compelling a woman to consult the doctor in attendance, along with an assistance service and a consideration term, its sponsors were very clear on the one and only thing that could justify an abortion: the woman's firm will (Senaat 1988, *Parl. Stuk.* 247–2). More than once it was stated that a woman could not be considered to be the

56

'envelope' or 'container' of a child that had an absolute right to live (Senaat 1989–90, *Parl. Hand.*, 24 October 1989).

Opponents had two images of women. One pictured an egoistic woman who puts her own comfort and well-being ahead of that of her unborn child. The other was the paternalistic image of a woman in distress, upset, and emotionally unstable, a woman who does not need an abortion but guidance and support (Senaat 1988, *Parl. Stuk.*, 247–2). Opponents of women's self-determination also added comments on the role and influence of the man—partner, husband, the child's natural father—in the abortion decision. They claimed that 'to exempt the man of all responsibility' would be very non-feminist because it would confirm the sex stereotyping in which women carry the burden only of children, making women the victims of legal abortion. The proponents of the reform replied that when there was a good relationship between the woman and her partner, he will automatically be involved in the decision. But when there was no healthy understanding, it would not be desirable for the partner to exert influence on the woman's decision (Senaat 1989–90, *Parl. Hand.*, 26 October 1989).

In this phase of the debate, not only the subject matter but the policy-making process itself was gendered. 'The woman is the most concerned party, but until now probably the one least listened to' (Senaat 1989–90, *Parl. Hand.*, 24 October 1989; author's translation). One Member of Parliament asked a rhetorical question: 'What right does a male parliament have to impose a law on the majority of women, to which they object with all their heart' (Senaat 1989–90, *Parl. Hand.*, 25 October 1989; author's translation).

❖ Policy outcome

On 29 March 1990, the Chamber passed the Lallemand-Herman-Michielsens bill to decriminalize abortion in the first twelve weeks by a majority that did not contain the governing Christian Democrats.[9] This very singular situation shook the foundations of the Belgian state. The government did not fall because of the abortion law, but it did result in a small royalty crisis. Whereas royal assent is required for a bill to become formal law, this process is usually a formality. In this case, however, the king refused to assent on 'moral grounds' and was thus 'temporarily considered incapable to reign'. After the Christian Democrats installed an Evaluation Commission to produce a report annually on the application of the law (Witte 1990: 474), the bill was ratified and enacted by the ministers united in Council (Witte 1990: 480–1).

❖ Women's movement impact

Women, as individuals and in groups, were actively involved in the decision-making process, in parliamentary debates, and in commissions.[10] One of the

❖ KAREN CELIS

MPs who submitted the proposal was a Socialist woman and all the reporters were women. Ms Hanquet was at the same time MP and president of the National Women's Council (the French wing). A memorandum putting forth the Council's position was included in the appendix of the official commission report (Senaat 1988, *Parl. Stuk.*, 247–2), and during the debate, references were made to this document. Appeals and petitions of women's organizations and lobbies in favour of liberalization also reached Parliament. Campaign slogans of women's and other organizations were introduced in Parliament during the discussions, but they were dismissed by some as 'extremist' and 'ultra-feminist' (Senaat 1989–90, *Parl. Hand.*, 27 October 1989).

Although the final law did not completely decriminalize abortion in Belgium, the content did coincide with women's movement goals. The right of women's self-determination was central to the 1990 law; only she can say whether her circumstances constitute a crisis situation entitling her to abortion services. This outcome coincides with the point of view of the Women's Council, which grouped together a large number of women's organizations and therefore can be seen as a representative of the women's movement. As a result, after April 1990 women's organizations' campaigns in favour of legalization ceased. The outcome of the debate constituted a dual response from the state to the women's movement.

❖ Women's policy agencies activities

The Commission for Women's Employment and the Consultative Commission for the Status of Women were still in existence during the late 1980s. However, nothing had changed with respect to their limited agendas and activities found in previous abortion-policy debates. Two new women's policy agencies were established in the mid-1980s, which appeared more likely to be involved with abortion policy reform on behalf of women and the women's movement. In 1985 and 1986 respectively, the government installed a State Secretary of Environment and of Social Emancipation and an Emancipation Council. Several authors regard these agencies as the start of the women's policy machinery in Belgium (Hondeghem and Nelen 2000). Compared with the earlier women's policy agencies, the sphere of action and the potential of the State Secretary and the Emancipation Council had increased substantially. The Emancipation Council came under the Ministry of National Health and Environment and functioned as a counselling body for the State Secretary of Social Emancipation.[11] The Council included delegates of the women's organizations of different ideological and socio-cultural persuasions. Its sphere of action was, in short, cross-sectional: everything, directly or indirectly, related to the emancipation of women. The Emancipation Council depended on the State Secretary: its advice could be made public only after reaching an agreement with the minister or the state secretary (Kuhl 1998: 14; Ministerie van Volksgezondheid en Leefmilieu 1987: 2). Both Miet Smet, the first State Secretary, and Ann Hermans, the first president of the Emancipation Council, were feminists, who had their roots in 'Woman and Society' circles—the women's wing of the Flemish Christian Democrats. A survey, conducted by Woman and Society, showed that an important number of its own members were in favour of a liberalization of the abortion law (Witte 1990: 454). This progressive standpoint differed radically from the conservative opinion advocated by the Christian Democratic party.

Despite these favourable circumstances, these new agencies did not take part in policy debates on the abortion issue. The abortion theme is completely absent from the Council's publications and actions (Kuhl 1998: 24–5). In Parliament several openings were created that could have enabled the State Secretary of Social Emancipation and the Emancipation Council to take part in the debate. For example, the State Secretary of National Health, among others, was asked for information concerning abortion, but the State Secretary of Social Emancipation was not approached. This absence is striking in the light of the relationship between the abortion issue and the emancipation of women, a relationship that was pointed out by several Members of Parliament. What makes the absence of any input of the Emancipation Council and the State Secretary of Social Emancipation—both official government bodies—even more remarkable is that the Women's Council, a non-governmental organization, did succeed in putting its memorandum in the official commission report.

With regard to the abortion debate we must conclude that the Emancipation Council and the State Secretary of Social Emancipation are symbolic actors. The reason the agency did not get involved can be understood in terms of the party system and the functioning of Belgian politics: the leaders of the agencies were bound by the political standpoint of the Christian Democratic Party, which was against a legalization of abortion.

❖ Women's movement characteristics

In the second half of the 1980s, the Belgian women's movement changed. The number of autonomous women groups decreased, whereas the number of integrated groups continued to increase. Financial necessity accounted for the use of less conspicuous organizational structures (Hooghe 1994: 150, 157). It is difficult, however, to characterize this phase in the Belgian women's movement as a decline, all the more so because activists were able to voice their opinions in the political arena. They brought their message to Parliament by means of memoranda to the person in charge of the formation of a new government, by using petitions, appeals, and awareness-raising campaigns (Socialistische

Vrouwen n.d.: 32–4; Witte 1993: 472). Despite this change that the women's movement went through, we can still conclude that it continued to be rather close to the left. The counter-movement, with Pro Vita at the forefront, campaigned heavily during this moment of the abortion debate, just as women's movement did. Every possible tool was used. It tried to get its message across by using phone calls, threatening and slanderous letters, pamphlets, and films. This campaign was so shocking by its brutality that it alienated many opponents of abortion reform (Witte 1990: 477–8). Tolerance toward legalization and a pragmatic solution grew amongst the Catholic part of the population, and the Christian Democratic women showed their dissatisfaction with the obstructional politics of their party (Socialistische Vrouwen n.d.: 35).

❖ Policy environment

The 1986–90 abortion policy debate took place successively in the Senate and in the Chamber. In this period a Liberal-Christian Democrat coalition was in power. Just as in the prior debates, the policy system was not entirely closed: there were committee hearings where movement leaders could testify; women's movements and other lobbies were able to formulate their point of view by means of direct representation in Parliament—for example, the stand, described above of the Women's Council by the presence of its president Hanquet—or indirectly through media, petitions, and appeals. This third debate was successful in changing the law because the dominant party coalition was divided. The Liberals and the Socialists came to a compromise while the Christian Democrats, who opposed liberalization of the abortion law, were losing electoral support, weakening their ability to negotiate. Eventually they were even passed over.

❖ CONCLUSION

In the abortion debates under study, the impact of the women's movement on the Belgian state evolved from cooptation to dual response. In all debates, women participated in the decision-making process, and the perspective of movement organizations was made known even in the closed structure of the SEP. It was not until the third debate that the Parliament was able to overcome the impasse among the traditional dominant parties and enact a policy that coincided with demands of the movement.

In contrast to the women's movement success, the Belgian women's policy agencies remained symbolic actors during all abortion debates. During the first two debates, this remarkable absence can be at least partially attributed to a lack of resources and influence, and a limited sphere of action. The obstacles facing these agencies became completely clear during the 1986–90 debate. The State

Secretary of Social Emancipation, although secondary to a minister, had access at high levels. In addition, she was supported by an Emancipation Council in which the different women's movements were represented. Despite having characteristics and opportunities favourable for exerting influence over the abortion debate, the Emancipation Council and the State Secretary of Social Emancipation did not participate. No structural reason whatsoever could be found that would explain the impotence of the women's policy agencies to intervene in this debate and to act as a mouthpiece for the women's movement.

The policy environment explains why the women's policy agencies were unable to act as allies of the movement. Specifically it was the fact that the Christian Democrats, rather than the leftist parties, dominated the coalitions and blocked any reform for many years. The women's policy agencies—Emancipation Council and a Secretary of State of Social Emancipation—were presided over by Christian Democrats. The state secretary as well as the president of the Emancipation Council were members of the Christian Democratic party. Although they were part of Women and Society, a Christian Democrat women's organization with more progressive ideas about the liberalization of abortion than the party leaders, they were bound by the official standpoint and could not advocate their more liberal opinions openly or act as representatives of the women's movement. The Belgian abortion case demonstrates very clearly that the positioning of the women's policy agencies at the highest levels of the political-decision making process, notwithstanding the fact that this was an explicit demand of the women's movement, can silence them, depending on the party coalition in power.

The favourable characteristics of the women's movement go a long way toward explaining its increasing influence over the abortion debate; in fact, in many ways, the women's movement coincided with the abortion struggle. The increase in numbers of the women's movement organizations and followers, its initial mediagenic and unceasing actions, together with its growing orientation towards the political decision-making process, in spite of a decline in autonomous discussion groups in the 1980s, brought the issue to the agenda, resurrected the 'battle' after political defeat, resisted the non-policy of the Christian Democratic government partner, and, in the end, brought about final, if partial, liberalization of the abortion law. In addition, the abortion question became the profiling issue of the women's movement which made it able to mobilize large groups of women.

❖ KAREN CELIS

❖ NOTES

With thanks to Petra Meier, Alison Woodward, and Tove Samzelius Jönsson.

1 At the end of the 1970s, some hospitals publicly announced that they performed abortions. During the same time period, polyclinical abortion centres, after the Dutch example, were opened (Witte 1993: 451).

2 The Belgian federal system can be called 'asymmetrical' because the substates—Flanders, Wallonia, Brussels, and the German-speaking region—have different competencies and different political institutions.

3 The number of private members' bills introduced by MPs, however, increased in the period 1968–90, but their success rate was significantly lower than the bills introduced by the government.

4 Integrated women's organizations are seen as organizations that are tied or linked to existing structures like political parties and unions. Autonomous women organizations are lacking these ties (Hooghe 1994).

5 In 1981, there were 33 female MPs in Belgium, 8.3% of the total (Van Molle and Gubin 1998: 367).

6 The Committee for the Suspension of Prosecution of Abortion Cases was founded 30 April 1978 by Monique Rifflet and Monique Van Tichelen. It was a pressure group with members from different interest organizations in favour of the legalization of abortion.

7 Senaat (1989–90, *Parl. Hand.*, 24–27 October 1989, 3–6 November 1989); Kamer van Volksvertegenwoordigers (1989–90, *Parl. Hand.*, 27–29 March 1990). The subsections 'Dominant frame of the debate' and 'Gendering the debate' are based upon these parliamentary debates in the Senate and the Chamber

8 Amendments were introduced to include the partner in the decision making process (Senaat 1988, *Parl. Stuk.*, 247–3, 247–5).

9 The law was accepted in the Senate with 102 votes in favour, 73 against, and three abstentions. In the Chamber, 126 MPs were in favour, 69 against, with twelve abstentions (Witte 1993: 473–4).

10 During this legislature, there were 33 female MPs in the Parliament, 8.3% of the total (Van Molle and Gubin 1998: 367).

11 A State Secretary, in the Belgian context, is subordinate to a Minister and is on the lowest level of a governmental hierarchy. The State Secretary is appointed to take care of a specific area of responsibility or a sub-sector of the ministerial responsibilities.

4 ❖ Of Rights and Power: Canada's Federal Abortion Policy 1969–1991

Melissa Haussman

❖ INTRODUCTION

Historically, as a British Dominion, Canada's legal framework, outside Quebec, was largely incorporated into the British one. The first criminal law on abortion enacted in 1869 followed Britain's 1861 Offences Against the Person Act and prohibited abortions with no exceptions. Similarly, the '*Bourne* defence' of 1939[1] (see Chapter 7) under which a physician could be excused for performing an abortion to save the life of the mother was incorporated into Canadian Criminal Code and practice.

Starting in 1931, with changes under Britain's Statute of Westminster, former colonies, including Canada, were given the right to pass any type of legislation, including that which might conflict with British statutes. In the 1960s, the Canadian federal government undertook a complete overhaul of the Criminal Code. Full constitutional independence was not granted to Canada until 1982, when, under the Constitution Act of 1982, Canada enacted the Charter of Rights and Freedoms, a supreme constitutional Bill of Rights, and got the power to amend its own Constitution without having to ask for British consent. The Supreme Court assumed the power of judicial review under the new Constitution.

The 1969 Criminal Code constituted the first instance of a reform of the strict criminal abortion law. In the ensuing evolution of the abortion issue in Canada, in terms of what area of the law should govern it and what, if any, restrictions should prevail, some questions have been effectively resolved, but others have arisen to take their place. There are two ways to look at the evolution of federal action on abortion policy during 1969–91. The first is that the 1969 reforms were a real watershed, and that the absence of an overarching federal law since 1988 is, essentially, a significant policy in itself. The second view, closer to that taken in this chapter, is that the 1969 reforms essentially codified the status quo—leaving it to physicians to determine who could 'qualify' for an abortion—and that successive federal governments never had the will to tinker with that framework. According to this view, the issue would probably not have come on to the federal agenda again, save for the new constitutional order of 1982 and a more activist Supreme Court acting to overturn the 1969 standards (Kellough 1996: 78, 180).

The Canadian framework since 1969 has been described as one where 'women won a symbolic right of access, without the corresponding right to choose' (Kellough 1996: 82). While the federal actions may be termed highly symbolic, the federal level is the one to determine the legality of abortion, and thus has been the one with the responsibility for framing the national system. It has also been the most vocal arena in which pro-choice and pro-life groups have combatted one another.

Two strands have persisted in the pro-choice framing of abortion policy, and have varied in their strength in different debates. The first is the liberal, rights-based framework of choice as a negative liberty, described in terms of women's freedom from state interference, and grounded in a conception of women as autonomous agents. The second view, more grounded in the traditions of socialism, the labour movement, and socialist feminism, tries to examine the 'actual circumstances of women who require abortions'. It recognizes choice not simply an individual right interpreted by a court, but as 'an enabling term' which often requires collective support—such as clinics and funding—for its implementation (Kellough 1996: 244–5).

In the women's movement, the rights-based view of reproductive choice has usually been represented by the Canadian Abortion Rights Action League (CARAL), many groups in the umbrella national women's movement, the National Action Committee on the Status of Women (NAC), and the Women's Legal Education and Action Fund (LEAF), a feminist national litigation organization founded after the enactment of the 1982 Constitution. The two national 'brokerage' mainstream parties, the Liberals and Conservatives, the only parties to have formed Canadian national governments to date, have also used the 'negative liberty' definition of women's reproductive rights. The second view of abortion, in terms of reproductive empowerment, has been most often voiced by the Ontario Coalition for Abortion Clinics (OCAC), unions affiliated with the Canadian Labour Congress, some Quebec pro-choice organizations, and the social-democratic New Democratic Party (NDP) among the national parties.

❖ SELECTION OF DEBATES

Overall, the most relevant public actors with decision-making powers in the abortion debate have been the federal Parliament and the Supreme Court of Canada. To situate the debate selection, the three debates chosen have occurred at the federal level since 1969. This is largely because this chapter is concerned with questions surrounding the legality of abortion in Canada, which is a federal power of criminal law. Under the founding framework of the British North America Act of 1867, the federal Parliament has the authority to adopt and amend criminal law, as embodied in the Criminal Code. After the Constitution Act of 1982 superseded the British North America Act, the Supreme Court of Canada was newly empowered to effect judicial review of statutes, particularly on civil liberties. The Court then joined Parliament as an actor on abortion policy.

Within the Canadian federal framework, provincial legislatures do not have authority to pass criminal statutes. Both the British North America Act of 1867 and the Constitution Act of 1982 assigned local matters, including hospital operations, to provincial jurisdiction. Before and after national policy-making episodes, provincial governments have maintained a 'hands-off' attitude toward the question of whether hospitals actually have to provide abortion services, giving them wide discretion.[2] Usually, at the provincial level, decisions about abortion provision as a health service occur out of the public arena, among doctors' associations or on hospital boards.

The universe of public policy debates at the federal level in the period under study includes the following:

(1) Reform/liberalization of abortion criminal code, 1966–9, Pearson and Trudeau Liberal Governments.
(2) Badgley Parliamentary Commission Report, 1977, assessing the workings of the 1969 reform; Trudeau Liberal Government.
(3) Conservative Government of Brian Mulroney 'sense of the House' debates 1988 producing no majority behind any option.
(4) Conservative Government of Brian Mulroney, Bill C-43 to reinstate criminal penalties for abortion in 1989–91.
(5) The Supreme Court of Canada review in Morgentaler, *Smoling and Scott v. The Queen* 1988—the *Morgentaler* case—of the 1969 Criminal Code provisions limiting abortions to hospitals.
(6) The Supreme Court decision in *Trembly v. Daigle*—the *Daigle* case—1989, concerning a father's rights and, more generally, the question of fetal right to life under the Quebec Charter.
(7) The Supreme Court decision in the 1989 *Borowski v. Canada* case concerning the question of fetal right to life under the federal Charter.
(8) The Supreme Court review in *R. v. Morgentaler* 1993 of a Nova Scotia law banning clinic abortions. At all levels of the Nova Scotia courts, and continuing to the Supreme Court of Canada, it was found that Nova Scotia's legislation infringed upon the federal government's power to pass criminal laws.

66

The following three debates have been chosen for analysis in this chapter: Reform/liberalization of abortion criminal code 1966–9; the Supreme Court cases of *Morgentaler* in 1988 and *Daigle* in 1989; and Bill C-43 to reinstate criminal penalties for abortion in 1989–91. By focusing on the question of legality versus criminalization, these debates have had the greatest impact on public policy regulating abortion in Canada. They also represent the two major institutional arenas making federal abortion policy.

These debates cover the life span of the question of abortion legality from the 1960s to the 1990s. They also show changes in the definition of the issue over time, especially in relation to the participation of women and the gendering of the debates. The first and third debates are two parliamentary actions— Omnibus Criminal Code amendments of 1969 and attempted re-introduction of criminal penalties into law by the Conservatives in 1989–91—that focused largely on doctors' fear of prosecution under criminal penalties. They show differences over time, however, in that women were sufficiently present in the 1989–91 debate to voice their concerns effectively about reduced access to abortion services. The two cases in the intervening, second debate, those of *Morgentaler* (1988) and *Daigle* (1989), are paired over the issue of autonomy and women's rights in the abortion process.

❖ DEBATE 1: REFORM/LIBERALIZATION OF ABORTION CRIMINAL CODE, 1966–1969

❖ *How debate came to the public agenda*

The abortion issue was brought to Parliament's attention by physicians, particularly the Canadian Medical Association (CMA), wishing to continue their de facto practices without being prosecuted. The British Columbia branch of the CMA began the call for reform of the laws then on the books, launching a debate which 'then became part of the internal politics of the association' (Kellough 1996: 78). Media attention followed the internal discussion documenting that doctors had long been informally practising a system which violated the Criminal Code. During the 1960s, 'eminent members of the profession regularly confessed in public that they were breaking the law', yet none of those performing hospital-based abortions was prosecuted (Kellough 1996: 78).

By 1966, the CMA put forth a resolution to legalize abortion, but rejected abortion on demand, 'which it define[d] as a situation in which a woman would have a right to have her pregnancy terminated' (Dulude 1975: 12). Rather, their resolution sought to formalize existing practices in three important ways: it would keep abortion procedures in hospitals, maintain the power of committees of physicians to decide whether an abortion were the right 'remedy' for the situation and thus could be performed, and empower the committee to require spousal or guardian consent. The Canadian Bar Association (CBA), which was mainly concerned about the physicians it was called upon to defend, joined with the CMA in its quest.

The impetus for the reforms in Parliament came initially from private members who had been working during the previous parliamentary mandate of 1965–8. In 1966 and 1967, two New Democratic Party (NDP) members, one a woman and one a male Liberal backbencher, proposed changes to the Criminal Code to allow abortion for the mother's health and well-being (Pierson *et al.* 1993: 3). The Liberal government then proposed omnibus amendments to the Criminal Code, including provisions to allow abortion where the pregnancy would endanger the life or health of the mother. When the Liberal government returned after the 1968 election with a large majority—155 of 264 seats—under the leadership of former Justice Minister Pierre Trudeau, it reintroduced its reform provisions.

❖ Dominant frame of the debate

The frame of this debate in the late 1960s was constructed largely through the interactions between the Canadian Medical and Bar Associations and some MPs. The rhetoric of the associations was based virtually exclusively on the needs of doctors under threat of prosecution for reform in the law. The CMA and CBA were in the controlling position to frame the debate in ways that coincided with concepts of hierarchy and scientific and male privilege (Jenson 1992: 24–6). Throughout, the dominant position of men in the House of Commons and the medical and legal professions was evident. There was no change in the terms of the debate from start to finish; it was mainly one about physicians and their fear of prosecution, even though women had been also liable to prosecution, or denial of an abortion, under the legal regime. While the Liberal government officially touted the need for Criminal Code reforms to benefit all Canadians, the consensus on this reform episode is that the order of lobbying importance was first, the CMA, and second, the CBA.

❖ Gendering the debate

A few women's organizations made submissions to the parliamentary committee considering the bill. The National Council of Women, a 'first wave' socialist feminist women's organization founded in 1893, viewed women primarily in relation to families, not as autonomous individuals. The Council had long criticized the abortion provisions in the Criminal Code as 'confused, conflicting, outdated, and cruel' (Jenson 1992: 31). The National Council was joined in parliamentary presentations by groups representing the liberation emphasis of part of the second-wave women's movement, including the Women's Liberation Group and Toronto Women's Liberation Group, the latter alone speaking of 'women's reproductive control' (Jenson 1992: 31). The Fédération des Femmes du Québec (FFQ), the largest umbrella women's organization in Quebec, supported legalization but not the complete removal of Criminal Code penalties. However, as Jenson (1992: 31) notes, 'none of these groups ever gained recognition as major actors in the debate'.

Inside Parliament there was little support for these organizations. Grace MacInnis, the NDP sponsor of the private member's bill which would have allowed for more liberalized grounds for abortion, was the only woman in the House. Among the parties, only the New Democratic Party consistently opposed Criminal Code sanctions for abortion and was most likely to argue against them on gendered grounds. It was, however, the third party in the House, holding only 21 seats. Thus MacInnis had little impact on the debate, being a marginalized member within a marginalized party, and women's concerns were not central to this debate.

❖ *Policy outcome*

Parliament passed the Liberal Government's proposed amendments to the Criminal Code on abortion in 1968; they were implemented in 1969. Under the new law, abortions had to be performed in qualified hospitals, and the request for the abortion had to be approved by the hospital's Therapeutic Abortion Committee (TAC), comprised of at least three doctors, none of whom could be the one to perform the abortion. The TAC would have to certify that continuing the pregnancy would endanger the life or health of the mother.[3] Physicians found guilty of 'procuring a miscarriage' without the requisite TAC approval would be liable to life imprisonment. A woman who did not get TAC approval, yet proceeded to have an abortion elsewhere, could be liable for two years' imprisonment. The amendments did not, however, codify a husband's right to be consulted in the decision, although this had been happening informally.

Decriminalization of abortion in 1969 established a system which provided few alternatives for women. Although the TAC system set up a way of gaining access to abortion services in approved hospitals, it did not require hospitals to offer the procedure. Further, there was no provision in the reform for non-therapeutic abortions, that is, those simply performed by women's choice; all had to be justified to protect the mother's health or life. Denial by a TAC was final; there was no appeals process. Finally, the TAC system gave legal legitimacy to the committee system doctors had been unofficially using and gave them a defence against criminal proceedings where previously there had been none.

As has been noted, this 'decriminalization' of existing laws effectively maintained the status quo as it had been practiced by doctors for years (Kellough 1996: 78). It also retained physicians as the gatekeepers to decide where and whether abortion services would be offered. While the decriminalization seemingly increased women's chances of obtaining safe abortion services, the lack of corresponding mandate that they be provided proportionately across Canada would soon become an evident problem.

❖ Women's movement impact

The women's movement impact on the 1967–9 debate was minimal and is classified as pre-emption. This is due to the fact that women were not involved in the debate in any significant sense, but that the government could claim that a form of decriminalization—abortion available to certain women and doctors following certain requirements—was a step in the direction of movement goals. As previously noted, however, most women's groups were not satisfied, and liberal, radical, and socialist feminist groups began organizing immediately following the bill's passage. However, the organizing space had been pulled out from under them since it was hard to argue that the government was completely unresponsive in the wake of the reforms.

❖ Women's policy agency activities

In 1967, the Liberal government appointed a Royal Commission on the Status of Women (RCSW).[4] In the Canadian political system, Royal Commissions tend to be the mechanism used by a government facing an election that wishes to appear committed to a controversial social issue, before proposing any legislation. Commissions are usually appointed for a long period, so that they report after the current government has faced an election (Pierson *et al.* 1993: 5).

There were seven commissioners, two of whom were men; only the Chair worked full-time, and the others included three professors, a judge, a homemaker, and an engineer. The mandate for the commissioners, with a C$3 million budget, was to 'inquire, report and make recommendations as to what steps the federal government should take to give women equal opportunities in every aspect of Canadian society' (Pierson *et al.* 1993: 32–6). The Commission travelled across Canada and heard from citizens, prepared briefings, and commissioned 40 studies from academics. Overall, its frame of reference was described by its Executive Secretary—later Cabinet Minister—Monique Begin as grounded in liberalism and the concepts of equal rights and opportunities.

Three years after the RCSW's appointment, it reported to Prime Minister Trudeau with recommendations clustered in five areas: economic participation of women; women in public life and the judicial process; education and training; family life and community services; and disadvantaged women (Paltiel 1997: 321–2). With respect to abortion, the RCSW recommended that, prior to twelve weeks of pregnancy, women should be able to request an abortion without medical advice. After twelve weeks, the basis for the required physician's consent should be that continuing the pregnancy would endanger the physical or mental health of the woman or that the child would be 'greatly handicapped', mentally or physically (Dulude 1975: 2). Jenson has written that of the Report's 167 recommendations, the two concerning abortion generated the most controversy and dissent for the commissioners (Jenson 1997: 297).

During the 1967–9 abortion reform debate, the RCSW was conducting its studies and its conclusions on abortion were significantly watered down in order to produce a consensus. By the time the Report's recommendations were made public, the Criminal Code reforms had taken place. Thus, the RCSW played a *marginal* role, articulating reforms of the law that coincided with the liberal wing of the women's movement, but unable to present these views in the parliamentary debates.

Overall, the resources given to the RCSW may be viewed as reasonably generous for 1969. Its mandate was clearly sweeping and multi-issue, as demonstrated by the 167 recommendations it issued. The Commission did not have close proximity to either Prime Minister it dealt with, neither Prime Minister Pearson, who appointed the RCSW, nor Prime Minister Trudeau, to whom it reported. Its Chair was considered to be feminist, while a few of the other commissioners had feminist leanings and at least two were not considered to be especially feminist.

❖ Women's movement characteristics

The Canadian women's movement at the time of the first debate was in transition between the older branch representing first-wave suffrage and Progressive activism, and the emerging second wave, which would ultimately include groups representing liberal, socialist, and radical feminism. No single-issue pro-choice group had yet been formed, which also meant that abortion rights were not the top priority for the groups in existence. This began to change only after the 1969 policy. Since the second-wave movement was not yet institutionalized, it was not yet very cohesive, although organizations from inside and outside Quebec did coalesce well in order to press for the Royal Commission.

There were early socialist feminist groups in existence, including the League for Socialist Action. These groups claimed that women's control over their reproduction was necessary to change unequal power relations, the contradiction between women's role in the private and public spheres, and, above all, the role of women *vis-à-vis* the state. They were, however, marginalized by two factors at the time (Adamson, Briskin, and McPhail 1988: 49, 97). The first was that the abortion discourse was framed around the needs of physicians for a criminal defence, and the definition of women's issues was resoundingly liberal. Second, the only possible ally among the parties was a new party with minority status in the House. Newly forming radical women's organizations were in a similarly marginalized position at the time. Therefore, the socialist women's movement may be described as having been close to the left at the time, but the NDP was a relatively new player in the House.

There was no effectively organized counter-movement at the time. Pro-life sentiment was represented by a few conservative, Social Credit MPs from Quebec, known as *Créditistes*. They did not tend to make much headway in the committee deliberations, but later presented arguments on the House floor. They did not sway many Catholic members of other parties, including the governing Liberals (Jenson 1992: 28–9).

❖ Policy environment

The Canadian parliamentary system, following the British Westminster system, is majoritarian where the governing party vests power in the executive, comprising the prime minister and the cabinet. By the time policy proposals are put before the House, they have been formulated by the prime minister and his or her leadership, including the deputy prime minister, with relevant cabinet members and committees, and support has been garnered from the deputy and assistant deputy minister level in the bureaucracy. The governing party has many resources at its disposal to control the parliamentary flow of legislation, including the expectation of party discipline in the House and the presence of the cabinet and executive departments such as the Prime Minister's Office (PMO) and the Privy Council Office (PCO). It is in a position to control the timing and outcome of legislation it puts before the House. There was little reason for the government to propose reform of a controversial social issue such as abortion if it had not carefully assessed its chances of winning beforehand. In this particular debate, the Westminster system worked as usual, contributing to a closed policy environment. The Liberals decided to introduce social policy amendments only when they had a clear majority in the House that would support their proposals. In addition to being tightly controlled by the governing Liberal party, the policy system was based on the consideration of proposals within the confines of liberalism and those acceptable to the CMA.

❖ DEBATE 2: THE MORGENTALER AND DAIGLE CASES, 1988–1989

The second debate involves two court cases: *Morgentaler, Smoling and Scott v. the Queen* (1988), 37 C.C.C. (3d) 449 (Supreme Court of Canada), and *Tremblay v. Daigle* (1989), 62 D.L.R. (4th) 634. They concerned, respectively, whether Dr Henry Morgentaler's freestanding—non-hospital—abortion clinics were a violation of the 1969 abortion law and whether women's male partners had the power to stop an abortion decision.

❖ *How the debate came to the public agenda*

A campaigner for increased abortion services, Dr Morgentaler began performing freestanding clinic abortions in Montreal immediately after the 1969
reforms. By the 1980s, Morgentaler had formed clinics in Ontario, Quebec, and
Manitoba.[5] From 1970 on he faced trials and appeals as authorities attempted to
stop him. In the *Daigle* case in 1989, an ex-boyfriend (Tremblay) who admitted
he was guilty of physical abuse nonetheless sued his former girlfriend (Daigle)
to prevent her from having an abortion. The Quebec Court of Appeal agreed
with Tremblay's arguments that 'the fetus was a distinct human entity'. By the
time Ms Daigle appealed to the Supreme Court of Canada, she was past the 20-
week cut-off for a legal Quebec abortion.

❖ *Dominant frame of the debate*

The 1969 Criminal Code debate had established the definition of the abortion
issue as a question of the rights, responsibilities, and authorities of physicians
over the procedure. In the course of his appeals, Dr Morgentaler combined his
defence of necessity, inspired by the *Bourne* precedent, with the claim that the
Criminal Code violated Section 7 of the 1982 Charter of Rights and Freedoms
which guarantees of 'life, liberty and security of the person' (Gavigan 1992:
123–4). In the *Morgentaler* case, there was a clash of opinions about the definition of the legal issue at stake. Dr Morgentaler's lawyer wished to emphasize
the narrow question of physicians' rights and their fears of prosecution which
had worked successfully in 1969. On the other hand, Section 7 of the Charter,
while gender neutral, provided a foundation for reframing the abortion question as a matter of human rights, specifically women's rights, to 'life, liberty
and security'.

The *Daigle* case was, on the facts, a disagreement between two ex-partners.
However, it also involved a clash between the Quebec and the federal Charters.
The central conflict was between a woman's right to choice, thought to be protected by the federal Charter of Rights and Freedoms, and the right to life of the
fetus, as argued by its father, based on right to life provisions of the Quebec
Charter. Tremblay, the ex-boyfriend, was financially backed by Quebec pro-life
groups in his quest (J. Brodie 1992: 93).

❖ *Gendering the debate*

The two main single-issue abortion-rights groups which were active in this
debate were the Canadian Abortion Rights Action League (CARAL) and the
Ontario Coalition for Abortion Clinics (OCAC). CARAL—formerly the
Canadian Association for the Repeal of the Abortion Law—was formed in
November 1974 to support Dr Henry Morgentaler's initial challenges of the 1969

framework on abortion (Dunphy 1996; Pierson 1993b). Stressing the liberal argument that choice in abortion is a woman's right, CARAL has worked with other groups, participating in both mainstream lobbying strategies and grass-roots actions such as candlelight vigils and marches.

The Ontario group, OCAC, disagreed with an emphasis solely on choice, viewing it as a liberal individualist argument divorced from social power relations (Kellough 1996: 214). It preferred to emphasize the concept of access, or what has been called the 'choice-as-access' or 'choice-as-empowerment' model, showing that choice realistically depended upon other components of society, such as willingness to fund and provide the services. As its name suggests, OCAC advocated the establishment of abortion clinics in Ontario in 1982 when they were illegal. CARAL and OCAC acted in coalition on numerous occasions, joined at times by the Quebec-based group, Coalition québécoise pour le droit à l'avortement libre et gratuit (Pierson 1993a: 102). Other multi-issue groups active in the abortion debate, especially in the courts, were the National Association of Women and the Law (NAWL), and the Women's Legal Education and Action Fund (LEAF). LEAF formed as a litigation group in 1985 to promote women's equality through the Charter of Rights and Freedoms.

There were essentially two ways in which women's movement activists could participate in these cases. The first was in the court of public opinion, the second as a participant in the court proceedings, whether as a litigant or as an interested third party, known as an intervenor. The Morgentaler defence team tried to prevail upon women's groups to keep a low profile, and pressed women's groups not to file supporting briefs in the case. While they were not allowed to intervene in the court proceeding, women's groups made their voices heard in other ways in the *Morgentaler* case.[6] In the public discourse surrounding the *Daigle* case, women's groups, possibly encouraged by the *Morgentaler* outcome, were even more overt.

In the 1980s, in order to emphasize the gendered nature of the issue, pro-choice organizations demonstrated in major cities across Canada, including in Quebec, against the Quebec court's decision in the Daigle case. They said it 'gave ex-boyfriends control over the most basic decision in a woman's life, and reduced them to walking wombs' (J. Brodie 1992: 94). Pro-choice arguments spoke of women's right to choice, and the fact that the male ex-partner was thus far successfully violating the right of women to autonomy guaranteed in *Morgentaler*. In what was said to be an unusual circumstance, the Supreme Court allowed all intervenor requests for the *Daigle* case (F. L. Morton 1992a: 277). The pro-choice intervenors were CARAL, LEAF, and the Canadian Civil Liberties Association.

❖ *Policy outcome*

On 28 January 1988, the Supreme Court voided the 1969 abortion law and its TAC framework. In its decision in the *Morgentaler* case, the Court contributed a new frame for the abortion issue in Canada—based on the rights of women— which followed liberal women's movement organization objectives. Five of the seven justices hearing the case in three separate majority opinions agreed that the operation of Section 251 of the Criminal Code violated a woman's right to 'security of the person' as contained in Section 7 of the Charter. Two of the opinions, comprising four justices, confined the 'security of the person' infringement to the criminal law context only, whereas the fifth, that of Justice Bertha Wilson, found that Section 7 conferred both the right to liberty and the right to security of the person upon women. She also found that the Criminal Code provisions violated women's freedom of conscience, as guaranteed in Charter Section 2a (M. Morton 1998, 3, 5–7).

All of the majority decisions noted that the justices had not been asked to decide whether the fetus possessed Section 7 rights, and while they were not undertaking this task, each acknowledged that 'the state interest in protecting the fetus through the criminalizing of abortion was important enough to over-ride the Section 7 rights of the pregnant woman'. Justice Wilson attempted to balance the woman's right to freedom from state interference in decision mak-ing with a potential increase in state interest as the pregnancy progressed, sug-gesting that the purview for making the distinction rested with Parliament, but also suggesting that the time for greater state scrutiny might occur 'during the second trimester' (M. Morton 1988: 11). The three opinions in the majority deci-sion seemed to walk the line between framing the decision in a 'right to choice' framework and in one that discussed access. Justice Wilson's opinion came down squarely on the side of women's right to choose, consistent with a liberal rights framework. The opinion of Justices Beetz and Estey stated that a right of access to abortion was only potential—with a potential, 'compelling' state inter-est in the protection of the fetus at some unspecified point. Only Chief Justice Dickson and Justice Lamer spoke of how Section 251 of the Criminal Code pre-vented access to local abortion facilities.[7]

The *Morgentaler* decision removed abortion from the Criminal Code, allowing abortions to be performed in non-hospital clinics and leaving it to provincial governments to decide under their powers under the Canada Health Act whether they wanted to provide and fund clinic-based abortions. The biggest change after this decision was that clinic abortions would no longer be illegal. However, access was really only theoretically improved by *Morgentaler*, given that the decision did not include a mandate for funding or establishing clinics (Kellough 1996: Ch. 6). The limitations of having 'no federal law', especially one that proactively addressed funding and access issues, soon became clear, since 'within a few months of the *Morgentaler* decision, every provincial government except for Ontario and Quebec had announced measures under their health-care jurisdiction to limit the funding and in some cases even the performance of abortions' (Mandel 1994: 424). Therefore, while *Morgentaler* codified the liberal right of choice, it did not address the question of access and clearly disappointed OCAC as well as some parts of CARAL.

As for the *Daigle* case, on the morning of the August 8 1989 court date, Ms Daigle's lawyer informed the court that Daigle had gone to Boston for an abortion. This action effectively mooted the arguments of the case, but Ms Daigle's lawyer chose to continue to push forward with it, arguing that injunctions against pregnant women were still a relevant issue (F. L. 1992a: 281). On 8 August 1989, the Court lifted the injunction against Ms Daigle and announced it would issue the rest of its decision later. On 16 November 1989, the Court found that there was not a fetal right to life under Quebec law and that the father did not have a right to act to protect fetal life under the Quebec Charter (F. L. Morton 1992a: 282). The Court also stated that the pro-life side's attempt to claim that there was a legislative intent to protect fetal personhood under the Quebec Civil Code was a 'fiction', being used to 'protect future interests of the fetus'; furthermore, 'the recognition of the foetus' juridical personality is only a "fiction of the civil law" which is utilized in order to protect the future interests of the foetus' (LEAF 1996: 115). Ultimately, the outcome of the case did follow women's movement goals. However, the parameters of the case did not reach the question of fetal personhood under the federal Charter, a question which both sides also wanted to see settled.

❖ Women's movement impact

The women's movement impact in this debate is assessed as a dual response, where movement organizations found opportunities to put their views before the state, both in public lobbying as in Morgentaler and as participants in the Court Challenges Program in Daigle. Women were less overtly involved in the former case than the latter since intervenors were prohibited. Yet some groups, especially OCAC and CARAL, still managed to hold public demonstrations in favour of the choice issue. The outcome of both cases may be said to have satisfied a reasonable percentage of the women's movement goals, even if not the whole spectrum. For example, OCAC wished that the Morgentaler decision had addressed the access issue, and both OCAC and CARAL wished that Daigle had included language about the fetus's right to life under the federal, not just the Quebec, Charter, since the federal Charter was the endpoint in the constitutional process.

❖ Women's policy agency activities

The Royal Commission's work in the 1960s led to the creation of four national agencies, all of which were in existence during the 1988–9 debate: the Minister Responsible for the Status of Women, the Advisory Council on the Status of Women, Status of Women Canada, and the Women's Program in the Department of Secretary of State. The Minister Responsible for the Status of Women, a cabinet position, was the apex of the women's policy machinery. Curiously, however, it was formed as an 'add-on' ministry, since its occupant has always held a primary portfolio elsewhere in cabinet, with the Status of Women as a secondary responsibility. It has thus been thought that the main way in which the Minister Responsible for the Status of Women is able to advocate women's concerns depends on the seniority of her primary portfolio. It is also true that the Minister Responsible for the Status of Women can convey Prime Ministerial displeasure—or approval—to the various women's agencies in the form of changing the issues for study or the time frame in which they are presented. Most of the time, however, the women's agencies function fairly independently, being outside the purview of the cabinet.

The Advisory Council on the Status of Women is funded and appointed by the government of the day and conducts research on issues of importance to the government. It advises the Minister Responsible for the Status of Women. Status of Women Canada was formed as a separate bureaucratic research agency in 1976. The Women's Program of the Department of Secretary of State is a means by which the government provides financial assistance for women's organizations (Geller-Schwartz 1995). One view of the Canadian women's policy agencies is that their very nature makes them part of the peripheral, non-mainstream governmental issues sector (Burt 1998: 136). This again makes them function fairly independently, and the communication between them and the cabinet is based on the ability and willingness of the Minister Responsible for the Status of Women to convey those concerns.

The relevant women's policy agencies in this debate were the Advisory Council on the Status of Women and the Minister Responsible for the Status of Women. They were cross-sectional with broad policy mandates, political rather than bureaucratic. There was moderately close proximity to power, given that the Minister Responsible for the Status of Women was at the time the most senior woman in cabinet; however, as an economic conservative, she did not support all women's movement concerns. The watchword of the Mulroney Conservative Government was loyalty to the executive; and this stance affected the strategies of women's policy agencies. In terms of resources, the Advisory Council on the Status of Women found itself in a similar position to some women's movement organizations in the 1980s, where support of the government's programme was rewarded. For example, in 1985–9, the Council's

Director took a conciliatory stance toward the Mulroney Government's philosophy, particularly on economic issues, and the Advisory Council received increased funding, more than ten times the initial figure of 1973 (Burt 1998: 120). At the same time, the leadership of these organizations could be characterized as interested in women's issues, but not consciously feminist. As Barbara McDougall, Minister for the Status of Women, stated: 'when we took office, we recognized that the women's movement was in a new stage, of dealing with economic and child-care reforms, rather than the issues of the 1970s'.[8]

Since its foundation in 1973, the Advisory Council opposed the presence of abortion provisions in the Criminal Code. At the same time, the Council adopted a stance of trying not to provoke controversy when dealing with the Mulroney Government, especially from 1985 onward (Burt 1998). The three-year strategic plan for the Council, published in 1987, did not mention abortion, although it was a prominent issue at the time. The Minister herself, likely in keeping with the Westminster model's discouragement of party or legislative involvement during judicial deliberations, did not publicly comment on either *Morgentaler* or *Daigle* in advance. While the Secretary of State's Women's Program provided funds, initially to pro-choice groups and later under Prime Minister Mulroney to pro-life groups, the women's policy agencies are classified as symbolic in this debate.

❖ Women's movement characteristics

During the second debate, the women's movement was in a stage of consolidation. While both the pro-choice sector and the National Action Committee on the Status of Women (NAC), the umbrella Anglophone organization, were growing in membership and activities, they had established an institutionalized presence with respect to the policy-making institutions. Of necessity, the strategies of consultation and lobbying used by the women's movement organizations during the Trudeau years began to change under the Mulroney Government. By the late 1980s, the relationship became adversarial, and movement access to politicians and bureaucrats was cut off (Bashevkin 1998). Because this abortion debate happened in the courts rather than in the House of Commons, however, both pro-choice and pro-life groups could choose to be publicly vocal.

The movement faced a strong counter-movement during the second debate. Among pro-life groups, the best-known outside Quebec since 1980 was the Campaign Life and its multi-issue successor, REAL Women of Canada. REAL Women was formed in 1983, standing against feminism, equality rights in the new Charter, federal initiatives to help women—on both libertarian and social conservative grounds—and abortion rights. One of the analogues in Quebec is the group Campaign Quebec-Vie. They were a strong presence in both cases. While most feminist groups distrusted the Tories, pro-life groups had found sympathetic ears among some social conservative members of the Conservative caucus.

Movement groups such as the socialist-feminist OCAC were overtly close to the left (the NDP), as were many members of CARAL. Consistently throughout these debates, the NDP never attained more seats than the third-party position in the House. Other members of women's groups worked with the Liberal Party. The evolution of abortion policy was clearly of high priority to the women's movement. Cohesion among women's movement groups was beginning to be tested at this time and during this debate in two significant ways. The first was the disagreement between CARAL and OCAC over how much to follow the strategies crafted by Dr Morgentaler's lawyer. Second, some women's movement activists in other groups were becoming sceptical about NAC's consistently adversarial position towards the Tory government, arguing that these actions could permanently 'freeze out' women's movement groups that had been accustomed to having a reasonably close working relationship with the state (Bashevkin 1998: 196).

❖ Policy environment

The policy arena for the second debate—the courts—was, potentially, an open sub-system especially with the provision for intervention by non-government organizations in cases. Unlike the Parliament policy sub-system, there was no internal control or single chain of command. On these two national test cases on abortion, the Supreme Court proved itself sympathetic to women's concerns. The national government had changed from Liberal to Conservative in 1984, but in both cases the majority of the Supreme Court were still Liberal appointees and ruled in favour of women's civil liberties. Participation of interest groups as intervenors was changing throughout this debate; from restriction during the *Morgentaler* case, where feminist groups participated publicly in other ways, to open-ended intervention rules in *Daigle*. Thus the policy environment for these matched cases is classified as moderately closed.

❖ DEBATE 3: GOVERNMENT BILL TO RECRIMINALIZE ABORTION, 1989–1991

❖ How the debate came to the public agenda

After the *Morgentaler* and *Daigle* cases, there were no federal guidelines on abortion policy. Realizing there was a policy vacuum, the Mulroney Conservative Government began quietly working to craft a new policy almost immediately after its return from the autumn 1988 election. The bill's formulation began in January 1989 with a cabinet committee that mirrored caucus divisions between social and economic conservatives but could not come to an agreement. Following that attempt, a specially selected caucus committee, headed by Senator Lowell Murray, was charged with drafting the proposal. Among the questions that had to be resolved was what language Catholic bishops would accept.[9] Highly-placed PMO members were conspicuously present at this committee, presumably to report back to the Prime Minister, as they would be during legislative committee deliberations later in the process.[10]

Bill C-43 was placed before the House on 3 November 1989. It was a proposal to return regulation of abortion practices to the Criminal Code, requiring that an abortion be performed by 'a qualified medical practitioner ... who is of the opinion that, if the abortion were not induced, the health or life of the female person would be likely to be threatened'. Health was defined to include physical, mental, and psychological health. Similarly, 'medical practitioner' was defined as one entitled to practise medicine 'under the laws of [any] province' (quoted in Brodie, Gavigan, and Jenson 1992: 149–50). Unlike the 1969 reforms, Bill C-43 did not require that abortion be performed in a hospital; if a province allowed the procedure in clinics, as most did, by then, that would be acceptable. Because it criminalized abortion performed outside the bill's guidelines, it was immediately opposed by pro-choice organizations and by many in the opposition ranks of the House of Commons.

❖ *Dominant frame of the debate*

The frame as a consequence of the Court's decisions in the second debate defined the abortion issue as a question of the rights of women to dignity and choice, recognizing the potential interests of the fetus at later stages of pregnancy. With Bill C-43, the Conservative government sought to reframe the issue as a question of health administration. It argued that the federal Criminal Code was the only vehicle through which to ensure national standards and prevent a 'patchwork' system of access, and that the recent Supreme Court decisions had left a policy lacuna which Parliament was required to fill. While the previous debate had centred around the choice issue from the beginning, the third debate shifted to new ground, emphasizing adequacy of services and women's access to them. The irony was that the bill did nothing to improve conditions of access, since it could not address provincial funding and licensing powers.

❖ *Gendering the debate*

OCAC and CARAL immediately became active on this proposal. CARAL challenged the government's effort to switch the frame established through the second debate. CARAL's brief to the special legislative committee emphasized women's rights in Charter Section 7, and Justice Wilson's opinion in

Morgentaler relating to the 'autonomy, integrity, dignity and equality of women'. The recriminalization of abortion was held to be against the Charter, viewed as undermining the doctor-patient relationship and ignoring the real causes of unplanned pregnancies (CARAL 1990). The two national feminist litigation organizations, NAWL and LEAF, stated that a return to the Criminal Code would again be found to contravene the Charter of Rights and Freedoms. In a fashion similar to its member organization CARAL, the NAC emphasized that majority opinion was against a return to the Criminal Code, and that 'the only standard the bill would enshrine was one of nation-wide dehumanization and deceit' (NAC 1990).

In keeping with its strategic tradition, OCAC used arguments relating to access. OCAC began to use the slogan that 'women are not criminals', and argued that returning abortion provisions to the Criminal Code was not the correct way to deal with the 'checkerboard system of justice' decried by the prime minister. Among the opposition parties, the NDP also emphasized the access issue. Like OCAC, the NDP's position was that the only acceptable national legislation on abortion would be under the Canada Health Act, requiring that hospitals and clinics offer the procedure to receive federal funds.

The CMA also opposed the government's bill. The CMA's position was that Bill C-43 singled out abortion 'as the only medical procedure to be labelled a potential crime' (Wilson 1989). Dr Judith Kazimirski, the CMA President, stated that it was likely that of the 375 physicians then performing abortion in Canada, many would stop (*Globe and Mail* 1990; Dunlop 1990). By June 1990, there were reports of doctors who either had stopped performing abortions or would stop performing them, in anticipation that the bill would continue its passage through Parliament. In Quebec, clinics claimed that they would defy the new law (McLaren 1990; Picard 1990).

The third debate was the first in which both physicians and women could be viewed as equal participants in shaping the discourse. Only the women's movement organizations tried to gender the debate to frame abortion policy in terms of its effect on women's rights and access. The women's movement would no longer let doctors claim that they were the only ones potentially harmed by the criminalization of abortion procedures. Another point was that doctors immediately threatened to withdraw services should the bill pass: in other words, punishing women who had no responsibility for the government's legislation.

In this debate, the movement advocates were more successful when they sought to gender the government's access frame relating to abortion policy than in their efforts to retain the *Morgentaler* frame of women's rights to dignity. All sides—the Conservative government, the CMA, and the women's movement organizations—dealt with access. The government claimed that putting abortion services back into the Criminal Code was the best way to ensure access. Opposition women MPs and women's groups dependent on party affiliation either took the position that abortion should not be governed by criminal procedures (Liberals) or that it should be totally up to the woman and, if any policy was needed, it should be governed by the Canada Health Act. The government responded that the national framework of the Criminal Code was needed to ensure access since the Health Act was administered by provinces and could vary widely.

❖ Policy outcome

The debate revealed extensive displeasure with the government's bill, even from pro-life forces who thought it too liberal. Officially, the government termed this a 'free vote' for its members, while most observers disagreed with this characterization; interviews have revealed the presence of a strong party whip. Despite the apparent dissatisfaction with the bill, it passed its second reading by a surprisingly healthy margin of 164 votes to 114 on 28 November 1989. The 'no' votes included pro-life defections from the Conservatives, 60 Liberals, and 42 New Democrats (J. Brodie 1992: 99). The starkest outcome under the government's theoretically 'free vote' for its members was the polarization by party, not gender. All of the Tory women, including the pro-choice ones, voted for Bill C-43 as required, and all of the opposition women voted against it. The only Tories voting against the Government bill were twelve pro-life members, who opposed the bill as too lenient. Bill C-43 passed the House on third reading on 29 May 1990 and was sent to the Senate, which conducted hearings from October to December 1990.

Prime Minister Mulroney undoubtedly expected Bill C-43 to pass in the Senate, given that he had appointed eight new Conservative Senators in September 1990 over the issue of the Goods and Services Tax (GST), giving the Conservatives a majority in the Senate. The Senate is Canada's 'chamber of sober second thought'. It is composed of 100 members representing the whole country but with attention to Canadian regions. In this manner, the Senate differs from the House, which is based on popular representation of each province. Senators were originally appointed for life but since 1965 until age 75. They must be property owners, and must demonstrate at least C$4,000 in assets. On the other hand, the Senate is not completely independent of the political forces controlling the House, for the prime minister appoints Senators. While originally envisioned as an independent actor, 'by the middle of the 20th century, it had arguably become a convention of the Canadian Constitution that the Senate must not oppose a bill that has the support of the House of Commons (Malcolmson and Myers 1996: 139–41).

In between the House and Senate action on Bill C-43, pro-choice forces outside and inside Parliament redoubled their efforts. Intensive pro-choice lobbying, and the fact that many of the new 'GST Senators' appointed in 1990 were pro-choice in addition to fiscally conservative, helped to swing the outcome. Many of them openly defied government pressure and voted against the bill. Bill C-43 was defeated by a tie of 43 votes on each side in the Senate on 31 January 1991. This was the first time the Senate had defeated a government bill in 30 years (J. Brodie 1992: 115).

❖ Women's movement impact

This policy debate was a success for the women's movement activists. They were involved in the policy process, presenting committee briefs and participating in public demonstrations. Their activism, linking up with pro-choice Senators, held the key to the outcome. The policy content of Bill C-43 violated the wishes of both the pro-choice and a significant part of the pro-life movements. The defeat of this measure coincided with the women's movement goals, making the movement's impact on the state a dual response. Had Bill C-43 not been defeated in the Senate, the impact would have been cooptation.

❖ Women's policy agency activities

In the debate over Bill C-43, the positions of the Advisory Council and the Minister Responsible for the Status of Women diverged. Since 1973, the Advisory Council's position had remained unchanged. In its brief on Bill C-43, it reiterated its opposition to including abortion in the Criminal Code, pointing out that 'this council has offered the federal government the same advice for the past 17 years' (Canadian Advisory Council on the Status of Women 1990: 2). The brief went on to assert that in December 1989 and February 1990, 'Council members told the Minister, "we feel that our voices on this issue have not been heard"' (Canadian Advisory Council on the Status of Women 1990: 1).

The Minister Responsible for the Status of Women, as a member of the government, chose to comply with the government's position and defended Bill C-43. The high-stakes nature of Bill C-43 for the Mulroney Government's programme, and the pressure placed upon cabinet ministers and others to support it, translated into pressure on other agencies in the women's policy sector, dividing their efforts and effects. The Advisory Council, on the other hand, felt no qualms about voicing its dislike of the government's actions.

If the Advisory Council were the only active women's policy agency, it would very likely have achieved an insider status in this debate. If only the Minister for the Status of Women were included, the classification would be symbolic, given that the minister did not adopt a position coinciding with women's movement goals or attempt to intervene in the debate to gender this debate or advocate women's movement goals. Combining the activities of these two, the women's policy agency activities in the third debate are classified

❖ MELISSA HAUSSMAN

as marginal. This is due to the fact that the gendering process and advocacy of women's movement goals, as promoted by the Advisory Council, were over-ridden in the House by the minister, but made themselves present in the Senate. Since the Minister Responsible for the Status of Women is considered the apex of the women's policy system, the actions of that minister are ulti-mately the ones that describe the degree of influence of the women's agencies in the debate.

The women's policy agency characteristics continued from the previous debate in the following ways. The scope was still cross-sectional, although most of the agencies privileged laissez-faire market analyses and downplayed radical feminist influence. Since the early 1970s, the proximity of the women's agencies as such to power had not been very close, with the degree of influence largely being dependent on the seniority of the cabinet minister and the minister's working relationship with the heads of the Advisory Council and the Department of the Status of Women. In the 1980s, resources had been increased for the Advisory Council but decreased for the Secretary of State Woman's Pro-gram, which directly funded women's movement groups. Most of the agency heads continued to be sympathetic to women's concerns, especially as expressed in the dominant liberal paradigm, with Status of Women Coordinators gener-ally being viewed as feminists.

❖ Women's movement characteristics

This category remained virtually unchanged from the second debate. Some of the pro-choice groups, such as OCAC, continued to support the NDP. The women's movement was said to be in a stage of consolidation, and the Bill C-43 debate was of extremely high priority not just to single issue groups such as CARAL and OCAC, but also to LEAF, NAWL, and NAC. Pro-life organizations were only moderately strong in that they did not like Bill C-43, thinking it was not restrictive enough, but were not able to mobilize enough MPs in the face of Westminster-style party discipline imposed by the prime minister.

❖ Policy environment

The policy sub-system operating in this debate was closed, with top-down exec-utive control through the prime minister and the PMO. Still, party divisions were a factor in the government's calculus. After the 1988 'free trade' election, the Conservatives had dropped from 211 House seats to 169. The Liberals doubled their representation, going up to 83 seats, and the NDP gained seats, going from 30 to 43. More pro-life members were elected in both the Liberal Party and the Conservative Party, and the social divisions previously present in the Tory Party became magnified. Prime Minister Mulroney identified himself as pro-life, although he also stated that 'no one had the right to impose their personal views on others' (DeSanto 1989). The pro-life MPs came disproportionately from the Conservative Party, but the pro-choice identifiers in the poll came mostly from the NDP, secondly from the Conservatives, and least often from the Liberals.[11]

The system in the Senate was moderately-closed, allowing access from interest groups, such as the CMA and OCAC, in defiance of the government's imposed party discipline. This was a strange development, given that typically the Senate, especially in a situation of same-party power, will uphold the wishes of the House. Part of this was due to the presence of feminist, pro-choice Senators, including Janis Johnson and Mira Spivak, who had made their pro-choice views known to the prime minister upon their Senate appointments.[12] Finally, Liberals who supported their party's position of no national legislation on abortion worked to defeat Bill C-43.[13]

❖ CONCLUSION

The policy cycle on the issue of decriminalization of abortion services in Canada began with federal action in the late 1960s, leading to the omnibus reform of the Criminal Code, setting up the TAC framework. The policy cycle culminated in 1991, with an uncharacteristic defeat by the government-dominated Senate on a tied vote of the government's Bill C-43 to return abortion services to the Criminal Code. In the intervening years, pro-choice women's organizations, like CARAL and OCAC, and multi-issue women's organizations, such as NAC, the FFQ, LEAF, and NAWL worked to keep the gendered nature of abortion policy before MPs and the courts, on at least two issue definitions: abortion rights as a choice issue, and the issue of access to publicly-funded services in hospitals and clinics.

In 1969, the movement was pre-empted, with the government liberalizing the abortion law but not opening up the process to women or women's rights advocates. Since it became institutionalized in the 1970s, the movement has been successful in its efforts to gain access for women to policy-making processes relating to abortion at the federal level in Canada, making abortion a women's rights issue and decriminalizing abortion regulations.

Women's policy agencies, which were plentiful and fairly well-funded during the 1970s and 1980s, were not instrumental in the movement's successes. They tended to adopt feminist positions on the issue of abortion, but either silenced themselves or were silenced by the policy environment restricting any possibility of gendering the debate on behalf of movement interests. The frame of the abortion issue in Canada places questions of women's reproductive rights at the centre of the conflict, but this has been done in a far more direct fashion by women's movement organization activism. In some instances, policy agencies indirectly supported women's organizations, but, outside of the Advisory Council, often could not do so publicly. Paradoxically, while the women's policy agencies are removed from the centre of power, they have been subject to top-down political control through the Minister Responsible for the Status of Women, acting as a conduit from the prime minister.

The combined forces of the strength of the women's movement and the openings in the policy sub-system in the second and third debates seem to account for the movement successes. The changes in the policy environment over the years mirror the changes to the Canadian political system. When legislative proposals were before the House in both the Trudeau Liberal and the Mulroney Conservative years, the system was closed. On the other hand, the Senate was at a crossroads in 1991 and acted more independently than had been seen for 30 years in allowing the movement to lobby and defeat the government's bill. Similarly, the opening of the system to include the Supreme Court as a strong policy-maker, and the willingness of particular Justices to take on that role, opened the second debate to women's voices and influence.

❖ Notes

1 R. v. Bourne 2 All ER 615 1938; 1 KB 687 1939.

2 The exceptions are that, in the last 1980s, post-Morgentaler, the provinces of British Columbia and Nova Scotia passed laws to limit funded abortions to hospitals, both of which were ultimately invalidated: the former by the British Columbia Supreme Court, the latter by the Supreme Court of Canada. Also, the British Columbia Provincial Assembly passed 'buffer zone' legislation in the early 1990s (Tatalovich 1997: 218–21).

3 Criminal Code, C. 38, S. 18, as cited in Mandel (1994: 408).

4 There is some debate on how internally receptive the Liberal government was to the idea of the Royal Commission, and hence to women's lobbying, at the time. One view is that the government had to be threatened with a two-million women march on Ottawa to proceed with the plans for the Commission; another is that an influential woman cabinet minister at the time, the Honourable Judy LaMarsh, was able to act as a conduit between women's movement groups and the rest of cabinet to help get the Commission off the ground (Pierson 1993c: 5).

5 Morgentaler had faced trials and appeals going back and forth in both Quebec and Ontario, where he was first acquitted in Quebec in 1973. This ruling was reversed on appeal the following year, sending him to prison under an 18-month sentence; he was then re-acquitted in 1976 when the separatist Parti Quebecois government came to power. The Supreme Court of Canada appeal came after he was first acquitted by the Ontario Supreme Court in 1984, and was then subject to a new trial ordered by the Ontario Court of Appeal (Pierson 1993a; Bourne 1993).

6 Under the federal Court Challenges Program, begun in 1985, groups wishing to challenge laws on either language or equality provisions of the Charter could be funded to do so. Equality challenges under this programme had to concern both federal laws and at least one of three sections of the Charter, including Section 15.

7 M. Morton (1998: 8). Also, different opinions within the Supreme Court seemed to reflect differences outside it. In Morgentaler, Justice Wilson spoke of women's rights as fundamental, and alluded to a framework balancing between liberty and state interest, similarly to that in Roe v. Wade. Another majority decision, by Justices Beetz and Estey, responded by quoting a dissent from Sandra Day O'Connor in one case that 'potential life is no less potential in the first weeks of pregnancy than it is at the first weeks of viability'. The Supreme Court Justices appeared to reiterate the public struggle to represent the 'authentic' women's voice (F. L. Morton 1992: 245).

8 Telephone interview with former Minister for the Status of Women, the Honourable Barbara McDougall, 4 May 2000.

9 Telephone interview with the Honourable Senator Lowell Murray, 29 June 2000.

10 Interviews with former and current Tory caucus members.

11 In the survey, of the 114 MPs identifying themselves as pro-life, 72 were from the Conservative Party, 39 were from the Liberal Party, two were from the NDP, and the other was the lone Reform Party MP. Of the 63 pro-choice MPs, 30 were from the NDP, 22 from the Conservative Party, and eleven from the Liberal Party. Of the 86 MPs favouring some restrictions on abortion access during later stages of pregnancy, 51 were Conservatives, 25 were Liberals, and ten were New Democrats. These figures were collected by the then National Coordinator of CARAL, Robin Rowe, and cited in Viennau (1989: A1).

12 Interviews with Senators Janis Johnson and Mira Spivak, Ottawa, 24–5 November 1998.

13 Interview with the Honourable Joyce Fairbairn, former Liberal government leader in the Senate, Ottawa, 25 November 1998.

5 ❖ Gendering the Abortion Debate: The French Case

Jean C. Robinson

❖ INTRODUCTION

Until the 1970s, the French abortion law was a modification of the 1920–3 laws that had criminalized abortion, with provisions for prison terms and fines for those performing abortions as well as for women having abortions. Although the law had been modified in 1955 by allowing therapeutic abortions when pregnancy threatened the life of the woman, abortion was still considered a criminal act.[1] With the passage of *la loi Neuwirth*, which legalized contraception in 1967, abortion law reform was thrust on to centre stage. The legalization of contraception raised the issue of what recourse women had if their contraceptives failed (Stetson 1987: 60). The resolution to that puzzle was *la loi Veil*,[2] which provided for legal abortion in the first ten weeks of pregnancy but did not erase the criminalization of abortion under other circumstances.

In 1971, 343 prominent women, including Catherine Deneuve, Simone de Beauvoir, Françoise Sagan, Gisele Halimi, and Yvette Roudy, earned the sobriquet of 'whores' (*salopes*) for issuing a manifesto, published in *Le Nouvel Observateur* (1971), affirming that they had undergone illegal abortions. With this act they called into question both the long-standing criminalization of abortion in French law, but also the claim that the interests of the French state should trump women's rights. The public debates that started prior to the legalization of abortion in the *loi Veil* continued long after, because the issues invoked were fundamental to political and social claims about the state, the Church, and the social order.

The Mouvement Français pour le Planning Familial (MFPF) and the Mouvement pour la Liberté de l'Avortement et pour la Contraception (MLAC) took the leading roles in promoting an activist agenda for abortion policy reform. The MFPF was initially an association devoted to providing contraceptive information and prescribing contraceptives. Conflict quickly arose between the medical and political goals of the organization: should it offer contraception and sexual information solely, or should it also promote abortion law reform? Members who believed that abortion reform was essential prevailed, and the MFPF became, by the early 1970s, the most organized voice for abortion reform (Hassoun 1997: 5–6).

MLAC began as a protest group arising out of the 1971 manifesto and demonstrations; by 1973 it was providing illegal abortions, thereby publicly questioning the morality of France's anti-abortion laws. This radical stance highlighted the problems of women facing unwanted pregnancies, and sought to force French institutions to recognize the need for change. MLAC's position has always been uncompromising: 'in order to suppress clandestine abortions, it is necessary that all abortions be on-demand and free' (Berger 1975: 122).

Where MLAC took the issue to surgeries and the streets, Choisir used the courts. Founded by Giselle Halimi, Choisir defended the women who signed the 1971 manifesto and represented people who were on trial for abortions. Halimi, echoing MLAC, has argued that abortion must be available since it is the sole recourse when contraception either is not practised or fails (Mossuz-Lavau 1991: 88). Choisir became nationally known especially through its involvement in the Bobigny trials, which provided grist for the ongoing debates.[3]

Debates on abortion and contraception have been framed by recurrent concerns about French demographics and the falling birth rate. The state has regularly encouraged pro-natalist policies in the face of decreasing birth rates among French citizens. Abortion reform also inspires claims about the fundamental rights of women as citizens, and thus invokes a legitimacy derived from the inspired traditions of the French revolutionary founding. All public conversations about abortion—whether in terms of decriminalizing, state funding, or access—inevitably raise these opposing claims: that abortion reform will destroy France and morality or that abortion access is fundamental to French rights.

❖ SELECTION OF DEBATES

Generally it has been the National Assembly that has made the most important decisions concerning abortion, whether it be funding, legalizing conditions, or ensuring access. Some policy decisions are administrative, made by the Ministry of Health, the women's policy agency, or an inter-ministerial group. Final resolution to almost all decisions have been taken by votes in the legislature and approved by the president. France has a mixed presidential-parliamentary system; the premier and cabinet provide policy leadership and command a majority of the National Assembly. It is the president, when he holds a 'presidential majority', who dominates the government with the Council of Ministers—the prime minister and the minister—under his direction. France is not a party state; the parties do not monopolize policy-making as they do in many other European countries. It is more often called an 'administrative state', indicating the strength of the civil service elite.

Since the first decision on abortion in 1975, there have been recurrent debates every few years. Most seem to have high salience for the public and for the women's movement, since abortion is one of its linchpin issues. These debates include:

(1) reaffirmation of the 1975 abortion law in 1979, in Parliament;
(2) removing abortion from the penal code, 1974–5; in Parliament, 1979–82;
(3) reimbursement for non-therapeutic abortion charges from the state social security, 1982–3 in Parliament;
(4) the production and distribution of RU-486, 1987–90 in the Ministries of Health and Women's Rights and the Council of State;
(5) anti-abortion 'commandos' obstructing access to clinics and leading to *la Loi Neiertz*, 1991–3 in the National Assembly;
(6) bio-ethical decisions in reproductive technology, 1976–94 in the National Assembly and Conseil d'État; and
(7) 'right to life' amendment to the French constitution, 1994 to the present in the National Assembly.

The three debates examined in this chapter are the 1979 debate culminating in *la loi Pelletier*, which was decided in the National Assembly; the 1982–3 debates over reimbursement of expenses; and the debate over commando-IVG culminating in 1993 in *la loi Neiertz*, which provided sanctions for obstructing access to abortion services. These three cases were critical to the abortion rights agenda: first, to secure a permanent law; second, to make abortion financially accessible; and third, to make access to abortion providers safer from protests and threats. They represent debates occurring in both major decisional systems, namely, the National Assembly and the ministries; all had high issue salience, and the cases together cover the time span of the universe from 1979 to 1993. Notably, these three cases also illustrate the importance to women's policy agency activities of the party or coalition that holds executive power. The first case, in 1979, occurs while a centre-right government is in power; the second case, 1982–3, takes place during the era of strong Socialist Party domination of both the executive and the legislature; and the third case, 1991–3, is during a period of increasing conservatism, just prior to a return to co-habitation in the National Assembly.

❖ Debate 1: Reconfirmation of the 1975 Abortion Legislation, 1979

❖ How the debate came to the public agenda

Although the 1975 *loi Veil* permitted abortion within the first ten weeks of pregnancy, it imposed certain requirements. The procedure had to be performed by a doctor, in a public or a private hospital, but doctors and other medical practitioners had the right to refuse to perform abortions. There were no public funds to support them. Upon consultation, a doctor had to inform patients wanting abortions of the medical risks, inform patients of the laws and policies supporting women and families, give advice on the possibility of adoption, and provide the patient with information on family planning centres and abortion clinics in her area. In the second trimester, abortions were allowed only for reasons of physical risk to the mother or risk to the fetus. The *loi Veil* also guaranteed that the question would come back to the public agenda after five years, when the National Assembly would assess the impact of the law and vote whether to reaffirm it. In late 1979, the question came to the Assembly. President Giscard d'Estaing appointed Monique Pelletier, the Ministère Déléguée auprès du Premier Ministre à la Condition Féminine et à la Famille (MDCFF), as floor manager for the bill.

The debate was already under way. Popular women's magazines, like *Elle*, covered the issue in advance of its appearance in the National Assembly. Feminist abortion organizations launched *manifestations* and sent letters to politicians and ministers. The sensational 'la Pergola' case, which involved the arrest for infanticide of two doctors who had performed late-term abortions, intensified the debate. The case received much press attention, and Pergola, the abortion clinic in the 18th arrondissement of Paris, became a symbol for all that was wrong with the 1975 abortion law. For those against legalizing abortions, this case re-imaged abortion as the killing of children. For those who wanted further reforms, the case demonstrated the farce of not allowing minors to make their own decisions about abortions, the lack of appropriate facilities to perform the procedure, and the failure to inform young women of their rights (*Le Matin* 1979; Collectif Féministe Contre La Répression et Coordination des Groupes Femmes Paris 1979).

Most of the major contenders in the earlier debates returned to the fray, joined by yet more activist feminist abortion groups in the streets. Conservatives and anti-abortion groups took this as an opportunity to restate their case against abortion. As in 1974, National Assembly deputies argued that abortion was murder, asking where this would stop. At the killing of handicapped children? With euthanasia? (*Journal Officiel* 1979: 10799). President Giscard d'Estaing proclaimed that there were four inviolable principles for the state:

respect life; help women who are physically at risk; enable every woman to raise her child under the best possible conditions; allow freedom of conscience for each and every doctor (Berger 1975: 165).

❖ Dominant frame of the debate

The dominant frame for the debate was provided by the centre-right government on the one hand, and feminists on the other. The government, in alliance with the Catholic Church and extreme right-wing parties, expressed its desire to limit abortion in light of both demographic and ethical issues and raised the question of values and national needs. Feminists, on the other hand, countered with the claim that abortion was a basic issue of women's rights that continued the trajectory from revolutionary ideals.

One of the primary concerns of the ruling centre-right government was a concern over the low population growth in France, an issue that has been raised by central French governments for centuries. While foreign residents were continuing to experience high birth rates, 'real' French had much lower birth rates. These demographic fears clearly influenced policy relating to women and families. Family stipends were strengthened, the women's policy agency was enjoined to find ways for women to both work and have several children, and, in the National Assembly, deputies spoke of a 'demographic crisis'. Not coincidentally these concerns brought together anti-abortion forces with members of France's extreme right, especially representatives of the National Front who had close ties to some anti-abortion groups. Amendments put forward in 1979 proposed that abortions be denied to married women who did not have at least two children; that abortions be denied families which had incomes that were four times the guaranteed minimum wage; and that all who sought abortions be given a lesson in the demographic straits of French society (Mossuz-Lavau 1991: 120). While the latter proposal was incorporated in the final 1979 version, the former two did not survive.

French feminists claimed that abortion reform was part of an unfinished agenda for women's rights. Abortion, even after the *loi Veil*, was neither on demand, widely available, nor accessible to poorer women. Despite the 1975 law that asserted that 'la femme est la seule juge de cette decision', in reality it was doctors who could decide whether she was at risk—during the second trimester—and it was doctors who could exercise the clause of conscience, leaving a pregnant woman to her fate.[4] Feminist groups wanted the government to address at least five areas: parental authorization for minors, residency requirements for foreign women, the conscience clause for doctors, the lack of social security reimbursement for the cost of the medical procedure, and, last but not least, the continuing criminalization of abortions.

❖ Gendering the debate

Gender was central to the debate in 1979, and an integral part of arguments for and against restrictions in abortion. The proposed pro-natalist amendments attempted to legitimize an image of women as fecund suppliers for the nation. Women's duty was to give birth; this was presented not only as a moral and Christian imperative but as a sacrifice required for the good of the nation. Simultaneously women were warned that they should not expect society to pay for their sexual activities. The conservative sexual views expressed in 1975, as when one member of L'union féminine pour le respect de la vie testified: 'Who will pay for these abortions? Social security? My husband said to me, "I will refuse to pay taxes for the pleasures of my neighbor!"' (Berger 1975: 135), continued to be voiced in 1979.[5]

Feminists argued that the abortion reform had fundamentally failed to protect and promote women's rights. If women were to be the autonomous beings that de Beauvoir and others had imagined, then certainly the autonomy of their own bodies was imperative. And just as certainly, they could not and should not be perceived or treated as vessels to produce children. An understanding of the ways in which gendered roles limited women's autonomy and potential shaped the feminist frame. For feminists the struggle was over more than a law, and it was more than a simple debate over abstract rights; rather, it was about the essence of their lives as human beings.

Minister Pelletier and the MDCFF did not engage in the rights discourse. Although Pelletier never disavowed the necessity for legal abortion, MDCFF was notably quiet during these public debates. The agency did provide statistics demonstrating that there had been no significant increase in the number of abortions in France since 1975, and in so doing attempted to defuse the pro-natalist argument. But neither did the MDCFF follow the lead of feminist groups in arguing that abortion was part of a package of rights due to women, although, when pressed, the ministry conceded that the abortion law had proved beneficial to women's health and that the number of cases of infection had diminished considerably. The women's ministry claim that legal abortions promoted women's health in fact moved the onus for promoting the legislation and defending the continuation of the Veil law from MDCFF to the Ministry of Health. Thus the most vocal proponents of the legislation in National Assembly discussions were from the Ministry of Health, not from the ministry responsible for 'women's condition'. The MDCFF, for its part, followed the president's lead and focused on proposals for facilitating adoption of 'unwanted' children (*Le Matin* 1979). While Pelletier accepted that 'it is no longer possible for a nation to increase its population by forcing women to have children…' (cited in Stetson 1987: 66), her promise was to find other incentives to address the pro-natalist demand.

❖ JEAN C. ROBINSON

❖ *Policy outcome*

In the end, the abortion law was recertified, by a slight plurality—255 for, 212 against, 8 abstentions—but with some significant new requirements.[6] Doctors were required to inform patients of the consequences of abortion, of the national demographic situation, and of every person's national obligations. The women's agency did not fight strongly against these provisions. Fines for illegal abortions were raised significantly in the 1979 law—by between 80 per cent and 120 per cent of the fines in the 1975 law—prefiguring debates to come. Decriminalizing abortion was not accomplished, and indeed criminal penalties were increased, probably because of the La Pergola case.

❖ *Women's movement impact*

For women's groups, the passage of the *loi Pelletier* was an incomplete victory at best. Abortion rights were minimally retained, but there remained significant barriers to women's free exercise of their rights. Furthermore, the dominant frame for the abortion debate ended up focusing on the demographic fears and pro-natalist mentalities that were abhorrent to groups such as MLAC, MFPF, and the Mouvement pour la Libération des Femmes (MLF). The conservatives succeeded in framing the debate in their own terms and sought to discourage abortions by requiring that doctors inform patients of the 'grave biological risk they were taking by intervening in a pregnancy' (*Journal Officiel* 1980). Pronatalism was embedded in the stipulation that women be informed of the support they would receive from state and society if they continued the pregnancy, and the duty they were fulfilling to the nation by having children. Clearly the policy outcome did not coincide with the women's movement goals: it was a partial and limited victory in the ongoing battle.

To an extent, one can argue that the policy content of the *loi Pelletier* coincided with women's movement goals, in that the abortion groups preferred having some legalized abortion to having none at all. And yet the provisions in the final document reflect the interests and concerns of conservatives and antifeminists; there is no evidence that women's abortion reform groups were involved in the final process to legislate a very limited abortion law. Since there is little evidence that women were accepted as primary actors in the policy debate, except Monique Pelletier, the 1979 decision yielded a non-response from the state to the women's movements goals.

❖ *Women's policy agency activities*

The MDCFF should be classified as non-feminist in terms of its failure to advocate women's movement goals and its effectiveness in gendering the policy debate in ways that the women's movement opposed. While the MFPF, left-wing parties—including prominently the Parti Socialiste—MLAC, and others attempted to gender the abortion debate by consistently referring to women's rights and women's control of their bodies, the state and the MDCFF, led by Monique Pelletier, were content to compromise on abortion policy by limiting its access and defining women's roles as primarily maternal. The MDCFF reinforced the gender ideas of government, sidestepping altogether the question of women's autonomy and control. It had a privileged place in the process as floor manager of the bill, making it effective in sustaining the dominant gender frame of women as mothers for the state. By acceding to the pressure to address pro-natalist demands, even if through mechanisms other than stringently restricting abortion, MDCFF accepted the pro-natalist stance, which inevitably framed women as primarily (potential) mothers.

The scope of the MDCFF was cross-sectional, with a mission to address all issues relating to women. Yet, to this agency, women as a category were not women as feminist groups understood the term: they were part of the family, neither oppressed members of society deprived of their rights, nor were they women in need of reproductive legal reforms. In fact, during this period the ministry was responsible for women and family issues. The emphasis on pro-natalism is then not surprising and betrays a very different perspective on women than that broadcast by the women's groups. Certainly Mme Pelletier supported equal rights for women, and in this sense was an equal rights feminist; but she did not see reproductive or sexuality issues as fundamental to women's self-expression. Despite advocating equal rights in terms of employment and legal access, Pelletier saw no conflict with accepting more traditional gender systems which posited women's primary maternal role.[7] MDCFF was not then an organization that sought to revolutionize the gender system; in this sense it was not a feminist organization. Instead, MDCFF was a marginal, underfunded administrative arm of the state to take care of issues related to women's maternity and employment.

❖ Women's movement characteristics

The women's movement as a whole was scattered and decentralized, and continued to decline from its high point of activism in the late 1960s and early 1970s. Feminist groups had splintered into contentious factions and were divided over strategies as well as tactics. For some groups, however, abortion was a top priority and threats to abortion rights quickly brought action from those groups and others interested in specific reforms relating to abortion and contraception. Both women's groups and family planning and abortion groups were close to the left, although the left itself was divided during this period. In their fragmented state, movement groups faced a strong and well-organized counter-movement. Although the priority of abortion was high on the agenda for feminists, the movement was neither strong enough nor cohesive enough to be able to push its own framing of the debate or its resolution.

❖ Policy environment

The policy environment, in both Parliament and the government, was moderately closed. Decision-making was dominated by ruling centre-right party politics, and, although compromises were made, the policy environment was defined and controlled by the Giscard leadership. During this period, the party in power was clearly not of the left. The centre-right coalition in the National Assembly found much greater comfort in siding with the counter-movement to abortion reform. Although President Giscard bowed to popular opinion by accepting that abortion could not be completely outlawed, his government wanted both to restrict abortion and to promote a pro-natalist agenda. A more liberal abortion law was not part of Giscard's agenda, and the centre-right control over the policy environment ensured that compromise was possible only at the margins.

❖ DEBATE 2: REIMBURSEMENT FOR NON-THERAPEUTIC ABORTIONS, 1981–1883

❖ How the debate came to the public agenda

When the Socialist Party (PS) won the 1981 elections, a change was presaged for women's policy. The PS had undergone a transformation of sorts, when its own Secrétariat des Droits des Femmes sponsored a congress for party delegates on women's rights in 1978; a rewritten platform on abortion was just one result.[8] By 1979, PS had proposed a new abortion rights agenda that started with the proclamation that 'La liberté de disposer de son corps est un droit inaliénable'—the freedom to control one's body is an inalienable right (Parti Socialiste 1979). Popular magazines took up the idea, with *Elle* publicizing the issue starting on 9 September 1980.

With the appointment of Yvette Roudy as the Ministère Déléguée auprès du Premier Ministre chargé des Droits de la Femme (MDDF) in 1981, the stage was set for abortion reform to proceed. Described by some as a militant feminist (Adler 1993: 194), Roudy had made her reputation in the PS by insisting that the party pay attention to women's rights. Her leadership of the women's policy agency demonstrated a determination to bring issues to the agenda even if they were controversial and thus at risk of failure in the legislature. She first emphasized the need to focus on dissemination of contraception and contraceptive information in order to diminish the number of pregnancies that might lead to abortion: by March 1982, 88 new family planning centres had been organized under the aegis of the MDDF. Then she sought to increase the number of hospitals that offered abortion services. Lastly, the MDDF launched a campaign in January 1982 to secure reimbursement from state funds for non-therapeutic abortion costs, for which there was still no state payment, although all other medical procedures were reimbursed either totally or in part by the social security system.

In March 1982, Roudy announced that an inter-ministerial council had approved the reimbursement of abortion costs, beginning in September. Prior to celebrating International Women's Day, Roudy remarked that 'March 8 is not just a symbolic day, but it is the start of a dynamic new era in the defense of women's rights' (*Le Matin* 1982a). Immediately anti-abortion groups launched street protests. Throughout the spring, the battle was played out in the press, among government ministers, and, later, in the National Assembly. In August, Social Security postponed reimbursement for abortion. Pierre Bérégovoy, Minister of Social Affairs, said the decision was not 'a question of money'. Rather, he said, it was necessary to consult with different '*familles spirituelles*'. The Catholic leadership took this as a partial victory and the left, including feminist groups and unions, saw the decision as an affront to women, the breaking of a promise (*Le Monde* 1982b). Yvette Roudy found herself stuck between angry proponents of abortion reform and those who wanted to stop abortion. Bérégovoy, a reluctant supporter of limited abortion reform, argued that, since it was a controversial issue, the decision should be made by Parliament.

❖ Dominant frame of the debate

At the end of the 1979 debate, the definition of the abortion issue involved ways abortion could be restricted to promote pro-natalist goals. In 1981, Roudy took the lead in establishing a new dominant—and gendered—frame in terms of women's rights and the class struggle. This view was soon countered by moral opposition to murder of 'innocent' life. Indeed the battle of reimbursement signalled a change in framing for the groups opposed to abortion reform. Rather than continuing to argue the case for pro-natalism, which had been addressed through the pro-family policies of the state, the framing of the opposition debate turned to one of preserving French morality and Catholic values. The anti-abortion discourse adopted the pro-life language emanating from the United States, just as it learned opposition tactics from these same American anti-abortion groups (Venner 1995).

After the postponement of Roudy's reimbursement plan, the battle grew more heated in the autumn: debates pro and con were published in journals ranging from *Le Quotidien du Médecin* to *Le Matin* and *Le Monde*. Popular women's magazines such as *Elle* addressed the reimbursement issue, as did organizations such as MFPF and numerous other associations (Bataille 1982:

6–10). In the Socialist government, the question required wrestling with whether abortion was a conventional medical practice or whether it was something extraordinary. Ultimately the decision concerning which fund would cover abortion reimbursement defined the terms of abortion in France. Bérégovoy and others in the government wanted to establish a special fund so that abortion could be separated from 'normal' medical procedures (Le Matin 1982b, c). On the other hand, the MDDF wanted to see abortion treated in the same manner as any other medical situation—as did organizations like Choisir, MFPF, and the PS platform.

❖ Gendering the debate

In the policy debates, women were depicted in two distinct images. One portrayed them as responsible people who have hard choices to make. Lack of access to subsidized abortions had made them criminals, or citizens unable to exercise their rights, or non-citizens unable to act as free adults. In this frame, the state had an inescapable duty to ensure that women become full citizens, with a citizenship that entailed the ability to control one's body and make decisions about sexuality and reproduction. The other image represented women as murderers who were trying to avoid their God-given responsibility and burden as females to 'give life'. According to this view, the state had the duty to restrain this trend by refusing to pay for abortions.

Yvette Roudy through the MDDF argued that reimbursement would make women 'equal before the law' and able to exercise their rights as French citizens, a description consistent with emancipatory feminist views. It was, simply put, a question of 'justice'. Roudy did not want women to become criminals by seeking illegal abortions or to have to go outside the country to obtain what was legally their right inside France. For Roudy, the important question to consider was not whether abortion was going to become a normal medical practice; for her it was, rather, whether class and sex would determine whether citizens' rights could be indeed be accessed. She continually argued that abortion was a legal right for women, but one that could be exercised only by those with money. The purpose of reimbursement was to elevate women's rights and overcome the 'immoral situation' where 'the law is not the same for everyone' (Le Monde 1982a).

Conservatives in the Senate described feminists as a 'phalange hystérique'. One Senator posed the moral problem of an infertile woman, faced with the pain of not being able to have a child, and having to pay taxes to aid in the 'death of an innocent' (Le Monde 1982e). The conservative view of women was that it is moral and natural and good that women be mothers and that it is sick and immoral if women choose to murder their children—a fetus was in this scenario no different than a child. This traditional gendered perspective still

98

presumed the female as mother and as citizen, but foremost as women-mothers (Fraisse 1995).

❖ Policy outcome

Minister Yvette Roudy initially approached the reimbursement problem as an administrative issue that could be handled without the National Assembly. After Bérégovoy's insistence that the National Assembly should vote on the issue, Roudy was still faced with persuading the Council of Ministers to proceed with her plan. The fear that reimbursement sent a signal that abortion was merely a routine medical procedure meant that Roudy faced a divided Council. Both Bérégovoy, a more senior minister, and Mitterrand, the president, shared this fear of 'banalization' (Jenson and Sineau 1995: 199–200). Roudy was eventually able to bring the ministers of Health and Women's Rights, Solidarity, Finance, and Budget together to create the compromise policy that was accepted by the Council of Ministers on 1 December 1982. The Council agreed to reimburse 70 per cent of the cost of abortion, with a woman paying the remaining 30 per cent; the reimbursement would not be from Social Security but from the general budget. The agreement was that the procedure would be treated as any other medical act. To avoid future confrontations over taxation and spending on abortions, Roudy hoped that the costs would be absorbed in the general budget and not be reported separately.[9] That proposal was discussed in the National Assembly on 10 December 1982 and adopted after a 'déclaration d'urgence'. It was then discussed and rejected in the Senate on 18 December 1982. The legislative history from that point forward included conference committee meetings; reapproval by the National Assembly on 18 December 1982; rejection again by the more conservative Senate on the same day; another discussion in the Assembly and adoption by 'second reading' on 20 December 1982.[10] The policy initiative was finally approved by President Mitterrand on 31 December 1982.

❖ Women's movement impact

The policy outcome was not all that women's organizations wished. Compromise meant that full reimbursement was not offered and that it could be subject to renegotiation since it was part of the budget rather than covered by Social Security. Nevertheless, the policy content of the MDDF as articulated by Roudy was in line with the goals laid out by organizations such as Choisir, MFPF, and umbrella abortion organizations (MFPF 1983). Furthermore, it is clear that women's movement groups were involved in the policy process: documents and letters from summer 1982 to spring 1983 demonstrate that the MDDF sought comments on the reimbursement proposals and that Roudy was contacted by most if not all of the groups engaged in promoting abortion law reform. The ministry paid careful attention to requests and concerns of groups such as MFPF, Confédération Française et Démocratique du Travail (CFDT), the National Secretariat for Women's Struggles of the PS, and Choisir (Bataille 1982). This debate then yielded a dual response, with the women's policy agency and women's movements working together, one from the outside, the other from the inside, to create a new policy. In a letter to Roudy dated 24 February 1983, the National Board of MFPF complimented Roudy's work, and that of the MDDF: 'we know the furious energy and will with which you and your ministers have defended the cause, and we thank you'.[11]

❖ Women's policy agency activities

Roudy was an avowed feminist and had good working relations with groups working on abortion and contraception reform. Although there was dismay among these activists that the MDDF was eventually forced to compromise and that, despite the new policy, lack of reimbursement continued beyond mid-1983, it is evident that the MDDF both advocated women's movement goals and effectively gendered the policy debate.

Roudy was successful in setting the agenda and making the policy despite internecine squabbling among ministers because she had the legitimacy of a party platform to stand on, an activist and relatively cohesive social movement that accepted her as a leader, and supportive popular opinion[12] that loomed larger than the anti-abortion demonstrations in Paris streets. Roudy not only set the agenda but found a way to keep the issue alive and to make it popular over a twelve-month period. She consistently used the rhetoric of women's rights, gendering the debate so that even in the National Assembly deputies spoke of women's rights and justice for women as the issue to be decided.[13]

The MDDF under the leadership of Roudy had a cross-sectional scope. As a junior minister reporting to the premier, Roudy would typically have had little influence in the government, but because the premier was a strong supporter of women's issues and Roudy herself an outspoken and effective advocate, she was able to make MDDF an agency to be reckoned with, at least on certain issues. The agency had an (influential) seat on the Council of Ministers and commanded a larger budget than previous women's agencies. The MDDF budget was over seven million FF, although this was but a tiny portion of total state budget. In terms of the MDDF's policy mandate, the ministry and Mme Roudy were adamant that women's status and position in French society should be considered separately from the interests of the family but saw every reason to include abortion and contraception as part of her policy mandate. After all, women's reproductive and sexual life was not about family, it was about being a woman.

❖ Women's movement characteristics

Although the broader women's movement remained in decline, the reimburse-ment issue elicited a growing response from both emancipatory women's groups and the popular women's press. Clearly, the reimbursement issue was brought to centre stage because the PS was pushed by its own female members to take a stand on the inequalities inherent in the then-existing abortion arrangements. The level of cohesion over this issue among the diverse family planning and abortion groups was very high, and all focused on Roudy and the MDDF as a realistic site for accomplishing something. Even Choisir, which remained quite sceptical of the government's promises, noted that 'After one year, the decision [to ensure reimbursement] is truly one of the sole concrete promises [followed through] by the MDDF . . . ' (Bataille 1982). The abortion movement in France revived during this debate and exhibited a cohesion that was evident in both formal and radical politics of the debate. In February 1983, the MFPF recognized the feminist contribution of the women's agency and characterized the battle over reimbursement as 'a victory of women against reactionary forces' (MFPF 1983). The MDDF presented itself as a feminist organization dedicated to ensuring that women's rights were protected and advanced. The discourse it used in framing this reimbursement debate reinforced that image; and it was a successful advocate for the women's movement.

Although the anti-abortion movement was active in presenting its opposition to the reimbursement, and was successful to the extent that it forced the press to engage in the debate about the 'banalization' of abortion, the counter-movement was not successful in stopping the policy initiative. It did effectively force a limited compromise in the final decision, however, and thus can be classified as moderately weak (*Le Monde* 1982b, c; *Quotidien du Médecins* 1982).

❖ Policy environment

The policy environment was shaped by the PS dominance of the presidency and the Parliament, and the organization of women within the party who were able to move into government positions after 1981. But the environment for this par-ticular policy debate was also shaped in large measure by the split within the PS itself over the reimbursement question. MDDF Minister Roudy and premier Pierre Mauroy agreed that abortion was a basic right for women, and that, in policy terms, it should be treated as a standard medical procedure. Pierre Bérégovoy, Minister for Social Affairs and National Solidarity, joined Mitterrand in his concern that abortion not become just another medical act. This split in perspective became public when Mitterrand reacted angrily to Roudy and Mauroy's announcement in early 1982 that non-therapeutic

❖ JEAN C. ROBINSON

abortion procedures would be covered under social security: 'I didn't authorize this decision; I am against any effort to make abortion a banal act; don't force this through.' For Mauroy, Roudy, and women in PS reimbursement was a simple act of equity and justice for all; for Mitterrand, abortion should not be treated ever as simple or an 'ordinary act' (Jenson and Sineau 1995: 200). The result was a policy environment in which the MDDF minister was faced with the task of convincing her own government. It certainly was advantageous that the PS was under pressure from women within the organization, and that it had a strong majority in the National Assembly. The PS election promises on abortion forced a moderately open policy environment in which external feminist organizing in concert with women within the PS could put effective pressure on the government. Thus, protests by feminist groups and left parties in autumn 1982 forced Mitterrand to accept the reimbursement compromise.

❖ DEBATE 3: ANTI-ABORTION COMMANDOS, 1991–1993

❖ How the debate came to the public agenda

Beginning in 1987, anti-abortion groups in France staged protests in urban streets and in front of abortion clinics and public hospitals, engaged in verbal and physical harassment of abortion clinic patients, and created blockages at hospitals and clinics.[14] Police and judicial authorities seemed unwilling to stop the protests, and abortion rights groups as well as women's media expressed alarm about the growing threat to abortion access and rights. The actions, called the commando anti-IVG,[15] sought to save the lives of 'unborn children' by occupying clinics, harassing clients, contaminating medical supplies, and chaining themselves to equipment, before finally being evacuated by the police.[16] SOS-Tout-Petit and La Trêve de Dieu, leading groups involved in commando operations, were joined by other organizations including Laissez-les-vivre and ACPER-VIE SOS Maternité, a Protestant anti-abortion commando group (*Golias Magazine* 1995). In addition to encouragement from the Catholic Church, the commandos received support and advice from American anti-abortion groups such as Operation Rescue. As in the United States, the anti-abortion actions were designed to deter women seeking abortions as well as to inhibit the participation of health-care providers in abortion provision.

In June 1991, within weeks of taking the leadership of the Secrétariat d'État aux Droits des Femmes et à la Vie Quotidienne (SEDFVQ), Véronique Neiertz issued a challenge to a commando operation at a Paris hospital. The secretariat not only judged the demonstration unacceptable, but Neiertz said she would work vigorously to stop the commandos. She hoped that the actions of the commandos would not pass without punishment and stipulated that the Ministry of Justice should systematically pursue the offenders.

Four days after Neiertz's communique of 21 June, the Health Minister Bruno Durieux and Mme. Neiertz issued a second circular, distributed to all regional and departmental prefects and directors of public hospitals. That communication instructed prefects and directors that blockages of hospitals and contamination of materials by anti-abortion groups were not to be tolerated, and that hospitals should take every precaution and measure to safeguard public hospital services—including abortion—and patients. Prefects were further instructed that 'in case of an incident, it is up to the hospital directors to immediately call the public security to reestablish the hospital's functioning and to record the nature of the acts committed and the identities of the troublemakers [fauteurs de troubles]'.[17] Administrators were further told to lodge systematic complaints for all infractions, destruction, and damage to material caused by the anti-abortion groups and to provide all information and support necessary to individual victims who desired to lodge complaints. In autumn 1991, Neiertz announced the formation of an inter-ministerial study group to look at judicial sanctions and concrete measures to be taken against the commandos engaging in 'opérations anti-IVG dans les hopitaux'. Ultimately the problem was brought to Parliament., where it came to a vote before the National Assembly. The inter-ministerial commission—regrettably, according to Mme Neiertz—decided that 'the majority of the commando actions did not correspond to the character of infractions recognized in the legal texts' (Le Monde 1992b), so that the issue had to be resolved by the legislative body.

❖ Dominant frame of the debate

The goal of the anti-abortion groups was to reframe the abortion issue in France to privilege the rights of the unborn over the rights of women. Secretary Neiertz cast the anti-abortion commandos problem in two ways: one was a reassurance to the abortion rights activists, using the rhetoric of women's bodies and rights, that she understood abortion access as a fundamental right of women; the other was to render the debate in terms of the state's legal authority, a move designed to deny legitimacy to these retrogressive anti-abortion activists. Throughout the debate, Neiertz continued to proclaim that the commandos' actions of 'intimidation' should not go unpunished (Agence France Presse 1991) and believed that the Gardes des Sceaux had the responsibility to ensure that women had safe access to abortion providers. Her invitation to Justice to do something about the commandos suggested an underlying question: what should the role of courts, police, and the state be when women's rights were threatened?

❖ JEAN C. ROBINSON

Abortion rights groups formed a new organization to coordinate their activities and put greater pressure on the government. The Coordination Nationale pour le Droit à l'Avortement et à la Contraception (CADAC) decried the violent action of commandos and demanded forceful action from the government to protect the hard-won right of abortion. More than 20 associations and unions, including MFPF, CFDT, Fédération de l'Éducation nationale (FEN), Grain de Sel, and Ligue des Droits d'Homme sent an 'open letter' to the premier and denounced 'the deterioration of the right to abortion' (Agence France Presse 1991). In particular, they called for the state to protect women's '*droit fondamental à maîtriser leur fecondité*' (fundamental right to control their fertility).

❖ Gendering the debate

The Secretariat gendered the debate publicly to the extent that it adopted the language and rhetoric of understanding women's roles as beyond maternity and home-making, and understanding women as individuals who would make responsible choices. In framing her arguments for parliamentarians and colleagues in the government, Neiertz focused on the legitimacy of duly enacted laws. Feminist groups also gendered the debate by reminding the public that women should have control over their own bodies and that abortion was a fundamental right that should be protected by the state, a claim supported by Neiertz. While both the women's ministry and feminist groups agreed on the need to ensure access to health clinics and on presenting women as responsible individuals not defined solely by the family or by state interests *vis-à-vis* natality, feminist groups framed the problem only in these terms. Feminist abortion groups wanted to ensure that the government actively protect all French women's right of access to abortion. The SEDFVQ for its part had another audience for which the legal authority argument was likely to be more compelling. Neiertz framed the issue foremost in terms of ensuring that state law be followed. The difference is slight, but for feminist groups the commandos were attacking abortion and thus women's fundamental rights rather than attacking the legitimacy of the state by subverting the law.

Neiertz recognized that the feminist gender frame was not effective in eliciting an appropriate response from Justice. She described the initial Justice response to the inter-ministerial commission as awakening to the reality, '*une certaine prise de conscience*' (Breen 1992). Neiertz further noted that once the state had made public its desire to address the legality of the commando action, the police response to individual actions became more reliable.

The anti-abortion commandos were gendering the debate to capture nostalgic views of women's roles, thus erasing the woman to save the unborn child. The anti-abortion groups focused on the immorality of abortion and returned to the theme of maternity and natalism. As in other debates, the issue was gendered by them to the extent that they understood women's roles as the bearers and producers of innocent children. The more dominant frame, though, for the anti-abortion activists was in terms of the moral need to save the unborn, innocent child. Neiertz, for her part, rejected these arguments.

❖ Policy outcome

Inter-ministerial commissions, hampered by political contestation and continuing controversy over the state's abortion policies, would not resolve the issue. Under continuing pressure from CADAC, Neiertz joined with the Ministry of Health in taking the issue to the National Assembly. In December 1992, the National Assembly approved a provision to the code of public health that created a '*délit spécial d'entrave à l'IVG*' (special offence of hindering access to abortions), with penal sanctions, and gave associations the right to seek remedies in civil courts as well (*Le Monde* 1992c: 8). This vote also included a decision to delete the portion of the penal code that made self-abortion a criminal offence. *La loi Neiertz*, effective on 27 January 1993, established fines from 2,000 to 30,000 francs for actions which sought to harass patients or workers or to prevent access to clinics. The law has been applied intermittently since 1983, but usually the fines have been suspended (Venner 1995, 147; *Actualités Sociales Hebdomaires* 1996).

❖ Women's movement impact

The policy outcome coincided with movement goals, but, despite the efforts of Neiertz and the SEDFVQ, they got little credit for this success. This frustration with the agency was also evident in popular women's magazines. *Elle*, for instance, covered the issue both before and after the Neiertz law was passed; in all cases, its theme was that abortion rights were in danger. During this period, the abortion rights groups experienced renewed support and carried out a large number of public actions to force the state to address the threat of the commandos.

For their part, the women's movement acted as outside initiators: within the secretariat action was ultimately predicated on the recognition that the problem would have to be addressed by SEDFVQ because no other ministry would take responsibility. While the policy content coincided with women's movement goals, women's organizations were somewhat peripheral to the policy process. Women's group representatives were not integrated into the policy process, and the ministry did not—or perhaps could not—invite women's groups into the inter-ministerial commission process. However, the SEDFVQ certainly recognized the feminists' influence and did act in response to them.

❖ JEAN C. ROBINSON

Despite criticism about the slowness of government responses, the state ultimately gave policy satisfaction to the movement, at least on paper, and thus this case can be categorized as dual response.

❖ Women's policy agency activities

The women's office had been downgraded from Roudy's time; under the new government of Edith Cresson, the agency reported to the Ministry of Labour, Employment and Professional Training. This implied a weakening of the women's rights agenda in terms of abortion and contraception and a refocusing on employment and labour-rights issues. However, Neiertz herself raised the question of abortion rights early in her interviews upon appointment as Secrétaire d'État, and evidently embraced reproductive rights as part of her portfolio.

Neiertz was asked by Mitterrand and Cresson to lead the newly renamed SEDFVQ in 1991, when the French economy was in difficult straits and the PS itself was pursuing a much more conservative agenda in economic and social policy. Neiertz was young and relatively inexperienced in terms of the women's rights agenda, especially compared with Roudy. Kept on even after cohabitation[18] returned in 1993, Neiertz did not present the profile of an outspoken advocate for women's rights (Adler 1993: 211–12). Nevertheless, she was forced into the fray by the increasing activism of abortion groups and by the increasing aggression of the anti-abortion commandos.

The mandate of the women's policy agency at this time continued to be cross-sectional, although its resources and power were downgraded from the Roudy period. The head of the agency was no longer a junior minister, as in Roudy's era, but demoted further to a Secretary of State, ranking near the bottom of the government hierarchy (*Le Monde* 1991). There continued to be field offices during this period but, because SEDFVQ was less engaged in pro-active leadership, the overall organization was more marginal than during the first years of Socialist rule.

At the beginning of her term, Neiertz set the tone in her framing of abortion as a fundamental right for women. She never backed down from this claim, but she also never seemed to have the support that her predecessor Roudy had. In standing up to the anti-IVG commandos, Neiertz was able to get support from the Health Ministry,[19] particularly in rallying opposition to the commandos from regional administrators. However she clearly faced more difficulty in getting the Ministry of Justice to respond.

It is not clear why Justice officials chose not to act in the face of hospital and clinic blockages, although later actions suggest that, in the face of controversy, Justice wanted a clear directive from authorities more senior than Neiertz (*Le Monde* 1992b). The initiative of SEDFVQ in calling for the inter-ministerial commission set the stage for an ultimate decision by the National Assembly. It was unthinkable that the women's rights secretariat could overrule the Gardes des Sceaux on this issue.

For her part, Neiertz did not respond publicly or strongly enough to suit the pro-abortion feminist groups. Rather she worked behind the scenes with the Ministry of Health to find solutions. The women's policy agency was a insider in that it did advocate women's movement goals in attempting to protect abortion rights and access; although it used non-feminist arguments it also gendered the abortion debate by framing the issue in terms of women's right to make decisions about her body and life.

❖ Women's movement characteristics

In this case, although a successful solution—a law—was finally reached, it is viewed by women's groups not as a victory of Neiertz but rather as a victory created by the re-mobilization of pro-choice groups in France. Indeed, the perception that abortion access and rights were in danger was the theme around which women's activities were organized. Former minister Roudy, for instance, declared in the mainstream and women's press that abortion rights were indeed in danger (Roudy 1991). Networks developed national umbrella organizations to coordinate political action and communication with SEDFVQ. Popular magazines took on the role of warning of the impending dangers to abortion rights. And yet, despite all this activity, even the active women's movement itself noted with alarm that 'there was a climate of demobilization among women, and especially among young women who are persuaded that abortion and contraception will always be there' (Le Monde 1992a). CADAC, announcing its January 1992 conference, despaired of the spirit of 'disengagement of the State'. It argued that the commando actions had been able to continue with impunity, and that the disengagement of the state constituted a grave risk to 'le droit de maîtriser leur fécundité et de décider de leur maternité' (the right of self-control over fertility and the decision to be a mother) (CADAC 1991). In framing the debate as a fundamental threat to abortion rights, the anti-abortion commandos issue became for a brief time a catalyzing force for women's groups. The movement remained, by its own analysis, weak and generally in decline, although it effectively pushed the SEDFVQ to action and experienced some renewal through this struggle.

❖ Policy environment

Certainly the PS was in a much stronger position in the early 1980s than when Neiertz came on the scene. Politics had grown more conservative, as had the PS in its years of power. A few months after the Neiertz law passed, the centre-right again gained majority control in the National Assembly. Although there remained an ideological commitment to women's rights within the PS, women's issues had dropped considerably in importance. The PS was facing a fight for survival and the abortion issue seemed to be too divisive to be a central theme. The women's policy agency was substantially downgraded under the government of Cresson, and this too limited its effectiveness in addressing controversial issues. The secretariat took the initiative in presenting the problem of sexual harassment and other labour and employment issues; it also sought to draw attention to issues of domestic violence, women's professional advancement, and contraceptive education and access. Most of these issues sat more easily under the portfolio of labour and employment than did abortion, and none was as divisive within and outside the government as abortion. The policy environment became more restricted under these political pressures, and was moderately closed to controversial initiatives.

❖ CONCLUSION

The cases presented here suggest that feminist movement impact on abortion debates is critical for effecting policy change. The *loi Pelletier* was passed in the National Assembly despite the inactivity of the women's agency and because of the feminist activism in rallying public support for abortion reform. The reimbursement for non-therapeutic abortions was approved because of the dual activities of both feminist groups and the women's ministry. The legal restrictions on anti-abortion commandos were achieved because of external pressure on the women's agency and the consequent inter-ministerial support for new legislation.

Even in a moderately closed policy environment, such as that experienced during the period of the policy against the anti-abortion commandos, feminist abortion groups were able to direct the attention of the women's ministry to problematic situations. However, it is the leadership of the ministry, and the political environment in which the women's agency operates, that are critical for agenda setting and for successful gendering of policy. A more open policy environment eases the routes for influencing policy; and the presence of a strong left-wing government makes it more likely that the environment will be open and the women's policy agency more feminist, but the presence of a left-wing government may not necessarily lead to sustained feminist domination of a women's policy agency, nor to a women's agency that has any status within the government.

When the political environment is more conservative, abortion debates are more likely to be framed in terms of health, law, and safety issues rather than women's rights. When the political environment is more liberal and the policy environment more open, the rhetoric sounds more feminist and the debate is framed in terms of rights, choice, women's bodies, and female liberty. The debates I have examined demonstrate that debates become gendered under specific conditions: when the left is in power and when the head of the agency is a confessed feminist with political connections and experience. Successful policies rely on more than this, though: they also depend on demonstrations of support from active social movements and evidence of supportive public opinion above and beyond those of activist groups. The women's movement itself does need to be cohesive and organized in order to influence policy, but this does not mean that a movement in decline cannot achieve a successful response from the state. Even a relatively small but focused movement can have an influence on the policy process within the women's agency.

Finally, the cases discussed here suggest that the women's policy agency is often the necessary intervening force for achieving policy success. Even when the agency subordinates a gendered discourse to other rhetoric, it can still engineer policies that are consonant with feminist movement goals. We have seen that the response to commandos was to engage in long negotiations with ministers, work through the Ministry of Health, and eventually craft legislation that would win the support of moderates. Without making the rights arguments that Roudy made, Neiertz and her colleagues relied on a different kind of politics. Born of the duty of government to ensure that its laws are enforced, the debate over anti-abortion commandos became a legitimate issue of preserving governmental integrity rather than the controversial issue of women's rights to access to abortions. Similarly in 1979, making the debate about health rather than women's rights again softened the radical character of abortion law reform and made it more palatable to moderates, if not conservatives.

The abortion debate in France as elsewhere mobilizes participation on both sides of the political spectrum. The French women's policy agency has the capacity under certain conditions to respond effectively to participation as well as to mobilize activism. The relationship between the agency and women is two-way: it is not just that the Ministry sets an agenda that the ruling government seeks to implement in terms of women's rights and opportunities. The Ministry, as in the case of the *loi Neiertz* and the social security reimbursement, also can react to and respond to what women are demanding. In this sense, a women's policy agency can play a critical role in making the French system more democratic. If, as many scholars have postulated, democratic development is incomplete because of women's relatively lower level of participation and representation, then by both representing women's interests and opening an arena where they can articulate their needs and interests women's policy agencies may well expand the possibilities for democracy.

✧ Jean C. Robinson

❖ NOTES

I would like to thank the Service des Droits des Femmes, Government of France, and the Office of International Programs, Indiana University, for funding this research. Special thanks to the Service des Droits des Femmes and their excellent Service de la Recherche as well as to the City of Paris Bibliothèque Marguerite Durand archives for providing me access to documents in Paris between September 1997 and May 1998. My research included qualitative discourse analysis of a variety of sources, including correspondence between the Ministry and lobbying groups, minutes of abortion reform and anti-abortion association meetings, mimeographs of materials produced by various abortion reform groups, collated newspaper articles and other reports; letters; collections of materials kept by CADAC, reports of MFPF, material from Collectif Nationale pour les Droits des Femmes; and internal ministry and inter-ministry circulars. Please contact me for a complete list of materials, beyond those cited here.

1 Although very few cases were prosecuted, the criminalization meant that hundreds of thousands of women each year had illegal abortions, many of them self-incurred (Stetson 1987: 61).

2 Simone Veil did not want the law named for her. She said, 'There is not a Simone Veil law; there is a law desired by the President of the Republic, deliberated and adopted by the Council of Ministers, and for which the entire government assumes responsibility' (Berger 1975: 260). Nevertheless, in research as well as public discussions the 1975 law enshrines her name.

3 This case tried a 16-year-old girl in juvenile court for obtaining an abortion; her mother, two women who referred her, and the person who performed the abortion were prosecuted in criminal court.

4 See the full text of the law, No. 75–17 of January 1975, in *Journal Officiel* (1975).

5 Embedded here was also conservative bourgeois concern about wanton and unrestricted female sexuality, although this was seldom raised publicly as an issue.

6 See the text of the law, No. 79–1204 of 31 December 1979, in *Journal Officiel* (1980).

7 Letter to Mme Colanis, of *Dialogue des Femmes*, 23 September 1980. (archives of the Services des Droits des Femmes, Government of France).

8 Appleton and Mazur (1993: 106) remark on the singular appearance of Mitterrand at a forum on women's issues sponsored by Choisir in 1981 during the presidential election campaign. Mitterrand was the only mainstream candidate to participate, although all candidates were invited.

9 It was decided that the code for recording the procedure was to be 'K30', the same as that used for circumcision.

10 'The NA can be asked to override Senate objections in definitive "second reading", thus reducing the action of the Senate to a mere suspensive veto' (Safran 1995: 211).

11 Other correspondence available in the archives of the Service des Droit des Femmes, Paris, reinforce this view. For instance, see the letter from Mme. Roudy to MFPF, 29 February 1983.

12 By mid-December 1982, opinion polls found that 56.4% of men and 57.8 % of all women were favourable towards the reimbursement by Social Security of abortion, just as with other medical procedures. Among women under the age of 34, a large majority (76.4%) favoured the proposal, and even 53.4% of Catholics were in support (*Le Monde* 1982d).

13 Although reimbursement was approved, obtaining the actual money continued to be a problem. By the mid-1980s, Roudy had been forced out, the Socialist government found itself in deep financial crisis, and rates for reimbursement of abortions, like other medical procedures, were not increased in response to inflation.

14 Venner's study of the anti-abortion movement in France counts 53 such incidents between 1987 and 1991, and another 69 between 1992 and 1995. Of these, about one-quarter involved violence, and 14 elicited counter-demonstrations, most of which occurred during the 1990s (Venner 1995: 141–6).

15 MLF used the term '*avortement*' throughout the campaign to get the 1975 law passed, but very quickly that word became associated with feminist radicals. The 'proper' term, quickly used by the National Assembly and more 'moderate' groups as well as in the press, became '*l'interruption volontaire de grossesse*' (IVG), 'the voluntary interruption of pregnancy'.

16 Dominique Frischer (1997: 145) suggests that there is a direct connection between the increase in commando attacks and the visit of Pope John Paul II to France in 1988. At that time, the Pope described France as having a 'culture of death' and called on the faithful to struggle against abortions even where they are authorized by law.

17 Archives of Service des Droits des Femmes, Circulaire DGS/2A/DH/9C/91, 25 June 1991.

18 'Cohabitation' refers to those periods when the two leaders of the executive—president and prime minister—belong to opposing political parties or coalitions.

19 The Service des Femmes archives include interministerial circulars and letters attesting to the effective working relationship between the Ministries of Health and SEDFVQ, as well as the lobbying efforts of groups outside the government. These include CADAC's mimeo: 'Avortement contraception: un droit menacé; une mobilisation necessaire' (30 November 1991); Circul'Info No. 9/ juillet 1991 (Ministère des Affaires Sociales et de l'Integration); Communique Secrétariat d'État aux Droits des Femmes et la vie quotidienne, 21 June 1991; Lettre ouverte à Mme. Edith Cresson, Premier Ministre, 11 June 1991; and Lettre à Mme. Veronique Neiertz, Ministre des Droits des Femmes, 11 June 1991.

6 ❖ Abortion Debates in Germany

Lynn Kamenitsa

❖ INTRODUCTION

When the feminist women's movement emerged in West Germany (Federal Republic of Germany, FRG) in the early 1970s, abortion was a central mobilizing issue. The feminists demanded the repeal of Paragraph 218 of the criminal code that had criminalized abortion as a felony since the 1870s.[1] Initially, the pregnant woman and the person performing the abortion could be imprisoned without exception, though an exception to protect the life or health of the mother was introduced during the Weimar Republic. During the Nazi era, penalties were severely increased, yet exceptions were made for genetic defects or other eugenic reasons. After World War II, the FRG adopted the pre-Nazi law until pressures from feminists and others led to the liberalization of abortion law in 1974. The following year, the Federal Constitutional Court (FCC) struck down the law, declaring that the constitutional protections of human life and human dignity applied to the 'developing life' of the fetus and mandating new legislation codifying its ruling.

The resulting 1976 law settled the issue for a time, but German unification brought it back to the national agenda in the 1990s. The ensuing debate ended with a 1992 law legalizing abortion in the first trimester with mandatory counselling. An immediate court challenge followed and the FCC declared the law unconstitutional in May 1993. Once again, the legislature was charged with crafting a new law to codify the court's decision (Goetz 1996). This debate ended with the passage of the current German federal law in 1995. It affirms that abortion is illegal according to Paragraph 218, but stipulates that neither the woman nor the doctor will be prosecuted if certain conditions are met (Bundesverfassungsgericht 1993; *Bundesgesetzblatt Jahrgang* 1995).

While the abortion issue coincided with the emergence and growth of the FRG women's movement, it has not been a unifying force as it has in other countries. Indeed, the movement has been a divided for much of the last 30 years. The core of the West German women's movement traces its origins to the anti-218 movement of the 1970s and has been characterized by autonomous groups focused on local women's projects rather than participation in 'men's' institutions (Ferree 1987). Later in the 1970s, a separate group of women, referred to here as mainstream feminists, rejected the autonomous feminists' strategy and instead opted to try to influence public policy by working within political parties, trade unions, traditional women's organizations, and state bureaucracies (Rosenberg 1996). These two groups had ideological and organizational disagreements not only with each other, but also with feminists associated with the Green Party that came to prominence in the 1980s (Altbach 1984; Kolinsky 1988; Pinl 1989; Meier and Oubaid 1987: 38–40). The events of 1989 added yet another faction to this already fragmented movement: in that year, an East German feminist women's movement emerged as one of the citizens' movements that helped topple the communist regime (Kamenitsa 1993; 1998; Kenawi 1995). Despite early gestures between eastern and western feminists, little actual cooperation occurred. Instead, different histories, perspectives, and goals led to much misunderstanding and acrimony on both sides (Rosenberg 1996; Chamberlayne 1995; Ferree 1995b; Kiechle 1991: 51–7). In sum, organizational fragmentation, ideological differences, and the willingness of several segments to question each other's feminist identities has meant that 'the' women's movement in the FRG is better understood as a collection of various factions, each of which has played different roles in the abortion debates.

❖ Selection of Debates

Major decisions regarding the legalization of abortion are made at the federal level, specifically in the lower house of Parliament (*Bundestag*) and the Constitutional Court. Individual federal States can regulate certain aspects of access to abortion in their territory, for example, the provision of pregnancy counselling services, but are not major arenas for abortion politics. Abortion-related policies made by Parliament and at other levels are subject to review by the FCC. The latter can use its extensive powers to make policy from the bench, often resulting the legislature's passage of another bill that formalizes what the Court has mandated. Federal ministries are often charged with drafting the legislation to be debated in the Parliament or providing expert testimony before parliamentary commissions considering abortion questions.

The major public policy debates in these institutions regarding abortion include:

(1) Parliament's decision to legalize abortion in the first three months of pregnancy, 1969–74;
(2) Federal Constitutional Court rejection of 1974 law, 1975;
(3) Parliament's legislation codifying the Court's decision, 1976;

(4) Parliament's post-unification legislation, an effort to harmonize abortion regulation in eastern and western Germany, 1990–2;
(5) Federal Constitutional Court decision overturning 1992 law, 1993; and
(6) Parliament enacts Pregnancy and Family Assistance Law Modification, 1993–5.

In this chapter, I analyze the three debates that resulted in federal legislation, representing the most important decisional system for abortion policy in Germany: (1) legalization 1969–74; (2) post-unification legislation 1990–2; and (3) Pregnancy and Family Assistance Law Modification 1993–5. I have not selected any debates exclusively from the FCC. The impact of the Court is evident in the policy debates analyzed here. In a sense, the Court is an actor in these policy debates by forcing certain frames and parameters on other actors and their agendas. Thus, by selecting debates that ended in parliamentary decisions, the Court's influence is included. On the other hand, the study of any Court ruling produced by the closed judicial process would tell us little about the parliamentary arena and the policy debate more generally.

These three debates have clearly been the most important ones regarding the legality and availability of abortion in Germany. Although both the first and the second debates ended with legislation that was later struck down, they produced wide-ranging public policy discussions of abortion unmatched in the three decades covered in this research. The third debate's importance stems from the fact that it resulted in the law that regulates the legality of abortion in Germany today. These debates also represent the range of the issue over the period under study. The first debate marks the beginning of the effort to decriminalize abortion in the 1970s. This was followed by a decade of relatively little public policy debate concerning the topic. The second and third debates represent the next and most recent appearance of abortion on the public agenda.

❖ DEBATE 1: *Bundestag* DECISION TO LEGALIZE ABORTION, 1969–74

❖ *How the debate came to the public agenda*

In 1970, a group of German and Swiss legal scholars released a proposed reform of the criminal code, part of the long-term post-war overhaul of the code (Schroeder 1972). This 'alternative draft', as their report became known, included two proposals for reforming abortion regulation: the periodic model, which would legalize abortion in the first three months of pregnancy, and the indications model, which would legalize abortion only when certain conditions or indications were present and verified independently. These models became the foundation for the abortion debate (Mattern 1991). Simultaneously, women's groups seized upon legal abortion as a central demand of their emerging movement and mounted numerous actions to gain public support. Meanwhile other groups, most prominently the civil rights group, Humanist Union (HU), also began agitating for legalization, with support from many legal and medical professionals. Finally, as other countries reformed their abortion laws in the late 1960s—notably, Great Britain in 1967—German media exposed the issue of illegal abortion. Magazine and newspaper articles told the stories of women travelling to London for abortions or procuring them illegally inside West Germany (FFBIZ e.V. 1991). The discussion of abortion reform gained more public and media attention in 1971, as the governing coalition of the Social Democratic Party (SPD) and Free Democratic Party (FDP) began drafting its reform of the abortion portion of the criminal code.

❖ *Dominant frame of the debate*

The dominant frame of this debate concerned preventing illegal abortions. Most actors, particularly lawmakers and legal experts, charged that the current, restrictive law did not prevent abortions but instead made criminals out of hundreds of thousands of women and their doctors. They argued that a law so widely violated, yet so infrequently prosecuted, must be flawed. The health risks to women of illegal abortions were mentioned as well. The dominant frame included the admission that the new regulations should 'protect life', as the German constitution required the state to do. Although there were discussions about whether that included 'developing life' or only existing life and the balance between those two, specific references to the life of the fetus were found mostly in the rhetoric of the churches.[2]

❖ *Gendering the debate*

Women's movement and civil rights organizations sought to gender the debate but were largely unsuccessful. Other important actors, including most legal experts, the churches, doctors, and the main party politicians resisted, managing to discuss abortion reform with minimal attention to woman *qua* women. Women's movement organizations were explicit in their gendering. They presented abortion as an issue of a woman's self-determination and control over her body. The slogan 'mein Bauch gehört mir!' ('my belly belongs to me!') was central to their protests and literature. They critically acknowledged women's roles as primary care-givers for children and the way that religion, society, and politics forced those roles upon them. For the feminists, criminalized abortion was a manifestation of patriarchal institutional control over women. The HU also included gendered frames in its debate contributions, but tended to focus only on women's right of self-determination without analysis of patriarchal structures. On occasion, however, the HU did discuss women's right to abortion as part of women's emancipation from oppression.

Except for rejecting assertions that the fetus is a 'part of the mother's body', statements by church leaders on abortion ignored women (German Bishops' Conference [1970] 1972). In one document, an association of Catholic medical professionals discussed the issue without mentioning once that it is women who get pregnant![3] Both the alternative draft of the legal experts and statements from professional medical associations acknowledged only the fact that women are the ones who get pregnant and, thus, could have abortions (Schroeder 1972: 46–57; Deutscher Frauenärzte 1972).

The rhetoric of the main political parties—the dominant rhetoric of the policy debate—likewise had few gender references. All major parties mentioned that women in 'times of need' might require additional social support, and all acknowledged that there might be a conflict of rights when a woman's life was endangered by pregnancy. The coalition parties went only a bit farther with the FDP rejecting state paternalism in favour of enabling women to make their own life decisions, and the SPD noting that reforming the law would not free women from 'antiquated subordination' (Jahn [1971] 1972: 162). The SPD's attention to gender reached its high point at the end of the debate when, in defence of the proposed periodic model, it explicitly acknowledged that social measures to ease women's domestic burdens could decrease the abortion rate by making motherhood a more viable option (Social Democratic Party of Germany 1974).

In sum, the efforts by the women's movement to gender the debate were unsuccessful. In the few cases where women's gendered roles were discussed, such as the late SPD rhetoric, there was virtually no discussion of gendered hierarchies, challenges to male domination, critiques of traditional gender roles, or abortion as a women's rights issue.

❖ Policy outcome

The road to a final decision in this debate was a long one (Muth 1994). The government proposed an indications model in 1971, but, at a party conference, the SPD rank and file roundly rejected it in favour of a periodic model. The SPD government's junior coalition partner also opted for the more liberal periodic model, whereas the opposition Christian Democratic Party (CDU/CSU) rejected the government's proposal as being too liberal. After parliamentary elections in 1973, the government declined to introduce its own bill, in allowing the SPD and FDP party caucuses in the Bundestag to present the periodic model in their own joint bill. A year of legislative hearings and debate about that bill ensued, along with alternatives introduced by the CDU/CSU and an SPD minority. The SPD/FDP bill finally received *Bundestag* approval in April 1994, only to be vetoed by the upper house, the *Bundesrat*, in May. In June 1974, however, the *Bundestag* overrode that veto and the Fifth Legal Reform of the Criminal Code became law.

Under this periodic model, abortion regulation remained in the criminal code, but abortion was not punishable in the first three months of pregnancy provided that a woman wanted the procedure, a doctor performed it, and she visited a counselling service. Thereafter, abortions were legal only if a specific indication was demonstrated, namely, danger to a woman's health or the presence of severe birth defects.

❖ Movement impact

Although the Fifth Legal Reform of 1974 fell short of the complete abolition of Paragraph 218 of the Criminal Code that feminist groups advocated, it was a significant liberalization of West German abortion law, thus achieving the minimal goals desired by movement activists. But anti-218 women's movement organizations were largely excluded from the policy process. Their activities and demonstrations were instrumental in gaining more attention to the problem of criminalized abortion, but their ideas and activists were seldom included in the policy debate in official arenas. Print media coverage, for example, tended to include feminist activists in two ways. One was to cover their demonstrations as news events without examining their impact on political decision makers. The other was to begin an article with one of the feminists' provocative slogans about women's self-determination, only to dismiss that position as too extremist before moving on to cover the activities and arguments of decision makers. Late in the debate, the SPD explicitly sought to distance itself from the women's movement positions (Social Democratic Party of Germany 1974).

Some women were involved in the policy debate. SPD women and the party's women's organization were among several vocal groups within the party that advocated a periodic model. Media interviews with, for example, Annemarie Renger, Member of Parliament and Chair of the SPD federal women's organization, and Katherina Focke, Minister of Family, Youth and Health, revealed women who publicly supported a periodic model. But these women were only part of the broader coalition within the party that helped shift the SPD's position from an indication model to a periodic one between 1971 and 1974. Indeed, less media attention was paid to SPD women than to the FDP and prominent SPD men who also advocated a periodic model. Furthermore, these SPD women did not present themselves as a part of the emerging women's movement. In sum, although some women were involved in the debate, women's movement activists were not accepted in the public policy process. Thus, movement impact on the state in this case is classified as pre-emption.

❖ LYNN KAMENITSA

Representatives of the movement were not directly involved in the policy process, but the policy content met their basic demand for the legal abortion.

❖ Women's policy agency activities

It is impossible to assess the activities of the women's policy agency (WPA) in this debate, since the FRG had no such agency in the early 1970s. The closest institution to such an agency, the federal Ministry for Family, Youth, and Health, did not yet have formal responsibility for women's affairs, and therefore does not meet the definition of a women's policy agency. Nevertheless, its two ministers—Käthe Strobel (1969–72) and Katharina Focke (1974–6)—had considerable involvement in the policy process, promoting a periodic model in keeping with women's movement demands.

❖ Women's movement characteristics

During this debate, the women's movement was in a growth stage. Dozens of groups were springing up throughout West Germany in the late 1960s and early 1970s, with the demand for abolishing Paragraph 218 as a main organizing and rallying point. Throughout the debate period, the legalization of abortion remained the central issue and a high priority of the new movement. Although excitement and mobilization were high, the movement was fragmented because the anti-218 groups were largely local in nature. There was little coordination among groups, despite periodic contacts and mutual inspiration. In addition, some feminist organizations that originated in the 1960s student movements were not fully integrated with the anti-218 groups. The women's movement groups tended to be suspicious of traditional institutions and hierarchies, and thus were not close to the political left, that is, the SPD and the trade unions. Finally, the women's groups confronted a strong counter-movement in traditional institutions that opposed legal abortion, including the two main churches, the CDU/CSU, and several physicians' organizations.

❖ Policy environment

The German policy environment in the early 1970s was mixed for social movement activists. On the one hand, the policy sub-system was a closed one, with political parties dominating the policy debate and determining its dominant discourse. While some outside experts—for example, law professors or medical doctors—participated, they did so only at the invitation of the political parties. Social movement groups were largely excluded as policy actors. On the other hand, the party of the left was in power, and the SPD/FDP coalition was amenable to reforming abortion law, despite internal disputes about the specifics.

❖ DEBATE 2: POST-UNIFICATION COMPROMISE, 1990–1992

❖ *How the debate came to the public agenda*

The FCC invalidated the 1974 reform, and a 1976 law designed to comply with the Court ruling again provided criminal penalties for abortion. Both a woman and her physician could be punished unless one of four indications applied: medical—threat to the woman's health or life; eugenic—grave birth defects; criminological—rape or incest; or social—when a woman was in distress (Klein-Schonnefeld 1994: 117). A woman was required to receive counselling from a physician and an aid facility before obtaining an abortion. Regulations governing the counselling content and facilities were established at the State (*Land*) level. The result was a regional divide in women's access to abortion: they could be relatively easily obtained in the largely Protestant northern States, but were difficult to obtain in the largely Catholic southern States.

The prospect of German unification in 1990 challenged this arrangement, because abortion was legal in the first trimester in East Germany (German Democratic Republic, GDR). The contradictory abortion laws were a serious point of contention in unification negotiations. The western CDU/CSU wanted to apply the FRG regulations to the East, as was done with other laws, but the GDR Parliament, along with some western political forces who saw an opportunity to liberalize the FRG law, resisted. A majority of East Germans, especially women, were steadfastly opposed to any restriction of their right to abortion (Kiechle 1991: 51–2). When the issue threatened the treaty's passage, negotiators agreed to leave existing laws in effect in eastern and western Germany until a jointly elected *Bundestag* passed new legislation, something it was obliged to do before 1993.

The policy debate took place in political parties, before a special parliamentary committee—the Committee for the Protection of Unborn Life—in the press, in the governing CDU/CSU and FDP coalition, in the *Bundestag*, and, most unusually, among women parliamentarians from several parties.[4] There was little consensus throughout the process, with debates and votes on seven separate bills in 1992.

❖ *Dominant frame of the debate*

At the end of the 1970–4 debate, the abortion issue had been defined as a question of providing assistance to women with problem pregnancies, primarily to avoid illegal abortions. The FCC decision in 1975 altered this framing by ruling that the state was obligated to protect 'unborn life' in compliance with constitutionally mandated protections of human life and dignity. The *Bundestag* incorporated this new frame into its more restrictive 1976 law, and put in place an indications model to allow women access to abortion

❖ LYNN KAMENITSA

only in situations where it would be unreasonable to carry a pregnancy to term. The unification treaty clearly reflected the Court's 1975 ruling when it directed the *Bundestag* to develop a law that would 'better guarantee the protection of prenatal life and the constitutional resolution of conflict situations of pregnant women' (*Vertrag* 1990). Thus the dominant frame at the beginning of the 1990 debate focused on fulfilling the state's obligation to protect unborn life, while acknowledging that women sometimes faced conflicts in pregnancy.

The specific policy choice was between the periodic model and the indications model. Regardless of which model was proposed, most debate participants framed their proposals with references to how they would better protect unborn life.[5] This was true of those who advocated a periodic model—the SPD, the FDP, most mainstream feminists, and the East German women's movement; those who supported various indications models—the CDU, the CSU, and those right-to-life advocates who would allow abortion to save a woman's life; and those who argued for criminalizing all abortions—a minority of CDU/CSU members and some right-to-life advocates. As the debate progressed, the framing tilted increasingly in favour of those emphasizing the protection of unborn life over those focusing on women's conflicts.

❖ Gendering the debate

With the idea of protecting unborn life dominating the debate, those who sought to incorporate attention to women faced an uphill battle. Gendering ran the gamut from feminist frames to those reinforcing traditional gender roles to those that ignored gender all together. The prominence of different gendered frames varied over time along with press attention to different proposals or public statements.

At one end of the gendering spectrum were the feminist images presented by the eastern women's movement and the political parties with eastern roots, the Party of Democratic Socialism (PDS), which was the successor to the communist party, and the Alliance90/Greens—a union of the western Greens and the eastern citizens movements.[6] These actors presented abortion as matter of 'women rights', 'autonomy', and 'self-determination'. Women were portrayed as citizens who needed the state's assistance to secure their full rights to 'self-determination over her body and her own life'.[7] The feminists critiqued the patriarchal structures of West German society and portrayed the effort to strip them of the right to abortion as an effort to return women to traditional gender roles.

At the spectrum's centre were SPD and FPD frames focusing on families and providing assistance to them as a way of addressing women's problems with 'pregnancy conflict'. At times, women disappeared entirely into these family frames. At other times, however, certain issues were presented as women's gender-specific problems, including pregnancy conflicts, childcare, and combining work and family. These debate participants argued that women's traditional responsibilities for children and households justified women's right to decide when and whether to have children. While this framing acknowledged women's gender roles, it did nothing to challenge them. There were no suggestions that men become more responsible for childcare or that they require assistance in combining work and family. Indeed, this gendering reinforced traditional gender roles by placing primary responsibility for parenting squarely on women.

The CDU/CSU and other right-to-life forces occupied the other end of the spectrum. Here gendering was de-emphasized. The emphasis was on families and the 'unborn child'. Women were subsumed under the 'family' category or ignored altogether. One bill, introduced by a conservative minority of CDU/CSU legislators, referred to the 'unborn child', 'pregnancy conflict', and even counselling services without even mentioning pregnant women! When women were present in these frames, they were portrayed as people who can be easily manipulated by others into having abortions or as people who are unable to 'make responsible decisions' without state intervention in the matter (Rönsch 1991a; Pursch 1992). Care for children was assumed to be the task of women, a task that the state could make more manageable with social assistance (Rönsch 1991b).

In sum, the prevailing debate discourse treated abortion as a family issue rather than a women's rights issue (Sauer 1995). When women were mentioned, they were portrayed in traditional roles or as needing to combine traditional and new roles. Women were discussed in connection with their children, but few speakers discussed fathers as parents or as people needing to combine family and employment. When men were mentioned, it was most frequently as possible sources of pressure on women to have abortions. In short, the efforts to gender the debate were largely unsuccessful.[8]

❖ Policy outcome

The final legislation emerged after more than a year of hearings, draft bills, and floor debates. Because party leaders had agreed that the *Bundestag* vote would be one of conscience rather than party loyalty, each bill was designed to woo one of the various constituencies within the Parliament. Finally a cross-bench coalition of women parliamentarians drafted a bill that, because it represented a compromise on several key issues, was acceptable to a majority of members. The legislation, which passed the *Bundestag* in June 1992, left abortion in the criminal code, thus signalling state disapproval of the procedure. However, it decriminalized abortion in the first twelve weeks, provided a woman underwent mandatory counselling, designed in part to inform her of the rights of the developing fetus, at least three days prior to the procedure. The authors sought to meet the Court-mandated state obligation to protect life through this more rigorous counselling requirement and though improved social welfare benefits ranging from free contraception for women under 20 to guaranteed day care and kindergarten places. Although the counselling was supposed to encourage the woman to continue the pregnancy, the final decision was left to her.

❖ Movement impact

This outcome was not in keeping with either the long-standing goals of any segment of the western feminist movement or the current goals of the eastern movement. The eastern women's movement, the most vocal and active during this debate, advocated a periodic model and the removal of abortion from the criminal code. The western autonomous feminists had long advocated abolishing Paragraph 218 on grounds of women's self-determination rights (Maleck-Lewy and Ferree 1996). Though some of them continued to advocate this position in the early 1990s debate, this core movement segment was strangely absent, and these claims were pushed to the edges of the dominant discourse (Sauer 1995: 173). Other feminists, particularly mainstream feminists, shifted their stance during the debate, moving away from the long-standing support for an unfettered periodic model and towards an expanded indications model or a periodic model with mandatory counselling. These women, some of whom played prominent roles in the debate, believed that only this compromise position had a chance of gaining a legislative majority and withstanding Court scrutiny.

The policy outcome, then, was in keeping with the short-term strategic goals of feminist politicians, but not with the women's movement's broader goals stated over time. The final legislation lacked the feminist emphases on women's self-determination, the removal of abortion from the criminal code, and women's right to abortion. It did not fulfil movement demands for access to abortion without the interference of and justification to an outside body. The goals of the eastern German groups—preserving eastern women's right to safe, legal, and free abortion and extending it to all German women—were clearly unmet by the new law.

Women were active participants in the policy process, particularly mainstream feminists and non-feminist women from the CDU. All political parties found it important to have women play visible roles in the process, so women acted as party spokespersons on the issue throughout the debate. For all but the CDU/CSU these included self-defined feminists. These spokeswomen, along with other prominent women in the FDP and the SPD, received enormous media attention and were ultimately responsible for the successful cross-bench proposal.[9] Prominent Christian Democratic women also played active roles.

Two cabinet ministers, Angela Merkel, Minister for Women and Youth, and Hannelore Rönsch, Minister for Family and Seniors, received continuous media coverage and were featured prominently in the parliamentary debates. Both were active in intra-party negotiations concerning CDU/CSU proposals. The *Bundestag* president and former women's minister, Rita Süssmith, a CDU member, received similar attention in the press.

Women's movement involvement was direct but ineffective. Feminists organized public protests, but these went largely unreported in the media. Only a few women's movement activists were invited to testify at the special committee hearings.[10] Issue spokespersons for both the PDS—Petra Bläss—and the Alliance90/Greens—Christina Schenk—were members of the main eastern German feminist organization, the Independent Women's Union (UFV). This gave the women's movement a direct voice in the process, but it went largely unheard due to the weak position of both parties and the distance of their frames from the dominant ones.

In sum, the impact of the women's movement on the process was one of cooptation. Feminist women were very involved in the policy process. The final policy outcome, however, was not in keeping with the positions long advocated by the West German women's movement or currently advocated by eastern feminists.

❖ Women's policy agency activities

The federal women's policy machinery originated in the 1970s, first with a small women's policy desk within the family section of the Ministry for Health, Family, and Youth, then, in 1979, as a separate unit within the ministry with a staff of eleven (*Jahresbericht der Bundesregierung* 1979). When Rita Süssmith, of the CDU, was appointed to head that ministry in 1986, she insisted that 'Women' be added to its title. Since then the ministry has been a cross-sectional one, dealing with various aspects of women's affairs ranging from employment to domestic violence.

As the leader of this large and powerful ministry, Süssmith was a 'very visible spokesperson on women's policy issues' until she was 'kicked upstairs' to become *Bundestag* president in 1988 (Ferree 1995a: 99). A cabinet reorganization in 1991 divided the ministry into the Ministry of Health, the Ministry for Women and Youth (BMFJ), and the Ministry for Families and Seniors (BMFS). The BMFJ became a middle-level ministry in terms of budget and staff. Many critics of CDU Chancellor Helmut Kohl believe that the timing of this reorganization was a conscious effort to divide a powerful ministry's resources and mandates in advance of the abortion debate.

The women's minister is a political appointment, though middle- and lower-level staff remain in their positions as ministers change. These civil servants include femocrats who, though bound to carry out ministerial directives, have some influence in shaping the proposals the minister forwards to the government. The use of this appointment for political ends was evident in the 1991 restructuring. The Ministry for Women and Youth was placed under the leadership of a young, inexperienced, eastern Christian Democrat, Angela Merkel, while the Family and Seniors portfolio was held by the more experienced Hannelore Rönsch of the CDU. As a personal protégé of Kohl, Merkel was promoted to minister very quickly. As concerns about unification's impact on East German women grew, it was politically strategic to have an easterner in charge of women's affairs. But Merkel's ability to represent eastern women's interests forcefully was limited by party discipline and her personal loyalty to Kohl. She was not a feminist minister.

The government determines ministries' mandates with some input from the ministers themselves. The regulation of abortion falls well within the purview of the women's ministry, but, because the debate entailed revising the criminal code, the Ministry of Justice had the primary mandate. The press covered a 1991 tug of war between Merkel and Rönsch over a secondary mandate. The more experienced Rönsch won, citing the family ministry's responsibility for the pregnancy counselling centres. Though not shut out of the policy debate completely, the women's policy ministry lacked the legal and political authority to represent the government on this issue. The importance of the mandate question was evident in interviews with ministry insiders, who revealed a long-standing feminist orientation in the women's section and a more Catholic orientation in the family section. In turn, Rönsch took a conservative stance in this debate and did not present herself as representing women. Merkel, influenced by her experience in the GDR, took a more liberal position focusing on abortion as a 'women's issue'. As political appointments, however, both were limited in how outspoken they could be.

The women's policy agency's mild effort to insert gender references in the policy debate was unsuccessful. Merkel explicitly identified abortion as a 'women's issue' because women 'are the ones who become pregnant and bring children into the world, they are usually the ones who are responsible for and bear the burden of raising them, and they are the ones who must bear the emotional consequences of an abortion' (Merkel 1991a). But her statements seemed designed more to justify her ministry's participation in the debate than to interject women's needs. Her most explicit efforts to gender were those emphasizing the importance of both parents taking responsibility for children and the need for social policies that enabled both parents to combine work and family life, something that challenged the dominant framing and the common reality of gender arrangements. This was not an effort to bring men's interests into the decision but rather an attempt to broaden the discussion from speaking only of the 'unborn child' or of mothers and their children to speaking of parents and their children.

GERMANY ❖

Merkel did not attempt to portray abortion as a women's *rights* issue. Instead she was careful to frame the issue in terms of balancing 'the need situation of the woman and also the protection of unborn life' (*Berliner Morgenpost* 1991). She conceded that women had a right to self-determination, but did so only indirectly through her criticism of the periodic model, which she claimed focused 'exclusively on women's right to self-determination'. She did not refer to it as the 'so-called right', as did others who opposed that framing, but neither did she embrace the self-determination and women's rights frames. Women were present in her framing as people who are conflicted and have abortions only if they 'see no other way out' (Merkel 1991*b*). This is in keeping with the dominant portrayal of women in this abortion discourse as being desperate and in deep moral conflict (Maleck-Lewy and Ferree 1996).[11] Merkel referred to women almost exclusively as 'women' or 'pregnant women' and only very seldom as 'mothers', the term preferred by Rönsch and other CDU actors, who often referred to women as 'mothers' regardless of whether they had children. But despite her efforts to cast abortion as a women's and parents' issue, Merkel's mildly gendered frames did not become important frames in the general policy debate.

Merkel supported an indications model with mandatory counselling, but allowed for flexibility. She accepted that the final decision should be left to the individual woman, who, in consultation with her physician, would determine which indication applied. Merkel argued that this process was inherently subjective and, thus, should not be subject to later review by independent experts as other proposals advocated. Merkel's stance was more liberal than those of most CDU politicians, but it did not coincide with the women's movement positions discussed above. She explicitly rejected a periodic model or any solution based primarily on women's self-determination rights. Her position was very similar to the short-term strategy adopted by some mainstream feminists in the debate, albeit with more restrictions and qualifications than they accepted.

In sum, the women's policy agency activities in this case should be classified as symbolic. The BMFJ neither supported women's movement goals nor was able to gender the policy definitions in the process. Indeed, in this case the government's symbolic use of the WPA was evident to observers at the time as Kohl placed an eastern woman in office but denied her the opportunity to represent eastern women's interests effectively.

❖ *Women's movement characteristics*

The German women's movement in the 1990s could best be characterized as fragmented and in decline. As mentioned above, this resulted from the long-standing divisions in the West German movement and from German unification. This fragmentation did not allow 'the' movement to speak with a single voice on abortion or any other issue. This, along with a lack of public support, put it in a poor bargaining position *vis-à-vis* policy makers.

The German women's movement was not close to the traditional political left during this debate. Many mainstream feminists were active in the centre-left SPD, but the movement as such retained its long-standing suspicions of such male-dominated institutions. Individual feminists played important roles in the Green Party and in the far left PDS. The eastern German feminists of the UFV were co-founders of the alliance of citizen movement groups known as Alliance 90. But each of these groups was peripheral to German politics during this debate and feminist relationships with them were fraught with tension.

In the abstract, abortion remained a high priority of the West German women's movement as it had been in the 1970s, and some hoped to reinvigorate the autonomous feminist movement around that issue in the 1990s. But the reality was more ambiguous. Abortion remained a priority for many mainstream feminists, whose activities were noted earlier. Abortion was also a priority for the East German movement throughout this period, as evidenced by demonstrations, manifestos, press releases, parliamentary testimony, and petition drives. But the lack of coordinated national activity and the relative invisibility of the autonomous feminist core of the West German movement make it difficult to argue that abortion was a high priority for the movement generally.

Advocates of more liberal abortion laws confronted a well-organized, institutionalized, and financed counter-movement that had mobilized in the 1980s. Kohl's conservative-led government bolstered the movement with pro-life public education and efforts to narrow the social indication, which abortion opponents believed women abused for their own 'convenience' (Kiechle 1991: 17–18; Czarnowski 1994). Abortion foes undertook efforts on several fronts: trying to restrict abortion access in CDU-controlled States, challenging the use of state insurance funds to pay for abortions, and campaigning to popularize the slogan 'abortion is killing' (*Abtreibung ist Tötung*). Key players included the Catholic Church, its bishops and other clergy, its grassroots groups, its elected representatives in State and federal offices, right-to-life legal and medical professional organizations, and the conservative political parties.[12]

❖ Policy environment

During the debate under study, the political right formed the government and controlled the lower, more powerful house of the Parliament. The governing coalition included the liberal FDP as the junior partner to the CDU/CSU. The SPD, however, controlled a majority of the seats in the *Bundesrat* for all but a few months of the debate period. The threat of an upper house veto gave the SPD some leverage in shaping the abortion legislation.

The policy sub-system surrounding abortion was a moderately closed one. The political parties and their parliamentary groups dominate the sub-system, determining, for instance, which interest group representatives testify at committee hearings. The involved governmental ministries also have substantial input in the process, particularly in drafting legislation for the government and in providing expertise in working groups and committees. Input from grassroots groups is limited by a neo-corporatist system in which major institutional interests have 'their' representatives in Parliament and lobbyists with long-standing ties to government officials (Conradt 1993; Dalton 1993). Thus the party in power and the established interests, notably including the churches in this debate, are able to exercise substantial, though not total, control over the policy sub-system.

❖ DEBATE 3: PREGNANCY AND FAMILY ASSISTANCE LAW MODIFICATION, 1993–1995

❖ How the debate came to the public agenda

In May 1993, the FCC struck down the 1992 *Bundestag* law, claiming that it did not provide constitutionally sufficient protection of unborn life, including protection against the fetus's mother. The justices set forth specific provisions that must be incorporated into new legislation including a prohibition of abortion, a legal obligation to carry a pregnancy to term, punishment of a woman's friends or family members who pressured her to have an abortion, and restrictions on the use of state health insurance funds to pay for abortions. The court also held, however, that an abortion was not 'unlawful' if it met either a medical or criminological indication. Furthermore, the state could use counselling and other social assistance measures to protect life rather than criminal penalties.

Another policy debate began immediately after the court announced its decision, and it lasted until a new statute became law in July 1995. This debate took place largely within and between political parties. The women's ministry played an important role, particularly after a government reorganization following the 1994 elections. Inter- and intra-party debates were covered in the press, but there was less press attention to other debate participants.

❖ Dominant frame of the debate

Throughout this debate all significant parties adhered to the court's stipulation that the focus of abortion regulation must be on protecting life, including unborn life. The dominant frame emphasized this protection of life, though generally with an eye toward how the state could achieve this protection by offering women 'help, not punishment' (*'Hilfe statt Straf'*) as the court had indicated. Much of the debate dealt with possible state means for achieving this, especially through the provision of counselling and emphasizing the point that life could be protected only 'with the mother, not against her'. Indeed, the terminology shifted from discussing periodic and indications models to discussing counselling models and social assistance. One of the measures from the 1992 law in particular, ensuring each child the right to a kindergarten place by 1996, became central to this debate and came to symbolize the assistance measures generally.

There was considerable discussion of specific policy proposals including financing of abortions, the punishment of a woman's family or friends, and language concerning the woman's role in the abortion decision. The SPD and FDP emphasized that she should have 'individual responsibility' for making the choice, while the CDU/CSU couched it as 'final responsibility', thus implying that the counsellor or doctor should have some say in the decision.

❖ Gendering the debate

The strongest efforts at gendering came from the Alliance90/Green parliamentary faction, which, along with the PDS spokespersons, continued to emphasize women's self-determination rights. The FDP and SPD presented gendered images only on rare occasions. As possible compromise gave way to campaign rhetoric, the SPD's gendering peaked in the summer of 1994 when its spokespersons briefly emphasized women's self-determination and individual responsibility in making the abortion decision, and criticized the CDU/CSU for its patronizing attitude toward women. SPD and FDP representatives frequently talked about the kindergarten provision as an important family assistance measure, but neglected to articulate the relationship to women's traditional gender roles or their decisions about having children. The only exception was in a parliamentary debate in February 1995, when SPD spokeswomen explicitly tied abortion to women's ability to keep their jobs and combine employment and family obligations. Generally, the debate implied that women are responsible for rearing children, but seldom explained that fully or appraised that role. Thus, women were largely absent from the discourse in this debate, except for their factual role as the people who get pregnant. While women were included as the 'pregnant ones', debate participants said little about their roles or social status beyond pregnancy.

❖ Policy outcome

Legislation introduced by the coalition government was passed in 1994, but was rejected by the SPD-controlled *Bundesrat* in advance of autumn parliamentary elections. After that election, the FDP introduced its own abortion bill rather than supporting a government bill as it had previously. Thus, both the SPD and the FDP were able to pressure the CDU/CSU to agree to compromise legislation, which was then approved by the *Bundestag* in June 1995 and, without additional debate, by the *Bundesrat* in July.[13] That law, currently in force, declared abortion to be 'unlawful, but not punishable' provided it met several criteria: it was conducted by a doctor at least three days after a pregnant woman underwent mandatory counselling, the doctor advised the woman about medical risks, and it took place during the first twelve weeks of pregnancy. Alternatively, an abortion was not unlawful if it met one of two indications: a medical indication—a threat to a women's life, physical or mental health—or a criminological indication—rape or incest. In perhaps the most controversial section, the law stipulated that the counselling must 'serve to protect the unborn life', provide the woman with information on social services available to families, and advise her of the fetus's right to life at all stages of development and, thus, that abortion could be possible only in an 'exceptional situation'. The counselling would, however, leave the final decision up to the pregnant woman. Finally, women were expected to pay for 'unlawful' abortions themselves rather using the state insurance funds that cover other medical procedures. Women with low incomes could have abortion costs covered by the state.

❖ *Movement impact*

This policy outcome did not meet the women's movement's long-standing demands for the legalization of abortion as a women's rights or self-determination issue, the removal from the criminal code, and access to abortion without the interference of or justification to an outside body. Instead, this policy explicitly criminalized the procedure and did not emphasize women's self-determination, although it did allow her to make the final decision. Further, it mandated counselling specifically designed to serve the fetus, which was conceptualized as a being with individual constitutional rights. In keeping with the court ruling, this legislation placed the constitutional rights of the fetus above the constitutional rights of the pregnant woman.

As in the early 1990s debate, women played an important role in this policy debate. All political parties again had women as their spokespersons on the abortion issue. All of these women received substantial media coverage throughout the debate and, with the exception of the CDU spokesperson, were feminists. Other prominent women in each of the parties gave frequent interviews to the press and had their positions and statements reported regularly. The Justice Minister, Sabine Luetheusser-Schnarrenberger, a member of the FDP, played a prominent and newsworthy role. Finally, the women's ministers before—Angela Merkel—and after—Claudia Nolte—the 1994 cabinet restructuring were important figures. Nolte, in particular, was very much engaged in the process and played an important role in crafting the compromise proposal.

❖ LYNN KAMENITSA

The women's movement, however, was essentially absent from the debate. Unlike the earlier debates, there was no media coverage of women's movement demonstrations, petition drives, or testimony. *Bundestag* members Bläss and Schenk, the eastern feminist activists, continued to speak out on the issue, but other movement activity was invisible. The movement seemed resigned to the fact that the eventual legislation would have to meet the Court's restrictive and specific criteria.

In sum, the impact of the women's movement on the policy process was one of cooptation. Feminist women were involved in the policy process, although the women's movement was not. Women, clearly, were viewed as belonging in this policy debate. At the same time, the policy itself was not in keeping with the goals the women's movement had advocated since the early 1970s.

❖ Women's policy agency activities

The women's policy agency assumed two different forms during the course of this debate. Through late 1994, the ministry remained the same as it was during Debate 2: the Ministry for Women and Youth (BMFJ) under the direction of Angela Merkel. After the 1994 election, a new government was formed with the same coalition partners but a reshuffled cabinet. The women's and family ministries were again combined to form the Federal Ministry for Families, Seniors, Women, and Youth (BMFSFJ) and placed under the direction of Claudia Nolte, a 27-year-old, eastern German, right-to-life activist.

In both its pre- and post-1994 forms, the ministry had the same characteristics outlined above. It was a cross-sectional, middle-level ministry. The minister, not a feminist, was a political appointment. Indeed, in addition to her adamant opposition to abortion rights, Nolte publicly advocated traditional family structures and conservative family values. The abortion issue clearly fell within the mandate of the reorganized ministry, since it was now responsible for women's issues, the pregnancy counselling centres, and family policy.

The women's policy agency's efforts to gender the policy debate varied slightly over time. While Merkel headed the Ministry for Women and Family, she made some efforts at identifying women as interested parties whose needs should be addressed by the new policy. Specifically, she greeted the 1993 Court decision not only for its protection of unborn life but also for its recognition that life can be protected only 'with, not against, the mother'. She praised the coalition's 1994 bill as a 'big improvement for the woman [because] the decision about abortion lies with her alone'.[14] With the abortion mandate clearly resting in the Family Ministry, however, her efforts were not as strong or visible as they had been in the early 1990s debate.

When Claudia Nolte took over the Ministry in 1994, the efforts at gendering decreased. Nolte narrowly defined the problem of abortion to be protection of fetal life and punishment of those whose underwent or encouraged abortions. Women were often absent from her framing. When they were present, Nolte portraying them as single, young, pregnant, and subject to the pressures of families and partners. In one instance, such a woman's 'life becomes more fulfilling' when she has a child. In the same speech, Nolte (1995) referred to a woman as 'the second victim of abortion' but did not articulate why this was the case. Similarly, she frequently referred to seeking a solution to the abortion debate that 'better protected unborn life [and] did justice to the woman', though she did not explain what that justice might entail. Nolte did not portray abortion as a women's issue, claiming instead that the fetus is actually 'independent' of the woman who carries it (Katholische Nachrichten Dienst 1995: 4).

The substance of the Ministry positions on policy debates was in keeping with the gendering efforts just discussed. Under Merkel, the Ministry advocated a policy that adhered closely to the Court decision by declaring abortion unlawful, but providing women room to make their own decision. Nolte, on the other hand, was opposed to any sort of periodic solution, rejected the notion of women's self-determination rights, advocated intervention by counsellors and doctors throughout the decision-making process, and supported continued criminalization of abortion. Neither minister's position coincided with that of the women's movement. The women's policy agencies' activities were, in conclusion, symbolic during this debate. The agencies neither advocated the women's movement goals nor were successful in gendering the policy debate.

❖ Women's movement characteristics

The state of the German women's movement in the mid-1990s was a direct continuation of its status in the early 1990s debate. It remained fragmented and in decline. The portion of the movement that was the most vibrant during the early 1990s, the eastern German movement, suffered internal fragmentation and organizational difficulties (Kamenitsa 1997). The various fragments of the movement remained suspicious of and distant from the political left. While the counter-movement was strong, well-financed, and active on this issue, the women's movement was largely invisible during this debate. Thus, one can only conclude that while abortion itself may have continued to be an important issue for various feminists, this policy debate, which they saw as a lost cause, was a low priority for movement groups.

❖ Policy environment

During the 1993–5 debate, Germany continued to be governed by a coalition of the CDU/CSU and the FDP. The SPD controlled a majority of *Bundesrat* seats. The policy sub-system surrounding abortion continued to be a moderately closed one. The political parties and their parliamentary groups dominated the sub-system, with the relevant governmental ministries also playing a role. Two additional groups were effective participants in the debate about eliminating the eugenic indication. The policy shift was largely the result of intense lobbying by the Catholic Church, an established institutional interest in German politics, and several groups supporting disabled rights, whose presence demonstrated that the policy sub-system was not entirely closed to grassroots input.

❖ CONCLUSION

Comparing the three debates discussed here goes a long way toward understanding the impact of the women's movements and women's policy agencies in the policy process. The movement's impact in shaping state responses has been mixed. In the 1970s debate, the state response was pre-emptive as the *Bundestag* passed legislation that coincided with movement goals, but women, and especially feminist and women's movement activists, were not involved in the policy process. Women's movement activism was important in drawing attention to the issue of criminalized abortion, keeping it on the front pages, and rallying the population, but it was not actually included in the process of making new policy.

Over the next two decades, women's movement activities, and the broader social changes they inspired, helped build support for the notion that women should be included in the process of policy-making on issues like abortion. This set the stage for the 1990s abortion debates, both of which resulted in cooptation by the state. In these debates, all the political institutions of the state that were involved, especially political parties and the government, recognized the importance of including women in this process. Even as the dominant discourse de-emphasized abortion as a women's rights issue, policy actors tacitly acknowledged that women's participation was necessary to gain credibility for the outcome. This opened the way for many mainstream feminists to play key roles. Yet neither resulting policy was the one desired by the women's movement groups.

To understand this outcome, one needs to examine both the women's policy ministry and the policy environment. There was no formal WPA during the 1970s debate, but agency characteristics are instructive in both 1990s debates. The political nature of the appointment, combined with the CDU-led government, meant that the ministers were non-feminist. The restructuring of the ministries in 1990 defused a potentially strong voice for women within the government. This institutional arrangement paved the way for the CDU-led government to use the WPA to further its own goals. The choice of Merkel as minister enabled Kohl's government to claim that an East German woman was overseeing important processes affecting eastern women's rights, even as it made sure that another ministry had the mandate for this issue. Minister Merkel was limited in her ability to speak out for movement goals or to frame abortion as a women's issue because of her party, cabinet, and personal loyalty to Kohl. During Nolte's tenure in the women's ministry, on the other hand, she was given much more latitude to present her anti-abortion rights views. Indeed she was even permitted to vote against the final compromise legislation passed in 1995. Interviews with ministry staffers verified that this was possible because Nolte's position was in keeping with the position of Kohl's government, a position that was more conservative than the compromise legislation. The case points to serious limitations of a women's policy agency's ability to shape the dominant discourse in directions beneficial to the women's movement goals when housed in a political executive controlled by a conservative party.

Policy environment was primary in these cases, particularly the party in power. During the first debate a party of the left, in coalition with liberals, was responsible for pushing through significant reforms regarding women's access to safe and legal abortions. In the 1990s debates, however, it was the control of a government led by the conservative CDU/CSU that was key. It was able to use the WPA for its political purpose and to further its own agenda. Yet the final state response was not exactly what the CDU/CSU desired in either of the 1990s debates. In both cases, the SPD's control of the upper house was a factor in the success of compromise legislation rather than government-sponsored legislation. Even so, it is clear that the party in power goes a long way toward explaining the different substantive outcomes in the 1970s compared with the 1990s.

The nature of the moderately closed policy sub-system limited the women's movement impact on policy discourse or content. In the 1970s debate, the dominant political parties and traditional established interest groups, especially the churches, dismissed women's self-determination frames. The Court, through its 1975 and 1993 rulings, directed attention in the 1990s debates toward the protection of fetal life, a position that no major actors in the debate challenged (Maleck-Lewy and Ferree 1996). This meant that, from the start, women's movement frames about women's integrity and self-determination rights were again marginalized. Furthermore, references to women as a category were nearly absent in the 1990s, thus making it difficult for the WPA to focus attention on their rights. Although women played public and leading roles in the abortion debate, the Court decisions and West German parties' priorities limited their ability to change the discourse and thus the content of the law (Maleck-Lewy and Ferree 1996, 32).

Finally, variations in women's movement characteristics are important in understanding these cases. Although fragmented and not close to the political left, the movement in the 1970s was growing and focused on the issue of abortion rights. This enabled it to play a role in getting abortion reform on to the political agenda and keeping it there. Established political actors did their best to exclude the movement activists and groups from the formal policy debate, but the feminists' continued agitation made abortion reform an issue that could not be ignored. In the 1990s, however, the fragmented movement lacked a concerted effort or voice in the debate, making it difficult for any feminists to influence the policy debate or outcome. Some feminists, like those from the East, who had advocated the long-standing women's movement frames and goals, were largely excluded from the process. The mainstream feminists who were involved accepted the institutional rules of the game and played strategically. This focus on strategy over principle helped to limit the discourse and exclude women's rights claims from the policy arena.

❖ Notes

1 For more detailed histories of German abortion regulation, see Klein-Schonnefeld (1994), Czarnowski (1994), and Maleck-Lewy (1995).

2 This is a sharp contrast to the 1990s debates analyzed below, in which the life of the fetus was a much more important element of the debate.

3 The references are to 'one's body' rather than to a woman's body (Katholischen Arbeitsgemeinschaft für Krankenpflege in Deutschland 1972: 103–4).

4 Transcripts of the public hearings and *Bundestag* debate are published in Deutscher Bundestag (1992) and Pursch (1992), respectively.

5 The court's ruling could be disregarded only by those who were unconcerned about constitutionality because, like the PDS, their position had no chance of becoming law, or, like Alliance90/Greens, they proposed amending the Constitution to guarantee abortion rights.

6 All the *Bundestag* representatives of this party were eastern Germans in this period.

7 Petra Bläss in a speech to Parliament reprinted in Pursch (1992: 45).

8 Sauer found that women were largely invisible in the parliamentary debate in which abortion and gender were separated (1995: 185).

9 Cooperation among parties is a common feature of Germany parliamentary politics, but such agreements are usually arranged among party group leaders. The fact that the cross-party cooperation took place among members—and women at that!—made it unique.

10 Feminist participation was hampered because each party could invite witnesses only in proportion to its legislative seats and because the public hearings reflected the existing frames of the debate with sessions devoted to topics like pre-natal diagnostics,

134

financing social measures, counselling, pregnancy prevention, sex education, and legal issues (Czarnowski 1994: 262).

11 Outshoorn (1996*b*) finds this to be a broader trend in European abortion laws.

12 For a thorough though one-sided discussion of these groups and their mobilization, see Frauen gegen den §218 (1991). For a summary of the right-to-life arguments, see Beckmann (1991).

13 Many members of the more conservative CSU actually supported a separate, more restrictive minority bill.

14 Interview with *Mitteldeutscher Express* (1994).

7 ❖ Women's Movements' Defence of Legal Abortion in Great Britain

Dorothy McBride Stetson

❖ INTRODUCTION

Historically, English common law did not prosecute for abortions performed before *quickening*. Yet as early as 1803, with Lord Ellenborough's Act, Parliament enacted statutes overriding this relatively lenient stance (Potts, Diggory, and Peel 1977). In 1861 the Offences Against the Person Act set full criminalization of abortion in England and Wales. Considered to be a codification of existing practice, the 1861 Act prohibited abortion with no exceptions, providing punishment for all involved: the woman, anyone performing an abortion, and all who assisted with information, instruments, or materials.

Between 1861 and 1967 there were some notable additions to the law. News stories of doctors killing babies in the process of delivery led to the Infant Life (Preservation) Act of 1929, which made it a life felony to destroy the life of a child capable of being born alive after 28 weeks gestation except to save the life of the mother. In effect, this Act established an upper time limit on abortion before abortions were legally permitted. In 1939, in the *Bourne* case, the courts signalled acceptance of a defence doctors could use against prosecution, that is, if an abortion were performed because of a threat to the mental or physical health of the mother.[1] As a result of *Bourne*, some abortions were performed in hospitals in England and Wales to save the life of the mother. In Scotland, until the 1967 Act, abortion remained governed by common law since these statutes and cases did not apply. In practice, however, prosecutors considered abortion a clinical decision of doctors. Thus, according to Simms (1994) abortions were performed in Scotland on much the same grounds as in England and Wales. When the Abortion Act of 1967 legalized abortion in Britain, it was, technically, an addition to, rather than a repeal of, this body of law.

With the passage of the 1967 Abortion Act, Great Britain became the first country to decriminalize abortion to any great extent. The story of the passage of the Act is a great one, told and retold in a number of places—but not here (Hindell and Simms 1970; Potts, Diggory, and Peel 1977; Cohan 1986). One of the reasons it's such a good political story is that it counters many of the standard 'truths' about British institutions and politics. Here was a major change in the law on a very controversial issue that was passed in one parliamentary session through a private member bill, chiefly engineered by a small interest group, the Abortion Law Reform Association (ALRA). Some of its essential features originated in the House of Lords, the institution many think to be an atrophied appendix on the British political body.

The Act, which affects England, Wales, and Scotland, was worded to provide exceptions to the general criminalization of abortion practice. No offence would be committed if two medical practitioners agreed that the pregnancy would involve risk to the life of the pregnant woman or injury to her physical or mental health or the physical or mental health of any children in her family or if there was 'substantial risk' that the child would be seriously mentally or physically handicapped. Two clauses in the bill proved to be especially significant to the ultimate impact of the reform on women's access to abortion. First, there was the so-called 'statistical argument': in determining the possible risk of a pregnancy to the mother, the doctor could justify abortion if it would be more harmful to continue the pregnancy than to terminate it. With advances in abortion technology, the statistical risk of abortion was always less than the risk of continuing a pregnancy to term. Second, in determining risk the doctor could take into account the 'pregnant woman's actual or reasonably foreseeable environment'.[2] These provisions turned out to allow doctors who wished to perform abortions to find a legal justification for just about every case. At the same time, a doctor could refuse; however, the burden of proof rested with the person claiming a conscientious objection.

The official purpose of the Abortion Act was to fix the problem of illegal 'back-street' abortions and the severe effects of these on the health of women. Advocates guaranteed that this moderate reform would merely help those women who would have had abortions anyway to have them in a safer way. It would not be 'abortion on demand' nor would there be an increase in the overall rate of abortion. Many of the ALRA activists were women, but their campaign has been criticized as not sufficiently committed to feminism (Francome 1984). The push to reform the 1861 abortion law began in the 1930s with significant support from feminists of the time. Several traditional women's organizations, such as the National Council of Women, the Women's Cooperative Guild, and the Family Planning Association, were allied with ALRA. Many members of the ALRA hoped for a complete repeal of the 1861 law, leaving the abortion choice to women. In the 1960s, to increase the chances of success in Parliament, leaders made the pragmatic decision to seek a more modest reform with a significant role for doctors in deciding whether to perform the abortion or not.

While the ALRA was launching its final campaign, the British women's movements already included traditional women's organizations influenced by feminist ideas, organizations with origins in the first wave beginning in the nineteenth century, and women in trade union and socialist circles (Lovenduski and Randall 1993). This was also the time when the second-wave autonomous movement, Women's Liberation, was emerging from the consciousness raising and leftist campaigns for working women (Coote and Campbell 1982). The first Women's Liberation conference at Ruskin College Oxford did not meet until 1970. While the older movement accepted the ALRA's compromise that handed over decision making authority in abortion to the medical profession, the autonomous movement did not and in 1970 made free abortion and contraception on demand one of its first four goals. Nevertheless, all these feminists have found it necessary to spend considerable time, resources, and energy in the last 35 years to defend the 1967 Act from tenacious anti-abortion activists. To this day, despite fairly open access to abortion services, many British feminists remain critical of the control that doctors and the National Health Service (NHS) bureaucracy retain over women's reproductive lives (Sheldon 1997).

❖ SELECTION OF DEBATES

In the British unwritten constitution, Parliament is supreme; therefore abortion policy is the responsibility of the national executive and legislature. Legally, Parliament enacts statutes and the Ministry of Health sets regulations for private clinics and runs the NHS, which provides public abortion services. Abortion is, however, a peripheral issue to the powers-that-be (Cohan 1986). One of those widely-held *conventions* so important in the British political process holds that abortion is primarily an issue of morality and even religious conviction. The majority party, which dominates the policy process for 90 per cent of the business of government, steadfastly refuses to take a leadership role in abortion debates, leaving the members of parliament to vote their consciences rather than respond to the party whips (Millns and Sheldon 1998). Instead of receiving government proposals already vetted through high-level civil servants and advisory committees, Parliament considers proposals for changes in the abortion law by means of the *private member bill*.[3] Unable to rely on party discipline, sponsors of such bills must push them through the first and second readings, committee amendments, committee report, and third reading during a single session in both houses of parliament. The governing majority allocates enough time for legislative action on fewer than ten private member bills during a session.

This chapter on the women's movements, women's policy agencies, and abortion politics in Great Britain includes three debates drawn from the universe of private member bills—including only those that went beyond first reading—submitted in Parliament beginning with the Abortion Act of 1967. Some bills stand alone as policy debates leading to government action in a single session, while others are part of a longer process over several parliaments. In all, there have been seven debates. The first led to the 1967 Abortion Act. The second in 1969 was Norman St John Stevas's failed attempt to restrict doctors from performing abortions. The third debate lasted from 1970 to 1975 and involved four bills, the last—James White's—leading to the appointment of a Select Committee. The fourth debate takes up the Select Committee report in 1977 and continues to 1979 and the defeat of the John Corrie restrictive bill. There were two separate debates: Richardson's to expand services debated in 1981 and Lord Robertson's to limit grounds in 1982; both ended in defeat. The last debate began in 1987 with the introduction of David Alton's bill to establish an 18-week limit for abortions and ended when the Human Fertilisation and Embryology Act included a provision for a 24-week limit. Two of these debates—1967 and 1990—changed the abortion law; two others—White and Corrie—attracted widespread attention in both Parliament and the press. The 1967 Abortion Act is a benchmark against which all other debates react, but it is not one of the debates selected for analysis. Since much of the policy controversy about the Act extends back to the 1930s, it is outside the scope of the book. All the other debates were efforts to change the scope and administration of this Act, and they all took place when both national women's policy agencies and the autonomous and traditional women's movements were active.

The following debates have been selected for study:

(1) 1970–5: the James White Bill including the Lane Committee Report that preceded it;
(2) 1975–9: the Corrie Bill and the two private member bills leading up to it; and
(3) 1987–90: the Human Fertilisation and Embryology Act and the Alton bill preceding it.

These represent the decisional system on abortion: they all take place in the House of Commons, and all involve private member bills. One includes an advisory commission report, the last was incorporated in a government-sponsored bill. They represent the major debates through the life cycle of the abortion issue since 1967; two are the immediate reaction to the 1967 Act at the height of women's movement activism in the 1970s. The third represents the most recent debate and the only statutory change since the 1967 act. The debates involve the most salient questions of abortion policy: limiting the grounds for abortion and instituting an upper time limit.

❖ DOROTHY MCBRIDE STETSON

❖ DEBATE 1 : LANE COMMISSION AND WHITE BILL, 1970–1975

❖ *How the debate came to the public agenda*

No sooner was the Abortion Act in place than the anti-abortion groups, especially the Society for the Protection of Unborn Children (SPUC), rallied to limit abortion (Soper 1994). Newspaper reports describing thousands of foreign women, mostly from Scandinavia, who were trafficked to London for quick abortions began to appear. There were claims of taxi drivers in the employ of private abortion clinics roaming the airports to pick up clients. Opportunities to question government ministers about alleged abuses conducted under the Act gave more publicity, and 250 MPs signed a petition for a government inquiry into the charges. In 1971 Sir Keith Joseph, the Minister of Health and Social Security, appointed a committee chaired by the only female member of the High Court: Mrs Justice Lane. Dissatisfied with the Lane Committee report, James White introduced his own bill to restrict abortion in 1975.

❖ *Dominant frame of the debate*

From the beginning, the leading participants in the debate focused on the problems with the Act itself. It was too liberal, they claimed. They expressed concern about the large number of abortions on demand, despite guarantees by MP David Steele who had sponsored the 1967 Act and others that there were ample safeguards to avoid such easy access. Many blamed unscrupulous private clinics and a few doctors for the abuses. In the middle of the deliberations by the Lane Committee, a sensational book, *Babies for Burning* (Litchfield and Kentish 1974), received extensive publicity, and the authors presented evidence to the committee's deliberations. They claimed that they had interviewed abortion doctors who not only promoted abortion on demand but for selective breeding and even sale of aborted fetuses to glue factories: 'Legalised, it is a filthy enough trade, without it being further prostituted by a casual attitude that reduces unborn children to the status of jelly babies' (Litchfield and Kentish 1974: 17).[4]

There were other, fainter, voices criticizing the law as being too restrictive and giving too much control to doctors over women's choices. They also were concerned that the NHS, upon which most women depended, did not provide enough services. They claimed there were significant regional variations in the ability of women to obtain abortions early in their pregnancies.

The Lane Committee issued its report in 1974. It was a disappointment to the anti-abortion groups. In the first place, the committee's report shifted the frame of the abortion debate away from the a focus on what was wrong with the Abortion Act to its overall goal: to balance the 'relief of the suffering of individuals as opposed to the sanctity of life' (Parliamentary Papers 1974: 18(6)). For the most part, the committee agreed that legalized abortion had great benefits and was unanimous in supporting the Act and its provisions. The committee stated that while there was a need for greater vigilance over the private clinics, the Act itself needed no amendment.

James White's private member bill in 1975 was intended to do what the committee refused to do: limit the grounds for abortion; require private clinics to use NHS consultants; limit access of foreign women to abortion services; bring private clinics directly under government control; and appoint a parliamentary select committee to further investigate the workings of the Act. In the debate on the White bill, the anti-abortion MPs sought to re-establish the dominant frame or definition of the abortion issue as the Abortion Act itself. In this, White even made a bow to the Lane Committee, admitting that abortion must be made available for women with problems such as 'bad housing, poverty and alcoholic husbands' but arguing that the abuses under the Act were of much greater importance (Parliamentary Debates 1975: 1757). One of these, claimed Leo Abse, prominent anti abortion MP, was abortion on demand, dismissing the Lane committee's claim that abortion on demand was not a problem (Parliamentary Debates 1975: 1777). Thus at the end of Debate 1, the frame for policy-making on abortion was in contention. Was the policy problem to choose between those who claimed the Abortion Act was too liberal and those who claimed it answered social needs of women? Or was the choice, as the Lane Committee asserted, to find a balance between individual needs and protecting the sanctity of life?

❖ Gendering the policy debate

Although women were mentioned in the arguments, ideas about women and their relationship to abortion were not central to the debate in the early 1970s. Anti-abortionist rhetoric pictured women either as carelessly pregnant or as victims abused by doctors and clinics, and referred to unmarried women as 'girls'. Supporters of the Act viewed its main clientele as women with problems who needed help. Basically responsible, these women found themselves in emotional turmoil, desperate enough to seek abortion at all cost.

The first Women's Liberation Conference in 1970 pledged to seek free contraception and abortion on demand. They formed a campaign organization, the Women's Abortion and Contraceptive Campaign (WACC) in 1971. WACC opposed all efforts to restrict the 1967 Abortion Act and developed a proposal to revise the statute in order to take control of the abortion decision from doctors and give it to women, increase services through the NHS, and expand contraceptive services. Their basic tenet was that women have a right to control their bodies and their fertility. Abortion was a positive vital service for women, they argued. Along with the ALRA, WACC participated in the debate by presenting both written and oral testimony to the Lane Committee. In the floor debate on the White bill, no MP sought to present the WACC position; Labour MP Renee

Short did argue that Labour women defended the 1967 Act and opposed the White bill because it gave working class women access to abortion services previously available only to the wealthy.

❖ Policy outcome

The statutory outcome of the first challenge to the Abortion Act of 1967 was to leave the Act unchanged. The Lane Committee was unanimous in its support for the Act, merely suggesting some increased oversight over the private sector by the Ministry of Health.[5] It recommended that the abortion decision remain a medical one, but that the woman's views should be given serious consideration. MP White's subsequent effort to amend the Act was unsuccessful, but he did secure the appointment of a select committee. Its report becomes the starting point of the next debate to be analyzed in this chapter.

❖ Movement impact

Using the two measures of women's movement impact—acceptance of women and women's movement organizations into the policy-making process and achievement of a policy outcome that coincides with movement goals—the 1970–5 debate led to dual response from the state. Women were active on both sides of the debate. They participated as Lane Committee chair and members as well as individuals presenting evidence to the committee. A wide array of women's organizations such as the League of Jewish Women, the Mothers Union, Catholic Women, the Midwives Association, and the National Council of Women constituted around 20 per cent of the submissions to the committee. SPUC itself was composed mostly of women. Women's movement organizations also presented evidence, and, once SPUC organized demonstrations and lobbies in support of the White bill, their activism in protection of abortion rights grew. Out of this effort a new organization—the National Abortion Campaign (NAC)— arose to rally activists and represent the women's movement position to the press and Parliament. Almost immediately the NAC became recognized as the feminist representative in the abortion policy-making process, allowing the women's movement to be a major player on the abortion issue.

The policy outcome, on the other hand, produced mixed results for the movements. The Lane Committee incorporated the movement frame of the debate: that the abortion issue pertained to women's interests. However, it did not go so far as to put those interests first, ahead of both the fetus and the medical profession, in controlling fertility. At the same time, the Lane Committee defended the Abortion Act, which coincided with the immediate interests of movement activists, and the defeat of the White bill in 1975 was viewed as a 'win' by those in the NAC.

❖ Women's policy agency activities

The Women's National Commission (WNC), an outgrowth of the Women's Consultative Council, was established in 1969 by Prime Minister Harold Wilson.[6] The WNC was intended to be a conduit for relaying women's opinion on public issues to the top executive levels of government. Its composition was limited to national organizations whose membership was 80 per cent women, had been in existence for 50 years, and were engaged in 'responsible' socio-economic or broadly educational activities. National and local women's liberation groups were not eligible; therefore the WNC represented many of the traditional women's movement organizations such as the National Council of Women and women in trade unions. An executive committee of about ten members organized the meetings and established ad hoc committees to work on specific policy questions. They surveyed the member organizations and translated their views into a set of recommendations to be submitted to the cabinet, advisory committees, the Law Commission, and the like.

There were two chairs: one appointed by the Prime Minister and the other elected by the membership organizations. In 1970–4, Prime Minister Edward Heath selected Margaret Thatcher, the Minister for Education and the highest ranking woman in the Conservative government. The other chair was elected by the membership, usually a leader of one of the major equal rights organizations such as the NCW. Since the elected chair was the de facto manager of the commission's work, the WNC can be classified as having feminist leadership, representing the equal rights and trade union movements, not the women's liberation autonomous or radical movements. The scope of the WNC was cross-sectional: 'to ensure by all means that the informed opinion of women is given its due weight in the deliberations of government and in the public debate on matters of public interest, including those which may be of special interest to women'(Women's National Commission 1974). It was an advisory body positioned close to the top leadership through its appointed chair. Resources were scant: a secretariat of no more than three staff to manage meetings and produce newsletters. There was no specific policy mandate and during the period of the first debate; the Commission considered and offered opinions on a range of issues such as divorce, adoption, litter clean-up, and anti-discrimination/equal pay legislation.

The WNC members took their charge seriously and, when the Lane Committee asked for their input, an ad hoc committee formed to draft an opinion paper. Since the issue was framed as a question of the status of the Abortion Act of 1967, the WNC weighed in in full support of the Act. Its report contained a strong statement that, while the ultimate abortion decision should remain a medical one, the 'views of the women' should be given serious consideration. The WNC was gratified to find that the Lane Committee's final report used

❖ DOROTHY McBRIDE STETSON

almost the same language: 'Every woman requesting abortion should have her wishes carefully considered.' From the minutes: 'the attention given by the Lane Committee to the view of the WNC was gratifying and members noted with pleasure the reaffirmation of the statements expressed' (Women's National Commission 1974). Thus the WNC did successfully gender a portion of this first abortion policy debate.

The women's policy agency's position, the extent to which it supported the Act, coincided with women's movement goals. But the campaign of the women's liberation branch sought to establish abortion as the women's choice, rather than under doctor's control. In this, the WNC's position did not reflect the autonomous women's view, but it did reflect the views of the traditional women's movement. Thus, on the basis of this evidence the WNC was an insider in the debate on the future of the Abortion Act of 1967.

❖ Women's movement characteristics

It is important to keep in mind when discussing the British women's movement that there are several movements. In the early 1970s, the traditional women's organizations were in a steady state, while both women's liberation and trade union women's activism were growing following their emergence in the late 1960s. Historically, many women's movement organizations had been close to the left, and this continued with the women's liberation and trade union women. However, the movement was so open in the 1970s that it grew outside the labour movement; the abortion campaign itself drew in many activists not affiliated with the left (Rowbotham 1989). The women's movements and the Labour movement were certainly not united on issues like abortion in the early 1970s. Many Labour MPs, including, notably, James White himself, opposed the feminist position on abortion.

Feminists faced a strong adversary on the abortion issue: the Catholic Church. Not only did the Church's adamant opposition to the Abortion Act of 1967 influence individual MPs of Catholic faith, it was a driving force behind SPUC, the anti-abortion campaign group, and LIFE, a support group for women with unwanted pregnancies. While not large in membership or deep in grass roots support, SPUC had many parliamentary contacts and seemed to have little trouble getting parliamentary representatives to defend its position and to introduce private member bills intended to limit women's access to abortion services. The infamous *Babies for Burning* was a product of this activism. The abortion issue was high on the agenda of the women's liberation movement, and while there were rifts growing in the autonomous movement between the radical feminists and the social feminists, they came together to support abortion rights campaign.

❖ *Policy environment*

As noted in the introduction, abortion policy is made in the Parliament, with the action centred in the House of Commons. The Prime Minister and Cabinet take no official stand on the issue, leaving it to the private member bill process and the MPs to vote according to their consciences, constituencies, lobbyists, or parties, depending on their wishes. In other words, the whip is off. The result is an open policy-making system, with backbenchers having equal chances to introduce legislation, and open access for groups to the Westminster lobbies. In this debate the government appointed a committee of inquiry, composed mostly of experts, which invited widespread participation from individuals and groups. A change in majority party occurred during the 1970–5 debate, Edward Heath's Conservative government in power during 1970–4 and Labour winning two general elections in 1974 to establish a working majority. For most of the period, however, the left-wing party was not in power.

❖ DEBATE 2: THE CORRIE BILL, 1975–1979

❖ *How the debate came to the public agenda*

The rejection of White's bill was not a complete defeat for the anti-abortion MPs. They made a deal with the Labour government to appoint a select committee of MPs to investigate the workings of the Abortion Act. The committee was sharply divided: nine for the White bill and six opposed. The entire committee issued a report in 1975 recommending little more than tweaking administrative processes relating to private abortion providers. When the majority of the committee succeeded in getting authorization for a second round of investigations, the minority members quit. The committee's second report was strongly anti-abortion. Armed with this report, the anti-abortion MPs tabled restrictive private member bills in 1977, 1978, and 1979. The first two were similar and stuck close to the Select Committee recommendations: upper limit of 20 weeks, restrictions on which doctors could certify abortion, and separation of pregnancy counselling services from clinics performing abortions. The Braine bill of 1978 added clarification to the conscientious objection clause.

By the time John Corrie introduced the third bill in 1979, a general election had changed the government and the composition of the House yet again. Conservatives took power under Margaret Thatcher and many supporters of the Abortion Act lost their seats. Sensing a better climate for their cause, the anti-abortion MPs promoted a bill that would strike at what they thought was the cause of abortion on demand: the 'statistical argument'. Recall that this provision of the 1967 Act permitted doctors to certify abortions for women if the risk of pregnancy was less than the risk of childbirth. They proposed adding restrictive adjectives: abortion would be legal only if the pregnancy involved *grave* risk to the life of the pregnant woman or *substantial* risk of serious injury to the physical or mental health of the pregnant woman or any existing children in her family. This amendment, along with removing the provision that put the burden of proof of conscientious objection on the person claiming it, curtailing the licensing of private clinics, and imposing an upper limit of 20 weeks, made the Corrie bill the greatest threat to abortion rights since 1967.

❖ Dominant frame of the debate

From the Select Committee deliberations in 1975–6 to the parliamentary consideration of the Corrie bill in 1979, the dominant frame of the debate posed a two-sided contest. One side, familiar from the first debate, was claiming that the policy problem was the Abortion Act itself and the abuses—ranging from administrative abuses to the immoral killing of unborn children—that were committed under it. At the same time, an equally dominant definition was the desire to keep the Abortion Act intact—although it would be nice if the NHS had more services—because it served women who must be able to decide to have abortions and have access to them. Restrictions would lead to more illness and death, sending women to back-street abortionists and bringing severely handicapped children into the world.

❖ Gendering the debate

Unlike in Debate 1, gender was central in Debate 2. Both sides brought gender into the discussion, but the abortion rights MPs, mostly women and all affiliated with the Labour Party, made it an indispensable part of the discourse. They portrayed abortion rights as central to women's needs and wants, especially working-class women. To them, efforts to restrict the 1967 Act were nothing more than men trying to control women and make them feel guilty for seeking abortions. A restrictive bill would take women's bodies away from them and condemn them to risk and delay in getting services. An anti-abortionist countered that the only right women had was the right to prevent pregnancy through contraception, not destroy a child. Corrie's supporters also tried to point out that they too were concerned about women because they were exploited by private clinics and faced with overwhelming remorse and depression as a result. But anti-abortion MPs were unable to shift the gendered frames toward this view. For Corrie's opponents, the only solution was to protect the rights of women by rejecting his and all other restrictive amendments to the Abortion Act of 1967. The MPs were thus responsible for gendering the dominant frame of the debate in terms compatible with the goals of the NAC and other women's movement activists. This is not surprising given the close ties between the NAC and MPs Jo Richardson, Renee Short, and Maureen

146

Coquhoun. They were sustained by widespread activism of NAC groups in lobbying, rallying local support, and managing large demonstrations. In many ways, the 1975–9 debate was the essential showdown between an active pro-life movement and a vital and strong abortion rights movement sustained by feminists and trade union organizations.

❖ Policy outcome

The parliamentary struggle over the Corrie bill was intense. Eventually the bill ran out of time. By the Report stage, only two of its original clauses remained: the upper limit which had been extended to 24 weeks and the revised language of the statistical argument, although 'substantial' risk had been changed to 'serious' risk. Many were surprised at this outcome because the Conservative majority plus the strength of the pro-life forces seemed to portend some sort of restriction. But Marsh and Chambers (1981) credit the expertise, strength and commitment of the feminist forces and their extra-parliamentary networks with the ability to stymie any of the efforts to derail the 1967 Abortion Act.

❖ Women's movement impact

Debate 2 is a double success for the British women's movements. Women were important participants in the policy debate, both as women and as representatives of movement branches. NAC rose to the status of official representative of the abortion rights movement, through its visible role in organizing support for the abortion rights MPs. As for the latter, most were Labour women and Vallance (1979) credits their work on the abortion campaign with developing a solidarity among women in Parliament that would be sustained through the next 20 years. This debate also brought a new leader to the fore—Jo Richardson—who became the staunchest advocate for the feminist position on abortion rights in the House. While the Labour Party had officially adopted a pro-abortion rights plank in its platform, there was little enthusiasm among the male Labour MPs. Thus these 'women of the House' were essential to a successful policy outcome. The defeat of the Corrie bill despite a Conservative majority and the Braine and Benyon bills before it was a success for the women's movement.

❖ Women's policy agency activities

The WNC continued its work into the late 1970s with little change to its organization or resources. It remained a cross-sectional, advisory agency composed
of women's organizations with a tiny staff. The elected Chair was Ethel
Chipchase, a feminist who was secretary of the Women's Advisory Council of
the Trades Union Congress (TUC) and a member of the Equal Opportunities
Commission (EOC). The EOC was another women's policy agency which was
established by the Sex Discrimination Act of 1975. The Equal Opportunities
Commission was a single-issue—granted, it is a large issue—administrative
commission located in a remote corner of the Home Office, with a large staff.
The Chair, although a member of the Labour Party, was not a feminist or supportive of feminists in the EOC (Lovenduski 1995). Neither of these agencies
was active or interested in the debate on the Abortion Act. The WNC, after the
Lane Committee submission, went on to other projects. The EOC was establishing itself as the chief implementer of the Sex Discrimination Act and stayed
away from controversial issues. Thus the women's policy machinery was largely
symbolic in the second debate.

❖ Women's movement characteristics

As we have seen, the women's movement branches were very active in the
campaign to protect the Abortion Act and defeat the Corrie bill. There was the
NAC, the non-hierarchal, feminist network that linked together nearly 350
groups, including many trade unions, in major towns and cities. Women in the
Labour Party and trade unions were active, and in 1976 the Labour Abortion
Rights Campaign formed, prompted by a party conference agreement to a
resolution for abortion on request. The NAC also organized the Campaign
Against Corrie to link together those not willing to get too close to the more
radical feminist groups. Co-Ord, the Coordinating Committee in Defence of
the 1967 Act, housed in the Birth Control Trust, included parties, unions,
abortion providers, social workers, and lawyers brought together in response to
the select committee battles in 1976. Finally, there were close ties between the
women's movement and abortion movement networks and Labour women in
Parliament, especially Jo Richardson and Renee Short.

At this time the women's movements were in a period of growth, expanding
their agenda to include seeking financial and legal information and freedom
from threat or use of violence. There was an increase in both the number of
groups and media attention, and the abortion campaign was a major contribu-
tor to this growth. The movement branches, always historically close to the
Labour Party, became very close during the debate as the party adopted a resolution incorporating the feminist position. It refused, however, to go so far as to

require Labour MPs to vote with the party leadership, continuing to claim that abortion was a moral issue of individual conscience.

Abortion remained a major, unifying goal of all branches of the women's movement, and, while a rift developed between radical feminists and socialist feminists in 1977, it did not derail the unity of the feminists against the Corrie bill and in support of abortion rights. There were conflicts, however, over the role of men in the campaign. These erupted in 1979, when the TUC sponsored a march of more than 60,000 against the Corrie bill. TUC leaders, mostly male, tried, unsuccessfully, to push them aside (Hemmings 1979). These activists faced a pro-life counter-movement that made up in persistence and intensity what it lacked in membership and party support.

❖ *Policy environment*

The policy sub-system on the abortion issue remained the same as in Debate 1. Parliament dominated, especially the House of Commons. The government treated the issue as non-partisan and ministers made it explicit that they would take no stand on proposals. The MPs voted according to conscience or in response to interest groups and lobbying. Thus the policy environment was wide open, within the limits on the time given to private member bills. The Labour Party was in the majority until the 1979 election, when several abortion rights Labour MPs were defeated. The Conservative Party majority, however, had little effect on the outcome of the final consideration of the Corrie bill. It refused to come to the aid of the advocates of change, thus giving the edge to those who could martial forces to delay and 'talk out' the pro-life effort.

❖ DEBATE 3: HUMAN FERTILIZATION AND EMBRYOLOGY ACT, 1987–1990

❖ *How the debate came to the public agenda*

Increased scientific knowledge of fertility and fetal development led to the most recent contest in British politics over abortion policy. While the result of this debate was the enactment of the Human Fertilisation and Embryology Act of 1990 (HFEA), the abortion part of the debate came to the public agenda in late 1987, when David Alton, a religious conservative, introduced a bill to reduce the upper time limit for legal abortions. The Abortion Act of 1967 had set no upper limit, so the Infant Life (Preservation) Act of 1929 prevailed, pro-hibiting the killing of a fetus either of 28 weeks of gestation or viable, that is, able to survive outside the womb. With more knowledge of fetal development and reduction of the age of viability, especially with advances in neo-natal care, SPUC and LIFE took the initiative to restrict abortions by focusing on what they called 'late' abortions. The Alton bill set the definition of 'late' at 18 weeks, and would prohibit abortions after that time except to save the life of the mother or if the child was likely to be born dead or would have extensive physical handicaps.

As usual, the government of the day took no stand on the issue of abortion or this effort to limit the time period for legal abortions. In fact the Prime Minister, Margaret Thatcher, refused to give the time needed to complete deliberations on the Alton bill. The government did, however, take on the problems and questions raised by rapid medical advances in assisted fertility, embryology, test-tube babies, and the like. The HFEA began as a government proposal in 1990 based on the Warnock Report.[7] In connection with this Act, the Government offered to include a provision regarding the upper limit on abortion and to provide time for the House to debate it. Motivated either by sympathy for the struggles of the pro-life organizations or by a desire to settle a nagging and highly conflictual issue, the government provided just what was needed to settle once and for all an aspect of abortion law that had been controversial since the Lane Committee recommendations of the 1970s. This section looks at the period from 1987 to 1990 as one policy debate.

❖ Dominant frame of the debate

Alton and his supporters made a major effort to establish the frame of abortion policy in terms of the medical knowledge of fertility and fetal development (Science and Technology Group 1991 ; Sheldon 1997). He described late-term procedures in gruesome detail, asserting that the fetus feels pain. His sentiments were not entirely without concern for the mother, emphasizing the physical and emotional consequences. But he quickly left the realm of science: 'Doctors and nurses are using their skills to extinguish life not cradle and care for it like they should' (Parliamentary Debates 1987–88: 1233). If successful, such a frame would establish that the fetus was a separate person, entitled to legal protection.

Alton's opponents fought to maintain the frame that prevailed before the Alton bill: that the abortion issue was an issue of women's needs and rights, and that any limitation would force women to unsafe procedures. This frame would cast the debate as finding a resolution between the rights of the woman and the rights of the fetus. When the question of upper limits came on to the floor during consideration of the HFEA in 1990, the choice was between those who wanted women's right to abortion on request and those who wanted to roll back the limits to pre-viability. Thus, by the end of the debate, the dominant frame remained the same one that had prevailed since the 1970s: a contest between women's right to decide and the life of the fetus.

❖ *Gendering the policy debate*

Gender was central to the arguments in Debate 3; despite pro-life attempts to medicalize the argument, the main issue that prevailed throughout was the significance of abortion to women's rights and status. Even the pro-life forces used gender to such an extent that feminist writers complained that feminist rhetoric had been captured to anti-feminist aims (Steinberg 1991). But it was the anti-Alton MPs, led by Jo Richardson, Teresa Gorman, and Harriet Harman, who prevailed. They portrayed women as deeply concerned about making the choice to have an abortion—the opposite of the anti-abortion assertion that abortion was a casual alternative to contraception.

For much of the period, pro-choice MPs steadfastly considered any upper time limits to be an interference with woman's right to control fertility and insisted on women's ability to follow their own consciences throughout pregnancy. This extended, especially, to the question of whether to give birth to a severely handicapped child. During the debate they found themselves trying to explain the incidence of late abortions. While opponents pointed to women's casual attitude to delaying abortion, the women's rights advocates portrayed women feeling trapped and frightened, or greatly distressed as a result of a rape. Eventually, they turned the tables on the pro-life group by charging that it was inadequate NHS services and the cumbersome process of getting two doctors to certify that pushed abortions into the second and even third trimesters. During the HFEA debate, MP Harriet Harman went on the attack, introducing an amendment that would permit abortion on request with consent of one doctor in the first twelve weeks of pregnancy. Although the amendment was defeated, it served to shift the blame for late abortions from the woman's irresponsibility to the difficulties with the system. Pro-choice activists considered the discussion on the Harman amendment an important victory.

The connection between abortion rights MPs and women's and abortion movement forces was very close, almost to the point of institutionalization. During the Alton discussion in 1988, the NAC and the Women's Reproductive Rights Campaign formed Feminists Against the Alton Bill. This led to the Pro-choice Alliance, which included MPs; the Alliance for the first time took a proactive approach. Rather than focusing only on defending the 1967 Act, it made a case for a law that maximized women's choice. 'Pro-choice Alliance believes the role of the doctor should be to help the patient come to her own decision and then provide safe medical treatment, not to decide whether she "needs" or "deserves" an abortion' (Pro-choice Alliance 1990). Coming out of Debate 3, the frame for the abortion issue was gendered to put women's rights at the forefront.

❖ DOROTHY MCBRIDE STETSON

❖ *Policy outcome*

The Alton bill passed second reading, and was close to completing the parliamentary gauntlet in the House of Commons when time ran out and the Conservative government refused to extend it. Instead, the government included an opportunity during parliamentary action on HFEA in 1990 for the House to agree, once and for all, on an upper limit. It organized a series of votes, with no party whip, to cover possible limits from 18 to 28 weeks. These votes were serial: 18, 28, 20, 26, 22, 24. Only 24 weeks—the last option voted on—passed. It amended the Abortion Act as follows: abortions cannot be performed on fetuses 24 weeks or more old except where there is danger of grave or permanent injury to the physical or mental health of the pregnant woman or the life of the pregnant woman, or substantial risk that if the child were born it would suffer from serious handicap. The effect of this amendment was to separate the Abortion Act from the Infant Life (Preservation) Act of 1929.

This outcome was the result of the framing of the debate as a question of the rights of women to seek abortion versus the rights of the fetus to be born. With this frame, MPs finally had to agree on a point of balance, and they selected 24 weeks with generous exceptions. The number 24 had received support from the Lane Committee in 1974, as well as a special inquiry by the Royal College of Obstetricians and Gynecologists (RCOG), as the point at which fetal rights are to be considered.

❖ *Movement impact*

From the introduction of the Alton bill until the enactment of the HFEA, women's movement representatives were integral to the policy-making process in the House of Commons during Debate 3. As we have seen, there were direct, institutionalized connections between abortion rights MPs and women's movement and abortion rights organizations, and they were successful in injecting feminist gendered ideas into the dominant frame of the abortion policy debate.

Whether or not the outcome coincided with women's movement goals is a little more tricky to assess. Certainly the defeat of the Alton bill was a major goal of the feminists, and they were successful in this. However, the eventual policy change was the establishment of a 24-week limit on abortions reduced from 28. Many pro-choice activists began by being firmly against any upper limit. When the dust had cleared after the serial voting in the House of Commons, the movement leaders inside and out declared a victory. The exceptions to the 24-week limit were generous enough to permit women to gain necessary abortions. And the fact that they had had the opportunity to debate abortion on women's request was also seen as a success, a first step toward the eventual achievement of a feminist goal. Both pro- and anti-abortionists agreed that the HFEA amendment liberalized the law of 1967. Jo Richardson (1990) focused on the shift in the frame of the issue: 'Anti-abortionists cannot claim they have not had fair access to parliamentary time. They have had and they lost. The debate has moved on and in future will focus on the real issue–women's choice.' The conclusion is that the women's movement obtained a dual response from the state in Debate 3.

❖ Women's policy agency activities

The WNC and the EOC continued to be the national women's policy agencies. Both machineries had expanded their policy activities in the decade since the Corrie bill debate. The WNC offered opinions culled from its member organizations on a wide ranges of issues, including many focusing on improving the status of women: women's representation in the parties, childcare, women in prison, and women in the media. The EOC had expanded its portfolio from giving advice to active involvement in enforcement of the Sex Discrimination Act (Lovenduski 1995). Neither agency, however, was involved in the issue of abortion or the policy planning on the Human Fertilisation and Embryology Act. Their activities were symbolic and their characteristics remained the same as in Debate 2.

Another agency that appeared in the 1980s deserves attention here. The Labour Party's Shadow Ministry for Women was not a formal government agency. Rather, it was a project of the opposition Labour Party leadership to give public attention to the status of women under the governing Conservative Party.[8] Given the institutionalized role of the loyal opposition in the British political system, a shadow ministry may be considered a quasi-state structure, and may, from the inside of the political establishment, serve as a liaison to facilitate women's movement success in seeking state response. Thus the shadow Ministry for Women will be included in the analysis.

Through its Minister, MP Jo Richardson, the shadow ministry was central to the debate in the House of Commons. Her leadership and that of other Labour women gendered the debate in favour of women's right to decide abortion. By privileging the feminist position on abortion through this structure, the Labour Party leadership signalled that, although there was not a formal invocation of party discipline during the votes, Labour MPs were urged to oppose the Alton bill and to support abortion on request. While Labour remained in the minority and not all MPs voted under the leadership direction, many did and provided a reliable base for women MPs to maintain their ground during the perplexing voting process on upper limits. Thus, the shadow Ministry for Women occupied an insider role as a quasi-governmental women's policy agency.

The shadow ministry was a cross-sectional political structure, remote from government power. During 1988–90, abortion rights was a major policy responsibility, along with questions of equality at work and status of home workers. The leader, Jo Richardson, was a socialist feminist and had been a committed activist for abortion rights for women since the early 1970s. For resources, it drew upon the Labour Party, which offered little more than a public relations staff to distribute a newsletter and position Richardson in the media.

❖ Women's movement characteristics

By the late 1980s, the autonomous women's movement—Women's Liberation—had declined. But other movements remained active, especially at the local level and in the trade unions and political parties (Lovenduski and Randall 1993). Most important for understanding the impact of the movement on the 1988–90 debate was the fact that many individuals and organizations of the women's movements have developed regular, almost institutionalized, relationships with government agencies at all levels. Thus, while the movements were not as visible as in the heyday of the 1970s, they consolidated their access to the policy-making process. The feminist groups inside the unions and the Labour Party attest to the continued close relationship with the left. With a strong position on the left, movement advocates faced a counter-movement that had lost some of its energy, although it maintained a core of MPs committed to restricting access to abortion. Abortion remained a top and unifying issue for the women's movement, which had continued to suffer from divisions among equal rights, radical, and socialist feminists.

❖ Policy environment

The policy environment comprised two stages in Debate 3. For the Alton bill, the usual abortion policy process was in place, that is, the open deliberations that are part of the private member bill tradition. For the HFEA, however, the majority Conservative Party in government set the stage, exerting nearly total control through its ministers and junior ministers. This process was not as closed, however, when the abortion amendments were being considered. True, nothing was going to get a hearing without the consent of the government. The Minister of Health, however, agreed to remove the whip and allow some play on the topic by MPs, in the style of the private member bill, maintaining firm control over the timing and agenda. There was no party whip on the abortion amendments. Thus we can classify the policy process as moderately closed. And, of course, the left was out of power.

❖ CONCLUSION

In Great Britain, since the legalization of abortion in 1967, the equal rights, socialist, and radical women's movements were consistently successful is achieving many of their goals with respect to abortion policy. In all three debates examined here, the movements secured a dual response from the state: women were included in the policy-making process and the policy outcome coincided with women's movements' goals. The content of these policy outcomes preserved the language of the 1967 Abortion Act: no restriction on grounds or services was put in place. An upper limit of 24 weeks was established in 1990, but with ample exceptions to permit doctors wide discretion. The movements were also successful in inserting their frame of the abortion issue—that abortion is primarily a matter of women's rights—into the dominant discourse used by policy actors. At the same time, they were not successful in achieving their long-range goal of changing the abortion statute itself to reduce the dominance of the medical profession over individual decisions about abortions.

With respect to participation, movement access has strengthened over the three debates. In the early 1970s, it was restricted primarily to individual women in Parliament and the Lane Committee—many not connected to any of the movements' wings—and a couple of campaign groups. By the 1990s, however, a network of feminist abortion rights activists was in place, linking prominent Labour MPs with the National Abortion Campaign and other activists of the women's movements and abortion reform movement. One of the two major parties had incorporated both the goals and the activists into its platform and organizational structure. After 1990, it seemed that any subsequent abortion debate would of necessity include this network.

The women's policy machineries played an occasional role in the abortion debates. In the early 1970s, the WNC was a conduit for important gendered perspectives from the traditional women's movement organizations to the Lane Committee. Later, the Labour shadow Ministry for Women, although a quasi-governmental agency, strengthened the Labour feminist voice in the 1990 debates. In 1970, it is hard to tell whether the Lane Committee would have included any gendered perspectives without the input from the WNC. Overall, however, the WNC opposed the women's liberation demand for abortion on request. The shadow Ministry played an insider role, but it was so closely identified with its leader and the other Labour women MPs that it was not, on its own, a vital interlocutor for the movement. The British debates, taken together, therefore, do not provide much support for a theory of state feminism on abortion.

If the policy machinery does not explain the success of the British women's movement in increasing descriptive and substantive representation, what does? As usual, it is a combination of factors. The essential variable is the policy environment, specifically the policy sub-system that makes abortion policy. The abortion issue is assigned to the open process that accompanies the private member bill in the Parliament. In this environment MPs from any party can be effective and the doors are open to both individuals and interest groups. There is so little organization to this process, however, that it is much easier to use parliamentary rules to prevent a bill from passing than to pilot a bill through complex legislative steps in a limited time.

The second necessary condition involved some characteristics of the women's movements. In the first place, the movements placed protecting the Abortion Act of 1967 as a high priority; second, they were united in this goal. It should be noted that their consistent success has been to prevent the anti-abortion movement from achieving any of its goals, with the exception of the upper limit. The feminist abortion rights activists have not been able to secure further liberalizing changes in the statute—that is, free abortion on demand, less control by doctors—in the statute.

That the movement was close to the left would not be a useful explanation, on the surface, given the fact that the Labour Party was not in power during the crucial stages of any of the debates. However, the fact that the Labour Party was willing to take a political stand on the issue, while the Conservative Party steadfastly remained de jure and de facto neutral, bolstered the efforts of abortion rights MPs in gathering their votes in crucial House of Commons votes.

Since the 1990 debate the evidence supports a conclusion that the policy makers have reached a resolution of the conflict over the abortion law. With the private member bill system, pro-life MPs present a bill from time to time, such as the attempt to ban partial birth abortion, which was inspired by US experience in 1996. But they warrant little more than a page in the legislative record. Public opinion and major political actors seem to accept the current law as it is implemented. The women's movements continue to speak for more control by women over the abortion decision and to complain about the uneven and inadequate services of the NHS. In 2000 the Ministry of Health, on advice of the RCOG, considered new standards for the NHS and private clinics, hailed by pro-abortion rights groups as 'a clear sign that the medical profession policy makers and society at large were beginning to accept abortion as part of essential reproductive health care' (Boseley 2000). The guidelines would set limits on the time women would have to wait after referral for a termination. In their recommendation, the RCOG advisory group's language demonstrates the success of the British women's movements in establishing a feminist policy frame: Abortion services should provide, they argue, 'high quality, efficient, effective and comprehensive care that respects the dignity, individuality and rights of women to exercise personal choice over their treatment' (quoted in Boseley 2000).

❖ NOTES

1 R. V. Bourne 3 All ER 615 1938; 1 KB 687 1939.

2 Ch. 87, sub-section 2.

3 There are two ways to introduce a bill. Members of the House of Commons participate in a lottery held annually at the beginning of each parliament to determine the order of consideration; MPs can also seek a vote on first reading of a bill under the 'ten minutes' rule'. On Tuesdays and Wednesdays at the beginning of the House of Commons business, members can move adoption of bills, with their speeches in favour limited—supposedly—to ten minutes. Only one bill per day is permitted and only one person can speak in opposition. The ten minutes' rule is used primarily to get some immediate publicity for an issue because it is rare that a bill under the ten minutes' rule goes on to further consideration (Wilding and Laundy 1972).

4 Eventually, the claims in the book were proved to be without substance and the authors lost in court in their efforts to counter attacks on their research (Sunday Times 1975: 1-2).

5 The committee recommended one amendment: to place an upper limit on legal abortions at 24 weeks. However, at this time the proposal was not taken up.

6 The Women's Consultative Council was a body of representatives of women's organizations established in 1962 to give their views on UK joining the European Community and other issues.

7 The government commissioned the study, headed by Lady Warnock, which formed the basis for the HFEA. A major issue of contention was trying to set an age for the embryo after which research would not be allowed. Pro-life organizations wanted the report to declare the exact date of the creation of human life, threatening the abortion time limits.

8 The establishment of a governmental Ministry for Women was a campaign pledge of the Labour Party throughout the elections of the 1990s. After Labour returned to power in 1997, Prime Minister Tony Blair named a Minister for Women to act as spokesperson on women's issues. Jo Richardson, who passed away in 1994, did not live to see this achievement.

❖ DOROTHY MCBRIDE STETSON

8 ❖ Abortion Debates in Ireland: An Ongoing Issue

Evelyn Mahon

❖ INTRODUCTION

Abortion has been a criminal offence in Ireland since the 1861 Offences against the Person Act, an act passed while Ireland was still part of the British empire (see Chapter 7). Under this statute, self-afflicted abortion is a felony, and, if convicted, a woman is liable to life imprisonment. Section 59 makes it a misdemeanour to assist a woman by procuring an instrument or poison, which is employed with intent to procure a miscarriage. This Act remained intact until the pro-life lobby successfully campaigned for a constitutional prohibition on abortion in the early 1980s.

Thus, Ireland is unique among the countries documented in this book in that it has not only not legalized abortion but has taken action to strengthen legal prohibitions in the period under study. Though abortion is prohibited, except to save a mother's life, the topic has been on the public agenda for a long time, and there have been several national policy debates. Meanwhile Irish women seeking an abortion are legally permitted to travel to Britain to have their pregnancies terminated under the 1967 British Abortion Act.[1] This has removed the urgency for an Irish reform that would resolve the conflict.

Ireland is an exception in another sense: abortion has been a marginal rather than a central feature of the women's movement. And, rather than directly advocating abortion reform legislation, the movement's role has been to generate empathy and understanding for women who have abortions. There are several reasons for this marginality. First, the women's movement had to face an extended campaign to attain other quite basic rights. To attain these rights it had to generate extensive broad support for its agenda by being as inclusive as possible. Second, pro-choice organizations found themselves on the defensive once the abortion issue came to the public agenda in the 1980s. The pro-choice lobby evolved from a section of the women's movement, Irishwomen United, which was set up in 1975. This was a radical group which in 1977 divided itself and its energies among a number of single-issue pressure groups. These were the Contraception Action Programme (CAP), which campaigned for the legalization of contraception; the Rape Crisis Centre, which supported victims of rape; and the Dublin Well Woman Centre, which offered contraceptive services, crisis pregnancy counselling, and, since 1978, abortion referrals to British clinics. Some members of these groups went on to form the Women's Right to Choose Group (WRCG) in 1980. In its initial stages WRCG was a pressure group established to achieve a right to free, safe abortion for Irish women. However, when the Pro-Life Amendment Campaign (PLAC) began, the WRCG became the counter-movement. Some of the radicals still followed the latter's 'right to choose' approach and continued to articulate it in the media until mid-1982 (Hesketh 1990: 86) while others feared that such an approach would be too antagonistic. Thus, rather than framing the debate in terms of the reproductive right to choose, networks of women and associations have worked to generate a pro-choice environment, while trying to avoid an aggressive divisive battle.

Third, international agencies such as International Planned Parenthood have answered the need for reproductive services. They initiated family planning centres in Ireland and established links with clinics in Britain. Along with activities of women's pro-choice groups, this has reduced the urgency for legislative reform. Since Irish women have access to British services, there has been no flouting of the law or health threats from 'back street' abortions. And there has been a noticeable absence from the debate, in contrast to France, of women who admit to having had abortions in defiance of the law. Only three women have publicly admitted to having had an abortion: a pro-choice activist, a pop star, and—more recently—a journalist.[2]

❖ SELECTION OF DEBATES

Because abortion politics involves criminal law, parliament—the Dail—composed of one elected chamber, the Oireachtas, and the Prime Minister (Taoseach) and Cabinet—is constitutionally charged with making changes in the law while the ministries, especially the Ministry of Health, are responsible for implementation. The major parties are the conservative Fianna Fail, the centre-right Fine Gael, and the left-leaning Labour Party. Other parties are the Progressive Democrats, who adopt a liberal approach to economic issues and a progressive one to sexual morality, and the Green Party, which included some members who were very opposed to any form of legislation on abortion. There are also a number of independent deputies who regularly support the minority government in Dail votes who are strongly opposed to abortion. They have repeatedly asked and were initially promised a new referendum on the issue. However, in the period under study, the abortion issue has primarily been a constitutional question. The constitution is amended through public referendums, and the High Court is charged with interpretation of the constitutional law. Since the 1970s, there have been five debates in these institutions:

(1) constitutional amendment to protect the unborn, 1981–3. There were three changes of government over these three years;[3]
(2) closing of pregnancy counselling services, 1983–92;
(3) X case, the Maastricht Treaty, and constitutional referendums on abortion and the right to travel, 1992;
(4) Regulation of Information (Services Outside State for Termination of Pregnancies) Act (1995) which 'does not permit counseling which promotes abortion or encourages the woman to select it in preference to other options or which amounts to direct abortion referral' (Hogan and Whyte 1994: 810); and
(5) C case and the Green Paper 1997–9, bringing the issue of abortion reform to government's official attention with publication of a Green Paper leading to a report on abortion by the All-party Oireachtas Committee on the Constitution (2000).

Three of these debates have been selected for analysis in this chapter. Ireland's unique position on abortion can be seen in the first debate: the constitutional amendment to protect the unborn, 1981–3. The second debate—the X case—took place in 1992, beginning with a legal interpretation of that amendment by the Attorney General, the public controversy it generated, and the subsequent Supreme Court ruling on the X case. This debate continued through a second phase in conjunction with the ratification of the Maastricht Treaty, which led to a referendum on abortion in 1995. The third debate, in 1997–9, began with the C case where abortion was once more on the public agenda and ended with the report of an Oireachtas committee in response to a government Green Paper.

These debates were chosen because they capture the key stages in the consideration of the abortion issue in Ireland. They take place primarily in the arenas of constitutional law and its interpretation, with the parliament and the cabinet as occasional participants. They also show the way in which the abortion issue was, tentatively, gendered over time, with a focus on the right to life of the mother and more recently to a more empathic understanding of crisis pregnancies which lead to abortion .

❖ Debate 1: Constitutional Amendment to Protect the Unborn, 1981–1983

❖ How the debate came to the public agenda

In 1979, the Supreme Court legalized contraception. Basing its ruling on a right to marital privacy, the Court exercised its powers, derived from a 1964 case, to determine which unspecified rights are protected by the Constitution. The legalization of contraception prompted conservative Catholics to establish the Society for the Protection of the Unborn Child (SPUC) in June 1980. SPUC sought to prevent any further escalation of liberalism, particularly with respect to women's reproductive rights. Data published by the Dublin Well Woman Centre established that at least 1,000 women were annually referred to Britain for abortion, and, simultaneously, the Women's Right to Choose Group had begun to campaign for the decriminalisation of abortion (Hesketh 1990: 5). SPUC's leaders feared that the right to privacy might be used by the Court to declare a woman's constitutional right to abortion, as had been done in the US. They decided to campaign for a constitutional amendment that would prevent the legalization of abortion in Ireland and that could not be overruled by either the Supreme Court or the European Court of Justice.

❖ Dominant frame of the debate

The initial dissemination of information on abortion in Ireland was shaped by SPUC in a campaign that spanned more than two years between April 1981 and September 1983. It argued that human life began at the moment of conception and that the right to life of the unborn should be protected by the Constitution. Though formal sex education at that time had not been introduced in schools, SPUC exhibited human embryos in schools and waged philosophical battles in the media over when human life began. Initially it acted like any other interest group. But a sense of urgency, agency, and possibility pervaded their activities and mobilized them into a social movement with a political agenda. They adopted the rhetoric of defence of traditional values, which they claimed were being eroded by the encroachment of European values.

SPUC formed the core of the Pro-Life Amendment Campaign (PLAC), an umbrella group for 14 associations. PLAC's goal was the adoption of a constitutional amendment which would guarantee 'the right to life of the unborn child' from the moment of conception. In addition to having a shared meaning based on this absolute right to life, it was also unified in its counteraction of secularising tendencies that appeared to be so strong throughout the 1970s. Abortion became the issue around which the maximum support for traditional values could be generated (Girvin 1986). As such, it was a strongly unifying issue which drew support from a variety of Catholic lay organisations and mobilized them into a concerted movement. Thus, this first debate established abortion within a frame of traditional Irish Catholic values versus secular inroads from abroad. Within this, the right to life of the unborn took a central place.

While SPUC was engaged in its public pro-life campaign, the chairperson of the Irish Catholic Doctors Guild, Julia Vaughan, opted, along with professional gynaecologists and lawyers, to lobby politicians. Although this approach met with some resistance from the more public SPUC, it gave to medical and legal members the major role of proceeding in a low key fashion, appearing responsible, and working with the government to develop a spirit of mutual cooperation and confidence. They met with leaders of Fine Gael and Fianna Fail, who committed their respective parties to a pro-life referendum. The Labour Party was more equivocal, but the leader, Frank Cluskey, and Barry Desmond, spokesman on justice, while indicating their opposition to abortion, agreed to consider the need for a referendum. Vaughan's success strengthened her position within the executive and among the medical patrons of PLAC.

In March 1982, Prime Minister Haughey announced in the Dail that his government intended to hold a pro-life referendum in 1982. In June, an official anti-amendment campaign was launched. Despite the parties' approval, the debate was a very protracted one. Eventually, the amendment appeared in four different versions. The first, proposed by PLAC, constituted an absolute ban on abortion: 'The State recognises the absolute right to life of every unborn child from conception and accordingly guarantees to respect and protect such right by law.' Protestant leaders opposed the SPUC approach as too strict, arguing that, while they were opposed to abortion on demand, in certain cases abortion may be permissible as the lesser of two evils.

Haughey worked on an alternative wording which would be acceptable to the Protestant community. On 2 November he proposed: 'The State acknowledges the right to life of the unborn and, with due regard to equal right to life of the mother, guarantees in its laws to respect, and, as far as practicable, by its laws to defend and vindicate that right.' Although PLAC disapproved of the compromise, liberal Catholics found it more acceptable.

Due to a general election in November, Haughey did not get an opportunity to put this compromise amendment before the people. A Fine Gael government came into power. Fine Gael itself was quite divided on the issue, some in favour of a very strong pro-life amendment with others opposed. The Attorney-General Peter Sutherland proposed a third version: 'The Oireachtas may, by its laws, prohibit the practice of abortion, and no provision of this Constitution shall be regarded as conferring any right to have an abortion'. This would have placed the responsibility to make laws with the Oireachtas and avoid making it a constitutional issue. An alternative constitutional draft was framed by the Minister for Health, Michael Noonan, which read: 'Nothing in this Constitution shall be invoked to invalidate, or to deprive of force or effect, any provision of a law on the grounds that it prohibits abortion.' Neither alternative wording got sufficient support and, in the end, the Haughey version was put to the people. By the time of the referendum, it had the support of both Fianna Fail and Fine Gael.

❖ Gendering the debate

The PLAC initiative put its opponents on the defensive causing a split in the women's movement over strategy. The Women's Right to Choose Campaign (WRCC) wanted to emphasize women's reproductive rights through a public campaign. Women's Right to Choose Group (WRCG), feared a right-to-choose approach might be 'grist to PLAC's mill' (Hug 1999: 149). WRCG instead joined the Anti-Amendment Campaign (AAC) and chose to emphasize liberal arguments that would challenge the anti-abortion groups' appeal to traditional values. The amendment should be defeated, they argued, because (1) it would do nothing to solve the problem of unwanted pregnancies; (2) it would allow for no exceptions; (3) it was sectarian; (4) it would prevent possible legislation on abortion; and (5) it was a waste of public funds. With this approach, they hoped to gain support from women opposed to abortion but who found a constitutional amendment an unwarranted intrusion of a moral issue into the Constitution. This indicates that their framing of the issue was a reactive one of containment.

To mobilize an effective campaign, women's movement activists made a conscious decision not to bring ideas about women and women's rights into the debate, with the exception of an assertion that the proposed amendment would put women's lives at risk. This indirect oblique or a 'causalist' approach, as described by Hesketh (1990), was clearly to be seen in Senator Mary Robinson's lengthy speech in the Senate. She opposed the proposed amendment by identifying the causes behind abortion, such as the lack of sex education, and argued that women could be victims of circumstances and that they should not be penalized for having children. She argued that while abortion was a problem, the pro-life amendment was not a solution. She also criticized the Catholic Church for backing an amendment, which would 'enshrine a moral issue in the Constitution, which would not acknowledge freedom of conscience'. Overall, the operational strategy adopted was to critique the referendum itself, which in turn evaded the need for any framing of the issue of abortion per se. This approach—rejecting a gendered discourse in favour of a neutral appeal to liberalization—was successful in building opposition to the amendment campaign. Groups of doctors and lawyers argued against their pro-life colleagues. In response, the government proposed a compromise wording that was put to the people.

❖ EVELYN MAHON

❖ *Policy outcome*

The amendment was carried by 66 per cent to 33 per cent, becoming Article 40.3.3 of the Constitution. There was, however, a comparatively low electoral turnout of 50 per cent. The anti-abortion movement achieved its objective, and its proponents hoped that this constitutional amendment would prevent any efforts to legalize abortion under any circumstances. The wording of the amendment included a gendered concession granted to those fearful of its effects on mothers, requiring 'due regard to the right to life of the mother'. Balancing the right of the mother with the right of the unborn set the context of all subsequent debates. The pro-life movement had made abortion a constitutional issue, and it was thus 'in a position to make further demands and adopt new goals' (Staggenborg 1991: 150). For example, it went on to successfully challenge abortion referral and information services, arguing that such services were unconstitutional under the new amendment IV. In 1988, SPUC successfully gained a Supreme Court injunction to prevent students at University College Dublin from publishing abortion information in student academic handbooks. In 1989, the Supreme Court granted a similar injunction against Trinity College Dublin students. In the High Court case which proceeded it, Justice Carroll had referred the matter to the European Court of Justice. In June 1991, the latter upheld the ban on abortion information.

❖ *Women's movement impact*

Women were active participants in both the pro-life amendment campaign as well as the anti-amendment groups. The two rival umbrella organizations—PLAC and AAC—were composed of women's groups. In addition, individual women such as Mary Robinson, Julia Vaughan, and Loretta Brown (SPUC) were prominent in the public discussions. This was the case despite the fact that the abortion issue was defined largely as a gender-neutral question. The policy outcome—approval of the pro-life amendment—did not, however, coincide with the goals of either the liberal or the radical feminist movements. The one concession to the moderates—balancing the right of the unborn with conservative language about the right to life of the mother—was too limited to constitute compensation to the feminists who saw the outcome as a defeat. This impact of the women's movement in the first debate is thus classified as cooptation.

❖ *Women's policy agency activities*

There was one women's policy agency in existence during this debate on the constitutional amendment. The Fine Gael government had appointed Nuala Fenell as Minister for Women's Affairs. Fenell had always been a liberal feminist but was not an advocate for the legalization of abortion. The position she held was junior, had few resources, and was remote from power in the government. She pursued liberal legislative reform in several other areas, but agreed with the party's support for the introduction of the amendment. The role of the Ministry of Women's Affairs was thus a symbolic one. This of course disappointed some women who thought that the Ministry should have played a more dynamic role.

❖ Women's movement characteristics

At the time of this first debate, the women's movement was at the stage of consolidation. The movement included well-established moderate and liberal groups who generally stayed away from the abortion issue. These groups were drawn from trade unions, journalists, and academics and were more left-wing in orientation. When the amendment campaign erupted, they supported the anti-amendment forces, adopting a causalist approach to the issue. By the 1980s, the movement also had a radical feminist component which had evolved from Irishwomen United. That group always took the pro-legalization line on abortion but, during this debate, this stance lacked any popular support. Abortion was thus a very divisive issue even among those who were members of the same party. Since the women's movement still had lots of other items on its agenda, abortion was not a high priority. When they were finally dragged into the amendment campaign, the experience did not unify them; instead it showed the polarization of attitudes and approaches among organizations. In addition, the women's movement was moderately close to the left, a position that gave them few resources since left-wing parties in Ireland have always been politically weak. The counter-movement for the amendment was very strong and organized. The insertion of an amendment into the Constitution was a priority for them and many women supported their cause.

❖ Policy environment

Ironically, the pro-life amendment's success opened up the policy sub-system on abortion. A proposed constitutional amendment entailed a public referendum which meant that parties did not have the dominance over the process that they would have in a legislative campaign. When the issue was considered in the legislature, the parties considered it a moral issue and allowed a free vote. Among the parties, only Fianna Fail held a unified pro-amendment position. Fine Gael was divided, and the left-wing Labour Party had no firm position on the issue. Many Labour Party politicians opposed the amendment, but the left-wing parties were not in power.

❖ EVELYN MAHON

❖ DEBATE 2: THE X CASE, MAASTRICHT, AND THE RIGHT TO TRAVEL, 1992

❖ *How the debate came to the public agenda*

At the beginning of the 1990s all information on abortion, even in magazines and books, was illegal in Ireland. *Our Bodies, Ourselves,* and similar women's health books were removed from public libraries. British magazines had to produce censored Irish editions. The pro-amendment group had been successful in its attempts to make sure that any abortion legislation would be anti-constitutional and that giving information on abortion would be illegal. In 1992, however, a crisis known as the X case put abortion once more on the political agenda. A 14-year old school girl revealed to her parents that she was pregnant, due to a rape in December 1991 by a friend of the family who had repeatedly molested her. Her parents had already arranged for her to have an abortion in England when they went to the police to report the rape and to make arrangements to procure fetal evidence that could be used in court to prosecute the case. Legal advisers informed the police that such evidence was inadmissible in an Irish court.

The Attorney-General applied to the High Court for an injunction which was granted by Justice Costello.[5] This actually restrained the defendant from leaving the jurisdiction for a period of nine months from the date of the court order (Hogan and Whyte 1994: 796). With this ruling, the effect of the 1983 amendment on a real person—a young girl—was evident, and there was a public outcry with meetings, protests, and a massive demonstration against the girl's internment. X was only 14, had been raped, and the public sympathized with her need to terminate the pregnancy. This afforded the Irish public the first opportunity to discuss abortion as embedded in a gendered social reality. Support and sympathy for X and her family led to questions about the fate of 4,000 other women who went annually to England for abortions. Would there now be pregnancy testing for all women leaving the country?

With the state offering to pay the costs, the family appealed their case to the Supreme Court, arguing that the rape and pregnancy had put their daughter's life at risk because she was liable to commit suicide. In a few days, by a majority of four to one, the Supreme Court decided that X could go abroad for an abortion. It concluded that 'if it is established as a matter of probability that there is a real and substantial risk to the life of the mother, which can only be avoided by the termination of her pregnancy, that such termination is permissible, having regard to the true interpretation of Article 40.3.3'.[6] The decision in this case led to a second phase of debate over the right to travel when the issue became conflated with the referendum over the Maastricht Treaty. Both phases of the framing of the debate are discussed here.

❖ Dominant frame of the debate: phase 1

The Supreme Court picked up the dominant frame of the abortion issue produced by the1981–3 constitutional amendment debate: that the question of abortion law was to balance the risk to the life of the mother with the right of the unborn. Article 40.3.3 prohibited surgical intervention against the unborn unless the pregnancy was a threat to the mother's life. In this frame of competing rights, the Court ruled in favour of the girl, interpreting her threat of suicide as a threat to her life. This judgement was an unexpected interpretation of the amendment, particularly for those pro-life advocates who had campaigned for its inclusion. Not only did the judges recognize suicide as constituting a real and substantial threat to the life of the mother; they also omitted any time limits on abortion in such circumstances. Justice McCarthy criticized the legislature for not enacting appropriate legislation; indeed, he described it as inexcusable that such a divisive amendment remained 'bare of legislative direction' (Hogan and Whyte 1994: 801).

❖ Gendering the debate: phase 1

The public definition of the issue in this case was thus very much on compassionate grounds. X was more commonly referred to as 'a child' rather than a woman. By seeking legal advice prior to procuring an abortion, the parents were seen as responsible citizens, who gained public support for their decision. Justice McCarthy's condemnation captured the tone of the judges who were influenced by this spontaneous expression of concern. Nevertheless, their opinion confirmed that abortion had a gendered dimension, not in terms of a woman's freedom to choose, but in terms of raising the status of woman's life to equality with the life of the unborn.

Although this frame had continuity with the right-to-life discourse, it produced a definition of the abortion issue that pro-life groups found difficult to accept. In the amendment campaign of 1981–3, the possible threat of pregnancy to the life of a woman had been discussed only in terms of a biological threat, not a self-induced threat. They accepted the legal possibility of abortion on this ground after reassurances by gynaecologists active in the pro-life movement that they had never encountered a pregnancy which was life-threatening in that way. However, the X case gendered the debate by its introduction of the risk of suicide, which arose because of the woman's reaction to the pregnancy. Further, to the alarm of pro-life activists, the judges involved the *Bourne* case as a precedent for their ruling.[7] *R. v. Bourne* in 1938 had liberalized the 1861 English criminal abortion law, which was still on the books in Ireland, by allowing doctors to perform an abortion if the pregnancy would turn a woman into a 'physical or mental wreck'. Even though the judges in the X case ruled that Article 40.3.3 of the Constitution meant there had to be a 'real and substantial risk to the life as distinct from the health of the mother which can only be avoided by the termination of her pregnancy' (Justice C. J. Finlay), the pro-life forces were alarmed that the constitutional amendment had been used to establish the constitutional right of the X case to have an abortion. Further, the Supreme Court decision in the X case had implications for the existing ban on the dissemination of information about abortion services abroad, as women whose lives were at risk could not be denied such information.

The liberals were also alarmed by the X case decision because, in their opinions, three members of the Court envisaged that the constitutional right to travel could be restrained in order to protect the right to life of the unborn. The implication of this was that only pregnant women whose lives were endangered could travel to secure an abortion in Britain. Accordingly, the Court ruled that the Attorney-General by his injunction had acted consistently within the Constitution. If legislation were ever enacted to bring this into effect, then thousands of women would be precluded from having abortions in Britain.

❖ How the debate came again to the public agenda

All sides of the debate were surprised by the court's ruling in the X case. Pro-life groups argued that nobody who had voted for the 1983 amendment could have anticipated the way it had been interpreted by the Supreme Court. They responded by proposing another amendment with a form that would preclude abortion under any circumstances be put to the people in a referendum. Liberals expressed surprise that the court had not specified any time limits on X's abortion in the judgement. Pro-choice advocates were relieved that the X case had procured a right to have an abortion under specified circumstances. However, they also realized that it was not a solution for all women with unwanted pregnancies because they would not be prepared to take their case to the Supreme Court. Of special concern was the threat to the right to travel to procure abortions abroad. In 1990, the European Community had defined abortion as a commercial service; within an internal European market Irish women had the right of access to services, including abortion, available in other Member States.

Despite the controversy raised by the X case, it is unlikely that the government would have responded were it not for the impending referendum on the Maastricht Treaty of Accession. The treaty, which promised to bind the states of the European Union even closer together in trade and policy, was due to come up for ratification in Ireland a few months after the X decision. The negotiations over the treaty had been handled by the then Minister for Foreign Affairs Gerry Collins. Because of the X case, it was revealed that in December 1991, Collins, under pressure from pro-life groups and without any public discussion, had surreptitiously inserted the following protocol into the Treaty: 'Nothing in the

Treaty on European Union, or in the Treaties establishing the European Communities, or in Treaties or Acts modifying or supplementing those Treaties, shall affect the application in Ireland of Article 40.3.3 [the anti-abortion amendment] of the Constitution of Ireland.' If *Maastricht* were approved, the legal implications of this protocol would be that Irish women could not seek to assert a Community right to travel to another Member State for an abortion, or receive information about abortion services there (Reid 1992: 33).

❖ Dominant frame of the second phase of the debate

The Maastricht Treaty took on a new meaning. What had been a fairly straight-forward referendum on a popular step towards greater integration with Europe and the formation of the European Union threatened to become a referendum on the X case, abortion, and women's rights to travel. The offending protocol had few supporters. For the pro-life group, the Maastricht Treaty would protect the pro-abortion ruling of the Supreme Court. SPUC immediately demanded another referendum, which would introduce a more explicitly anti-abortion amendment. The liberal community was pleased with the Court judgement on abortion, but feared that approval of the Maastricht Treaty would severely limit women's rights to travel and information. Thus in this second phase of the debate, another definition of the abortion issue was added to the dominant frame of competing rights to life of mother and child: the right of Irish people to travel within the European Union, a definition which threatened support for the Maastricht Treaty in the important referendum.

The government wanted at all costs to ratify the Maastricht Treaty in June. At that stage, the Danes had voted already against ratification, and it was portrayed by the media as if the future of the European Union depended on Ireland endorsing the treaty. First, the government tried to renegotiate the protocol, but this was rejected. The best that could be achieved was an insertion of a Solemn Declaration, which permitted travel and information on services available legally in the other Member States. It included an agreement that, if a future amendment of Article 40.3.3 were voted on in Ireland, the protocol could be amended. This was designed to please both sides, women who did not want to vote away their rights under the European Union (EU) legislation and the SPUC group which hoped to have a new referendum that would revert matters to how they were understood to be prior to the Supreme Court decision.

❖ Gendering the second phase of the debate

At this point, women's movement activists stepped in to change the government's plans. Under the leadership of Frances Fitzgerald, the National Council for the Status of Women, a national federation of women's groups in Ireland, played a strategic role in the campaign against the protocol by identifying and generating 'a middle ground' on the issue. She argued that the Council and its affiliated groups had a long and consistent history of supporting women and mothers, and raised questions about the motives of certain pressure groups that presumed to tell Irish women about their responsibilities as mothers. At no stage did the Council positively endorse abortion. Rather, it cogently argued that women should be able to make up their own minds on the matter, thereby gendering the debate over Maastricht.

Thus, as the time for the referendum approached, the National Council for the Status of Women held that it could not recommend that women support the referendum unless women could be formally included in decisions relating to EU expenditure. It also wanted a referendum that would give women a right to travel and to information on abortion. Under this pressure, the government pledged to submit three referendums in the autumn regarding the right to travel, the right to information, and the 'substantive' issue of abortion per se. With this guarantee the Council encouraged women to vote in favour of Maastricht. Although SPUC supporters called for a 'no' vote, the electorate approved the Maastricht Treaty. Settling the abortion issue depended on the outcome of three referendums planned for November 1992. Unexpected political upheavals meant that the vote was held on the same day as the 1992 general election. The vote was preceded by vigorous arguments from both sides with far more women active than in the past.

❖ *Policy outcome*

The voters approved the amendments guaranteeing the rights to travel and to information. These were signed by the President in December 1992:

> This subsection shall not limit freedom to travel between the State and another state.

> This subsection shall not limit freedom to obtain or make available, in the State, subject to such conditions as may be laid down by law, information relating to services lawfully available in another state.

The voters rejected the third amendment which would have excluded suicide as a grounds for abortion. It read:

> It will be unlawful to terminate the life of the unborn unless such termination is necessary to save the life, as distinct from the health, of the mother where there is an illness or disorder of the mother giving rise to a real and substantial risk to her life, not being a risk of self-destruction.

Opinion is divided about the basis of the voters' rejection of this amendment. A liberal explanation claims that the electorate did not want the Supreme Court's decision—which allowed abortion if the mother threatened suicide—changed or rolled back. Irish women thus obtained a constitutional safeguard that their right to life was equal to the right of the unborn. However, an alternative inter-pretation claims that the electorate rejected any form of abortion, even in cases where the mother had suicidal tendencies. Yet even the anti-abortion groups were split, some seeing a 'yes' vote as a restriction on abortion and others seeing it as a reduction of restrictions.

The liberal interpretation is consistent with the findings of the European Values study carried out in 1990, which found that 65 per cent of Irish respondents, compared with 95 per cent of Europe generally, approved of abortion when the mother's health was at risk from pregnancy (Hornsby-Smith and Whelan 1996: 36). Nevertheless, Irish tolerance of abortion was strictly limited. Only 32 per cent approved of abortion where it was likely that the child was handicapped, and 8 per cent where the mother was not married or where a married couple did not want to have more children (Hornsby-Smith and Whelan 1996: 36). This survey supports the conclusion that the public's approval or disapproval of abortion is dependent on circumstances and that, by rejecting the amendment, the Irish people did not endorse ' woman's right to choose' abortion in all circumstances in 1992.

❖ Women's movement impact

Women participated actively on both sides of the debate. The government, how-ever, especially depended on the National Council for the Status of Women to gain the necessary portion of the women's vote to pass the Maastricht Treaty. Thus, when the Council and women's pro-choice groups brought up the impli-cations of the Irish Protocol to the Treaty for women's rights to travel, the gov-ernment listened. These women's movement groups gendered the debate and were accepted as legitimate participants in the policy debate leading to the referendums on abortion and travel. In addition, the outcome of the debate coincided with the goals of the Irish women's movement, which had not adopted a clear right-to-choose position on abortion. In accord with the moderate demands of the movement groups, Irish women gained a constitutional right to travel to procure an abortion and to information on abortion services. Moreover, they defeated an effort to reduce the significance of women's right to life and health in the abortion law derived from the precedent in the X case. Based on this information it is clear the movement obtained a dual response from the state in this second debate.

❖ Women's policy agency activities

In 1992, there was no longer a Ministry for Women's Rights. Instead, that role was subsumed under the Department of Justice, Law and Equality. The only women's policy agency was the Joint Oireachtas Committee on Women's Rights (JOCWR). This was an all-party committee established in the legislature and charged with reviewing bills affecting the status of women. With a small budget, it studied and published reports on ways of improving the status of women (Mahon 1995). Generally the leadership stuck to a liberal feminist approach. Since the committee represented all the parties and had an accommodating style to their work, they never took up the divisive issue of abortion. Thus, since they took no stand on the issue and did not participate in the debate, the JOCWR's role was symbolic.

❖ Women's movement characteristics

The women's movement in the early 1990s was in abeyance (Mahon 1995). The main section of the movement active in this instance was the National Council for the Status of Women, a non-governmental organization which represented a variety of women's associations. It had benefited from EU funding under the New Opportunities for Women (NOW) programme and was emerging as one of the social partners. The election of Mary Robinson as President of the Republic in 1990 had given the movement activists a psychological boost, and women as individuals and in groups were involved in a variety of issues. The women's movement groups were not essentially left-wing, though many of them were oriented towards the left. Others, especially those in Fine Gael or who later joined Fine Gael, were very socially concerned and sought a 'just society'. Abortion was still not a high priority issue. The Council on the Status of Women became an important policy actor in the debate only because of the oblique way in which the abortion issue came to be connected with the Maastricht Treaty. In its campaign, the Council benefited from the overwhelming public reaction to the X case. Although the counter-movement remained strong, the government realized that if the Treaty were to be signed, it could not rely on the pro-life forces to make up for the opposition voters swayed by the Council on the Status of Women. As a result of this debate, the Council became the executive agent or officer of the women's movement.

❖ Women's Policy environment

The policy sub-system was similar to the first debate. The main institutional arenas were the prime minister and cabinet, the Supreme Court, and the constitutional referendum. Also as in the first debate, the system was an open one. Not only did the referendum process open the arena to participation by a wide number of voices, but a Fine Gael-Labour-Democratic Left coalition was in power, setting quite a different tone from that of the more conservative Fianna Fail government during the early 1980s. The highest number of women—20—had been elected to the Dail, many of them topping the polls in their constituencies. The left—Labour and Democratic Left—also occupied a number of key ministries.

❖ Debate 3: C Case and the Green Paper, 1997–1999

❖ *How the debate came to the public agenda*

In early November 1997 the Eastern Health Board (EHB) sought guidance from the High Court in relation to the case of a 13-year-old member of the travelling community who was under its care. This young woman, known simply as C, was pregnant as the result of an alleged rape. She developed suicidal intentions as a result and wished to have an abortion. Despite the passage of the right-to-travel referendum following the X case, the EHB was informed by its legal advisers that, as a state agency, it could not assist in the procurement of an abortion. A voluntary agreement, which was drawn up between the EHB and the woman's parents allowing her to be released back into their care, quickly fell apart when the woman's father changed his mind, informing the Court that he now did not wish his daughter to have an abortion. This change of mind co-incided with the appearance in Court of the woman's parents accompanied by prominent anti-abortion campaigners including the groups Family and Life and Youth Defence. Considerable confusion ensued, resulting in the Children's Court extending the EHB's care order after the young woman's legal representatives, her parents, and the EHB failed to agree on a course of action.

On 21 November 1997 the case was referred to the District Court. The psychiatrist in the case gave strong evidence that the 'child is likely to commit suicide unless she has a termination of pregnancy'. Justice Mary Fahy directed that C be allowed to travel for the purpose of termination of her pregnancy while under continued supervision by the EHB. In response, the parent's legal team alleged that Judge Fahy had no jurisdiction to make this order and the case was immediately referred to the High Court. On the 29 November 1997, just under two weeks after this case first came to light, Mr Justice Geoghegan upheld Judge Fahy's order and the right of the District Court to make a decision on the case. He took the view that 'the termination of pregnancy which was authorised by Judge Fahy was one which both in her view and in my view, was lawful under the Irish Constitution'. Justice Geoghegan added that he failed to see 'how any judge could have avoided the conclusion that as a matter of probability there was a real and substantial risk to the life as distinct from the health of C, which could only be avoided by the termination of her pregnancy'.[8]

This case drew attention to work under way in the Ministry of Health over the issue of abortion. In mid-1995, the Minister for Health had commissioned a study on crisis pregnancies in Ireland in order to identify the factors which contributed to 'the incidence of unwanted pregnancies' (*Irish Times* 1996). The purpose of the research was to assist in the development and planning of future health policy with a view to reducing the incidence of abortion among Irish women. Published in 1998 under a different government, the report revealed that the majority of abortions were carried out for social reasons, specifically the personal and family stigma of lone parenthood and its impact on women and their children, the difficulties of reconciling work and anticipated mothering or family life demands, and the financial difficulties attached to lone social motherhood (see Mahon, Conlon, and Dillon 1998). The Crisis Pregnancy Study exposed a somewhat unpalatable truth about abortions: that the majority of abortions obtained by Irish women would not be covered by limited or restrictive legislation.

The new Fianna Fail Minister for Health asked a civil service committee to produce a Green Paper on abortion, which invited submissions from interest groups. When published in 1999, the Green Paper formed another stage in the institutionalisation of the issue. It was a very comprehensive document, which primarily addressed the political and legal context of the discussion of abortion in Ireland. The final chapter presented seven possible constitutional and legislative approaches that could be taken. The public and interest groups were invited to make submissions focused on the seven options outlined to the All-Party Oireachtas Constitutional Committee on abortion (Green Paper on Abortion 1999).

❖ *Dominant frame of the debate.*

During the C case the question to be settled was the same as that developed in the previous debate: the competing rights to life of mother and unborn child conflated with whether or not a woman had a right to travel abroad to obtain an abortion. SPUC warned that the state would be acting as an 'executioner' if it allowed the woman to travel to obtain an abortion. Other anti-abortion groups such as Youth Defence criticized the EHB for offering nothing but a solution of 'violence' to a crisis pregnancy (*Irish Times* 1997a). The Irish Council for Civil Liberties expressed concern at the apparent 'moral tug of war' that had taken place 'over the body' of the thirteen year old pregnant girl. It called on the Oireachtas to legislate immediately for abortion in the circumstances provided for in the judgement on the X case (*Irish Times* 1997b).

With a growing public as well as political interest in the C case, The Minister for Health said in the Dail that the Government 'will initiate public debate on the issue with the publication of the green paper and the intention is to refer the matter at that stage to the all party Constitutional Review Group' (Dail Reports 1997: 1527). He framed the issue in terms of the need to settle a contentious issue referring to the 'difficult journey of building consensus on how to deal properly and adequately with the issue'. But he also emphasised that it was not possible to deal with the issue by way of consensus without 'giving the people a say in the matter'. Any 'proposed legislation would have to be put to the people by way of referendum. This is the view of the government' (Dail Reports 1997: 1532). The framing by the Government was articulated in terms of process i.e. that the people should decide, rather than substance.

The Green Paper combined these frames. The seven options were presented within the legal and political context in which the issue has evolved in Ireland and ranged from abortion on demand to an absolute prohibition. Submissions were invited from the public. But the All-Party Constitutional Review Committee's goal was to present options that had a chance of bridging the highly polarized conflict. One submission would retain the legal compromise achieved in the X case. In particular, the Irish Congress of Trade Union submission, the Adelaide Hospital Society, and T. K. Whittaker, who chaired the review of the Constitution, all recommended legislation based on the X case.

In addition to the pro-life groups who had actively campaigned for a referendum, the main objections at the oral hearings to legislating on the grounds of the X case came from the gynaecologists. Abortion on suicidal grounds was also vetoed by psychiatrist Professor Anthony Clare. The views of these spokespersons—all men—reflected the biological model upon which the medical community operates. They could see a pregnancy only as providing a biological rather than a psychiatric threat to a woman's life.

Psychologists for Freedom of Information countered that it was possible to clinically establish risk of suicide. Such assessments were already utilized as part of the Mental Health Act in cases of committal. In their actual submission, women spokespersons recommended that abortion be permitted 'where there is a serious risk to the mental health of a woman pregnant as a result of rape or incest' (All-Party Oireachtas Committee on the Constitution 2000: A264).

❖ Gendering the debate

During the Courts' proceedings, it was highlighted that C, the young woman concerned, had threatened suicide if she were prevented from proceeding with her abortion. This discourse was quite similar to that expounded by the Court in the X case and made the life of the mother of paramount importance. Pro-choice groups throughout Ireland welcomed the High Court decision. They criticized the actions of anti-abortion groups such as Youth Defence and Family for Life for their 'very gross and direct intervention in a case in which they had no place . . . they have plumbed to new depths of extremism and poor taste' (*Irish Times* 1997d). The Dublin Abortion Information Campaign said that 'it [government] must legislate for the right to have an abortion in Ireland, and stop trying to export the problem' (*Irish Times* 1997a). Conversely, the anti-abortion lobby groups expressed 'dismay and disappointment' at the decision; a Youth Defence spokesperson stated, 'it's a tragedy for Ireland, for this girl and for her baby', while Family and Life was 'profoundly disappointed' (*Irish Times*

1997d). The Catholic Church's response to this issue was delivered by the Archbishop of Dublin, Dr Desmond Connell, who was 'greatly saddened' by the High Court's decision, stating 'the rights of the unborn child in Ireland are now very vulnerable'. In a similar vein, Canon Kenneth Kearon of the Church of Ireland outlined his disapproval of the use of the Constitution as a means of dealing with an issue as complex as the individual case of a 13-year-old rape victim who had decided to have an abortion, noting that 'the apparent attempt by other groups to influence that decision must be a cause for concern' (*Irish Times* 1997e).

The National Women's Council of Ireland (NWCI, formerly CSW) did not have a unified position on abortion policy, and focused instead on the unequal access of Irish women to abortion abroad. The NWCI chairperson, Noreen Byrne, stated 'it was assumed that the right to travel and to information had been completely clarified in 1992, but now we find that those rights may not extend to the most vulnerable in our society' (*Irish Times* 1997b). In a similar vein, one *Irish Times* commentator, Nuala O' Faolain, went as far as to state that: 'the raped thirteen-year-old is an emblem, not a person. Let her stand for all travellers, all people at the bottom of all societies, all the multiple disempowered' (*Irish Times* 1997c).

Submissions on behalf of women were made to the Green Paper committee and the Oireachtas committee examining the abortion question. The pro-choice groups, such as the Woman's Health Council, attempted to remind the committees that abortion was a woman's problem and to generate a sympathetic response to women faced with crisis pregnancies. The Irish Family Planning Association recommended that the 1983 constitutional provision be repealed, effectively removing the issue from the Constitution. The result was that the seven options produced in the Green Paper included demands for abortion on demand as well as more moderate options focusing on women's health.

❖ Policy outcome

Not surprisingly, the Oireachtas committee did not produce a consensus plan for abortion policy. Rather, it outlined three different options. The first proposal, backed by Fianna Fail, recommends that, to restrict or counteract the X judgement, a referendum be held for an absolute ban on abortion. The second recommendation is to retain the status quo and have the state initiate an active policy to assist women with crisis pregnancies. This proposal builds on the findings of the study on crisis pregnancy and puts the needs of the pregnant woman at the centre. It also offers a consensus middle ground on the issue. However, it can be contended that this option is only feasible while access to British abortion services is available. It puts off any legislative change, while implicitly acknowledging the reality of Irish abortion rates.

The third option is proposed by the Labour Party, which argues that legislation as prescribed by the X case judgement should be introduced. This would permit abortion in restricted circumstances when the mother's life was in danger, including a risk of suicide. It would not include abortion on grounds of rape or other social factors. However, proponents of the referendum approach suggest that this approach is 'unregulatable'. This stems from a view that many women could claim to be suicidal and it would in effect secure an abortion on social grounds.

❖ Women's Movement impact

Many individual women and leaders of organizations participated in the third debate, especially through the formal channels to the Green Paper and Oireachtas committees. Women's Aid, Women's Counselling Network, Dublin Abortion Rights Group, the National Organisation for Women, National Women's Council of Ireland, Women's Education Research and Resource Centre, and Trinity College Women's Group made submissions to the Green Paper. These organizations had ties with the original broad feminist movement. There were also submissions from many women's groups that came into existence after, or as a result of, the 1983 referendum and were pro-life, such as Feminists for Life Ireland, Irish Family League, Christian Family Association, Family Prayer Movement, and Family Solidarity.

The Green Paper incorporated all views in its document. One can, however, regard such a document as at least facilitating debate and promoting an understanding of the viewpoints of others. However, the Oireachtus committee eliminated the more gendered options. As a parliamentary document, the report may be closer to reaching a final policy outcome on abortion. If so, then the conclusion would be that the outcome did not coincide with the views of most organizations in the movement which sought an expansion of conditions under which abortion could be performed. Thus, the third debate has again produced cooptation as the Irish women's movement activists continue to struggle with the highly divisive issue.

❖ Women's policy agency activities

Although the Joint Oireachtas Committee on Women's Rights was still in existence during this debate, it played a symbolic role on the abortion issue. It had the same characteristics as in the previous debate: a cross-sectional, all-party political group, remote from power, with a mandate that excluded abortion. It was, however, the All Party Oireachtas Committee on the Constitution that considered the Green Paper and invited submissions on the seven options outlined in it. So, while there is not a women's policy agency in existence, this committee constitutes an important institution which offered the public a range of options on abortion legislation.

❖ Women's movement characteristics

The women's movement remained the same as in the earlier debate. It was in a stage of consolidation, only moderately close to the left, and faced a moderately strong counter-movement. The proliferation of special interest committees has diluted the cohesiveness of the movement, which continued to find it difficult to reach a consensus on abortion. Nevertheless, the participation of feminist women has promoted a wider involvement of all women in the policy-making process.

❖ Policy environment

This third debate began in the courts, moved to the Health Ministry and finally to a parliamentary committee. At this final stage a centre-left Fianna Fail-Progressive Democrat Party-Independent coalition formed the government with, Fine Gael in opposition. The power structure remained open, facilitating wide-ranging debate and discussion. It tends to remain open because, given the polarization on the topic, without a consensus the parties hesitate to use their legislative resources to introduce legislation. At the end of this third debate, the parliament was presented with three options drawn more or less along party lines. With this situation, the issue of abortion could become a major focus of the next general election, in 2001 or very early 2002, something all parties would like to avoid.

❖ CONCLUSION

Using a cross-national standard of policy content—decriminalization of abortion furthering women's right to choice—the women's movement in Ireland has had little success. Demands for abortion law reform have divided rather than unified the movement, and it has not made the push for abortion on demand of its counterparts in other countries. There have been few women's policy agencies and those that existed have been weak. Beyond that, they have avoided the issue as too divisive, preferring to address what they consider more pressing demands, in light of the safety-valve of legal abortion in British clinics for Irish women. In terms of the policy environment, the left is weak, and has never formed a government on its own, although a left party participated in the coalition during the X/Maastricht debate.

Despite this conclusion, the movement has been successful in bringing women into the policy-making process. The open policy sub-system on the abortion issue gave voice to feminist groups. In turn, they paved the way for all women to become more involved, and this became especially notable with their visible participation in the pro-life movement. Further, while the legislative issue remains unresolved, the debate has been gendered with a focus on the mother's life receiving constitutional protection and, more recently, by seeing abortion as an outcome of a crisis pregnancy. The latter view has finally been a unifying theme among all groups, so that abortion is now considered to be a socially constructed rather than a moral outcome. Such debate, of course, has been possible only because Irish women have access to abortion services in Britain, which Irish law over time has recognized.

❖ Notes

1 This entails considerable financial cost for women both because of the travel and accommodation and because they attend the abortion clinic as private patients. The typical cost of an abortion includes an initial £45 consultation fee plus £320 for an abortion up to 14 weeks gestation with an overnight stay in the clinic which is obligatory for non-UK residents; £430 for an abortion over 14 and up to 20 weeks or; £510 for an abortion over 20 and up to 24 weeks. Travel and accommodation would generally cost women another £200 as well as the cost of travel and accommodation for any companion.

2 This silence was eventually broken when, in 1995, the Minister for Health funded a large study on abortion and crisis pregnancy, the findings of which were published in 1998 (Mahon, Conlon, and Dillon 1998).

3 In 1980 there was a Fianna Fail government in power. A general election was called in June 1981 and both Fianna Fail and Fine Gael had included support for an pro-life amendment in their pre-election material. In June 1981 a Fine Gael-Labour coalition was instated. This, however, was defeated in a vote on the budget in January 1982 and another general election was held in February 1982. This returned a Fianna Fail minority government. It too was short-lived. and was defeated on a censure motion in November 1982. A Fine Gael-Labour Coalition was returned to power and this ran until 1995. Then a Fianna Fail-Progressive Democrat Coalition was formed which is still in power.

4 SPUC & Attorney General v. Open Line Counselling and Dublin Well Women Centre.

5 Attorney General v. X and others [1992] I IR I.

6 Ibid.

7 In R. v. Bourne 3 All ER 615 1938; 1 KB 687 1939, a girl of 14 had become pregnant as a result of multiple rape and the jury acquitted the defendant who performed an abortion. The judge gave the jury the following directions: under the Offences Against the Person Act of 1861, 'In relation to a criminal prosecution under section 58 of the 1861 Act, the prosecution had to prove beyond reasonable doubt that the abortion had not been carried out in good faith in order to preserve the life of the mother. Moreover, he said that a surgeon would be obliged to carry out an abortion where the consequences of the

pregnancy would make the mother a physical and mental wreck' (Hogan and Whyte 1994: 790). 'In the instant case, a girl of fourteen had become pregnant as a result of multiple rape and the jury acquitted the defendant who performed an abortion' (Hogan and Whyte 1994: 791).

8 High Court, unreported, 28 November 1997, reprinted in full in *Irish Times* (1997d).

9 ❖ Debates and Controversies on Abortion in Italy

Marina Calloni

❖ INTRODUCTION

The legal history of *procurato aborto* (procured abortion) in Italy reflects the different and conflicting legal codes and cultures that have ruled Italy. During the Roman Republic, abortion was not considered as a crime but only as an 'immoral act'. The fetus was determined to be an integral part of the 'mother's viscera'. During the imperial age, in the second and third century, emperors Antoninus Pius and Septimius Severus introduced a legislative 'restriction' regarding abortion because it was considered as an offence against the *pater-familias* who could be deprived of an heir. During Giustiniano's empire (528–65) abortion started to be persecuted as a crime, as stated in the *Digesto* (no. 498, 8, fr. 8)—a systematic collection concerning issues of Roman law— reflecting the increasing moral influence of Christian doctrine according to which the fetus was God's creature.[1]

Christian doctrine thus became the dominant framework for religion, jurisprudence, and the state. In the Middle Ages, abortion started to be condemned as culpable homicide and punished according to canon law. The fetus was in fact considered as a *person*, meaning a body supplied with a soul. Yet this question was the 'big issue' precisely because the soul was supposed to be the part connecting a human being with God also after his or her death. The soul was thus connected with the idea of having a life and being a person. However, the Church adopted over centuries two different approaches to this question: the idea of *immediate animation* and that of *late animation* (Sardi 1975; Tettamanzi 1975). While under the former idea, supported by the Popes Sisto V and Gregory XIV in the sixteenth century, the fetus is considered as having from the beginning a life or a soul, under the latter, supported by Pope Innocent III, in the twelfth and thirteenth centuries, the fetus is considered as having a life or a soul only when the quickening of the fetus can be felt. This second interpretation derives from Aristotle's philosophy, which states that a male fetus acquires a soul 40 days after his conception while a female fetus obtains hers 80 days after. Yet in 1869 Pope Pius IX chose definitively, on the basis of the new dogma of the 'immaculate conception' of Mary, the version of the immediate animation of the fetus. Since then, the Catholic Church has espoused the protection of human life from its conception. Indeed, in modern times as well legislation has indicated very clearly the connection made by the state between public codes and private morality. In 1532 Charles V, the Holy Roman Emperor, stated in *Carolina*, the criminal code that he promoted, that abortion was homicide and was therefore to be prosecuted. This law was extended to all his domains.

All these traditions became embodied in the Italian nation state which was created in 1871 with Rome as its capital. The first national Italian penal code, adopted in 1889, condemned abortion as a crime. Later, in 1930, during the Fascist regime (1924–44), a new penal code, the *Codice Rocco* (Rocco Code), came into force. Abortion was included in Arts 545–51 as one of 'the crimes against the continuity, integrity and health of the race', one of the means the regime used to increase the 'population', meaning the 'race'. In addition to prohibiting abortion, the state provided incentives for women to have as many children as possible. This pro-natalist policy coincided with the long-standing position of the Catholic Church (Palini 1977).

Public policy debates on abortion in Italy reflect these Roman, Christian, and Fascist traditions as well as contemporary effects of social change, especially in women's roles, since World War II. In 1946, Italy became a republic after a popular referendum, and women were for the first time recognized as citizens having political rights (Zincone 1992; Bimbi and Dal Re 1997; Commissione per le Pari Opportunità, 1998). On 1 January 1948 a democratic constitution came into force. Nevertheless, many Fascist laws remained on the books, including Art. 547 of the Rocco Code stating 'a woman, who commits an abortion, can be sentenced from one up to four years of imprisonment'.

Throughout the post-World War II period, Italy has continued to have a Catholic culture in which the pope, although technically head of another state, is very influential in public issues and national policies. At the same time, the period has been marked by strong social movements and left-wing parties, especially the Communist Party. These powerful forces have struggled over a variety of social reforms affecting women, including family law reform and reproductive rights. The cases discussed in this chapter reflect deep economic and cultural upheavals in Italian society, the changing role of the women's movements, and the transformation of public opinion over the years. In 1978, abortion was partly decriminalized and legally recognized by law no. 194, titled *'Norme per la Tutela Sociale della Maternità e sull'Interruzione Volontaria della Gravidanza'* (Norms for the Social Protection of Motherhood and about the

Voluntary Interruption of Pregnancy). Note that legal abortion is referred to in Italian as *Interruzione Volontaria della Gravidanza* (IVG).

Since then, as in other countries, debates about abortion have revolved around efforts to overturn or defend legal abortion. Women's movements and feminists, both activists and theorists, have participated in all these debates in important, yet ambivalent, ways. The beginning of the abortion struggle, aimed mostly at its decriminalization, signified a sort of 'emancipation' of the feminist movement from the traditional left-wing parties. The women's movement therefore reacted in two different ways: one sector stressed a radical and anti-institutional position, while the other decided to continue to work within political parties, institutionalizing gender policies. This constitutive ambivalence of the Italian women's movement has characterized the last three decades, challenging the idea of a unified approach to women's rights. After parliamentary approval of the law in 1978, the major interest of women, in both movements and political parties, became the defence of legal abortion. They have not been unified, however, as throughout these struggles the radical feminist wing has criticized law no. 194 as a product of what it calls a 'state compromise' against women.

Women's policy agencies did not appear in Italian governments until the mid-1980s, and thus did not participate in the debates surrounding the legalization of abortion. The first agency, Commissione per le Pari Opportunità fra Uomini e Donne (Commission for Equal Opportunity between Men and Women), which was instituted in 1984 (Guadagnini 1987) steered clear of the issue, reflecting different political and moral beliefs among commissioners regarding abortion. This situation changed after 1996 in the first post-war governments not dominated by the Democrazia Cristiana (DC, Christian Democratic Party). The centre-leftist 'olive tree' coalition established a Ministry for Equal Opportunities and appointed several female secretaries of state. Thanks to recommendations of the United Nations, the directives of the European Union and various UN world conferences and programmes—UNIFEM (url), Women Watch 2001 (url)—devoted to women's status, gendered issues and human rights became more accepted in Italian national policy debates, and women in government publicly defended the law on abortion.

❖ SELECTION OF DEBATES

Alongside the debates in the public arena and the various interventions of social movements, the political institutions making abortion policy were the parliament (Senate and Chamber of Deputies), popular referendums, and the government (Cabinet). Governments are always either composed of one party or coalition of parties, and, in most of the period under study, the Christian Democrats provided the leadership role. The universe of abortion policy debates in these institutions is quite complex (Calloni 2002). Indeed, starting from the 1960s many bills for decriminalizing or for prohibiting abortion were presented in successive parliamentary sessions by MPs belonging to different and opposed political parties.[2] Most of these bills were not approved, and so did not become law.

From this universe of debates, the following case studies have been selected for analysis:

(1) the legalization of abortion, 1971–8;
(2) the popular referendum to repeal legal abortion, 1980–1; and
(3) in vitro fertilization and abortion, 1996–9.

These cases represent the decisional system: the first and the third are centred in Cabinet and Parliament, while the second occurs in the forum of a popular referendum, a crucial policy arena for social and moral issues such as abortion. In addition, they cover the range of issues over three decades. They comprise decriminalization, the initial Catholic/conservative backlash to that policy, and the questions raised about abortion by new reproductive technologies, which are, without doubt, the crucial steps in the formulation of public debates on abortion in Italy. In addition, these debates indicate paradigmatically the changing dynamics between the women's movement, counter-movements, national Parliament, and various governments. Indeed, these cases also stress the shifts in the relationship between civil society and the state over the last 30 years.

The debates drew many participants, both for and against abortion, into the political arena and civil society for the first time. They represent the controversial cosmos of the Italian policy debates and the conflicting relationships between different political and institutional organs and a more and more divided public opinion. In fact, the debates on abortion affirm a 'bottom up' democracy, where political institutions are forced to discuss social and gender issues, revolutionizing the previous structure of political debates, institutional proceedings, and decision-making.

❖ DEBATE 1: DECRIMINALIZING ABORTION, 1971–1978

❖ *How the debate came to the public agenda*

In the 1970s the abortion issue was a part of a broader socio-political conflict related to civic campaigns struggling against both the confessional power of the Catholic Church over society and class/patriarchal domination over women's sexuality. After the recognition of their political rights in 1946, Italian women, mostly belonging to trade unions and the communist or socialist parties, had started new campaigns for promoting socio-economic rights and different reproductive policies (Ravera 1979). Work and family were central issues in women's political debates from the 1950s on. By the 1970s, a decade characterized by major change in Italian society in the family and female identity (Caldwell 1991; Ginsborg 1998; Barbagli and Chiaraceno 1997), public debates on specific laws concerning gender relations increased.

The first 'revolution' in Italian family law was legal divorce (*Disciplina nei casi di scioglimento del matrimonio*, law no. 898, 1-12-1970). The struggle over divorce reform emphasized the secular/leftist and Catholic/conservative split in Italian society and stressed the difference between law, morality, and religious belief.[3] The abortion debate also coincided with approval of a general reform of family law in 1975 overturning previous discriminatory articles contained in the civil law of 1942 which were based on the principle of the *patria potestas* (father's authority). The new family law acknowledged equal rights and duties for women and men and the possibility for children born either outside marriage or to parents married to other people to be recognized as legitimate by their biological fathers or mothers.

A third area of reform during this period was the development of family planning. The use of contraceptives became a public issue while the Catholic Church continued to impede it—which it still does. However, in 1975 law no. 405, referring to constitutional Arts 31 and 32, established *consultori familiari* (family consulting centres), reforming the previous National Health Service (Francescato and Prezza 1979). They have four main aims: socio-psychological assistance for women and men, protection of motherhood, family planning, and information about the use of contraceptive methods. For the first time the concept of 'responsible procreation, with respect to ethical convictions and physical integrity of the users' was introduced in the Italian legal system (Calloni 1998). Moreover, the use and propagation of information about contraception were not only allowed but this issue became one of the main tasks of the new health public structures.

The first bill designed to decriminalize therapeutic abortion was submitted to Parliament in 1971 by a socialist MP, Loris Fortuna. The proposal immediately raised constitutional questions since abortion was a crime; and it was submitted to the Constitutional Court for a ruling.[4] However, in 1975, in response to a specific case, the Court declared that Art. 546 of the Rocco Code, which criminalized abortion, was unconstitutional because it did not allow a woman voluntarily to interrupt her pregnancy—that is, to seek an abortion—in cases where the pregnancy would be dangerous, as certified by a doctor, to her health or life (Corte Costituzionale Italiana 1976).

This decision opened the way for advocates of reform to move ahead with proposals for a new abortion law. This new consideration of abortion was helped by changes in the party composition of the Italian Parliament. Of special importance was the increasing power of the Italian Communist Party (PCI), whose moderate leader, Enrico Berlinguer, introduced the idea of a possible *compromesso storico* (historic compromise) in Italy and euro-communism in Europe. In the national election on 20 June 1976, the PCI received 34.4 per cent of the votes, while the Italian Socialist Party (PSI) 9.6 per cent. Sixty-four women—6.7 per cent of the total—were elected to Parliament. The Christian Democrats remained the dominant party, but this new political scenario permitted a pro-reform coalition. Communists, socialists, social democrats, and liberals reached an agreement and unified their different proposals in a single text.

❖ Dominant frame of the debate

Initial discussions of abortion reform were part of a more general process of modernization of social relations, especially concerning the status of women in the family and society. Left-wing and radical parties initiated parliamentary debates, sustained by activists from the newly energized women's movement. Meanwhile the Constitutional Court provided the first official framing of the abortion reform issue. The 1975 ruling confirmed both the legitimacy of therapeutic abortions and the priority of the *diritto alla salute* (right to health) of the mother, who is a born person, over that of the fetus, which has yet to be born. Politicians like Giovanni Berlinguer, doctor and spokesperson in Parliament on behalf of reform, supported the proposal in order to eliminate back-street abortions, reduce inconsistencies in the law, offer social and health assistance to women, and develop new policies for family planning.

❖ Gendering the debate

In Italy the growing debate on abortion was quite similar to what was occurring in other European countries in the 1970s when abortion became a prominent issue on the political agenda of many governments and a cause for mass mobilization. Many considered it to be mainly a political fight against the state and its undemocratic structure. Yet the debate on abortion also permitted the emergence of new female identities, the recognition of the centrality of women as a political subject, and the affirmation of feminism as a public discourse.

Since the inception of the debate on abortion, the actions and strategies of women's movement groups and feminists were mainly aimed at decriminalizing abortion and constructing a women-friendly society against patriarchal culture. Yet many of them did not agree with legislation which was supported and later voted for by radical and left-wing parties. This diversification among feminist collectives became evident during the 1970s.

Rivolta Femminile was the first example of a feminist collective which took a public position on abortion in 1971 (Rivolta Femminile 1971; Lonzi 1974). The Movimento per la Liberazione della Donna (MLD), later related to the Radical

Party and the Fronte Italiano di Liberazione Femminile, connected to the Lega dei Diritti dell'Uomo, initiated their pro-abortion activities in the early 1970s. The Radical Party played a central role in the campaigns, together with the MLD and Rivolta Femminile. At the time the PCI was devoted to more conventional issues connected to the emancipation of women, like education, work, and health, rather than reproductive rights. However, its women's wing—Unione Donne Italiane (UDI) (Ravera 1979)—started a strong debate within the PCI in support the new issues on reproduction (Pieroni Bortolotti 1963, 1978; Frabotta 1975, 1976).

In February 1971 the MLD started its action for decriminalizing abortion and the use of contraceptives. Many lawyers and doctors became activists supporting these campaigns. Women initiated a plan to confess to having had an abortion (Faccio 1975a, b), a tactic which started in France with the *Manifesto* published by the *Nouvel Observateur* in 1971 (Associazione 'Choisir' 1974). Illegal centres, like the Centro Italiano per l'Aborto e la Sterilizzazione, were promoted for helping women, increasing self-help methods (Gruppo Femminista per una Medicina della Donna 1976). Other groups of women started to organize travel abroad for women to countries like Switzerland and Great Britain, where abortion was allowed.

On 22 February 1973 the Collettivo Femminista Milanese based in Via Cherubini 8 published a leaflet demanding the abrogation of all punitive laws against abortion and the creation of an autonomous women's organization. This document was crucial because it signified the beginning of the radical critique of traditional left-wing parties by feminists and extra-parliamentary groups like Lotta Continua, Il Manifesto (Rossanda 1978) and Potere Operaio. Meanwhile Lotta Femminile (Feminine Struggle) changed its name to Lotta Femminista (Feminist Struggle) and the numbers of new feminist collectives grew exponentially in many cities, in both north and south Italy.

As reconstructed by the Libreria delle Donne di Milano in 1987, 'the *autocoscienza* groups had very valid reasons for keeping their distance from the Radical Party mobilization ... When we talked about abortion among ourselves, we discovered how varied experiences were, depending on our different social locations' (Milan Women's Bookstore Collective 1990: 61). The legalization of abortion was considered another way for patriarchal society to dominate once again the body of women, as stressed by the feminist magazine *Sottosopra*. The proposal was for an abandonment of a 'sexual culture, which legitimizes the existing procreative structure'. 'Abortion is any solution for a free woman', because 'woman continued to be colonized by the patriarchal system' (Chinese *et al.* 1977: 122).

❖ Policy outcome

Seven years after the beginning of the feminist debate, there were divisions over abortion policy among feminists, political parties, and even Catholic groups. Finally, in January 1977, with the support of the centre and left-wing parties, the Chamber of Deputies approved a reform bill. However, it had to be approved also by the Senate, a chamber with similar multiparty representation. The divisions among protagonists continued. Leaders of the UDI, the PCI's women's organization, began to mobilize in support of the bill in the Senate. They were joined by feminists in the Radical Party and Democrazia Proletaria despite their doubts about the proposal. On the other side, pro-life and Catholic doctors, lawyers (Unione Giuristi Cattolici Italiani 1975), and activists of Comunione e Liberazione and Movimento per la Vita (MpV) (Pirovano 1981) reinforced their campaigns. Not all Catholics opposed the bill, many supporting women's freedom to choose (Gozzini 1978). The situation on the street became very tense, and police intervened in demonstrations on many occasions. In the Senate, female politicians played a fundamental role in working for a 'quick approval of the law' and overcoming the parliamentary obstructionism of both Catholic Democrats and the neo-Fascist party (Movimento Sociale Italiano). The Senate rejected the first bill and the reformers had to start again with a new text in the Chamber and submit it to the Senate. The struggle continued for another year. After many consultations and compromises, a law on IVG finally passed on 22 May 1978.

The 1978 law did not remove abortion from the criminal code, but it did establish a number of conditions under which legal abortions were permitted:

> A woman can be administered a voluntary interruption of pregnancy by the first 90 days of her pregnancy, when circumstances can prevent the continuation of her pregnancy, birth, mothering/motherhood and put in serious danger her physical or mental health, in relation to her health state, economical/ social/ family conditions, circumstances in which the conception has happened, expectations of anomalies or malformations by the conceived. The woman can turn to a public consulting structure, a socio-medical structure, fully licensed by a region, or to a physician in attendance. (Art. 4, law no. 194)

There is a conscience provision giving doctors opposed to performing abortion the right to decline to participate (Martini and Dell'Osso 1979). Due to the fact that abortion was 'limited' once again by a law, some autonomous feminists and the Radical Party demanded national referendums in 1975–8 to repeal the articles (nos 546, 547, 548, 549.2, 550, 551, 552, 553, 554, 555) criminalizing abortion. Yet this request was not considered valid by the Ufficio Centrale per il Referendum (ordinance 26-5-1978) because of the existence of the law no. 194 which allowed abortion under specific constitutional restrictions.

❖ MARINA CALLONI

❖ Women's movement impact

Eight years after the beginning of feminist claims, institutional quarrels, and mass mobilization, the first phase of the abortion debate came successfully at an end, thanks to the support of left-wing political parties, women's movements, and a sector of civil society. In this case the women's movement was successful through its public mobilization and influence on parliamentary debates. Members of the women's movements—the leftists and the autonomous movements—worked closely with reform supporters in Parliament as well as providing a background of grass-roots support through street demonstrations. Women, as individuals, in parties, and in feminist groups, were active in the debate and were accepted by the political parties as legitimate participants on the abortion issue. This was facilitated by the fact that the abortion reform issue was defined as a question of women's health and psycho-physical integrity.

The policy outcome placed abortion reform among the new policies adopted in the 1970s regarding women's health and social issues. Yet the result—the achievement of a parliamentary statute—did not realise the aim of the radical wing of the autonomous feminist movement. On the one hand, it wanted the total decriminalization of abortion, while on the other it did not recognize the legitimacy of a law seen as a 'political—and patriarchal—compromise'. Recognizing that while the abortion reform was an improvement over the 1930 punitive law coinciding with demands of sectors of the movement, it did not achieve the goals of many radical and separatist feminists to liberate women completely from state control. For these reasons this first debate is classified as a *dual response.*

❖ Women's movement characteristics

The abortion debate of the 1970s coincided with the emergence and growth of the women's movement in Italy. A dominant feature of the movement in this period was the split between activists in political parties and trade unions on the one hand and autonomous feminists in various collectives on the other. The party movement was very close to the left while the autonomous groups were openly critical and separate. Abortion was a high-priority issue for both wings, but for different reasons. The Marxist approach to the class struggle was radicalized through the critique of a patriarchal society and male domination (Spagnoletti 1978). Autonomous feminist groups radicalized the issue of self-determination starting from the praxis of *autocoscienza,* the affirmation of sexual freedom and the necessity for self-control of reproduction (Bono and Kemp 1991). The 'repossession' of the body became the basis for a new female subjectivity and the discovery of the 'unconscious'. Thus there were many splits in feminist groups, who agreed only on the necessity to decriminalize abortion while they disagreed among themselves about many other issues, beginning with the possibility of promoting a liberal law in Parliament. Thus the cohesion of the movements on the abortion issue was sorely tested (Ergas 1992, 1996). Activists faced solid Christian Democratic institutional opposition but a relatively weak grass-roots counter-movement.

❖ Policy environment

The policy-making sub-system in this first debate was moderately closed. It was based on strict party organization, yet insider activists were supported by free agents, like feminists and members of social groups, to reach the common aim of the abortion campaigns. In this way, the abortion debate altered the previous institutional structure of parliamentary organizations, and new links between political parties and social movements became crucial to the policy-making process.

Giulio Andreotti was the Prime Minister leading his fourth government in the VII Legislature (1976–9), composed only of Christian Democrat MPs, with left-wing parties in the opposition. New forms of coalitions among different parties were needed for reaching a majority in the Chamber of Deputies as well as in the Senate to approve the law, creating a sort of sub-system. At this time women's representatives were not strong enough to lead this struggle on their own, so that the parliamentary debates were conducted mainly by male MPs. Left-wing parties' networks supported specific requests of the feminist movement regarding the liberalization of abortion. Yet, with the exception of the Radical Party, they rejected radical versions and searched for an 'acceptable' compromise. Leftists, especially the PCI, were criticized by many of their activists because of their too centralized and hierarchical structure. However, at the end of the debate the common goal was obtained.

❖ DEBATE 2: POPULAR REFERENDUM TO REPEAL LEGAL ABORTION, 1980–1981

❖ How the debate came to the public agenda

The second debate involves the attempt by pro-life forces (Liverani 1979; Lombardi Valluari 1976) to abrogate the abortion law by means of a referendum.[5] The approval of law no. 194 in 1978 did not bridge the deep social divisions over abortion. On the contrary, the law left much discontent and many seemingly unresolvable questions. Based on proposals from the Catholics and the Radicals, the 1981 referendums offered voters the opportunity both to restrict and to liberalize the law. This section focuses on the proposal to restrict the law because this was by far the more important debate for the women's movement (Damiani and Graziosi 1981).

❖ MARINA CALLONI

In the *Libro bianco sull'aborto* (White Book on Abortion), published in 1977, Christian Democrats in the Chamber of Deputies called abortion a 'tragedy for the Italian conscience'. This book (Gruppo Democratico Cristiano alla Camera dei Deputati 1977) collected all documents related to parliamentary debates in Legislatures VI (1972–6) and VII (1976–9) on abortion, reporting the reactions and speeches of interested MPs. These documents confirm how parliamentary debates reflected the increasing tension between the state, the government, and civil society. As soon as constitutionally permitted, those groups unhappy with the 1978 abortion reform proposed nullifying referendums to change it. By 1980 there were seven different referendum requests: four by the Radical Party (Passeri and Pergameno 1981) to remove restrictions and three by the Christian Democrats in collaboration with the pro-life movement to prevent the institutionalization of a system of legal abortion.[6]

The maximal proposal was intended to completely erase the law while the minimal proposal was intended modify it in a restrictive way. The contents of these proposals were similar in their reference to the protection of the unborn (Busnelli 1988), defined as human life since its conception. The Constitutional Court rejected the maximal proposal presented by the MpV (sentence no. 26, 10 February 1981) because it would have meant the total abrogation of law no. 194, which had been previously judged as constitutionally sound and legally enacted. Therefore, only the minimal proposal aimed at reducing the impact of the law was submitted to the voters. It would reject the principle of the women's self-determination and permit abortion only for therapeutic reasons, giving the physician the power to make the decision.

❖ Dominant frame of the debate

At the end of the first debate, the frame of the abortion issue was gendered, based on the notion of women's prior needs. According to this frame, abortion law should place a woman's life and health before that of the fetus, and the state had to be involved by providing information, social services, and assistance to women. Once the law was enacted, providing abortion services became a legitimate responsibility of the state. In presenting their referendum proposal, the Christian Democrats and their pro-life allies sought to change the frame of the debate by advancing the interests of the fetus and countering the view that assisting women to obtain abortions was a legitimate state function. Their position was that the fetus is a person who must be protected.

Pro-life Catholics launched a major campaign to convince people to vote affirmatively for restricting the law. Against these campaigns, those parties which had sponsored the 1978 law—in particular Socialists, Communists, and Liberals—and sectors of the women's movement organized initiatives for defeating the referendums. This was necessary despite their fear that, after the years of exhausting debates and negotiations that preceded the 1978 law, the hard-won compromise would be thrown aside by a new conflict on this hot topic in Italian civil and political society.

❖ Gendering the debate

Their success in 1978 meant that advocates for women had to shift their use of gender topics from seeking to change a law by gendering an ungendered debate to using gender to defend an existing law. This task was made even more difficult because of the split between the movement and a section of radical feminists who supported another referendum to achieve total decriminalization of abortion. Since the pro-life referendum involved all citizens qualified to vote, the main strategies of women activists were directed toward persuading public opinion to vote 'no'. They organized a strong mass mobilization on various fronts in the public arena. The separatist wing of feminism maintained its distance from the institutional process of referendums, continuing to be critical of the law as a whole. In general, however, the women's movement found new energy for representing the public defence of the abortion law as a gender issue and the fruit of women's struggles (De Musso and Pasotti 1989).

❖ Policy outcome

Seventy-nine per cent of qualified electors voted on 17 and 18 May 1981, resulting in a defeat for all referendums. The defeat was crushing for the pro-life Catholics: more than 60 per cent voted against, with 32 per cent in favour and 7.7 per cent blank or invalid votes.[7] Thus, the Italian electorate confirmed the legitimacy of legal abortion and law no. 194 remained in force. Abortion would be covered by national insurance but, first, new health services and family planning centres had to be constructed. The positive outcome, arising from the negative results of the referendums, illustrated the necessity to reinforce welfare services in all Italian regions—the difference between northern and southern Italy was quite strong also regarding family planning.

The debate and the outcome of the referendums revealed the increasing polarization in Italian society and a decisive transformation in the Catholic movement and party. Many Catholics now had to admit the reality of a new society and female identity. Christian Democracy was the majority party in power, but it was forced to apply a legitimate law it bitterly opposed. The pro-abortion vote was evidence of the growing political and cultural opposition to the Christian Democratic political hegemony that had prevailed since 1948.

After two defeats—the approval of the law and the failure of the referendum—Catholics realized that they had to reframe their approach to changing Italian society by reconceptualizing the theory and strategy based upon the 'culture of human life' (Casini and Quarenghi 1981; Palo 1977; Traverso; Galli 1978).

❖ MARINA CALLONI

Consequently some theological assumptions were redefined in the shift from the pontificate of Paul VI, who wrote the encyclical *Humanae Vitae* in 1968 (Paolo VI 1968), to that of John Paul II, who initiated a persistent campaign against abortion using a new language: 'absolute respect of human life from its conception' (Caprile 1981). This new theological, communicative, and cultural transformation also reflected the fact that there was no longer a general agreement even among Catholics about divorce, abortion, and the family (Zarri 1981), so that new strategies were needed for recomposing the Catholic doctrine. Therefore, while feminist/women's movements continued their usual action in support of abortion, the Catholic Church was reframing its cultural strategies for fighting legal abortion (Congregazione per la Dottrina della Fede 1974, 1987; Fiori and Sgreggia 1975).

❖ Movement impact

The end of the debate coincided with the goals of the activists who supported the new pro-abortion law campaign. The policy outcome of the referendum concerned not only the protection of the abortion law but mainly the perspective of increasing social services connected to health and gender issues. Indeed, the results of the referendum stressed indirectly not only the legitimacy of the law but mainly the necessity to apply it, following its directives. Campaigns against the referendums became in fact for women occasions for discussing the necessity to implement the existing law. The women's movement activists felt stronger after this confirmation by the public acceptance of a topical gendered issue aimed at increasing socio-economic rights. Women also participated actively in the referendum debate. The movement showed its ability to mobilize people and resources to overcome the pro-life campaigns of MpV. Thus, as a result of the debate on the pro-life referendum, the movement achieved a dual response from the state.

The debate also meant the establishment of a new socio-political force in opposition to legal abortion. Therefore, the law had to be defended. The liberalization of laws on divorce, family law, contraception, and abortion did not have the catastrophic effect on Italian society foretold by the opponents of these measures (Sanna 1989). And although the counter-movement had lost the referendum campaign, it had been successful in changing the frame of the debate on abortion in Italy by introducing the very powerful slogan: 'protection of human life since the conception'. The women's movement would ultimately have to face this new challenge.

❖ Women's movement characteristics

During the second debate, both women's movements—socialist/communist and radical/separatist—were in the growth stage. They were successful in the face of a strong and cohesive counter-movement with roots in the dominant Christian Democratic Party and Catholic Church. The non-autonomous wing remained closely allied with left-wing parties and made the defeat of the pro-life referendum a top priority. This campaign, however, was the last political action of Italian feminism as a mass movement in coalition with left-wing parties. While this referendum campaign demonstrated the increasing capacity of women for public mobilization, at the same time it marked a change in the politics of mass feminism. Indeed, after this referendum the women's movement disappeared from the *piazze* (Valentini 1997), that is, from the public arena, for years.

After 1981, differentiation among women according to their beliefs, practices, theories, and political engagement became more and more evident and relevant. Many radical feminists left the debate disappointed at the 'bad compromise' that, for them, codified the state's control over the female body and denied women's self-determination and individual freedom. Feminists, such as Libreria delle Donne di Milano and Diotima collectives, started to elaborate theories and practices within closed, separated, and restricted groups, so that a distinction between 'thought and life' (Rossi-Doria 1996) became quite visible. The ambivalence and tensions developed within women's movements between a defence of the law and its critique (Peretti and Socrate 1988) characterized the 1980s.

❖ *Policy environment*

The policy sub-system connected with referendums was open to widespread participation. Other than the need to gain approval from the Constitutional Court, social movements were free to express their policy goals, promoting activities and mobilizing people to prohibit abortion on behalf of the unborn, to defend the law, or to decriminalize abortion altogether. At the time of the abortion referendum (17 May 1981), Arnaldo Forlani, a Christian Democrat MP, was the prime minister, leading a coalition with the PSI, the Italian Social Democratic Party, and the Republican Party (VIII Legislature); these parties were promoters and defenders of the abortion law. At that time the political situation was very tense due to the increase in both right-wing and left-wing terrorism, political scandals, and corruption—as in the case of the Masonic secret lodge P2—and the attempt against the life of Pope John Paul II in May 1981.

❖ DEBATE 3: IN-VITRO FERTILIZATION AND ABORTION: 1996–1999

❖ *How the debate came to the public agenda*

In the 20 years following the legalization of abortion, there was a decline in both legal and illegal abortions performed in Italy. Rates of legal abortion fell from

❖ MARINA CALLONI

15.9 per cent per 1,000 Italian women in 1980 to 9.3 per cent in 1998 (ISTAT 2000). Back-street abortions, while still performed, are much reduced as well.[8] Yet also the national birth rate is dramatically decreasing: 1.2 per cent, the lowest in the world with Spain (Delgado and Livi-Bacci 1992; Sabbadini 1998) and the use of contraceptives is not increasing (Barazzetti and Leccardi 2000).

Divisions over abortion and social modernization revealed by the 1970s debates persisted into the 1990s. Pro-life parties have incessantly promoted parliamentary bills for a radical transformation of law no. 194 and Catholic doctors in some cases have tried to obstacle the application of the low in public hospitals (Salemi 1989). Their arguments were reinforced by Pope John Paul II's theological message (Magli 1995) aiming at the absolute protection of the human life from conception, as asserted also in encyclicals like the *Evaneglium Vitae* about the value and inviolability of human life (Giovanni Paolo II 1995). The challenges to Catholic doctrine presented by dramatic increases in medically assisted reproduction, specifically in-vitro fertilization (IVF), provided addition evidence to the pro-life forces that the government needed to take action. As well, it was due to the moral-political debate relating to the necessity to regulate IVF processes.

Unlike the debate on abortion, which started in the civil society and was later taken up in parliament, the debate on IVF began with a government bill and later became a controversial issue for public opinion. A Bill concerning *Norme sull'inseminazione artificiale, la fecondazione in vitro e il trasferimento di gameti ed embrioni* (Norms about artificial insemination, in vitro fertilization and transferring of gametes and embryos) (no. C.1560) was announced in Parliament on 20 June 1996. Abortion opponents found the occasion an opportunity to push back the liberal abortion law. Women's organizations moved to protect women's rights. The familiar battled was waged in very new political territory. With the demise of the polarization between Communists and Christian Democrats under the change of ideologies and the growing scandal of corruption and ineptitude, all 'old' parties transformed their previous names, composition, and political alliances. Christians from the former DC split into several smaller often conflicting parties (PPI, UDEUR, CCD). While PPI and UDEUR joined a centre-left coalition called *Ulivo* (Olive Tree), CCD allied with the renamed right-wing Alleanza Nazionale, conservative (Forza Italia, led by Silvio Berlusconi) and separatist (Lega Nord per l'Indipendenza della Padania) parties, constituting a coalition called *Polo* before and *Casa delle Libertà* (House of the Liberties) later.

The front in favour of maintaining a liberal law on IVG and approving tolerant legislation on IVF was composed of Democratici di Sinistra (part of the former PCI), Verdi (Greens), Partito dei Comunisti Italiani, Rifondazione Comunista, and a part of the '*gruppo misto*', a mixed parliamentary grouping of liberals, socialists, republicans, and so on.

❖ Dominant frame of the debate

The 1981 referendum had established a gendered frame for the abortion issue. However, one of the goals of the pro-life forces was to replace that definition with an exclusive focus on the fetus. Once abortion was raised in the context of the IVF controversy, they posed the moral question of the life of embryos inside and outside the womb. While in the past the dispute between the Catholic Church, conservatives, the pro-choice movement, left-wing groups, and feminists concerned differences over questions of liberation and sexuality, in the 1990s the clash concerned control of the 'reproduction of life' (D'Orazio 1989; Rodotà 1993, 1995). The development of research in genetics, promotion of biotechnologies, discussions on bioethics, discoveries in embryology, and the possibility of maintaining the life of a fetus of five to six months also raised questions regarding the role of doctors and their potential to eliminate or select embryos.

Debate over the new parliamentary issue of abortion/IVF came to the floor of the Chamber of Deputies during the XIII Legislature. The prime minister was Romano Prodi (17 May 1996–9 October 1998), leader of the centre-left coalition Ulivo. In March 1997 Marida Bolognesi, an MP belonging to the Democratici di Sinistra-Ulivo, was nominated speaker and chairwoman of the Commission XII, whose task was to prepare a bill to be discussed and approved by the Chamber of Deputies. This process did not run smoothly. Eventually, Bolognesi resigned because the majority of the Chamber of Deputies approved an article of the bill which neglected the *fecondazione eterologa*, which meant that only gametes belonging to married couples could be used for IVF. Hon. Alessandro Cé, a Lega Nord MP, replaced Bolognesi. This created a radical shift in the composition of the Commission from a female pro-abortion speaker in favour of a liberal IVF law to a male pro-life conservative speaker in favour of restrictions. The result was approval on 26 May 1999 by the Chamber of Deputies of a very restrictive IVF law by 266 votes to 153 with 28 abstentions. Not only did the law restrict use of embryos; it allowed the possibility of adopting them. The debate was much more contentious in the Senate, which failed to agree on any final approval.

❖ Gendering the debate

This shift in the public debate toward emphasis on embryos and fetuses brought about a change in feminist discussions. Their challenge was to re-gender the frame of the abortion debate to restore the situation of women in the discourse. Feminists and female left-wing MPs underlined once again the necessity for women both to protect their rights and to struggle against restrictions regarding human reproduction. After many years, feminist demonstrations were back, events for reaffirming that woman has the right to 'the first word and the last word' regarding her reproductive decisions and life.

❖ MARINA CALLONI

At the political level women activists tried to construct a common platform for preventing a restrictive law on IVF, for avoiding the approval of any amendments which would threaten the 1978 law, and for protecting its fair application. The dispute on a restrictive law about *riproduzione medicalmente assistita* gave a new impulse to feminist debates. While in the 1980s women seemed unable to reconstitute a mass movement, in the 1990s they used new issues to try to find common strategies and language. They wrote new proposals for definitively removing abortion altogether from the penal code (Boccia 1993; 1995; Chiaromonte *et al.* 1993; Ferrajoli 1976, 1999; Pitch 1998), indicating the ambiguities of law no. 194 (Tatafiore and Tozzi 1989; D'Elia 1996) and/or criticizing radically liberal laws on abortion and reproduction at all (Diotima 1987; 1995; Cavarero 1990). A concept of *diritto sessuato* (gendered law) was also theorized (Democrazia e Diritto 1993; 1996).

After the approval by the Chamber of Deputies of the law on IVF, the participation of women in the abortion debate concerned also the publication of several documents and appeals (Il Foglio del Paese delle Donne 1999). These new campaigns aimed at opposing the 'new patriarchal' intention 'to dominate once again the female body and to control all reproductive processes' (Associazione Orlando 1999). Activists reaffirmed that freedom of procreation should not be arbitrarily restricted by law. For this reason the document mentioned above affirms: 'No to the law! No to any reductive and restrictive revision of the law no. 194'.

❖ Policy outcome

At the beginning, the IVF bill concerned only the regulation of centres devoted to IVF and the protection of the health of patients. During the legislative debate, the bill changed from being a technical proposal to a proposition for a restrictive law with an ethical character. In fact, it had to concern only married people or '*coppie di fatto*'—stable couples living as husband and wife—medically certified infertility, adoptability of frozen embryos, the protection of the unborn (Art. 1), the moral limits of science, and the centrality of the family.

Through the debate the frame changed due to approval of amendments extraneous to the original project. Indeed, the main intent became not only an ethical restriction on IVF but also a strong attack against the abortion law. The opponents of abortion included some women who were part of the governing Olive Tree coalition. Such was case with Irene Pivetti, a Catholic, former President of the Chamber of Deputies under the Berlusconi Government, while a member of the Lega Nord; she became later president of the UDEUR, part of the former DC, which supported the centre-left coalition. During session no. 542 on 26 May 1999, Irene Pivetti proposed an amendment to deny the right to abort a fetus produced by IVF for ethical reasons. Yet this amendment was defeated for two main

198

reasons: first, it was extraneous to the topic under discussion, that is, IVF; second, it implicitly abrogated law no. 194 and therefore was not constitutionally admissible.[9] This indirect attack against law no. 194 was unsuccessful and therefore 194 remained in force. Still, the outcome of the debate on IVF was mixed. Although the effort to restrict abortion failed, approval of such a restrictive law by the Chamber of Deputies indicated the presence of a pro-life majority.

❖ *Women's movement impact*

As a result of this third debate, the state and its institutions, that is, the centre-left government, continued to implement the 1978 abortion law. However, due to a complex and ambivalent dialectic between state, government, Parliament, and the women's movement over IVF and IVG, it is difficult to classify the debate according to the categories of movement impact. Nevertheless, if we consider only the debate on abortion—specifically, the limits on abortion proposed within the regulatory scheme for IVF—then the outcome does coincide with long-standing movement goals to defend the law while proposing more reforms. However, given the remoteness of movement activists from the debate on IVF and abortion in parliament, there is little evidence that, when abortion was on the agenda, women as individuals, groups, or formal organizations were accepted as legitimate spokespersons on the issue. Thus, this case is classified as pre-emption.

❖ *Women's policy agency activities*

At the time of the third debate there were three women's policy agencies at the national level in Italy. The members of the Commission for Equal Opportunities are appointed by the prime minister for a five-year term. The Commission is charged with furthering equality and equal opportunities between women and men and is cross-sectional. The Equal Status Committee specializes in equality issues at work and is located within the Ministry of Labour. Both agencies were established in the 1980s. In 1996, the prime minister established a Ministry for Equal Opportunities, in compliance with the UN Platform for Action adopted at the 1995 Beijing Conference. Hon. Anna Finocchiaro, a lawyer by training and a feminist, was appointed for the first time as a secretary of state.

In 1999, Prime Minister Massimo D'Alema, former speaker of the PCI, appointed Laura Balbo, professor of sociology, former MP and feminist, as Secretary for Equal Opportunities, one of seven women secretaries of state in the D'Alema Government: Interior, Health, Culture, Regional Affairs, Social Affairs, and European Policies. The parliamentary debates on IVF took place when two centre-left governments were in power, the Ministry for Equal Opportunities was established, and femocrats started to be involved in the design of gender-oriented policies.

❖ MARINA CALLONI

Under both Anna Finocchiaro and Laura Balbo, the Ministry took a stand in defence of the abortion law. On the other hand, the Commission for Equal Opportunities, headed by former Christian Democrat Hon. Silvia Costa, did not express public support for either abortion or IVF. In fact, however, both gender-oriented institutions were more interested in the elaboration of broader gender policies, developing international directives, and organizing awareness campaigns. They introduced some new gender issues in the public arena, aimed at stressing and bringing on to the political agenda questions and concepts belonging to women's experiences and the history of Italian feminism (Ingrao and Peretti 1998) in the light of international debates regarding women's rights, empowerment, and mainstreaming. Therefore, the two secretaries of state at the Ministry for Equal Opportunities supported the two main cores of the feminist tradition: on the one hand the theory of *sexual difference*, conceived as the basic distinction between women and men, as theorized by the political and radical feminism of the 80s; on the other the theory of *double presence*, which means the possibility of combining work and family, according to a conception of equality, as traditionally supported by the left.

Women's policy agencies did not, however, promote a women's coalition in Parliament to oppose new gender restrictive laws. These agencies played a *marginal* role in the debate on IVF.

❖ Women's movement characteristics

The characteristics of the women's movement at time of the debate on IVF were quite different from those during the previous controversies on abortion in Italy. Indeed, a strong autonomous feminist movement no longer existed. Although feminists organized demonstrations, they had lost their capacity to mobilize public support. Rather, the movement was at the consolidation stage as, with increases in the number of women secretaries of state, femocrats, and feminist advisers, gender issues and concepts became part of the state.

Abortion was no longer a priority issue. Yet one thing had not changed: women's organizations and feminist groups were split again between a radical critique and a strong defence of the law on abortion, and the non-radicals were close to the left-wing parties. The influence of the women's movement was limited to the defence of an existing law; it did not extend to blocking a new restrictive pro-life law on assisted procreation. The main reason was the strong counter-movement led by a cross-parties alliance between Catholics—some of whom were member of the coalition in government—and conservatives in the Chamber of Deputies. In the debate on abortion and IVF, the pro-life groups were composed of Catholics and conservatives belonging to both opposition and government parties.

❖ *Policy environment*

The policy sub-system in Parliament was closed and left-wing/feminist public opinion was unable to change the strategies of the pro-life majority in the Chamber of Deputies. As mentioned above, due to political scandals connected to public corruption which characterized Italian society in the early 1990s, the political environment and parties' composition changed dramatically in this decade. A government led by Silvio Berlusconi from 10 May 1994 to 22 December 1994 in the XII Legislature (1994–6) was ousted after a national election by a centre-left coalition, Olive Tree. Romano Prodi became prime minister, serving from 15 May 1996 to 9 October 1998. Yet at the same time the number of female MPs fell in both the Chambers of Deputies and the Senate. They amounted to 9 per cent in 1992; 13.1 per cent in 1994, when a quota system was adopted but later rejected by the Constitutional Court as unconstitutional; and 10.3 per cent in 1996. After a government crisis, Massimo D'Alema became Prime Minister on 21 October 1998, serving until 18 December 1999 (first Cabinet) and from 22 December 1999 until 19 April 2000 (second Cabinet), when he was replaced by Giuliano Amato (25 April 2000–12 May 2001), who belonged also to the Ulivo, because of problems within the Olive Tree coalition.

However, this new political situation—the existence of a centre-left coalition—led to a sort of paradox. In fact, from the mid-1990s gender and family issues found institutional recognition in ministries and commissions, but at the same time the issue of abortion and human reproduction became again a topical public question and was seriously challenged in Parliament. Indeed, the centre-left government included both former communists and Catholics who were pro-life and in favour of strict control over IVF. Therefore, any cultural-moral cohesion was impossible even in the Cabinet.

❖ CONCLUSION

In the 1970s the issue of abortion was related to the struggle against the state which treated abortion as a crime. Therefore, social actors demanded either its decriminalization or a more favourable law. In the 1980s the question concerned a state which allowed abortion but permitted it either in a too restrictive way—as the Radicals and radical feminists argued—or in a too permissive manner—as the pro-life Catholics claimed. Therefore social actors challenged the law and the state from two opposite sides and ideological convictions.

Without any doubt, the debate on abortion in Italy has played a crucial role for decades in changing Italian society, transforming politics and contributing to a new female consciousness. The civic campaigns, the *autocoscienza* groups and the mass mobilization in support of reproductive freedom were a fundamental step in the affirmation of post-conventional women's identity (Pattis

1995). For the first time in the history of the Italian Republic, women developed an original discourse, becoming influential in public campaigns and mass demonstrations, mobilizing public opinion, constituting networks, and forming lobbies. Moreover, women became a pressure group in the public arena, promoting petitions and projects to be discussed by MPs.

In particular, female MPs tried to find among the different groups a common basis for agreement on a law. Yet traditional politics were radically questioned and abortion caused a split among feminist groups. Over the years this fracture provoked both a theoretical and a pragmatic distinction between separatist and anti-institutionalist feminists—against a quota system and equal opportunities—referring to a radical interpretation of the '*teoria della differenza sessuale*' (Muraro 1988; Bono and Kemp, 1991; *Sottosopra* 1983; 1996). Some feminist groups were based on the *autocoscienza* (*Memoria* 1987, 1989; Melchiori 1995; Lapis 1998; Paolozzi and Leiss 1999), while others opted for institutional parties (Ravera 1979) and the *doppia presenza* (Balbo et al. 1983; Beccalli 1984).

However, in the 1980s the conflict over abortion led to a paradox: it helped to build a conscious, strong, and post-conventional 'female identity' but it was not able to reinforce the unity of the women's movement. On the contrary, it was one of the main reasons for the split of the feminist movement into distinct groups. Yet the 1980s are crucial for the development of social policies, which started to take into account the presence, interest, and needs of a 'political gendered subjectivity'.

After the approval of law no. 194, the women's movement, left-wing parties, and feminists became 'reactive' whenever the law was endangered and tried to defend it, as happened with the pro-life referendum in 1981 and the debate for a restrictive IVF law in 1996–9. Italian women still seem to be united in the defence of the abortion law, even though a better implementation of it has been often requested and some limits of it were indicated. However, an 'embryo' of 'state feminism' has emerged since the establishment of a Ministry for Equal Opportunities in 1996 and the engagement of female researchers and activists in many commissions and working groups. This new step of the women's movement has been considered to be a shift from policies based on the 'protection' of women to the 'mainstreaming' politics and policy as stated by law no. 125 (1992) regarding a new meaning of equal opportunities and the introduction of gender issues in decision making and parliamentary bills. At the end of the 1990s formal and informal networks of feminist workers, scholars, politicians, and activists are increasing in number and working together in common, often not-for-profit projects in NGOs, civil society and political institutions.

❖ NOTES

1 The oldest Christian document which explicitly condemns abortion is the *Didaché*, the doctrine of the twelve apostles, probably written in the first century (Sgreggia 1974).

2 The bills from Senate (S) and Chamber of Deputies (C) in this universe are: V Legislature (1968–72): S.754, S.351, C.1313, S2020; VI Legislature (1972–6): S.429, C.3582, C.2893, C.646, C.1655, C.3435, C.3651, C.3654, C.3661; VII Legislature (1976–9): Law no. 194; VIII Legislature (1979–86): C.0570, C.0627, C.0905, C.2351; IX Legislature (1986–7).

3 After the approval of Parliament, the law on divorce came into force on 1 December 1970. The DC immediately started a campaign against this law, organizing a referendum for its repeal on 12 May 1974. On this occasion, many of the demonstrations were organized by women, whose socio-political influence also in mass mobilization was increasing. The DC referendum was unsuccessful: 40.74% voted against divorce, while 59.26% voted for maintaining the law. It was the first political and cultural defeat for Catholics in Italy, even though some left-wing Christians, like those associated with the Florentine magazine *Testimonianze*, affirmed that divorce was 'a matter of individual conscience and responsibility'. As well, evangelical/Protestant minorities in Italy have supported over the years the law on abortion and the principle of the self-determination for women, also in the case of IVF. See Gruppo di Lavoro sui Problemi Etici posti dalla Scienza (1996).

4 No bill can be considered by Parliament unless it is constitutional. The role of the Constitutional Court, composed of 15 judges, is thus to consider the constitutionality validity of a bill. As well as resolving institutional conflicts, the Constitutional Court must intervene when a judge believes that in a trial, as indicated by an interested solicitor or barrister, a juridical norm contravenes a constitutional principle. In such cases the trial is deferred until the Constitutional Court has given a judgement.

5 Article 75 of the Italian Constitution permits popular referendums whereby people can give direct expression of their will about a specific law after its approval and implementation. A referendum can nullify an existing law; it cannot be used to create a new law. A petition for a referendum must be signed by at least 500,000 eligible voters. Their signatures are checked prior by the Corte di Cassazione (Cassation Court). If they are in order, then the Constitutional Court judges the validity of the petition, determining whether or not it is permitted by the constitution. Referendums for repealing fiscal and budget laws, amnesties, and international treaties are not allowed. The results of the referendums are considered valid only if a majority plus one of eligible voters has cast votes. The question takes the form: 'Do you want the law X to be abrogated?' If a majority of voters votes 'yes', the law is annulled. Otherwise the existing law remains in force.

6 The pro-life proposals were: (1) request for a referendum by the MpV, founded in 1977, 'minimal' proposal' (*Gazzetta Ufficiale* 1981); (2) request for a referendum by the MpV, 'maximal' proposal; and (3) request for a referendum by the Alleanza per la Vita.

7 The defeat was even worse for the Radicals: 88.4% voted no, with only 11% in favour.

8 Seventy per cent of illegal abortions are performed in southern Italy due to cultural prejudices and lack of social services, and 20% by teenagers. The main reasons why these

women do not turn to public health structure are: 34% do not know about the existence of a liberal law; 41% do not want to endure the long wait to have an abortion in hospital; and 27% prefer to remain anonymous (ISTAT 2000). As well, there is a new phenomenon due to increasing human mobility, namely, the increase in the number of illegal abortions performed by migrant women, who often do not have regular residence permits: in 1980 there were 4,500, while in 1998 there were an estimated 20,480. Along with the persistence of back-street abortions, these rates suggest that legal abortion is regarded as legitimate by the majority of citizens.

9 Legal abortion was considered by the Constitutional Court to be compatible with constitutional principles. Therefore, another law could not prohibit it unless the Court issued a new ruling.

10 ❖ Policy-Making on Abortion: Arenas, Actors, and Arguments in the Netherlands

Joyce Outshoorn

❖ INTRODUCTION

In 1966, in a letter to the editor of a progressive magazine on the emerging debate on abortion in the Netherlands, a young woman academic complained that all kinds of opinions were being expressed except those of the women concerned: 'if ever a woman is being regarded as a voiceless being instead of an autonomous individual, it is in this area ... Legalize abortion ... but in all cases the central criterion should be the explicit wish of the woman concerned' (Smit 1966: 720–1). The correspondent was Joke Smit, soon one of the founders and leaders of the emerging women's movement. She was the first to argue for law reform to provide abortion on demand. At the time, other opinion leaders were still wondering whether there should be any legal reform at all of the 1911 statute.

This statute, which allowed abortion only if a woman's life was endangered by her pregnancy, was one of the 1911 Morality Acts, which also outlawed contraception, brothels, and homosexuality. It was the result of a campaign by doctors and religious leaders who believed abortion was on the increase and that the older statute of 1886 contained too many loopholes. The 1911 Morality Acts symbolized the new-found majority of the religious parties in Parliament in the early years of the twentieth century.

Smit's call for reform was soon joined by others, and by 1970 the abortion issue had become one of the most topical issues in national politics. This remained so till 1984, when the Abortion Act of 1981 was finally implemented, allowing abortion more or less on demand.[1] The 1981 act has managed to pacify the abortion issue; none of the politicians from any of the major parties has made any serious attempt to reopen the issue since then and public opinion on the whole has been supportive of its content.[2] Elsewhere I have analyzed this successful resolution and explained why the issue proved so intractable: this can be attributed to the dominant definition of the issue in terms of power and to the particularities of the party system (Outshoorn 1986a, b).[3]

The re-emergence of the abortion issue in the Netherlands more or less coincided with the re-emergence of the women's movement. Both had their roots in the profound social and cultural changes of the period, and the movement put abortion on demand at the top of its agenda. It argued that the woman herself was the best authority on whether or not she should have an abortion. This framing made abortion a lay affair, taking issue with rival framings in terms of morals or medical and psychiatric pathology. Abortion came to be defined in terms of control—who has the power over the decision: the woman or not?

At first, both cabinet and Parliament tried to ward off the issue by maintaining it was a legal and medical problem, preferring to leave it to the legal experts to find ways around the old statute and to doctors to develop criteria to filter requests for abortions. However, in 1970 the cabinet acknowledged its responsibility by appointing a special commission, Commissie Kloosterman, to study the issue: a classic delaying tactic. Its deliberations lasted two years and it failed to achieve consensus. Meanwhile an alliance of progressive doctors, sexual reformers, and feminist women found allies among the Social Democrat parliamentary party, which was in opposition at the time. When, in that same year, two of its members, Lamberts and Roethof, launched a private member's bill in Parliament to allow for abortion on demand, the parties making up the cabinet could no longer ignore the issue. During the same period a liberal interpretation of the 1911 statute by a leading legal scholar, Enschede (1966), encouraged hospitals, on an experimental basis, to allow therapeutic abortion using so-called abortion teams consisting of doctors and psychiatrists. By 1971, however, it was evident these efforts could not meet the demand for abortion or provide precise or equitable criteria for allowing it. Moreover, the first groups of the women's movement had put forward the demand for legalization and turned it into a highly publicized issue. When, despite the law, progressive doctors started a chain of private clinics allowing abortion on demand, it was evident that a decision about law reform was inevitable, and cabinets could no longer resort to the politics of delay. It was time for a cabinet proposal, but, as we shall see, this was no simple matter.

❖ SELECTION OF DEBATES

In the Netherlands abortion law is in the Penal Code, and changing the code always requires a parliamentary act. This made Parliament and the cabinet, which submits the overwhelming majority of bills to the Second Chamber—the lower house—of parliament, the primary policy-making arena for abortion law reform, the first chamber being mainly a house of review. Private member bills are quite unusual. The Netherlands has a multi-party system, in which no one party has a majority by itself; coalition government is therefore inevitable in order to obtain a parliamentary majority. The leadership of the coalition partners draws up the pact for each new cabinet, which determines the political agenda to a very large extent for the next four years. Party discipline is strict in order to maintain the pact, and only on matters of individual conscience is it relaxed. Forming a cabinet is no simple matter as the party system is based on two cleavages—a socio-economic divide and a religious-secular divide—which have to be accommodated. This process usually takes weeks or even months to succeed. Until 1994, in practice coalition governments always involved the three major religious parties, which since 1977 have been united in one party—the Christian Democrat Appeal (CDA)—ruling with either the Liberals or the Social Democrats as partners.

Debates in the parliamentary arena started in 1967 with MPs posing questions about reform, and lasted until the settlement of 1984. From 1971, the issue haunted all the negotiations of coalition pacts because, defined as a moral problem, it cut across the socio-economic divide which usually determines the outcome of the coalition formation. Since the abortion issue touched on the religious divide, it meant that the Christian Democrats could veto reform even if their coalition partner was in favour. On several occasions the issue endangered the life of incumbent cabinets.

Policy-making on the abortion issue predates the establishment of women's policy agencies in the Netherlands. Well before the first national women's policy agency, the Directie Coordinatie Emancipatie (DCE, Directorate for the Coordination of Equality Policy) was established in 1978, the issue was already on the agenda, hotly debated and framed in a feminist way (Outshoorn 1995). If one were to select only debates after the agency was in existence, one would not do justice to the also required representativeness of the range and saliency of debates. It would also be hard to understand how the successful framing of the issue by the women's movement came about in the first place. Therefore it is necessary to consider all debates in Parliament from the time the issue of reform came to the public agenda.

Thus, the universe of debates on abortion in the Netherlands comprises all those which led to some kind of official output over the whole period from the first call for reform to the present. Using these criteria produces a list of nine policy debates:

(1) the establishment of the Commission Kloosterman to advise the cabinet on abortion policy, 1967–70;
(2) Stuyt/Van Agt cabinet proposal for limited reform, 1971–2;
(3) Cabinet pact to stop enforcement of 1911 law and leave matter to parliamentary initiative, 1973;

(4) parliamentary debate on closing of an abortion clinic performing second trimester abortions, 1974;
(5) parliamentary debate on Justice Minister's attempt to close same abortion clinic, 1976;
(6) cabinet pact pledging to bring abortion reform after failure of parliamentary initiatives, 1977;
(7) reform of abortion law, leading to the 1981 Act, 1978–81;
(8) implementation of 1981 Act by executive order, 1981–4; and
(9) funding of abortion by national health insurance.

After 1984 there were no debates leading to official output, 1980–5.[4]

For this case study I have therefore also looked at debates prior to the DCE's establishment and selected from the whole range of policy debates. The debates chosen are:

1. The 1971–2 debate on the first cabinet proposal —Stuyt/Van Agt,[5] named after the ministers of health and justice—in Parliament, introduced by the cabinet-Biesheuvel (KVP-ARP-CHU-VVD-DS'70)[6] in June 1972. The starting point of this debate was the national electoral campaign of 1971, followed by the cabinet formation of 1971, when the five coalescing parties agreed to submit a bill. The bill never came to a vote, as the cabinet fell and its successor withdrew it.

2. The 1978–81 debate ending in the successful reform of 1981, the cabinet proposal Ginjaar/De Ruijter.[7] This debate started in January 1978 when a new Christian Democrat-Liberal cabinet (Van Agt I) pledged to introduce a new proposal, after private member bills foundered in Parliament in 1976.

3. The 1981–4 debate on the implementation of the 1981 statute. The law could become operative only after an executive order (Algemene Maatregel van Bestuur) on the registration and licensing of abortion facilities. The executive order was enacted by the cabinet-Lubbers I (CDA-VVD) in 1984, the end of the third debate.

The selected debates are representative of the decisional arena—given that these are mainly made in the Second Chamber, among the party elites and in cabinet—and of the range in time. One can argue about saliency. The importance of the 1971 debate or the reform bill debate of 1981 will be hard to dispute. The implementation debate is preferred to the notorious formation debate of 1977 because without the executive order there would have been no act at all. The 1977 debate was also mainly about the procedure for achieving a reform, and not about the substantive content of the proposed reform.

❖ Debate 1: The Cabinet Proposal Stuyt/Van Agt, 1971–1972

❖ How issue came to the public agenda

This debate started during the national election campaign of April 1971. As mentioned in the introduction, a cabinet reform had become inevitable because of social developments, including the increasing sympathy of doctors to women's demands for abortion. However, it was a Social Democrat private member bill in parliament that would have legalized abortion on demand which pushed the cabinet to action. The cabinet leaders realized that, based on the Liberals' support for women's self determination, there was the possibility of a majority in favour of what they considered a radical reform. The Christian Democrats, of course, were loath to reform, but realized that a modest reform bill as part of the cabinet coalition pact would prevent more sweeping change. A small working party from the elites of the three major confessional parties and the Liberals[8]—all men—drew up the rough outline for the abortion paragraph of the pact. The result was a compromise that would allow abortion only where pregnancy posed a threat to women's physical or mental health. The Liberal Party reneged on its own party programme, which saw abortion as a private affair between the doctor and the 'married and unmarried people' involved, an interesting gender-neutral definition (Outshoorn 1986a: 192), letting socio-economic issues prevail in its decision to stay in power.

❖ Dominant frame of the debate

The explicit purpose of the cabinet-Biesheuvel proposal was to bring the current abortion practice, which in effect was illegally giving women abortion on demand, under control. It presented its proposal to Parliament in June 1972.[9] It allowed for abortion if the mental or physical health of the woman was endangered by the pregnancy and if her 'interests' were more important than those of the fetus, as judged by a multidisciplinary team. The abortion had to take place in a hospital or approved clinic and all had to be registered.

During the first debate there was not yet an organized counter-movement, only some scattered interest groups,[10] but there was still a very strong mobilization of bias against legalizing abortion. In the eyes of many, abortion remained an immoral act; if reform was considered, it was only for a small number of victims of unfortunate circumstances. The weak mobilization of anti-reform groups was directly related to this bias; it did not seem necessary to organize against reform. Doubt about the solidity of the opposition to reform started to develop when the three confessional parties proposed their modest reform platform in 1971. It was fuelled when anti-abortion activists realized that, in line with legal custom, no prosecution of abortions would take place while Parliament was officially deliberating a reform bill.

Only then did counter-mobilization develop on a larger scale, leading to a coalition of anti-abortion groups in 1974. This coalition was called the Comité Redt het Ongeboren Kind (Committee to Save the Unborn Child), of which the Vereniging voor de Bescherming van het Ongeboren Kind (VBOK, Society for the Protection of the Unborn Child) was the prime mover. The latter had a popular following among the orthodox Protestant segment of the population (Outshoorn 1986a: 204–5). Roman Catholic opposition was less well organized, despite explicit pronouncements against reform by the Catholic hierarchy. The Roman Catholic People's Party (KVP), was divided, and split on the issue in the early 1970s, the split-off Roman Catholic Party of the Netherlands (RKPN) gaining one seat in parliament in 1972 (Outshoorn 1986a: 186).

Thus, the abortion debate was already beginning to polarize in 1971 as widely different views emerged regarding what the problem was and how it should be solved. For the confessional parties abortion was not just a medical problem but also a moral problem, which meant that any abortion practice had to be carefully policed. In their eyes only a small number of deserving women required help and the interests of the woman had to be weighed carefully against those of the fetus. This was essentially because, true to a time-honoured discourse about selfish women not wanting a child for reasons of luxury and laziness, they viewed women as irresponsible. Socialists and liberals initially considered abortion to be a medical problem, making doctors the experts. As the debate progressed, they soon came to accept that abortion was an affair between a woman and her doctor and required total repeal of the 1911 Act.

❖ Gendering the debate

At first the debate was about morals and then about doctors who wanted to be able to perform abortions without running the risk of prosecution. But it became gendered very quickly. Once the debate moved on to consideration of the permissible conditions for abortion, talking about women could no longer be avoided. Before the debate reached the parliamentary arena, it took place mainly in the media. Several gender meanings circulated. The traditional left portrayed women in a class discourse as too poor to afford safe abortions. The emerging women's movement introduced a new feminist meaning, seeing women as mature moral agents, not the time-honoured victims of illegal practices. Both meanings led to the same demand: that the woman should be able to determine whether she needed an abortion. Sexual liberationists constructed an active sexual woman who should not have to shoulder the burden if contraception failed. Among members of the Nederlandse Vereniging voor Seksuele Hervorming (NVSH, Dutch Society for Sexual Reform) this was a popular view.

Sexuality was viewed as a positive force in people' lives and both sexes should be able to enjoy it. Finally, there was the mentally unstable woman of medical discourse and much confessional debate. Early research on abortion influenced politicians and offered what appeared to them to be an acceptable explanation of why mothers, of all people, should want to abort: they were mental cases.

Political parties drew only partially on these meanings when they formulated their platforms on abortion in time for the elections of 1971. The Christian parties, retaining the woman-as-victim view, resorted either to supporting the 1911 statute or to allowing therapeutic abortion under very narrow circumstances. The secular parties shifted to pro-demand positions, whether for women or, assuming consensus among partners, couples. The Christian parties prevailed, and the cabinet bill was an attempt to maintain the earlier frame of abortion as a special medical procedure with moral aspects. While apparently they could no longer ignore the fact that women were involved and granted them an 'interest' in the matter, their bill empowered medical experts to overrule that interest in favour of the fetus.

❖ Policy outcome

Opposition to the cabinet bill was extremely strong. A parliamentary hearing scheduled on the private member bill of Lamberts and Roethof for abortion on demand turned into an indictment of the proposal.[11] The general feeling was that the bill was already outdated by current abortion practice and its arguments refuted by contemporary research findings. Stimezo,[12] the association of abortion clinics that had pioneered and developed the practice of liberal abortion, provided the research; it dispelled many of the myths about abortion (Ketting 1978: 121). For instance, the research showed that 'high risk' groups for abortion were young teenagers and women in their late thirties with completed families, and not the category in between. This disproved the idea that these women would become careless about contraception if abortion became available. It also showed that women seldom change their minds once they have decided to have an abortion, making obligatory use of counselling superfluous. But in 1972, before further action could be taken, the cabinet unexpectedly fell over its fiscal policy, and with it the bill died a silent death. In January 1975, the bill was formally retracted by its successor, the cabinet Den Uyl (Labour-KVP-ARP-PPR-D'66).[13]

The bill was the last attempt in the Netherlands to contain abortion within the frame of the terms of public morals, state intervention, and restricted medical abortion. From then on, one can say that the matter of control over an abortion became the central cleavage of the debate, and all subsequent policy proposals were first and foremost judged by the criterion of 'who decides?' (Outshoorn 1986a: 197). Abortion could no longer be viewed as a personal problem, but became solidly linked to women's status and rights (Ketting 1978: 8).

This framing of the issue cleared away all attempts to formulate 'objective criteria' for an abortion, eliminating a possible middle ground in which to forge a compromise.

❖ Women's movement impact

Women fully participated in debate outside Parliament, both as individuals and as group members, and also became involved in the anti-abortion groups.[14] But in the policy arena itself men dominated. There were no women cabinet ministers; the working party, the cabinet—save for one token junior minister— and the party leadership of all the major parties were all male. In the legal and medical debates among the professionals, no women were involved either. In the cabinet bill the movement's demands were ignored by the government. It can thus be concluded that in this first debate, despite its increasing public voice, the women's movement had no impact on the bill. In no way were its demands met and neither were women represented in the policy-making as the bill was drafted within the inner circle of the party elites. There was no women's policy agency to intervene on behalf of the movement, leading to a case of *no response*.

❖ Women's movement characteristics

The period of the first debate coincided with the rise of the women's movement, generating huge publicity. The first groups, Man-Vrouw-Maatschappij (MVM, Man-Woman Society) and Dolle Mina[15] were soon surrounded by a proliferation of other groups, making for loose and temporary coalitions. All of these organized and joined in demonstrations, meetings, and media debates. Moreover, the new feminism revitalized the organizations of women within the Social Democrat Party (the Red Women), the Liberal Party, the smaller left-wing parties, and the secular trade union movement. MVM was close to the Social Democratic Party; several of its leading members were also party members. Dolle Mina had originated in the student movement and shared the latter's distrust of parliamentary politics and traditional lobbying practices. Many women participated without joining an organized feminist group or set up their own informal group at the local level. Although women in the 'movement' were united on the issue of abortion on demand, one cannot speak of a cohesive movement at this stage. MVM, Dolle Mina, and Red Women cooperated on abortion but there were major ideological differences on other matters such as the position of men in the movement, on tactics, and on radical feminism.

❖ Policy environment

The coalition pact meant that when the ministers of justice and public health set their civil servants to work on the proposal, there were already strict guidelines

❖ JOYCE OUTSHOORN

negotiated by the party elites. Cabinet and the party elites were the site of the debate and determined the policy environment, which was very much a closed system. In this period there was no women's policy agency which could have intervened to open channels for movement demands. At this time, in addition, the left-wing parties were in opposition, leaving the power to the Christian Democrats and their Liberal allies.

❖ DEBATE 2: THE CABINET PROPOSAL GINJAAR/DE RUIJTER, 1977–1981

❖ *How the issue came to the public agenda*

Abortion remained a major issue in national politics between 1972 and the 1977 election. It had been agreed during the cabinet formation of 1973, in the absence of a consensus between the cabinet partners, that abortion reform would be left to Parliament. In the meantime there would be no prosecution of the clinics except in cases of medical malpractice. Although Parliament had the initiative of submitting reform bills in that period, all attempts at reform failed. A combined Social Democrat-Liberal private member bill was passed by the Second Chamber in 1976 with a comfortable majority, but it failed that same year in the First Chamber when the Liberal vote split. Major upheaval was also caused in 1976 by two attempts by the Minister of Justice, Van Agt, to shut down a clinic performing second trimester abortions. A sit-in by feminists from the movement frustrated the minister's efforts. Many parliamentarians held Van Agt to have contravened the cabinet pact, but the majority of the Social Democrats was not willing to risk a cabinet crisis and refused to vote for a motion of confidence against him (Outshoorn 1986a: 221–5).

During the coalition negotiations following the 1977 elections, the Social Democratic Party and the CDA reached a procedural agreement on how to settle the issue. The new cabinet was to come up with a proposal, no longer leaving reform to private member bills. Further negotiations failed, however, and the CDA turned to the Liberal Party to form the new cabinet—Van Agt I. This new CDA-Liberal coalition pact included the same procedural agreement negotiated between the Social Democrats and the Christian Democrats and promised a new proposal before 1 January 1979. Two ministers—Ginjaar, a Liberal at the Ministry of Public Health and De Ruijter, a member of CDA at the Ministry of Justice—without their civil servants but closely watched by the cabinet and their parliamentary parties then drafted the bill 'en petit comité'.

The bill was introduced to Parliament in February 1980.[16] The major point of this bill was to leave the decision about an abortion to the woman and her doctor, but the woman would have to observe a five-day wait to reflect on her decision before she was granted her request. In order to guarantee standards, the abortion would have to take place in a hospital or clinic with the appropriate licences, with registration and price controls. After 13 weeks of pregnancy the abortion would have to take place in a hospital. The national health inspectorate was to monitor all of these procedures. Abortion would remain illegal if it took place after viability of the fetus—not specified in terms of weeks in the bill—or if the abortion were performed outside of licensed premises.

❖ Dominant frame of the debate

The cabinet bill framed the issue in terms of the rule of law, defining the policy problem as the discrepancy between the restrictive legal situation and the rather liberal practice of abortion in the Netherlands. This inconsistency was seen to undermine respect for the law, lead to legal insecurity for citizens, and make it difficult to prevent obvious malpractice. A point of departure in the debate was policy actors' recognition of both the need to help the woman in an 'emergency situation' and the need to maintain respect for human life. To guarantee 'conscientious decision making', the bill proposed a whole set of procedures. These were drawn up to convince the moderate reformers among the Christian Democrats that the bill was a compromise and in no way a sell-out to abortion on demand, so that they would provide the necessary support to pass the bill.

For the opponents of abortion any reform was anathema, and, among the CDA supporters, many wanted to curtail the liberal practice which had permitted, in effect, abortion on demand since the early 1970s. As for the women's movement and radical reformers, there was consensus on the necessity of reaching a definite settlement in order to create a safeguard against ministerial intervention in the future. They were well aware that, in the previous cabinet term, the former minister of justice, Van Agt, now the prime minister, had twice attempted to close down an abortion clinic performing second-trimester abortions. Generally, because it was the political parties that had failed to resolve the issue, 'politics' was held to blame for the stalemate. The women's movement and its allies blamed both the Liberal Party, which had voted down a promising proposal in the first chamber in 1976, and the Christian Democrats, who, because they were pivotal to coalition formation, were in a position to block any proposal.

A huge part of the debate centred on the interpretation of the vital clause in the bill about the decision to abort: does the woman decide, or the doctor, or is it a joint effort? Those in favour of women's control could, as evidence of the right of the woman, point to the clause in which a doctor has to refer the woman to another doctor if he or she refuses to help her. The moderate reformers interpreted that clause to mean that ultimately it is the doctor who decides once he or she is convinced, after listening to her story, that there is no alternative to an abortion to solve her emergency situation. To ward off attempts to curtail current practice, Social Democrats and Liberals in Parliament sought to insert into the bill a definition of abortion as a regular medical practice, requiring no special treatment or extra safeguards. Despite this medical slant, the feminist framing of the abortion issue remained intact, and control over an abortion remained the overriding issue.

❖ Gendering the debate

The bill and the debates contained several gender meanings, to which all protagonists in the debates in Parliament contributed. In the memorandum to the bill there was the portrayal of a woman in distress deserving help who must not be left out in the cold. At the same time, as with the five-day waiting period, there was the view of a woman who cannot be completely trusted even if she does carry the responsibility for human life. The five-day waiting period was designed to stop her from acting impulsively, which she may well do because of her state of distress. In all these views, the 'woman' operates more or less on her own; there was little mention in the bill or in the debate of men, whether as husbands or as fathers. There was, however, a brief reference to the woman's 'kin', a group not to be completely trusted, as evidenced by provisions requiring the doctor to ascertain whether the woman was being pressured into having an abortion or acting out of free will. In parliamentary debates it was mainly the CDA which propounded these views. Social Democrats and Liberals, on the other hand, maintained that abortion was a matter best left to the woman and her doctor, but they differed over the necessity of legal hurdles such as waiting periods. Liberals backed these as a way to persuade the CDA to vote for the bill.

Among feminists a new gender meaning, which can traced in the documents of We Women Demand (Wij Vrouwen Eisen, WVE), the feminist abortion coalition, emerged alongside their usual portrayal of the woman seeking an abortion as a mature and moral person who makes her own responsible decisions (Outshoorn 1986a: 257–8). This new view was the 'intuitive Woman', a representation developed to counteract the implications of the proposed viability limit and the five-day waiting period. Defining legal limits was not necessary, they argued, because this 'Woman' had her own intuitive limits—she felt what was right—and her sense of responsibility guaranteed proper moral behaviour and care for the fetus. Finally, in anti-abortion discourse of both the orthodox Protestant parties in Parliament and the VBOK the image of the selfish 'Woman' of earlier anti-abortion discourse was now joined by a 'dangerous woman' who was a threat to unborn life and needed to be stopped.

❖ Policy outcome

After a series of amendments focusing mainly on the crucial article about the decision over an abortion, the second debate came to an end in December 1980 when the Second Chamber passed the bill by 76 votes to 74.[17] Then, in April 1981, the First Chamber passed it with a majority of only one vote.[18] These minimal majorities were the result of the fact that the left, the orthodox religious right, and a number of Liberals voted against the bill, for different reasons. For the orthodox the bill was far too liberal, whilst the left objected to the five-day waiting period, as did some of the Liberals. For the members of the Liberals and the Christian Democrats party discipline prevailed, with some exceptions allowed for those who had very strong conscientious objections.

The 1981 Act allows abortion up to viability if the 'emergency situation' of a woman asking for abortion makes this unavoidable; the doctor has to determine whether she is acting out of 'free will' and has considered other 'alternatives'. She has to observe a waiting period of five days to avoid rash decision-making. In fact she has the final say, for if a doctor does not grant her request, he or she has to refer her to another doctor. The abortion has to be performed in a licensed clinic or hospital.

❖ Women's movement impact

Since 1974 there had been a coalition of women's groups on abortion, WVE, an umbrella organization organizing women from various second-wave groups, such as MVM, Dolle Mina and the Feminist Socialist Platform, non-aligned feminists, and representatives from the left-wing parties and the secular trade unions.[19] The WVE alliance formulated three demands: abortion was to be removed from the Penal Code, it should be financed by national health insurance, and the woman was the person to decide about an abortion. The three demands confirmed the issue in terms of power and they came to dominate both parliamentary debates and public discourse. From the mid-1970s, all proposals were judged by all concerned, including the media, on these three criteria.

The act met part of these demands. On the touchstone question 'who decides' there was a success. The act provides that the woman can make her own decision, and abortion is no longer an offence in the Penal Code unless the terms of the act are transgressed. Although a considerable part of the second debate was about technical aspects and clauses aiming at compromise, it was the very strong presence of the women's movement in public debate outside parliament that in the end preserved these demands for women's rights.

At the same time, WVE actually opposed the bill, as had the left in Parliament, because of the compromises inserted to appease the CDA. Feminists did not like the five-day waiting clause because of the implicit insult to women being seen as vacillating creatures and because of the resulting (intended) barrier to women coming from other countries. In the course of the 1980s it proved to be ineffective in practice; women from Belgium and Germany actually formed the majority of the abortion cases in the clinics. Finance also remained an issue for feminists; it was not provided for by the 1981 Act, despite a parliamentary majority in favour of funding by national health insurance.

In this second debate, women's participation increased considerably in comparison with the first debate. Real progress had already been made in the 1975–6 debates, when many parliamentary parties had women as their speakers in Parliament and there was a woman minister of health, Vorrink (Social Democrat), a feminist in favour of abortion on demand. Women were prominent in the public debate, and they also gained presence in the policy arena itself. There was still only one woman minister at the cabinet level, Gardeniers-Berendsen (CDA, health), who was in favour of only limited reform, but there were several women as official spokespersons for their parliamentary party—Social Democrats, Democrats '66, and Radicals (PPR) in the second chamber, CDA and Social Democrats in the first chamber. The clause to ensure that a doctor was obliged to refer a woman if he or she refused to meet her request was inserted by a female Social Democrat MP.

However, despite recognition of the fact that abortion was a women's issue and that many women were active in the parliamentary parties, neither they nor movement activists had any access to the cabinet which settled the issue. This makes the second debate a case of pre-emption. One can qualify this by pointing out that the parliamentary rank and file and other interest groups were also resolutely excluded as the cabinet reverted to summit politics.

❖ Women's policy agency activities

The women's policy agency, the DCE, was established in 1978. It received a cross-sectional policy mandate and was not formally limited to any issue area. Its task was to coordinate women's policy across the ministries and to develop the major equality policy plans. It obtained a considerable budget to fund women's initiatives (Outshoorn 1995). The political head was a junior minister for equality policy, who could sit in on cabinet meetings when issues concerning women's status were debated. The DCE was part of the regular national bureaucracy and had direct access to cabinet through its minister. During the second debate she was Ms Jeltien Kraaijeveld, a CDA parliamentarian with a background in a large Protestant women's organization. According to the civil servants of the DCE and as evidenced by interviews she gave in the press, she adopted feminist views in the course of her incumbency.[20] On abortion she was a moderate reformer. The first director of the DCE was a female professional civil servant who had served as the permanent secretary of the Emancipation Commission, the predecessor of the 1981 Emancipation Council.

Despite these promising assets, the DCE did not get involved in the second abortion debate; and there was no mention of the issue in any of its policy papers. Thus it is classified as symbolic. This was not for lack of conviction about the issue: most of its femocrats were feminists. Two senior femocrats, commenting on the lack of activity of the DCE on the abortion issue, claim that successive cabinets deliberately kept abortion out of the equality policy network within the national government (Dijkstra and Swiebel 1982: 55). By the time the DCE was established, the highly politicized issue was firmly in the hands of the cabinet. The director of the DCE recalls that there was a tacit consensus among senior femocrats to leave the issue untouched because of its controversial nature; their task was already controversial and arduous enough. There was also the feeling that the DCE should cater for all women, and it was well aware that a substantial part of the traditional women's organizations were opposed to abortion on demand.[21] Moreover, the junior minister also subscribed to this latter position. In retrospect, attempts to influence the civil servants of another ministry concerned with the issue would have foundered as the proposal was being drafted by the ministers themselves. Their own civil servants were outsiders to this process and consequently also not in the position to lobby.

❖ Women's movement characteristics

During the debate on the bill, WVE upheld its three demands and the secular political parties presented and elaborated on them during the parliamentary debates in 1980–1. Stimezo also supported the demands, adding its own critique of the government's plans for licensing abortion facilities. As the bill had been drafted within the cabinet, both 'outsiders' and 'insiders' had to resort to public protest, the one route open to influence the drafting. In the past WVE had maintained good informal contacts to the Social Democrats, now in the opposition. WVE and most other women's groups had little access to the governing parties.

WVE was the only national umbrella organization of the women's movement at this stage. The movement, although at its zenith, remained an 'archipelago of many islands', the metaphor coined by Joke Smit in 1977 to describe the state of the women's movement (Smit 1984). Major movement debate was on the use of parliamentary strategies and the rise of state feminism (Outshoorn 1995:179–82). A serious rift in WVE occurred during the cabinet formation of 1977, when the Red Women backed the compromise drawn up by their party and the CDA during the ill-fated negotiations about a new cabinet. This was seen by many feminists as a form of treason. Abortion remained the number-one issue of the movement, the issue on which all feminists agreed; in fact, it almost a litmus test for being a feminist at the time. Disagreement was on tactics, not on ends.

At the same time, the women's movement met more serious opposition from anti-abortion groups than during the previous debates. Opponents of reform realized that their cause was no longer safe in the hands of the CDA, and a strong counter-mobilization got under way. They pressured the CDA and found a willing ear among a substantial section of the party and its elite, most prominently prime-minister Van Agt.

❖ Policy environment

The resolution of conflict and settling of the direction of abortion policy during the second debate was turned into the province of the cabinet, with the exclusion of the civil servants normally involved in drafting legislating, and as such it was a closed system. Although there was public debate on government proposals, these had little impact on the outcome of the process. The cabinet practised a type of 'summit' politics which restricted access from interest groups as well as the rank and file of political parties. The policy environment for this important abortion policy reform in the Netherlands also included a majority coalition that excluded the major left-wing party, the Social Democrats.

❖ DEBATE 3: THE EXECUTIVE ORDER TO THE 1981 ACT, 1981–1984

❖ How issue came to the public agenda

The third debate selected covers the implementation measures which had to be taken before the 1981 Act could take effect. The act left several technical points, such as the licensing of abortion facilities and the registration and monitoring of the incidence of abortion, to be operationalized in an executive order. A draft version of the order was published in the week the act passed (Staatsblad 1981: 257). During the debates on the 1981 act in the second chamber it emerged that these matters were not to remain technical because the hard-liners in the Christian Democratic Party intended to use the order to restrict the scope of the act. The main thrust of its offensive was to insert the requirement of 'objective grounds'—the act refers only to the 'emergency situation' of a woman—into the regulations. Their goal was to reframe the issue as a special medical procedure to be handled by the experts that left the woman out of the decision. Their other goals were to prevent hospitals from asking for licenses to perform abortions, to include conscience clauses in the order enabling personnel in the hospitals to opt out of delivering abortion services, and to prevent funding from national health insurance. Needless to say, this met with determined opposition from those favouring abortion on demand, who saw it as an effort to detract from the act that would shift the balance of power to the medical profession. The draft order provoked prolonged debate, and it was finally settled in 1984 under the cabinet Lubbers I (CDA-VVD).

❖ Dominant frame of the debate

The third debate can be seen as a contest between those who presented the issue as a regular medical procedure, in which women wanting an abortion were seen as normal patients who should be treated like any other patients—the position taken by the two advisory bodies on health (Outshoorn 1986a: 279)—and the hardliners of the CDA and its allies in the anti-abortion front. In the view of the cabinet-Lubbers I, the executive order had to guarantee the quality of the facilities and to safeguard the intent of the Abortion Act. However, there was dissent among the CDA cabinet ministers about whether to support a strict or moderate interpretation of the Abortion Act. Minister of Welfare, Health and Culture Brinkman (CDA), along with a considerable minority of the parliamentary party, wanted a strict interpretation of the law. In their view, the act allowed for abortion on demand, for which they blamed permissive doctors and insistent women. In the eyes of the Liberals and the left-wing opposition, the CDA was to blame for the persistence of the conflict. They saw the CDA as a poor loser that would not accept a parliamentary decision. The stalemate finally ended when a majority of the cabinet and the party elites lost patience and wanted the issue settled once and for all; this was the same mood that helped to pass the 1981 Act. In a parliamentary system which is dependent on coalition cabinets to govern, abortion is too disruptive an issue to keep recurring on the agenda. Because it cuts across the prevailing left-right spectrum, it makes for continual tension in the inevitable negotiations and compromises required for coalition rule.

❖ Gendering the debate

All sides in the debate worked to remove gendered references, not add to them. The successful conclusion to the debate on the 1981 Act—abortion defined as a women's issue and a statute providing for abortion on demand—meant that the women's movement and the women's policy agency were in the position of defending their gains. Ironically, they allied with those who defended the law and its gendered frame by seeking to degender the debate. By advocating the normalization of procedures, those in favour of the 1981 Act defined women seeking abortions as 'normal patients'. Those opposing the act also degendered the issue by shifting control to medical experts who were to determine the 'objective' grounds for allowing abortion. They had their allies in Parliament among the confessional right. Nearly all were orthodox Protestants as the organized Catholic opposition had all but disappeared.

❖ JOYCE OUTSHOORN

❖ Policy outcome

The final draft of the regulations passed the cabinet in May 1984 and the debate over implementation finally ended in July 1984 when the Council of State approved the executive order. The Abortion Act of 1981 took effect on 1 November 1984.[22] Both the act and the executive order encoded the abortion practices which had developed since the early 1970s: a network of clinics and hospitals which provided abortion on demand, usually after a visit of the woman to her doctor, who referred her. The framing of the issue in terms of control also remained intact, despite the intricate wording of the crucial article of the act and the fight over the objective grounds in the executive order. They amounted to the defeat of the Christian Democrats and the anti-abortion groups, as abortion on demand in the Netherlands was widely available for all women residents. The executive order did not include further requirements about the reasons for an abortion, save the 'emergency situation' required by the 1981 Act, and provided a licensing system which left all abortion facilities, including those providing second-trimester abortions, intact.

❖ Women's movement impact

In the end the women's movement received a dual response by having its goals fulfilled as well as having been involved in the policy debate through its institutionalized manifestation. Abortion remained accessible for all women needing one, as facilities were left untouched and the law gave women options by requiring doctors to refer women to other doctors if they were not willing to grant their requests. The five-day waiting period proved ineffectual in limiting access to the procedure.

Feminist women had access to the policy arena through institutionalized channels. Because the cabinet expanded the debate on the administrative rules to consult the corporate institutions and because the issue was considered a woman's matter, the Emancipation Council (Emancipatieraad, ER)—the corporate advisory body for women—took part in the process. Most of the council's members and its staff identified as feminists and its report backed the demands of WVE, as well as monitoring the debate on the executive order. Involvement in the policy debate had its limits though: movement representatives did not have direct access to the powerful health care councils. And there was still only one woman cabinet minister and one junior minister, for equality policy. Parliamentary parties did continue to recognize the issue as a women's issue, as witnessed by the considerable number of women speaking for their party in Parliament. Perhaps the greatest impact of the movement was indirect: all actors in the relevant policy arena were well aware of its presence and its potential to mobilize again.

❖ *Women's policy agency activities*

In this debate, the women's policy agency, the DCE, now having insider status, advocated the movement's goals and, along with the advisory Emancipation Council, functioned as watch-dog on the progress of the issue. In 1981 the DCE was relocated to the Ministry of Social Affairs and Employment; it kept its cross-sectional mandate and its expertise, as most of its personnel made the move to the ministry. Both the staff and many feminists welcomed this move and expected that the agency would now be in a better position to intervene in the major policy debates concerning women's employment and social security. Its political heads were able to strengthen the DCE's position by producing a seminal policy paper on the position of women which did much to acquaint other ministries with the issues. Moreover, the junior ministers for women's affairs had direct access to cabinet when women's issues were addressed.

When the cabinet Lubbers I (CDA-Liberal Party) took power in 1983, Annelien Kappeyne van de Coppello (Liberal Party), a prominent and forceful parliamentarian, became junior minister and head of the DCE. She took a liberal feminist stand on women's issues and on abortion, which she considered to be a woman's right. In the cabinet debates on the executive order and on the funding issue she soon came into conflict with the hard-line CDA ministers, especially Brinkman, the Minister of Health. He tried to push the executive order through the cabinet when she was absent from the meeting, but this attempt at exclusion failed (Outshoorn 1986a: 283–4). When cabinet negotiations on the funding issue broke down, Kappeyne was included in the 'summit' of the cabinet to solve the issue and she threatened to resign if abortion funding was not included in the national health insurance (Outshoorn 1986a: 280). From these events and from the fact that the Emancipation Council was consulted, one can conclude that abortion was now indeed recognized as also being part of women's policy.

❖ *Women's movement characteristics*

In this third debate, the women's movement was in the consolidation stage, and continued to stay non-aligned, evenly distant from the major parties and critical of the left. The conflict about state feminism—the debate about movement strategy and the state—having been settled in favour of the 'reformists', women's groups started to make use of the regular policy channels to lobby and use government subsidies to maintain issue networks and service projects (Outshoorn 1995). The radical feminist tendency disappeared in the early 1980s, but new alliances emerged with the traditional women's organizations, involving new mobilization around socio-economic issues. With this shift the closeness of the movement to the left diminished. At the local and national levels, second-wave feminists now cooperated with the other parties, depending on the issues at stake.

Thus, movement activists did not become directly involved in the question of the administrative regulations. After the 1981 act, interest in abortion declined, other issues taking priority. The national alliance of WVE was reduced to a group of only the most highly involved WVE women who kept a critical eye on events subsequent to the 1981 victory. They still faced some relatively strong counter-movement organizations and broader anti-feminist activity from the orthodox Protestant militants.

❖ Policy environment

The executive order was handled in cabinet, the Ministry of Health, and Parliament, which made the highly unusual request to see the draft order before it took effect. The cabinet was the CDA-Liberal Coalition of Lubbers I, with the Social Democrats firmly entrenched in the opposition. The site of debate expanded as the corporate health institutions—Centrale Raad voor de Volksgezondheid (Central Council for Public Health) and the Gezondheidsraad (Council of Health)—of the Dutch political system had now to be heard on the draft. The former was a typical corporatist body made up of the representatives of the various medical professional groups, the organizations of the institutions providing health care, and of the social partners, health care insurers, patients' and consumers' platforms. The latter sets standards for medical procedures and is dominated by top clinicians and medical researchers (Kirecjzyk 1996: 73, 76–7). Women's interests were not represented in either, and at the time only about 10 per cent of the members were women.

The cabinet also formally sought input on the order from the Emancipation Council, as the official advisory body on women's policy, an implicit acknowledgment that abortion was a woman's affair. Civil servants from the Ministry of Health had tried to prevent this, so the Emancipation Council could intervene only at a late stage, delivering its report in 1983.[23] Although it was opposed to the 1981 Act, the report, by providing arguments against the attempts of the CDA to reinsert 'objective grounds' in the order, stimulated public debate.

The policy environment was thus characterized by the advisory bodies and the preponderance of the medical profession and the civil service. The DCE could not have lobbied the advisory bodies—it was considered not done. So while the DCE was an insider as it had a direct and effective line to the cabinet, in the corporatist scene it had to rely on the members of the Emancipation Council. Fortunately all three councils advised against introducing 'objective criteria' and other trappings which would have redefined abortion as an exceptional medical practice. Moreover, the power of the advisory bodies—abortion still being a topical political issue—was more closely supervised by cabinet and Parliament than normally occurs.

❖ Conclusion

In the Netherlands the abortion issue was finally settled in the mid-1980s, with an outcome which met the major demands of the women's movement: abortion is available on demand, without barriers to women's control over the decisions or access to services, and the costs of an abortion are covered by national health.[24] Abortion is generally defined as a women's issue, and, since the 1970s, the women's movement, along with its allies from the pro-choice movement, succeeded in making the matter of control over the decision the primary issue. The 1981 Act is widely accepted in Dutch society, and, with opposition confined to the religious orthodox minority of the population, there has not been a threat to abortion rights since its implementation in 1984. Despite the availability of abortion on demand, the Netherlands has had the lowest rates of abortion in the world,[25] which can be accounted for by the widespread use of contraception and sex education in schools.

The outcome of the abortion issue can be attributed to the fact that the life cycle of the issue was in tune with the emergence and growth of the women's movement. In the first debate, on the restrictive government bill of 1972, the movement was becoming highly visible, but had not yet gained access. It had no impact on the policy formation of the government bill; the latter was drafted within the inner circle of the party elites. There was no women's policy agency to counteract it. The first debate is a case of no response.

This situation had changed radically at the time of the second debate. In the intervening years, the movement had grown to its zenith, and its major demands had come to dominate the debate on abortion. In terms of its demands, it received near full policy satisfaction. But despite recognition of the fact that abortion was a women's issue and the presence of many active women in the parliamentary parties, there was no access to cabinet—the token CDA woman minister shared the views of the more conservative section of her party on abortion—where the issue was settled. The second case is therefore one of pre-emption. This time there was a women's policy agency, but, as described, it was kept out of the relevant arena and its leadership did not challenge this. It did not gender the policy debate, nor did it advocate the abortion demands of the women's movement. So the second debate meets the case of symbolic representation.

The third debate, on the executive order to implement the act, ended highly successfully for both movement and agency. The women's policy agency advocated the movement's goals and kept the issue gendered, which makes for the case of insider status. The women's movement received a dual response by having its goals fulfilled as well as having been involved in the policy debate through the advisory body.

Finally, two further points are in order. First, it is striking how much abortion was always an issue of parties, cabinet, and Parliament in the Netherlands. The major decisions were all taken in that arena, which is typical of the category of regulatory policy as described by Lowi (1963) and Smith (1975). It makes for conflictual and usually open politics as decisions are made in the legislature. It means social movements and interest groups have easy access, bypassing the usual corporatist structures. Attempts of the political elite to return to closed politics were only partially effective as Parliament refused to allow this and the women's movement countered on several scores. Once the arena closed again, the wisdom of having institutionalized feminism within the government bureaucracy became evident.

Second, it is clear that women are still seriously under-represented in the policy arenas. Despite the very vocal presence of women in the public debate and their gradually improving numbers in Parliament, the party elites and the cabinet remain male preserves. This also applies to the corporate channel and the professional arenas. As long as men are in a position to say there are no suitable women to fill the positions in the elites, the women's movement will have to counter by attacking the criteria for selection, as the crux of the problem is now more clearly than ever located in the power of determining who is allowed access.

❖ Notes

1 The funding issue was settled in 1985 by including the costs of an abortion in the coverage provided by the national health insurance.

2 The most recent poll (1998) shows that 49.8% of the Dutch are of the opinion that a woman should have an abortion if she wants it, 13.3% strongly disagreeing. Unpublished figures supplied by Saskia Keuzenkamp of the Sociaal en Cultureel Planbureau. This hardly differs from the findings of the National Election Survey of 1981 where 48% said a woman should be the one to decide and 14% wanted to prohibit abortion (Outshoorn 2000: 146).

3 Both contributions were based on the policy documents and draft bills, parliamentary debates, documents, and articles of all major actors, newspaper clippings covering the entire period, interviews and secondary sources, used in an earlier study (Outshoorn 1986a). For the period after the 1986 book, similar source material has been collected. For an overview of developments since 1986 see Outshoorn (2000).

4 The present cabinet—Social Democrats, Liberals, and Democrats '66—agreed in 1999 to extend the scope of the 1981 act to make abortion possible after viability in cases of extremely serious fetal defects, but the proposal has not yet been introduced in Parliament (Outshoorn 2000: 145–6).

5 Handelingen Tweede Kamer (HTK) (1971–2: 11890), Wet Afbreking Zwanger-schap (Pregnancy Termination Act), Nos 1–3, 23 June 1972.

6 KVP: Catholic People's Party (Katholieke Volkspartij); ARP: Anti-Revolutionary Party (Anti-Revolutionaire Partij); CHU: Christian Historical Union (Christelijk Historische Unie); VVD: People's Party for Freedom and Democracy (Volkspartij voor Vrijheid en Democratie); DS'70: Democratic Socialists 70 (Demokratisch Socialisten 70).

7 HTK (1979–80:15475), Wet Afbreking Zwangerschap, Nos 1–3, 16 February 1980.

8 It consisted of four men, one from each party; DS '70 was not represented.

9 HTK (1971–2: 11890), Wet Afbreking Zwangerschap, Nos 1–3.

10 The first single-issue anti-abortion group—the name the groups preferred until the mid-1980s, when they started calling themselves pro-life—the Stichting voor het Ongeboren Kind (SOK, Foundation for the Unborn Child) was founded in 1970, con-sisting of notable medical professionals and others from the social elite. Its discourse was a combination of medical-biological and ethical discourse. The Vereniging ter Bescherming van het Ongeboren Kind (VBOK, Society for the Protection of the Unborn Child) was founded in 1971 and is much more popular and activist in style. It wants to maintain the 1911 statute (Outshoorn 1986a: 176–7).

11 HTK (1971–2: 10719), No. 4. Verslag van een openbaar verhoor (Report on a hearing) (September 1971).

12 Stichting voor Medisch Verantwoorde Zwangersonderbreking (Foundation for the Medical Interruption of Pregnancy).

13 PPR: Politieke Partij Radicalen (Radical Political Party); D'66: Demokraten '66 (Democrats '66).

14 This was also the case in the VBOK, as opposed to early anti-abortion groups, in which elite males predominated. Like the political parties, the VBOK was quick to take on women spokespersons to increase legitimacy after the rise of the women's movement.

15 'Mad Mina', a reference to Wilhelmina Drucker, one of the most famous feminists of the first wave of feminism at the end of the 1890s.

16 HTK (1979–80: 15475), Wet Afbreking Zwangerschap, Nos 1–3, 16 February 1980.

17 HTK (1980–1: 2318), 18 December 1980.

18 Handelingen Eerste Kamer (HEK) (1980–1: 829), 28 April 1981.

19 The women's Liberal Party auxiliary, Vrouwen in de VVD, originally a member, left in 1975 after a split between Social Democrats and Liberals on strategy in the second chamber.

20 Interviews held in 1993–4 during a project on 'femocrats' (Outshoorn 1994; 1998).

21 Interview with Ms. E. J. Mulock Houwer, former head of the DCE, 14 July 1998.

22 HTK (1983–4: 18386), No. 1, 6. Besluit van 17 mei 1984, houdende vaststelling van een algemene maatregel van bestuur ter uitvoering van de Wet Afbreking Zwanger-schap. For the politics around it, see Outshoorn (1996a: 284–5).

23 It opposed the draft, as it did not do justice to the current abortion practice. For

the same reason, the Council opposed the implementation of the 1981 act (ER Advies 1983).

24 The costs are not covered by the Ziekenfonds, the compulsory national health insurance scheme for low- and middle-income earners, but are covered by the Algemene Wet Bijzondere Ziektekosten (AWBZ, General Law on Special Medical Costs). For the woman having the abortion this makes no difference, but note that abortion is thus considered a special medical act. Higher-income earners are insured by private insurance schemes, and most of these cover the costs of an abortion if it is within the limits set by the 1981 act.

25 The rate is now 6.5 per 1000 women between 15 and 44 years of age (Henshawe, Singh, and Haas 1999: 34).

11 ❖ Gendering Abortion Debates: State Feminism in Spain

Celia Valiente

❖ INTRODUCTION

There has been punishment for abortion in Spain since medieval times. With the first penal code in 1822, the state punished those performing abortions with prison terms, and subsequent legal reforms changed this criminalization only slightly until the 1980s. However, there is a precedent for reform that dates back to the 1930s when, during the civil war of 1936–9, a decree in Catalonia permitted abortion on grounds of the woman's health when she did not want the pregnancy and when the child would have physical defects. Given the upheaval that ensued, the reform was implemented in a very limited way (Nash 1986: 227–38).

From the mid-1930s to 1975, Spain was governed by a right-wing authoritarian regime that actively opposed the advancement of women's rights and status. On 24 January 1941, voluntary abortion was again defined as a crime. In 1944, this anti-abortion act was repealed, but the articles related to abortion were included in the Penal Code. The 1944 Penal Code punished abortion with prison for between six months and six years. Abortion was a crime with no extenuating circumstances for the woman, unless she became pregnant while unmarried and subsequently had an abortion (Barreiro 1998: 35).

A partial decriminalization of abortion took place in 1985. Since then, abortion has been a crime punishable by the Penal Code except on three grounds: when the woman has been raped—so-called 'ethical abortion'; when pregnancy seriously endangers the physical and mental health of the mother—so-called 'therapeutic abortion'; and when the foetus is deformed—so-called 'eugenic abortion'.

Most groups in the Spanish feminist movement have been united in calling for abortion on demand since the 1970s, when Spanish feminists first mobilized in favour of decriminalizing abortion (Sundman 1999; Trujillo 1999). The main women's policy machinery at the central state level, the Women's Institute (Instituto de la Mujer), established by the socialist government in 1983, managed to influence the debate prior to the regulations of the implementation of the 1985 decriminalization of abortion, facilitating women's access to abortion services.

Unlike in the United States, Germany, or Ireland, the abortion issue no longer provokes intense conflict in the policy-making process. Although feminists continue to advocate abortion on demand, and some pro-life groups are active, the political controversy on abortion has been deactivated since the late 1980s. The Catholic Church does not agree with some acts of the Spanish state on moral matters, such as the act that legalized divorce in 1981 or the one that partially liberalized abortion, but it has not made a big effort to reverse them. Catholics' resistance to these public policies has been more moderate in Spain than in other Western countries (Linz 1993: 44).

❖ SELECTION OF DEBATES

The period of study for this chapter is post-authoritarian Spain, from 1975 to the present. Two institutions dominate the policy area regarding the termination of pregnancy at the central state level: Parliament and the government, composed of the prime minister, the cabinet, and ministries. Acts of Parliament set forth the general legal framework while the ministries—in the case of abortion, the health ministry—establish regulations to implement the law. Royal decrees, enacted by the government, are the highest-ranking regulations emanating from national government departments (Newton and Donaghy 1997: 66). These institutions are the arenas in which major debates over abortion take place.

Parliament is composed of two chambers: a lower chamber called the Congress of Deputies, and an upper chamber called the Senate. In practice, although not in constitutional theory, the former is much more important than the latter, and the Congress of Deputies has precedence over the Senate in most matters. Members of the Congress of Deputies are elected by proportional representation under the D'Hondt system with closed and blocked lists. The province serves as the constituency. The vast majority of senators are elected by a majority system. The province is again the constituency, and each province elects four senators, although each voter casts votes for only three senators. The remaining senators are elected from among the members of regional parliaments according to the population of the regions and the political composition of regional parliaments.

Parliament functions in both plenary sessions and committees. Most parliamentary work takes place in committees, the majority of which are legislative standing committees. Different units have the power to initiate legislation: government, Congress of Deputies, Senate, and regional parliaments. However, in post-authoritarian Spain the constitution set up a political system which includes a strong executive and a weak parliament, so that most laws have been initiated by government. The dominance of the executive is further strengthened by the dominance of political parties. There are strict controls on individual MPs. For instance, only parliamentary groups—in general composed of deputies and senators from a party or coalition—are allowed to introduce legislation. During 1982–93 the socialist party had an absolute majority in the parliament, and the independence of the parliament and opposition MPs declined even further (Heywood 1995: 99–101; Newton and Donaghy 1997: 45–72).

The universe of policy debates on abortion in Spain is small, especially in comparison with other countries in Europe and North America. For one thing, the democratic period when such debates came to the agenda began only in the late 1970s. In addition, the dominance of the parties in government—first the socialists and then a centre-right coalition—have left little policy space for either advocates or opponents of liberalized abortion. That abortion was a potentially extremely divisive issue was apparent early in the formation of the democratic state. During the process of drafting the constitution, between 1977 and 1978, abortion was an issue that, together with education, regionalism, and divorce, among others, divided the left and the right to such an extent that it threatened to derail the constitutional process. Given this conflict, the political parties agreed that the constitution would not explicitly say anything about abortion. Conflict was therefore avoided by postponing it.

The first important piece of legislation on abortion was the organic Act 9/1985 of 5 July, on the reform of article 417bis of the Penal Code—hereafter 'the 1985 abortion act'. The 1985 abortion act decriminalized ethical, therapeutic, and eugenic abortion. The 1985 act, however, does not say anything more concrete about the implementation of abortion with respect either to the conditions under which health personnel could refuse help in abortion cases for reasons of conscience, or to the characteristics of clinics where performance of abortion would be permitted (Barreiro 1998: 238). Therefore, regulations were necessary for the implementation of the 1985 act. The government prepared these regulations, which were adopted in 1986.

Since 1986, there have been several failed attempts by left-wing parties to reform the 1985 abortion act. Although they presented bills to parliament, the reformers knew that without a majority to approve them their efforts would be symbolic. Thus, there have been no subsequent changes to the 1985 abortion act.

Two debates have been selected to represent abortion policy making in post-authoritarian Spain. The first is the debate beginning in 1983 leading to the 1985 abortion act. This debate is central to the issue, but it does not provide an opportunity to examine state feminism because the women's policy agency—the Women's Institute—was in the process of being founded during the debate and had little chance to participate. The second important legal piece in the policy area under study here is the regulations of the implementation of the 1985 abortion act: Royal Decree 2,409/1986 of 21 November.

Given the small universe of abortion debates in Spain, two debates, rather than three as in the other chapters in this book, adequately represent the policy-making process on the issue. These debates fulfil the criterion of issue salience. According to scholarly secondary sources (Barreiro 1998; Marín 1996), the 1985 abortion act and its regulations are the main measures taken in post-authoritarian Spain in the policy area of termination of pregnancy. The criterion of decisional system importance is also satisfied since the main institutional site of the 1985 debate was Parliament, and that of the 1986 debate was the executive. Given that the government's attention to the abortion issue was concentrated in the 1980s, selecting these important debates also, in effect, represents the narrow range of debates.[1]

❖ DEBATE 1: DECRIMINALIZATION OF ETHICAL, THERAPEUTIC, AND EUGENIC ABORTION, 1983–1985

❖ How the debate came to the public agenda

Although the socialist party—Partido Socialista Obrero Español, PSOE—had not included references to abortion in its 1977 and 1979 electoral programmes, other party documents issued in the 1970s, such as the resolutions of federal congresses, advocated radical reforms, for example, abortions provided free of charge by the public health system. Nevertheless, the party was divided mainly between supporters of a broad abortion liberalization and supporters of a more limited reform. In the context of electoral competition, PSOE leaders took the latter position. This was part of their overall strategy to convert the PSOE into a moderate catch-all party capable of achieving power (Barreiro 1998: 172–7).

In order to fulfil a compromise included in its 1982 electoral programme, the socialist government presented a bill on the reform of the Penal Code on 25 February 1983. The bill contained an article that decriminalized abortion on ethical, therapeutic, and eugenic grounds (Barreiro 1998: 183–4). This parliamentary debate began six years after the first democratic elections were held in Spain, and four months after the PSOE first came to power, which it retained until Spring 1996. The debate started eight months before the Women's Institute was established.

❖ *Dominant frame of the debate*

The dominant frame of the debate was composed of two types of arguments. Supporters of the decriminalization of abortion argued that, since abortions would be performed no matter what the laws said, it was reasonable to adapt the law to this social reality. They maintained that this reform would make Spain more like other European countries, which were economically more developed and had a longer democratic past. On the other hand, pro-life MPs often couched their support for the criminalization of abortion in terms of the defence of the fetus's rights.

The PSOE defended its reform bill in the Congress of Deputies arguing, among other things, that the reform was constitutional and that according to opinion polls it was supported by the majority of the population.[2] Socialist leaders emphasized the moderate character of the bill, pointing out that, apart from three exceptions, abortion would still be a crime punishable under the penal law. Only the communist party advocated abortion on demand in the first three months of pregnancy performed free of charge in public hospitals.

Among the chief opponents of the bill was the main political party in opposition, the conservative Alianza Popular (AP). Most, although not all, AP deputies were against any sort of decriminalization of abortion. Members of the centre-right Unión de Centro Democrático and the Basque Nationalist Party (Partido Nacionalista Vasco), parties with fewer seats than AP, also took a pro-life position. A division of opinion characterized—and still does—the Catalan nationalist coalition (Convergència i Unió). MPs from the Christian Democratic Unió opposed abortion. While some MPs from Convergència were pro-life, many others were pro-reform and liberalization. The main arguments of the opponents of the decriminalization of abortion were, among others, that the bill was unconstitutional and that abortion is murder, because, according to them, life starts at the moment of conception. In the Senate, arguments for and against the bill were similar to those advanced in the Congress of Deputies.[3] Amendments from the opposition of similar content were also defended and defeated (Barreiro 1998: 217–9).

❖ **GENDERING THE DEBATE**

On the whole, the debate was not gendered, with a few exceptions. At times MPs supporting reform described women as people with the right to choose whether or not to continue an unwanted pregnancy. Members of the communist party—but not of the socialist party—sometimes used the argument made by the feminist movement that women had the right to freely dispose of their own bodies. Otherwise, references to the constitution, the foetus, doctors, and public opinion far outnumbered references to women.

When MPs who supported liberalization explicitly referred to women, they tended to talk in the context of social class. Socialist and communist MPs denounced the fact that rich women could afford a safe abortion performed abroad while poor women had to suffer unsafe clandestine abortions at home, calling it a socio-economic injustice. In fact, they tended to be more concerned with class inequalities than with gender differences. They portrayed women as weak people experiencing anxiety, insecurity, and distress before abortion. They asserted that women opt to have an abortion only in very extreme circumstances: otherwise, all women really want to give birth to their babies because nobody would want to have an abortion. To them, it seemed as if women were forced by disturbing and unbearable circumstances to get rid of their pregnancies. Women were never presented as serene people who in ordinary circumstances would rationally opt for an abortion as their first choice. These ordinary circumstances seemed not to exist.[4]

Pro-life MPs mentioned women only in terms of their anatomy, specifically their wombs. A pregnant woman was, in effect, two people because the fetus in a woman's womb was independent from the moment of conception. Sometimes, pro-life MPs portrayed Spanish women as ignorant of contraceptive devices or unable to have access to them. Thus, unwanted pregnancies were likely. So, if the act were passed, women would try to cheat on the law in order to have abortions on grounds not permitted by the law. Pro-life, but not pro-choice, MPs also talked about men as fathers, demanding fathers' consent in abortion cases.

❖ Policy outcome

Since the PSOE had an absolute majority in Parliament, the abortion reform bill was approved in the Congress of Deputies and sent to the Senate. On 30 October 1983, the Senate approved the bill. Two days after this approval, but before the bill was enacted, conservative MP José María Ruiz Gallardón, supported by 54 MPs, lodged an appeal before the Constitutional Court (CC) on the ground that the bill was unconstitutional. The CC has a responsibility equivalent to that of the Supreme Court in the United States, that is, to be 'the supreme interpreter of constitutionality', and can rule that laws are unconstitutional and invalid. It reviews laws made by the Spanish Parliament, the national executive, and regional governments, and its decisions apply to the whole territory of Spain and cannot be appealed (Heywood 1995: 105–6). The abortion reform policy-making process was stopped until the CC pronounced its sentence (Barreiro 1998: 219–20).

It took a year and a half, but on 11 April 1985, the CC made public its decision. The Court declared that the bill would be constitutional provided that it was modified to require that abortions be performed in authorized private or public centres. The Court went on to require a medical report certifying the grounds of the abortion prior to the procedure in the case of therapeutic and eugenic abortion, in order to provide more protection for the fetus (Barreiro 1998: 219–27, 231).

After the CC ruling, the socialist government revised the bill in accordance with the CC recommendations and again submitted it to Parliament. The debates in the Congress of Deputies and the Senate were less virulent than before the publication of the CC sentence.[5] The reason is that, around this time, the conservative party changed its position. If before 1986 the AP had frontally opposed any attempt to decriminalize abortion, it softened this opposition afterwards. After deliberation and approval in Parliament, the abortion act was enacted on 5 July 1985; it decriminalized abortion on grounds of the physical and mental health of the mother, the deformity of the fetus, and pregnancy due to rape.

❖ *Movement impact*

Representatives of the women's movement did not directly participate in the parliamentary debate that preceded the 1985 abortion act. The movement did mobilize, demanding decriminalization of abortion and organized pro-choice street demonstrations. Some members of the parliamentarian elite noted their activities, and a few times pro-choice MPs referred to the women's movement as a collective actor outside parliament that denounced gender inequalities and mobilized to remedy them. These references to the women's movement were complimentary.[6] However, the overwhelming majority of the numerous participants in the debate were men. A male deputy from the Mixed Parliamentary Group Bandrés Molet publicly noted and denounced the lack of women's voices. Only three female MPs participated in the very long debate: deputy Pelayo Duque, Senator Ruiz-Tagles Morales, and Senator Sauquillo Pérez del Arco. All were pro-choice.

The policy content of the 1985 abortion act coincides with women's movement goals but only to a certain extent. An overwhelming majority of groups in the women's movement supported the decriminalization of ethical, therapeutic, and eugenic abortion. However, most feminist groups also supported and mobilized for a further decriminalization of abortion, that is, abortion on demand. Thus, with a liberalized abortion law, but not admitting women or movement groups to the policy process during this important debate, the state's response to the women's movement was one of pre-emption.

❖ *Women's policy agency activities*

The Women's Institute (WI) was officially created in 1983 (Act 16 of 24 October). It took almost two years from its foundation to hire the whole staff and to establish the directive organs. Therefore, the establishment of the WI partly

SPAIN ❖

coincided with the debate that preceded the 1985 abortion act. The scope of the WI is very broad, since the WI has five comprehensive goals: to promote policy initiatives for women through formal enactment of policy statements; to study all aspects of women's situation in Spain; to oversee the implementation of women's policy; to receive and handle women's discrimination complaints; and to increase women's knowledge of their rights. The WI was a permanent bureaucratic agency and not a political appointment. Since the WI was in a ministry rather than having a cabinet position, it has always been distant from major power centres. Up to 1988 the WI was a part of the Ministry of Culture and between 1988 and 1996 a part of the Ministry of Social Affairs. These ministries are two of the least important in the Spanish state.[7] In the mid-1980s, the WI had not yet acquired an extensive staff and budget.

The leadership of the WI between 1983 and 1988 had much to do with the agency's activities. The director in that period, Carlota Bustelo, revealed a good deal of knowledge and understanding of gender inequality. She could identify openings of policy windows to push for reforms. She often gave the personal impression of having power and was likely to be obeyed. She made a number of initiatives and promoted demands on many fronts: education, labour market, reproductive rights, and so on. For allies, she chose former members of the women's movement. Bustelo was a well-known former PSOE deputy and feminist activist. Abortion was one of the top priorities of the WI in the mid-1980s.[8]

During the early period of the debate under study here, the Women's Institute did not exist and, in the later stages, formally existed but was still in the process of formation. Thus the WI had very few chances to participate in the debate. In line with the concerns of the women's movement, however, the WI did put pressure on the PSOE government to take the lead on the abortion reform question. After the decision by the Constitutional Court, WI director Bustelo urged the government to move more rapidly to solve what she termed the grave problem that the criminalization of abortion caused for many women (Barreiro 1998: 228). Thus, by adopting a position on the issue allied with the women's movement but being unable to gender the dominant frame of the abortion debate, women's policy agency activities were marginal.

❖ Women's movement characteristics

After emerging in the 1960s and early 1970s, and growing from 1975 to the early 1980s, by 1983–5 the women's movement was in a stage of consolidation (Rosenfeld and Ward 1996).[9] Nevertheless, the Spanish feminist movement, while not negligible, has been historically weak, its activities involving only a minority of women. The movement has occasionally shown some signs of strength, however. For example, it has organized national feminist conferences regularly attended by between 3,000 and 5,000 women. Nevertheless, in comparison with other

Western countries, the movement in Spain has not achieved high visibility in the mass media or initiated many public debates. In the 1980s, most of the feminist groups were very close to the left, and abortion was a priority for the women's movement. The Catholic Church was the main pressure group against the decriminalization of abortion and led a strong counter-movement to reform. Recognizing this, the PSOE moderated its position on abortion before the 1982 election in order to attract Catholic voters and avoid a frontal clash with the church. Once in government, the PSOE went on to seek legal abortion but only on limited ethical, therapeutic, and eugenic grounds (Barreiro 1998: 19,189).

❖ Policy environment

The debate under study took place in Parliament, which has some characteristics of closed policy environments: parliamentary proceedings are codified through regular meetings and rules, and participation is limited to leaders of political parties with parliamentary representation. However, it would be an over-statement to say that one major actor—the PSOE—controlled the policy space and parameters of the arena. Theoretically, parties other than the PSOE could affect the content of the bill through amendments. Practically, this was very unlikely, because the PSOE had an absolute majority in Parliament and could use it to block any amendment. But the system was opened a little because opposition parties could appeal to the CC. Since the beginning of the parliamentary debate, the conservative Alianza Popular declared that it would appeal to the CC, which it in fact did.

On other hand, as mentioned, at the time of debate prior to the 1985 abortion act the party in office was the socialist party, which had the absolute majority of seats in both chambers. Generally speaking, left-wing parties are considered to be more receptive to social movements than conservative parties, and in this case the left-wing party arrived in office with abortion reform on its agenda.

❖ DEBATE 2: THE REGULATIONS OF THE 1985 ABORTION ACT, 1986

❖ How the debate came to the public agenda

The rules involving of the implementation of the abortion legislation are very important, because they determine whether access to abortion services is easy or difficult for women. As Joyce Outshoorn (1996b: 150) explains, the implementation of legislation 'mainly revolves around the question of whether sufficient hospitals, clinics, and doctors willing to perform abortions are available. Institutional factors such as different hospital systems, the possibility to set up private clinics, and the presence of trained personnel are key factors here. Of

238

extreme importance are the attitudes of hospitals and clinic boards and personnel'.

The Ministry of Health and Consumption—hereafter called the Ministry of Health—had the responsibility of issuing these regulations. First, the ministry set forth the material and human resources required in clinics for the performance of abortion.[10] These clinics were required to have a doctor specializing in obstetrics and gynaecology; several nurses and nursing assistants; adequate facilities and tools to perform abortions; a clinical analysis laboratory; a unit for anaesthesia and resuscitation; a blood bank; and a hospitalization unit. Clinics were also required to have a social service unit themselves or to have access to external social services. These requirements were more extensive than what was necessary from a health point of view. The Ministerial Ordinance also established that an assessment committee (comisión de evaluación) composed of five members selected from health personnel must be present during the process leading to each induced abortion. The purpose of these committees was officially to facilitate the implementation of the act and to inform and give advice on problems of implementation.

In August 1985, the Ministry of Health made public a very broad conscience clause. According to this policy, health personnel, without giving concrete reasons, could refuse help in abortion cases pertaining to any of the three grounds. They could express this refusal in writing or by any other means, provided that the refusal was made directly to the head of the clinic, and could refuse to perform either specific abortions or abortions in general.

The WI monitored the implementation of the 1985 abortion act, and, according to Victoria Abril, the technical adviser to the Institute's director, found grave insufficiencies.[11] In September 1985 the WI drafted the first of a series of internal reports on the problems of the implementation of the 1985 abortion act to be sent to the Ministry of Health.[12] On 10 July 1986 the WI sent to the Ministry of Health draft legislation on the implementation of the abortion act (Instituto de la Mujer 1986a).

❖ Dominant frame of the debate

The debate dealt mainly with the difficulties that appeared when the abortion act was put into practice. In its reports, the WI identified three main problems, among others. First, the assessment committees exercised powers they did not have according to law. It was they, not the doctors, who decided case by case whether abortion should be performed or not. Second, due to the excessive resources requirements, very few public clinics, and no private clinics, were performing abortions. Third, the breadth of the conscience clause meant that very few abortions were actually performed in the very few public hospitals with adequate facilities (Barreiro 1998: 244–6; Instituto de la Mujer 1985; 1986 d, e).

In its reports, the WI made recommendations to facilitate access to abortion including, but not limited to, suppressing the assessment committee to simplify the bureaucratic procedures and increasing the number of authorized centres. In 1986 the WI took an even greater step by asking the government to change the statute itself by adding a fourth ground for abortion: the socio-economic circumstances of the pregnant woman (Instituto de la Mujer 1989c: 173; 1989d.). The Institute's position on abortion and this demand for a more permissive act created serious tensions between the government and the WI.[13] As a result, the WI put aside its demand for greater liberalization of the law and concentrated its efforts on influencing the regulation of the implementation of the existing act.

❖ Gendering the debate

The WI put the abortion debate where, according to feminists, it belonged: at the heart of the discussions on women's rights. The leadership strongly denounced other political and social actors for being overly concerned with other people's rights—for example, those of physicians. An example will illustrate the Institute's role. When the leaders asked the government to further decriminalize abortion, they justified this liberalization in terms of developing the 'fundamental right of the free development of personality [of the woman]', legalizing abortion on demand leaving it 'up to the free decision of the pregnant woman' if this decision was taken 'in a period during which the viability of the fetus only depends on the woman's will'—that is, when the foetus is not viable outside the woman's body (Instituto de la Mujer 1986e: 7).[14]

❖ Policy outcome

Following in some degree the recommendations of the WI, the Ministry of Health prepared a new draft decree pertaining to the implementation of abortion policy (Ministerio de Sanidad y Consumo 1986b). Subsequently, the WI sent other reports to the Ministry of Health with comments on the ministry's proposals. Eventually the government approved Royal Decree 2,409/1986 of 21 November on the implementation of the 1985 act, which substituted for the previous Ministerial Ordinance of 31 July 1985 (Ministry of Health and Consumption). The new regulations made access to abortion easier by suppressing the assessment committees. It also cut back on the material and human resources required for clinics to have the right to perform 'low-risk abortions', that is, up to twelve weeks of pregnancy.

❖ Movement impact

The negotiation between the Ministry of Health, the Women's Institute, and other policy actors was a process closed to the public. Representatives of organizations of the women's movement were not invited to participate in the negotiations. However, before taking state responsibilities in the WI, Carlota Bustelo and most members of the first directorate had for years belonged to women's movement groups. In addition, feminist groups kept up the pressure on the Institute to make further efforts regarding the decriminalization of abortion.

As I have explained elsewhere (Valiente 1995), Spanish feminists did not make a strong unified call for the creation of women's equality institutions in the 1970s and early 1980s. A sector of the feminist movement—namely, a part of the radical branch—was clearly against the creation of the WI and constantly accused it of being too moderate regarding some issues. This radical sector chose the issue of abortion to fight against the WI, in order to show that the women's policy machinery meant the deradicalization of the movement. According to these radical feminists, the WI and the socialist government would always promote measures that were far behind what radical feminism wanted, that is, abortion on demand performed in the public health system and free of charge. This radical sector was composed of very few women, but some of them were 'historical feminists', that is, comrades in political battles in the 1970s and early 1980s of some feminists who later became members of the first WI directive team. A few were active in Madrid, where the headquarters of the WI are located. These radical feminists always criticized WI's motives on abortion, which were considered too moderate for their radical taste. It is hard to measure the impact of radical feminism on the WI, but the impact probably existed.[15] For all these reasons, I conclude, but with reservations, that representatives of the women's movement participated in the policy process during the second debate.

The policy content of the 1986 Royal Decree, as it was de facto implemented, partly coincided with women's movement goals without fully satisfying them. It is true that most feminist groups mobilized in favour of abortion on demand, which was not provided by the 1986 Royal Decree. Nevertheless, the decree helped to make access to abortion easier. The loose implementation of the Royal Decree in practice made possible the performance of abortion on certain grounds not permitted by Spanish legislation. Therefore, the debate that preceded the second debate studied in this chapter lead to a dual response with respect to the movement impact.

❖ Women's policy agency activities

As during the first debate, during the second debate the scope of the WI was very broad. The WI was a bureaucratic part of the state and not a political appointment, and the WI was distant from major power centres. During the second debate, the WI was slightly better organized than during the first debate, since it had more staff and resources. The agency's position coincided with, if not completely fulfilling, women's movement goals in the policy-making process, that is, abortion on demand. However, although the WI sought a more permissive abortion act, it concentrated most of its efforts on obtaining final regulations for the existing act which would make access to abortion easier. This choice was probably the most radical option among the feasible alternatives available to the WI, given that, generally speaking, the PSOE refused to allow passage of a more permissive abortion act.

Due to previous experience, Carlota Bustelo and members of the WI directive team were well aware of the importance of intervening in the process of rule-making for such acts of parliament. Let me illustrate this point with the example of the legalization of contraceptives. When the first democratic parliamentary term started in 1977, the selling and advertizing of contraceptives was a crime punishable under the Penal Code. In Parliament, Carlota Bustelo advocated the decriminalization of contraception. Although the reform was eventually approved in 1978, it was not an easy battle. Afterwards, Bustelo and the defenders of the decriminalization of contraception found with dismay that the reform had been very poorly, if at all, implemented. Family planning centres were not set up, and doctors in public hospitals refused to prescribe contraceptives for conscience reasons (Bustelo 1979: 4). Therefore, access to contraception was still very limited, so much so that this issue became another priority of the WI, and a topic to be regularly discussed and negotiated with the Ministry of Health. This experience, along with others, probably made Carlota Bustelo and her team aware of the importance not only of asking for good acts but also of demanding good regulations for the implementation of any act which could enhance women's position.[16] Thus, the Women's Institute influenced the terms of the debate by bringing the Ministry of Health to accept a gendered definition of the problem of implementation. The WI also included the experiences and points of view of women who had abortions or wanted to have them in the debate (see, for instance, Instituto de la Mujer 1985). Thus the role of the Women's Institute can be classified as insider.

❖ *Women's movement characteristics*

Women's movement characteristics were unchanged from the first debate. The movement was in the stage of consolidation. The movement was not a mass movement—but was not a negligible movement either; it was very close to the left; and it made abortion one of its priorities. The Catholic Church itself acted as a strong opponent of any form of abortion liberalization.

❖ *Policy environment*

The policy sub-system of these health regulations in the bureaucracy was closed. The decision system was organized through regular meetings among policy-makers. Participation was limited to a few agents, that is, policy-makers. The Ministry of Health was the principal actor in the debate and controlled the policy space and parameters of the arena. Since its establishment, the Women's Institute had, however, made conscious efforts to build institutional channels of communication with other state units, especially the Ministry of Health. There were periodic meetings between the members of the WI directive team and personnel of the Ministry of Health to discuss a variety of matters including abortion.[17] Nevertheless, the reader should not infer that the relations between the WI and the Ministry of Health were strong, friendly, and cooperative. Very often the WI directive team got the impression that the Ministry of Health did not welcome WI proposals, or that the ministry politely heard them but did not have any intention of putting them into practice.[18] Nevertheless, channels of communication existed and were of crucial importance in influencing policy-makers in the debate on abortion. Thanks in part to these institution-building efforts, the policy environment around the regulation of the implementation of the 1985 abortion act was open to insider feminist activism.

❖ CONCLUSION

This chapter has discovered that state feminism led to a dual response in one of the two policy decisions in the area of abortion in Spain in the mid-1980s. With only a marginal agency during the debate leading to the 1985 abortion act, however, the state pre-empted the movement's demands without accepting women or movement activists into the policy-making process.

The findings of this chapter suggest at least three conditions that are necessary for the WI to successfully gender policy debates and to have policy influence on a specific matter. First, the WI directive team has to show a pronounced interest on the topic. Since the WI is a small institution—the whole staff is slightly more than 150 people—this interest in the issue is in part related to the personal interests of the WI director and members of the WI directive team. As shown, in the mid-1980s abortion was a top priority for the WI.

Second, in order to successfully gender policy debates, the WI has to have created institutional channels of communication with other institutions in the specific policy area. The WI managed to do this regarding abortion. Since its establishment, members of the WI directive team periodically met with personnel of the Ministry of Health to discuss issues including abortion.

Third, obvious as it might be, the knowledge of the WI directive team on specific topics and policy areas is very important. The WI directive team needs to know a lot about specific topics, for instance abortion. But the WI also needs to know the characteristics of the policy areas around concrete issues. Crucial here is the knowledge of the institutional capacity of the state to intervene regarding any given problem, the range of feasible alternatives to solve problems, and the possible difficulties that can be present at the implementation stage of the policy. The empirical case of abortion policies shows that this knowledge existed in the mid-1980s in the WI, and contributed to the successful advancement of feasible demands that were satisfied. In any case, more research is needed on state feminism and political debates in different policy areas, national cases, and chronological periods in order to reach more nuanced conclusions on women's descriptive and substantive representation emanating from women's policy machineries.

As a result of WI's influence, the human and material resource requirements for legal abortion were lowered, and private clinics became interested in becoming authorized centres for performing abortions. Since then, private clinics have performed the overwhelming majority of abortions. In 1998, 53,847 abortions were reported in Spain, a rate of six abortions per 1,000 women of reproductive age. The actual total number of abortions is probably higher. Ninety seven per cent of reported abortions were performed in private centres, and the remaining 3 per cent in public centres. Almost all—97.32 per cent—reported abortions were officially granted because of risks of pregnancy for the physical or mental health of the mother, 2.27 per cent were performed because of presumed deformity of the fetus, 0.03 per cent were performed because of rape, and the remaining 0.38 per cent for unknown reasons (*El País* 2000: 22). Thanks to the loose implementation of the 1986 Royal Decree, access to abortion is easier than before, and very often goes beyond what is permitted by the 1985 Abortion Act. Most cases officially registered as abortions performed on the ground of the physical and mental health of the mother are in reality performed on socio-economic grounds, which is a type of abortion not permitted by law (Barreiro 1998: 248–52).

There remain serious barriers to abortion. One of them is cost. Private clinics charge fees while public centres do not. Since most abortions take place in more costly private centres, some women cannot afford an abortion. A second barrier is the scarcity of authorized clinics in some cities, towns or regions; abortion rates vary widely among different regions (*El País* 2000: 22). Third, because many abortions are performed for reasons not permitted by law, doctors and women are under continuous threat of prosecution. Only a reform in the 1985 abortion act can remedy this situation (Barreiro 1998: 248–52).

❖ Notes

1 A seminal Ph.D. dissertation written in Spanish, 'Democracy and Moral Conflict: The Politics of Abortion in Italy and Spain' (Barreiro 1998), has been of immense value for the writing of these empirical case studies. I follow this dissertation very closely when I describe the two abortion debates in this chapter. The sources for this chapter also include published and unpublished documents from the Women's Institute, a parliamentary debate, legislation, unpublished documents from the Ministry of Health and Consumption, and press files.

2 This part of the debate in the Congress of Deputies can be consulted in DSCD (1983*a,b,c,d*; 1985*d*).

3 This part of the debate in the Senate can be consulted in DSS (1983: 1852–1906).

4 The representation of women who have abortions as people under stress and in need of help is common in policy statements issued in other Western countries (Outshoorn 1996*a*).

5 The debate in the Congress of Deputies can be consulted in DSCD (1985*a*; 1985*b*). The debate in the Senate can be consulted in DSS (1985: 5994–6030).

6 See, for instance, interventions of: deputy Bandrés Molet from the Mixed Parliamentary Group (DSCD 1983*a*: 1870); (female) deputy Pelayo Duque from the Socialist Parliamentary Group (DSCD 1983*c*: 2927); and deputy Pérez Royo from the Mixed Parliamentary Group (DSCD 1983*c*: 2938).

7 In 1996, the Ministry of Labour and Social Security and the Ministry of Social Affairs were merged into the Ministry of Labour and Social Affairs.

8 Many sources document this priority status. For instance, most issues of the WI periodical journal Mujeres (Women), published in Madrid, contain pages on the topic. According to the Women's Institute, Mujeres had a circulation of 8,000 copies in 1983 and of 20,000 copies in 1986. Pages on abortion can be consulted in Mujeres (1983: 6, 9–11; 1984*a*: 32–33, *b*: 15–17, 27, 32, 49, *c*: 72). For more information on the women's institute, see Threlfall (1996; 1998) and Valiente (1995; 1997).

9 For accounts of the Spanish feminist movement, see: Durán and Gallego (1986); Escario, Alberdi, and López-Accotto (1996); Folguera (1988); Kaplan (1992); Scanlon (1990); Threlfall (1985, 1996).

10 Ministerial Ordinance of 31 July 1985, Ministry of Health and Consumption.

11 Personal interview, Madrid, 14 August 1998.

12 The series comprises: Instituto de la Mujer (1985, 1986*a*, *b*, *c*, *d*, *e*, *f*, *g*).

13 This information was provided by WI director Carlota Bustelo in a personal interview conducted by the author in Madrid on 6 April 1994 (Valiente 1995).

14 Author's translation.

15 This description of radical feminism in Spain and its position and tactics regarding abortion and the WI is drawn from a personal interview the author conducted with Justa Montero on 25 May 1994 from the Pro-Abortion Commission (Valiente 1995).

16 Carlota Bustelo's understanding of the significance of the implementation of acts is contained in some of her writings (Bustelo 1986: 275; 1987: 15; 1988: 281–2).

17 Published WI documents mentioned these meetings as early as in 1984: for instance, Mujeres (1984*a*: 32–33).

18 This description of the relationships between the WI and the Ministry of Health is drawn from the interviews conducted with Victoria Abril in Madrid, 14 August 1998, and Carlota Bustelo in Madrid, 6 April 1994 (Valiente 1995).

12 ❖ US Abortion Debates 1959–1998: The Women's Movement Holds On

Dorothy McBride Stetson

❖ INTRODUCTION

It is almost impossible to overstate the significance of the abortion issue in the political life in the United States. Since its arrival on the public agenda in 1959, abortion has never left and it remains 'politically charged and morally problematic' (Condit 1990: ix). It permeates every political arena: legislative, executive, judicial, interest group, and bureaucratic at federal/national, State, and local levels (Craig and O'Brien 1993). It has claimed attention in every sort of political process: electoral, legislative, judicial and executive appointment, constitutional, political party, interest group, budgetary, administrative, federalist. It has infiltrated debates on nearly every other issue: education, welfare, sexuality, science and medical research, licensing of professionals, health care, military, foreign aid, labour, taxation. Political leaders have considered and made policy on every aspect of abortion: regulation and legalization; funding; access to services; limits on protest; family planning; reporting requirements; advertising; fetal research; parental consent and notification; spousal consent and notification. Potentially, every time the abortion issue is up for discussion it pulls in the major religious, moral, and cultural divisions of American society. No wonder it has been called the major conflict of the post-war era in the United States.

Initially, the objects of controversy were laws in every State, enacted between 1821 and 1880, that criminalized abortion. Most permitted abortion on therapeutic grounds, typically if the pregnancy threatened the life of the mother. It is important to realize that earlier in American history, however, in the absence of effective contraception, many women had come to rely on obtaining abortion from a variety of practitioners. The common law that prevailed in the colonies and the early days of the union did not prosecute when the termination was done early in pregnancy, before quickening (animation). It was the American Medical Association (AMA) that led the campaign to criminalize abortion in the 1850s, declaring the fetus a 'living being' and, simultaneously, driving other practitioners, such as midwives, out of the business (Mohr 1978).

While feminists in the nineteenth century opposed abortion and did not protest against its widespread criminalization, the contemporary women's movement has been involved on the abortion issue on behalf of women's rights since the 1960s. In the early years, demands for legalized abortion were a unifying issue in the growth phase of the movement. At the same time, a separate movement developed to seek relief from strict laws, which included doctors, population control groups, and other advocates for repeal of criminal abortion. Women's movement groups joined with the abortion repeal groups to form the pro-choice movement. The central pro-choice organizations have been NARAL[1] and Planned Parenthood Federation of America, and several women's rights organizations have remained their stalwart allies: American Association of University Women (AAUW); National Organization for Women (NOW); and the National Women's Health Network. Thus the pro-choice movement and the women's movement overlap, and the feminists have had a great deal of influence over pro-choice activism (Staggenborg 1991). But these movements are not the same, and the distinction between them will be made throughout this chapter.

When an issue with the political significance of abortion in the US draws the attention of not one but two pro-woman social movements, it could mean that they would not need any help from women's policy agencies in order to have an impact on the state. But these movements face an exceptionally strong counter-movement, called the 'pro-life' movement which has, since the early 1970s, periodically threatened to overwhelm advocates for abortion rights for women. Despite their efforts, the pro-choice movement and its feminist allies have so far prevailed. In 2001, abortion remains legal in the US and, in comparison with other countries, relatively unrestricted. Have the pro-choice and women's movements had any help from women's policy agencies and other femocrats within the state? In reviewing several policy debates, this chapter shows that the women's rights advocates have periodically found allies inside the state who have made the difference between success and failure. But usually their allies have been either the president or congressional representatives rather than the specialized women's policy agencies, which tend to be weak and, at best, peripheral to the process.

❖ SELECTION OF DEBATES

The period of the study of abortion policy debates is 1959–98. In the United States, decisions pertaining to the abortion issue are taken in nearly every public arena by every type of government actor. Four main institutions dominate. First, the federal courts, especially the Supreme Court, issue 'landmark rulings' that set the limits on governmental policy options in all other arenas. Second, Congress sets guidelines for the use of federal funds, and, through its constitutional authority to regulate interstate commerce, can regulate abortion services. Third, the president sets regulations for the implementation of congressional policy that have wide impact. The fourth set of institutions is the State governments which enact the laws that directly regulate the legality of, and access to, abortions and serve as important policy forums on the issue (Merz, Jackson, and Klerman 1995). The States are not, however, the last word, and their policies must be within constitutional and federal guidelines set by federal courts and Congress.

This study will focus on the institutional arenas in Congress and in the US Supreme Court. The congressional arena encompasses activities by the executive branch, and States operate within guidelines set by these powers. And, given the fact that thousands of policies have been debated during the period of review and the need to select no more than three debates, the study will select debates that represent consideration by these two most authoritative institutions. Both arenas have the potential to be open to participation by women's policy agencies: Congress through hearings and the courts through assisting in presentation of *amicus curiae*—friend of the court—briefs.

The universe of debates will include regulation, funding, and access to services, because these are the abortion policy debates where the subject is exclusively about abortion. The universe does not include the many instances in which questions of abortion have been raised in the course of debating another issue, such as education, the military, family planning, or foreign aid. Such a wide array of abortion-related debates is the result of the high politicization of the issue in the US and including them in the universe of debates would make the US case less comparable with other countries in this study. All debates end in a statute or court ruling.

Within these parameters, the following comprise the universe of policy debates in the United States:

(1) legalization of abortion leading to the Supreme Court decision *Roe v. Wade*, 1959–73;
(2) restriction of federal funding for abortions by Congress: Hyde Amendment, 1974–7;
(3) Supreme Court rulings clarifying the scope and application of *Roe v. Wade* and the Hyde Amendment: *Planned Parenthood v. Danforth*, 1976; *Beal v. Doe*, 1977; *Belotti v. Baird*, 1979; *Harris v. McRae*, 1980;
(4) Supreme Court rulings on constitutionality of administrative barriers to abortion procedures: *Akron v. Akron Center for Reproductive Health*, 1983;

Thornburgh v. American College of Obstetricians & Gynecologists, 1986; Webster v. Reproductive Health Services, 1989;

(5) congressional deliberations on the Freedom of Choice Act to write guidelines from *Roe v. Wade* into federal statutory law, ending with a Supreme Court ruling upholding and adapting *Roe* guidelines in *Planned Parenthood v. Casey*, 1991–2;

(6) congressional enactment of Freedom of Access to Clinic Entrances, providing federal remedies to criminal obstruction of access to clinics, 1992–4; and

(7) congressional enactment of Partial Birth Abortion Ban Act, criminalizing a late-term abortion procedure, vetoed by the President, 1995–8.

Three of these debates have been selected for study here: *Roe v. Wade* (1973) 1959–73: the Supreme Court decision prohibiting States from criminalizing abortion in the first two trimesters of pregnancy; the Hyde Amendment 1975–7 restricting public funding of abortions sustained by Supreme Court decisions; and the Partial Birth Abortion Ban Acts, 1995–8. These debates represent decisional system importance by including one from the Supreme Court and two from Congress. In the case of the Hyde Amendment, the congressional debate was affected by a decision in the Court. The debates represent the life cycle of abortion, from the first significant debate over legalization to the most recent regarding the banning of a specific late-term abortion procedure. However, rather than spacing debates evenly over the life cycle, the criterion of issue salience took precedence by including the initial withdrawal of federal funding (Hyde Amendment). The selection does not include debates on access, whether physical access to a abortion clinics or where the debate pertained to parental consent, spousal consent, or other administrative hurdles. Given the limits in resources, I have chosen to concentrate on legalization and funding, which constitute the foundation of policy on the abortion issue in the US.

❖ DEBATE 1: CONSTITUTIONALITY OF ILLEGAL ABORTION, 1959–1973

❖ *How the debate came to the public agenda*

Beginning in the 1930s, hospitals tightened standards and required doctors to consult with other doctors before performing abortions. Gradually, for doctors to perform legal abortions, they had to comply with these standards, reducing their discretion within the realm of private practice. During the post-war period, demand for abortion increased, medical procedures improved, and physicians and psychiatrists began to criticize, if quietly, the restrictions on their medical judgement. The issue arrived on the public agenda in 1959 when doctors called for liberalization and the American Law Institute (ALI) issued its draft reform law (Stetson 1997; Garrow 1994: 277). This model law expanded the conditions for therapeutic abortions to include preserving the physical and mental health of the mother, if the pregnancy was the result of rape or incest and if there was likelihood that the fetus would be deformed. Beginning with California in 1967, 15 States passed abortion reform laws based on the ALI proposal.

'Abortion on demand' was one of the first goals of the Women's Liberation Movement, as the autonomous or 'younger' branch was called (Freeman 1975). The National Organization for Women, formed in 1966, added abortion rights to its agenda in 1967. A strategy of constitutional litigation—seeking statutory change through judicial review by the federal courts—had proved to be extremely successful for the civil rights movement. Women's rights attorneys and civil liberties advocates adopted a similar strategy to challenge laws that discriminated against women. Until the 1960s, seeking reproductive rights through this strategy was largely untried. In 1965, family planning advocates achieved a striking success when the Supreme Court legalized contraceptives for married couples.[2] In 1971, two young feminist attorneys brought a constitutional challenge to the Texas criminal abortion law in the case of *Roe v. Wade*.[3]

❖ Dominant frame of the debate

Initially, challengers to restrictive laws focused on the need for doctors to have more legal leeway to respond to increasing demands from patients for exceptions to the strict ban on abortion, in most States available only to save the life of the mother. The defenders of the laws, drawing strength and support from the Catholic Church, maintained that fetal life was absolute with no exceptions. Thus, when it arrived on the public agenda, abortion law reform was framed as a desire for giving expanded discretion to the medical profession and was opposed by groups who saw abortion as murder. During the 1960s, however, the scope of the conflict about these laws expanded as many new perspectives came into public discussion. With the Sherry Finkbine case, doctors sought to demonstrate the problems of middle-class married women faced with the birth of a deformed child.[4] Population control advocates wanted legal abortion as a means of family planning. The women's movement began to raise questions about women's reproductive rights.

The decade of the 1960s was a period when the conflict was not only over what the law should be, but what the frame of the issue should be. Was it an issue of doctor's rights? Was it a problem of married couples faced with problem pregnancies? Was it part of women's liberation? Advocates for change took their battles to State legislatures seeking reform or repeal of abortion laws. But it was not until the constitutional appeal of a criminal abortion law by Jane

Roe against Attorney General Henry Wade of Texas reached the Supreme Court that a national institution was an arena for this 'conflict over the conflict'.

The briefs challenging the constitutionality of the Texas law argued that illegal abortion was a problem because it violated individual privacy protected by the Constitution. Building on the precedent in *Griswold v. Connecticut*, challengers went on to say that guarantees of privacy included the right to terminate an unwanted pregnancy and claimed this marital and personal privacy for women. Second, they pointed out that illegal abortion infringed on a physician's right to practice medicine without state interference and the patient's right to medical treatment. Challengers elaborated on the safety of abortion, arguing that it was an accepted medical procedure, dangerous only when illegal. Some briefs likened illegal abortion to involuntary pregnancy, involuntary servitude, and compulsory child-bearing.

Defenders of illegal abortion offered fewer arguments, focusing on the humanity of the fetus. Their main point was that illegal abortion protected the right to life of the fetus which, they claimed, was a person under the law according to scientific evidence. They responded to each of the challengers' points: (1) personal and family privacy are not absolute, but life is; and (2) physicians should have discretion to treat their patients, but in the case of pregnancy they have two patients, mother and child, and the law should protect both. Simply put, defenders claimed that what was at stake in the legalization of abortion was allowing the child in the womb to be killed.

❖ Gendering the Debate

Both challengers and defenders attempted to gender the debate. Challengers, in support of Jane Roe, included medical groups, such as the American College of Obstetricians and Gynecologists, the American Medical Women's Association, abortion reform groups such as the National Abortion Action Coalition, population groups such as Zero Population Growth, and women's movement organizations such as NOW and the Women's Health and Abortion project. These interests, which eventually came together as the pro-choice movement, painted an image of women overwhelmed by the problem of illegal abortion. Since pregnancy had such an impact on women, they argued, illegal abortion meant involuntary pregnancy, with the pregnant woman's body in a state of service, made a victim by the law. The defenders were fewer: Americans United for Life, National Right to Life Committee, and 'Certain Physicians and Professors'. The defenders portrayed women, as mothers, to be passive carriers of another human life. Scientific evidence was called upon to demonstrate that the fetus was in charge of the pregnancy, not the mother.

❖ DOROTHY McBRIDE STETSON

Challengers tried to compare women and men, pointing out that men and women have equal responsibility in sexual intercourse and conceiving a child, but that women endure the entire burden; sometimes, they said, this burden is a punishment which women must bear alone. They deplored illegal abortion which made women into unwilling incubators or forced them to give up their children, drawing analogies to breeders. Challengers emphasized the need to give choice in abortion. Defenders suggested that while women had choice over their fate, they had to make this choice before they become pregnant. Thus, gendering was central to the debates in the *Roe v. Wade* briefs. Challengers especially emphasized the effect of the law on women in their gender roles and their rights in reproduction. The defenders focused more on the rights of the fetus but also engaged in a gendered debate.

❖ *Policy outcome*

On 22 January 1973, the Supreme Court, ruling seven to two, overturned the Texas law and established guidelines for States' regulation of abortion. The justices did not permit the States to enact laws that restricted abortion before the third trimester of pregnancy. In the third trimester, the State governments could prohibit abortion but must retain exceptions for the life and health of the mother. The Court's decision in *Roe v. Wade* established the dominant frame of debate on the question of illegal abortion. Justice Harry Blackmun's opinion agreed with the challengers that, first and foremost, the question of illegal abortion was a question of a violation of the right of privacy for women. But the Court also decided that there were other problems that must be part of the debate: these were the physician's rights to practise medicine, the State government's interests in the health of mothers, and, only at the end of pregnancy, the State's interest in protecting fetal life. According to the court, the frame did not include the rights of the fetus as an autonomous person. Only through the intervention of the State government could the interests of the fetus be considered. This decision thus set forth the hierarchy of interest: first, woman's privacy; second, doctors' professional status; and third, the States' interests.

❖ *Movement impact*

The debate over the constitutionality of criminal abortion laws culminated in a Court ruling, not a legislative statute as in many other countries. In this, however, the state provided a *dual response* to both the women's movement and the pro-choice movement. Through presenting *amicus curiae* briefs, women as individuals and in groups—American Medical Women's Association, New Women Lawyers, NOW, and the Women's Health and Abortion project—were accepted into the judicial policy process.[5] And, of course, the ruling in *Roe v. Wade* which placed women's right to choose abortion at its centre, coincided with, while not completely satisfying, women's movement demands and definition of the abortion issue.

❖ *Women's policy agency activities*

The women's policy agency that may have been able to participate in the debate over the constitutionality of criminal abortion was the Secretary's Advisory Committee on the Rights and Responsibilities of Women appointed by the Federal Secretary of Health, Education, and Welfare. It was a cross-sectional, administrative committee composed of representatives of agencies and organizations within and outside of government. It occupied a low position in the government hierarchy, and had no independent resources. Its leaders were Republican Party feminists. Its primary policy responsibilities were equality in education, national health insurance, social security, and career advancement within the department. Thus abortion rights was only peripheral to the committee mandate. In its 1973 report, the Committee declared that women must exercise choice in child-bearing, but the agency did not participate in the constitutional debate and therefore did not successfully gender the debate (Department of Health, Education and Welfare 1974). Thus the women's policy agency's role can be classified as *marginal* in the achievement of a dual state response in this first abortion policy debate.

❖ *Women's movement characteristics*

In 1959–72, the women's movement was *emerging*: the autonomous movement was in its heyday with vast expansion of local women's liberation groups. NOW formed in 1966 and its chapters were growing in the States. The movement formed outside the two dominant political parties, and in 1972 made efforts to influence both parties at their national conventions to equalize representation for women. While they were more successful in the Democratic Party, they were often ignored by its presidential candidate George McGovern. Therefore the movement was not close to the left. There was a counter-movement on the abortion issue—right to life—but it was not very strong or well organized before the *Roe v. Wade* decision. The issue was a high priority unifying issue for the women's movement's older and younger branches.

❖ *Policy environment*

Between 1959 and 1973, Democrats retained control of both houses of Congress, while the presidency shifted between Democrats and Republicans. In 1973, Republican Richard Nixon was in the White House. The composition of the

Supreme Court, where the debate took place, reflected choices by both Republicans and Democrats, with Warren Burger, Nixon appointee, as Chief Justice. Legal structures which focus on the justiciability of an issue dominate the arena. Precedent is extremely important in the process, and there is collegial decision-making among the justices. The legal culture is based on texts and argument, and seeks a regulated and limited approach to policy making (Scheppele 1996). This might signal a closed environment of legal experts applying narrow rules. Nevertheless, through conscious strategies of litigation and presentation of *amicus curiae* briefs, social movement activists have found the constitutional court to be an environment for seeking reform of laws they are unable to change through legislative arenas. Thus, for these reasons, the policy sub-system relating to Debate 1 was moderately closed.

❖ DEBATE 2: FEDERAL FUNDING OF ABORTIONS, 1974–1977

❖ How debate came to the public agenda

Roe v. Wade set guidelines that prohibited States from proscribing abortion before the third trimester of pregnancy and stimulated opponents of legal abortion to action. A strategy of the so-called pro-life movement was to use federal laws to restrict access to abortion in every way possible. By 1974 there were proposals in Congress to restrict Medicaid funds along with discussions of a constitutional amendment to return power to the States to make abortion illegal. Here we examine the debate over what came to be known as the Hyde Amendment after its chief sponsor, Representative Henry Hyde of Illinois. Rather than a separate bill, this proposal was a floor amendment to the annual appropriations bill for the Department of Health, Education and Welfare. It prohibited Medicaid funds to be used to pay for abortions.[6] Therefore there were no public hearings; senators and representatives articulated their views on the floor.

❖ Dominant frame of the debate

Proponents of the Hyde Amendment opposed legal abortion and sought to change the debate frame established by *Roe* in order to recognize the right of the fetus to life as being at least coequal with the right of the mother to privacy. Although they tried to substitute taxpayers who were morally opposed to abortion as the proxy victims of abortion funding, it was the right of the fetus to life that emerged as the top priority in floor debates throughout 1975, 1976, and 1977. Echoing the defenders of criminalized abortion in the Roe briefs, proponents of the Hyde Amendment argued that a woman's right to control her body to achieve her own interests ends at conception and that she has no right to terminate life 'for convenience'.

THE UNITED STATES ❖

Opponents of the Hyde Amendment defended the dominant frame established in the *Roe* decision: that what the abortion debate was about was the rights of women to make decisions about abortion. They claimed that denying Medicaid funds for abortions deprived poor women of a fundamental constitutional right. Poor women alone would face the consequences of back room/back alley abortions with coat hangers and knitting needles.

Proponents of Hyde blanketed the rhetorical space with references to the fetus as human life, the 'innocently inconvenient' defenceless human being, tiny human waiting to be born, new and unique genetic package, weak and vulnerable. Abortion was portrayed as elimination of people, execution, destroying our young, snuffing out lives, violence, killing the next generation, taking of human life, calculated killing of innocent inconvenient human beings, fetal euthanasia: in short, morally and ethically VERY wrong. Opponents had nothing to say about the fetus, and portrayed legal abortion as safe and illegal abortion as dangerous to women.

❖ Gendering the Debate

As in the *Roe v. Wade* briefs, the floor debate on the Hyde Amendment was gendered. Proponents of the Hyde Amendment articulated images of women as mothers whose function was to give themselves to their children before and after birth. 'For nine months the mother provides nourishment and shelter, and birth is no substantial change, it is merely a change of address' (*Congressional Record* 1976: 20410). But they also saw another, bad, woman, the one who seeks an abortion, ' . . . when the mother who should be the natural protector of her unborn child, becomes its adversary . . .' (*Congressional Record* 1976: 26785). Opponents of the Hyde Amendment made references to poor women forced to carry unwanted pregnancies to term because they could not afford to pay for abortions. They also portrayed poor women as exposed to risk of unnecessary death or severe emotional complications because they could not use their right to abortion.

❖ Policy outcome

During the debates in the Congress, the Supreme Court ruled on the constitutionality of restrictions on Medicaid funding laws that had been previously enacted in the States.[7] According to the justices who ruled in these cases, government was under no constitutional obligation to help women get abortions. '*Roe* did not declare an unqualified "constitutional right to an abortion" ... Rather the right protects the woman from unduly burdensome interference with her freedom to decide whether to terminate her pregnancy' (*Maher v. Roe*).[8] This decision strengthened the case of the proponents of the Hyde Amendment because opponents could no longer claim a constitutional right to obtain abortion or to warn that any congressional restrictions were unconstitutional.

The 1977 debate over the Hyde Amendment became a stalemate between the House of Representatives and the Senate that tied up the Health, Education and Welfare appropriation bill from September to December. The struggle was not over whether to pass a restriction on abortion funding but over what exceptions would be allowed. The House version, pushed by active pro-life congressional representatives, allowed funding only for abortions deemed necessary because the life of the mother would be endangered if the pregnancy went to term. The Senate wanted more exceptions, including paying for 'medical procedures'— read: abortion procedures—for victims of rape and incest. The final compromise coincided more with the Senate version than the House version. Neither side was happy. Henry Hyde introduced his amendment again the following year and secured a ban with an exception only when a mother's life was endangered. That version became the standard enacted in every session of Congress for the next decade. The US Supreme Court, as expected, upheld the constitutionality of the Hyde Amendment in 1980.[9]

❖ Movement impact

The Hyde Amendment debate was a failure for the women's movement. Women—individuals or in groups and networks—were not admitted to the policy process in Congress where the decision was made. The only two women who participated in the debate were Representatives Bella Abzug and Patricia Schroeder, but, with the tiny representation of women in the Congress, they were clearly outnumbered.

President Carter announced his support for the Supreme Court's decision to uphold the constitutionality of States' restricting abortion funding. When asked in a press conference about the fairness of funding restrictions on poor women he replied 'There are many things in life that are not fair' (*New York Times* 1977: 10:3). This apparently callous remark provoked a strong reaction from women's movement activists and even women in his administration. Their protest made news, but this was far removed from the policy arena.

Women's groups also participated in the public discussion of the Hyde Amendment. NOW and the National Women's Political Caucus strongly opposed the cut-off of funds for abortions, but they did not get access to the policy process either. The outcome—the passage of the Hyde Amendment nearly eliminating federal and, consequently, State funding of abortion for poor women—was a rejection of the demands by movement advocates. Therefore this debate resulted in no response with respect to the movement impact.

✧ *Women's policy agency activities*

The National Commission on the Observance of International Women's Year (IWY) was the only agency with the potential to be involved in the debate. Congress established the committee to prepare for the US participation in the United Nations IWY conference in Mexico City. It was a cross-sectional, advisory commission, remote from power. Congress appropriated funds only to finance IWY conferences in every State and a national conference, so its resources for other activities were limited. The two chairs, Jill Ruckelshaus, a Republican, and Bella Abzug, a Democrat, were both feminists. The commission reports dealt with a wide range of policy issues, but they were propositions only. The commission, which disbanded in 1977, had no mandate to follow up on its policy recommendations.[10]

The commission had sponsored the National Women's Conference in 1975 in Houston and published a wide-ranging report on the goals and demands of the women's movement and a national plan of action (National Commission 1976; 1978). The IWY commission urged the federal government and the States to provide abortion services under Medicaid funding; this was a part of their more general support for wider reproductive rights and coincided with women's movement goals. Their resolutions had little impact on gendering the discussion over the Hyde Amendment, and their activities were marginal to the policy debate.

✧ *Women's movement characteristics*

In the mid-1970s, the women's movement was in a full growth stage as indicated by expansion of feminist consciousness, increase in number of movement organizations, and the large number of movement events and activities (Rosenfeld and Ward 1996). The movement's participation in the Democratic Party was growing as well, but there were conflicts between feminist groups and the party's leader President Carter, especially over abortion funding. At this time, the influence of the anti-feminist New Right, in league with a very strong counter movement (pro-life), was growing in the Republican Party, and the women's movement bipartisan strategy waned, bringing it moderately close to the left during the Hyde debate. The abortion issue remained a top-priority, unifying issue for the women's movement.

✧ *Policy environment*

The Democrats were in the majority in the Congress and held the presidency during the debate. The policy sub-system for consideration of the Hyde Amendment, however, was the appropriations process, a closed policy process no matter which party holds the majority. In appropriations, debates take place in committees and on the floor of both houses, and there is input from executive agencies, but few public hearings or opportunities for voices from outside Congress. A budget reform in 1974 meant that appropriation bills were bundled into huge omnibus packages and few people knew what was in them. Financial discourse dominates. The debate on the Hyde Amendment disturbed this process by interjecting a substantive policy debate, one that was divisive and upheld the health, education, and labour budget for several months past the beginning of the fiscal year. It also demonstrated that the appropriations policy sub-system can be used by congressional leaders—in this case pro-life advocates—to achieve a social or behavioural outcome.

❖ DEBATE 3: THE PARTIAL BIRTH ABORTION BAN ACT, 1995–1998

❖ How the debate came to the public agenda

During the 1980s, as the pro-life activists sought to further restrict access to abortion, women's movement advocates for choice in abortion were in a defensive mode. The counter-movement's campaign to overturn *Roe* by changing the composition of the Supreme Court was moving along, and, in 1989, the decision in *Webster v. Reproductive Health Services* augured success. The decision itself did not make abortion illegal but a plurality of four justices invited States to bring challenges to the central holding in *Roe v. Wade*. The case provoked strong reaction from the pro-choice movement and woke up many to the real possibility that abortion would once again be criminalized in the US. Allies in Congress immediately introduced the Freedom of Choice Act (FOCA) which would guarantee legality of abortion before viability of the fetus through a federal law. The intent was to codify the court's decision in *Roe v. Wade*, taking it out of the reach of the pro-life justices. Hearings and floor debates were held in 1990, 1991, and 1992. Before action could be taken, however, the Supreme Court issued its ruling in *Planned Parenthood of Southeast Pennsylvania v. Casey*,[11] upholding the legality of abortion established in *Roe*. Apparently, the justices succeeded in finding a compromise because neither the pro-choice feminists nor the pro-life activists were happy with the Casey ruling. However, with the election of pro-choice President Bill Clinton in 1992, after twelve years of presidents sympathetic to the pro-life movement, the pro-choice organizations switched their attention to issues of access to abortion services.

Not so with the pro-life movement. With the decision in Casey and defeats in efforts to obtain a return to criminalization of all abortion, the pro-life advocates switched their strategy. In 1992, Martin Haskell, MD presented a paper titled 'Dilation and Extraction for Late Second Trimester Abortion' at a seminar sponsored by the National Abortion Federation, a provider group. It described an alternative to the standard dilation and extraction (D&X) surgical procedure for ending second-trimester pregnancies, and the author claimed to have performed 700 of these procedures with few complications. Both standard and modified D&X procedures, faster than other methods and performed in doctors' offices under local anesthesia, were developed in response to the lack of hospital facilities for second trimester abortions. The National Conference of Catholic Bishops, aiming to persuade nominally pro-choice voters that abortion was abhorrent, distributed articles describing D&X in extremely gruesome terms. They renamed this procedure 'partial birth' abortion and, taking advantage of the Republican majority in both houses of Congress after 1994, pro-life representatives introduced a bill that would bring criminal prosecution to any doctor using the procedure.

❖ Dominant frame of the debate

In 1992, the 'troika' (see Scheppele 1996: 32) of Supreme Court justices who wrote the *Casey* opinion had provided a revised official frame of the abortion issue in the United States. For them—Justices Sandra Day O'Connor, David Souter, and Anthony Kennedy—the challenge for policy-makers regulating the legality of abortion was to find the proper balance between women's liberty to make decisions about their pregnancies—as opposed to the privacy frame of *Roe v. Wade*—and the obligations of States to protect the life of the fetus.

Pro-life advocates developed a strategy aimed at re-framing the issue of abortion by describing the procedures of late-term abortion in the most gory detail possible. They hoped the following definition of the procedure would make the need for a ban self-evident: 'An abortion in which the person performing the abortion partially vaginally delivers a living fetus before killing the fetus and completing the delivery' (House of Representatives 1995: 1). Restated, they said, the procedure takes the life of the 'baby' while in the birth canal. It is 'three inches' away from homicide. In introducing the Partial-Birth Abortion Ban (PBAB) Act, pro-life advocates sought to introduce a new definition of abortion regulation into the public debate, portray the procedure and doctor's use of it as an attack on the lives of the nearly born, and thereby change the dominant definition of the issue of abortion regulation to eliminate reference to women's rights.

In 1995, opponents of the ban struggled to reclaim the definition of abortion regulation as a matter of women's rights. They warned that the PBAB Act was bad public policy and an intrusion into women's medical treatment. It would tamper with the right of women to choose abortion, thus increasing medical risks to women. It also, they argued, interfered with physicians' rights and was so vague that it might ban many abortion procedures. In fact, many maintained, such a procedure as partial-birth abortion did not exist at all: it had no relevance to medical procedure. Further they charged, no doubt accurately, that the intent behind the act was to begin to criminalize abortion, one procedure at a time, until all abortions were prohibited.

❖ Gendering the debate

Both sides brought gender ideas into the debate. The proponents of the ban used imagery similar to debates 20 years earlier, that is, seeing woman as mother, the natural protector of the child in the womb, turned by legalized abortion into her child's deadly adversary. Opponents maintained that abortion was a deeply personal decision for any woman and should not in any way be proscribed by government. They brought out their conventional arguments that any ban on abortion increased medical risks to life and health of women and would restrict their right to obtain needed health care. They reasoned that since late second-trimester abortions were a last resort due to serious risks to the mother by continuing the pregnancy, denying this procedure would especially risk a woman's future ability to have children. This bill allowed no exceptions when the procedure might be necessary to save a woman's life or protect her health and ability to have more children. It merely said that when a doctor was charged with the crime, that excuse could be used as a defence against a conviction.

Although the opponents of the PBAB Act strove to attract attention to the gender questions they raised, gendering became marginal to the emerging frame of the 1995 debate. Most attention was paid to the question of the rights of the fetus to life against the rights of doctors to choose to use the procedure. Depictions of the procedure reduced women to their somewhat romanticized body parts: womb, cervix, 'birth canal'. There was little attention to whole women. The procedure became the issue, described by proponents as inhuman, gruesome, horrible, violating everything good to the human community. It is killing, homicide, infanticide, a procedure designed to produce a dead child. And they presented evidence to support their claim that the fetus 'perceives and appreciates pain' and by the procedure is reduced to human rubble.

The bill passed both houses of Congress, but President Clinton vetoed it, as promised. In delivering his veto message, he took the opportunity to reinsert gender into the debate. The White House Office of Women's Initiatives and Outreach recruited women who had had late-term abortions to tell their stories at the veto session and to show why they needed the procedure to protect their lives or health. This effort was effective because a House committee immediately convened to counter Clinton's claims that the PBAB would harm women and that the issue was really about women's health. PBAB Act proponents stressed that an exception to the ban on the procedure for women's health was a 'lethal loophole' large enough to permit any abortion. They persisted in claiming that the partial-birth procedure was violent and completely unnecessary. Participation by feminist pro-choice groups who had been excluded from 1995 hearings brought gender back to a central place in the frame of the debate. This regendering, while successful, had narrowed the definition of women's interests in abortion to that of health. In the end, most opponents of PBAB were just trying to get a health exception, having already given up hope of defeating the ban.

❖ Policy outcome

The PBAB Act was passed twice by both houses of Congress and vetoed twice by President Clinton, in 1996 and 1997. Calling the procedure 'potentially life-saving', he had pledged to veto the ban as long as it did not include an exception to use the procedure for protecting women's health. Congress failed to override the veto in 1998, when the Senate majority fell short of the necessary two-thirds. Partial-Birth Abortion Ban Acts have been passed in some States. In 2000, the Supreme Court ruled Nebraska's partial-birth abortion ban unconstitutional (*Stenberg v. Carhart*).[12] Nebraska's statute was nearly identical to the PBAB vetoed by President Clinton in that it defined the procedure in the same terms and allowed no exception for the health of the mother. The Court found the statute to be vague and ban procedures used for abortions on pre-viability fetuses in opposition to the guidelines in *Casey*. Further, it was ruled that the failure to provide for uses of the procedure in cases where a woman's health was at risk was an 'undue' burden—also prohibited under *Casey*—on woman's right to make an abortion decision. While no US statute has been reviewed by the Court, *Stenberg v. Carhart* puts in doubt the constitutionality of the PBAB Act, without the exception for women's health, should it pass Congress and get presidential acceptance.[13]

❖ Movement impact

The outcome of the specific bills introduced in Congress in 1995 and 1997 was a victory for the women's movement. But it didn't feel like a victory to them. At first, a collapse was in the offing, until Clinton's veto managed to change the terms of debate and allow women representing pro-choice groups some access to the important committee hearings. Pro-life forces had twice, in 1994 and 1996, won large majorities in Congress. More significantly, they have reframed the debate on abortion, initially, to eliminate any gendered references, and, finally, by forcing pro-choice advocates to accept a narrow construction of women's right to seek abortion. But the Clinton vetoes have meant that the outcome—no change in law—was a victory that coincided with women's movement goals and completed the *dual response* by the state.

❖ DOROTHY McBRIDE STETSON

❖ Women's policy agency activities

The women's policy agency, the Office of Women's Initiatives and Outreach in the White House, began as a campaign organization for the president in the 1996 elections and remained to develop support from female constituencies for President's Clinton's policy proposals until the end of his term in office. It was a cross-sectional, political office, placed low in the White House hierarchy. The head in 1995–8 was Betsy Myers, the sister of Clinton' first press secretary, appointed for her political rather than feminist connections. She had a record of promoting the interests of women business owners. The mandate of the office was 'bridging the gap between women's groups and the administration and to report back to the president on the dialogue' (Morris and Norton 1998: 17).

President Clinton used the Office of Women's Initiatives and Outreach successfully to gender the succeeding policy debate on proposals to ban partial-birth abortions. The position of the Office was that it was acceptable to prohibit the late-term procedure as long as doctors were still able to use the procedure to preserve the pregnant woman's life or health. This frame was a narrow slice of the feminist position on reproductive rights, but it did not contradict movement goals, being better than nothing. Therefore the women's policy agency in this third debate played an insider role.

❖ Women's movement characteristics

Since the early 1980s, both the pro-choice movement and the women's movement had become institutionalized, regular participants in policy communities relating to abortion issues. After twelve years of confrontation with the New Right under the Reagan and Bush administrations, pundits declared feminism was dead. The Washington women's lobby was criticized as being out of touch with the rank and file, and there was tension between the tactics of insider groups and outsider demands. In other words, the women's movement had a seat at the table, but it struggled to retain its base in constituencies (Spalter-Roth and Schreiber 1995). With the election of President Clinton in 1992 came some relief, although the counter-movement retained a strong foothold in Congress. Some things had not changed: the movement remained very close to the Democrats, and abortion continued to be a high-priority item on the movement agenda, if not the unifying issue it once was.

❖ Policy environment

Democrats were in the White House, but Republicans controlled both houses of the Congress. The policy sub-system was moderately open, the same as in the second debate. In other words, the action centred on congressional committees which allowed participation by outside groups. Individual initiatives within

Congress remained essential to the process, and the majority party usually had an advantage in the scheduling of the testimony of individuals and representatives of interested groups. With abortion regulation a partisan issue, a change in the majority in either the White House or Congress can have a remarkable effect on the outcome.

❖ CONCLUSION

In the major debates on abortion regulation, the pro-choice and women's movements have been successful in achieving dual responses from the federal government: incorporation of movement organizations into the policy process, and policies that coincide with their goals. They achieved this success with both insider and marginal women's policy agencies. The movements suffered one complete failure, in the enactment of the Hyde Amendment, with the women's policy agency playing a marginal role.

Explanations for these movement successes and failure must take into account changes in the strength of the counter-movement and the relationship of the abortion debate to political parties. In the first two debates, in the 1970s, the key to success or failure was the strength of the counter-movement. In Debate 1, over *Roe v. Wade*, the pro-choice and women's movements were emerging, united, and believed that abortion regulations to favour women's rights were a top priority. The issue was non-partisan, especially in the policy arena of the federal courts. By the time of Debate 2, the counter-movement had become strong; other factors, however, remained unchanged, including the fact that abortion was a non-partisan issue: both parties had pro-choice and pro-life advocates. The key factor leading to movement defeat was that pro-life legislators dominated debate in the closed policy sub-system of budget appropriations.

In the 1980s, abortion became a partisan issue, with the pro-life advocates dominating the Republican Party and pro-choice prevalent among Democrats. Another change was the institutionalization of the women's movement lobby and pro-choice movement organizations in the policy community on abortion in Washington. Thus, the outcome of abortion policy debates depends on the placement of party leaders in the executive and legislatures. Until 1994, the women's movement could rely on the strength of the left-wing majority in congress. In 1995–8, it was a pro-choice Democrat in the White House, despite the pro-life Republican majority in Congress, who led the effort to return women's rights to health care to a central place in the policy debate. The fact that the president used a women's policy agency to convey this message allows us to count Debate 3 as an example of state feminism, but the weakness of all women's policy agencies in abortion debates was a feature of the three debates studied in this chapter.

❖ DOROTHY MCBRIDE STETSON

This longitudinal analysis of policy debates on abortion regulation and funding reveals significant changes in the frame of the debate and especially the place of gender in that frame. As a result of *Roe v. Wade*, abortion was framed, for the first time in history, in feminist terms as an issue of women's civil rights and health. Subsequent debates have weakened the feminist elements of the frame. For most of the period under study, women's rights and status have shared equal billing with the rights and status of the fetus—or unborn—thus narrowing pro-choice movement claims to nothing more than shoring up their argument under frequent attack by an exceptionally strong counter-movement. The last debate, however, has inflicted the most damage on the feminist frame. Rather than defending a comprehensive view of reproductive rights for women as framed by women's movement organizations, the institutionalized movement lobbies have moved only slightly away from the corner they were backed into by the partial-birth abortion ban proposals. Finally, with President Clinton's help, they were able to defend an explicit demand for protecting women's lives and health in the last stages of pregnancy. The 2000 elections, however, made a critical change in the all-important placement of party leaders in the national policy arena. The majority of the Congress supports many pro-life positions; most are Republicans but there are also a few Democrats. More importantly, the Republicans have control of the executive, and the pro-life advocates hold key places in the abortion policy network under President George W. Bush, who campaigned in support of pro-life principles. The likelihood is slim that women's movement activists can recapture control over the definition of the issue of abortion any time soon.

❖ NOTES

1 The acronym NARAL has evolved to reflect changes in the scope of the demands: National Association for the Repeal of Abortion Laws (1969); National Abortion Rights Action League (1973); National Abortion and Reproductive Rights Action League (1993).

2 *Griswold v. Connecticut.* 381 US 479.

3 410 US 113, 1973.

4 Sherry Finkbine took the tranquilliser thalidomide while pregnant and later learned that this greatly increased the chance of fetal deformity. She sought an abortion but was denied at her local hospital. Eventually she sought a legal abortion in Sweden.

5 These friend-of-the-court briefs are the only way for groups not directly party to a case to gain access to judicial decision making (see O'Connor 1980).

6 Medicaid is the national health-care policy for the poor. It is funded by contributions from both the federal and State governments. Since women with children are the majority of the poor, they are the majority of the Medicaid clientele.

7 *Maher v. Roe* 432 US 464, 1977; *Beal v. Doe*, 432 US 438, 1977.

8 432 US 464, 474–5.

9 Harris v. McRae, 448 US 297, 1980.

10 To implement the IWY Houston recommendations, Carter appointed the National Advisory Committee for Women (NACW) in April 1978 with Bella Abzug as Chair. By January 1979, Abzug had been fired and the subsequent protest led to the disbanding of the NACW and its replacement with a restricted President's Advisory Committee on Women, the last national women's commission in the US. See House of Representatives (1990a).

11 112 S Ct 2791, 1992,

12 120 S.Ct. 2597, 2000.

13 President George W. Bush, who took office in 2001, indicated in his campaign that he would sign the Partial Birth Abortion Ban Act should it pass.

❖ DOROTHY MCBRIDE STETSON

13 ❖ Conclusion: Comparative Abortion Politics and the Case for State Feminism

Dorothy McBride Stetson

❖ INTRODUCTION

State feminism is defined as the effectiveness of women's policy agencies in assisting women's movements in achieving their procedural and substantive policy goals. The excellent studies of abortion politics in the preceding chapters classify the major abortion debates of the last 30 years in eleven advanced industrial democracies according to the variables of the state feminism

Women's movement impact (dependent variable)

> Dual response, co-optation, pre-emption, or no response impact

Activities and characteristics of women's policy agencies (intervening variables)

> Insider, marginal, non-feminist, or symbolic activities
> Scope, type, placement, resources, leadership characteristics

Characteristics of women's movements (independent variables)

> Stage, closeness to left, issue priorities, cohesiveness, counter-movement

The policy environment (independent variables)

> Policy sub-system, left in/out of power

Figure 13.1. State feminism: conceptual framework

Table 13.1. Abortion policy debates by country

AUSTRIA

AU 1   Social Democratic Party Draft Liberalization, 1970–2
AU 2   People's Initiative (anti-abortion) and National Council reaffirmation of legal abortion, 1975–8
AU 3   Regulation of mifegyne: abortion pill, 1998–9

BELGIUM

BL 1   State Commission for Ethical Problems, 1974–6
BL 2   Detiège bill to suspend prosecutions, 1981–2
BL 3   Reform of abortion law, 1986–90

CANADA

CA1   Reform of abortion criminal code, 1966–9
CA2   *Morgentaler/Daigle* cases (constitutionality of criminal code), 1988, 1989
CA3   Bill to reinstate criminal penalties for abortion, 1989–91

FRANCE

FR1   Reaffirmation of legal abortion in first trimester, 1975–9
FR2   Reimbursement of abortion expenses, 1982–3
FR3   Commando-IVG and *Loi Neiertz* (sanctions for obstructing access), 1993

GERMANY

GR1   Legalization of abortion, 1969–74
GR2   Post-unification liberalization, 1990–2
GR3   Restoration of limited abortion law, 1993–5

GREAT BRITAIN

GB1   White bill and Lane Committee investigation into 1967 act, 1970–5
GB2   Corrie bill to restrict abortions, 1975–9
GB3   Human Fertilisation and Embryology Act: upper limit, 1987–90

IRELAND

IR1   Constitutional amendment to protect the unborn, 1981–3
IR2   X and Maastricht Treaty referendums on abortion and right to travel, 1992–5
IR3   C and Green Paper on abortion policy, 1997–9

ITALY

IT1   Legalization of abortion, 1971–8
IT2   Popular referendum to repeal legal abortion, 1980–1
IT3   In vitro fertilization and abortion, 1996–9.

THE NETHERLANDS

NE1   First cabinet proposal for limited reform, 1971–2
NE2   Reform of abortion law, 1978–81
NE3   Implementation of statute to register/license abortion facilities, 1981–4

SPAIN

SP1   Abortion Act, 1983–5
SP2   Implementation regulations, 1986

UNITED STATES OF AMERICA

US1   Legalizing abortion, *Roe v. Wade*, 1959–73
US2   Hyde Amendment, 1975–7
US3   Partial Birth Abortion Ban Act, 1995–8

framework (Fig. 13.1). This concluding chapter compares the measurements from these studies to examine a series of propositions designed to explore the extent to which state feminism has existed and how it has varied, and to assess explanations for that variation. These propositions comprise the following steps in building a foundation for a theory of state feminism: determining impact of movements on policy-making; examining the influence of women's policy agencies in that success; comparing the characteristics of agencies associated with influence; finally, assessing the validity of the state feminism explanation of women's movement success in contrast to explanations derived from resource mobilization and political opportunity structure theories.

Before analyzing these propositions, we will begin with a comparison of abortion politics across the eleven countries using information on all debates. Table 13.1 will help the reader keep track of 32 debates from eleven countries over 30 years that will be analyzed. This information on the politics of the abortion issue provides the context for the theoretical analysis. The section 'Abortion Politics' will review the institutional arenas in various countries, how abortion problems arrived on public agendas, and the dominant frames and definitions of these problems. This comparison shows that there are many similarities in the way abortion questions reach public attention and the institutions that deal with them.

The second and third sections of this chapter, 'Gendering the Abortion Issue' and 'Women's Movements', use the data from the preceding chapters to examine some assumptions of the research design and the state feminism framework. It is important to examine these assumptions because if the evidence does not bear them out it would undermine any conclusions reached in examining the hypotheses. The first of these is the assumption that the way policy debates are gendered affects both policy content and procedural access. The framework's typology of the effectiveness of women's policy agency activities is composed of two variables: whether the agency adopts a gendered position in the debate that coincides with women's movement goals and whether the agency is successful in inserting those ideas into the dominant debate frame. The framework assumes that such activities will be equal to effectiveness in assisting movement activists in achieving their goals for content and participation in the policy-making process. But this will be the case only if the way debates are gendered opens up access for advocates for women and leads to gendered policy outcomes. In 'Gendering the Abortion Issue' the comparison of patterns of gender ideas, inserted both successfully and unsuccessfully into dominant debate frames, shows the extent to which policy actors have defined abortion in terms of feminist ideas of women's rights and status. It will also show connections between the frames of the debates and substantive and descriptive representation. This section will conclude with a review of the policy outcomes and the extent to which they have coincided with women's movement demands.

The second assumption pertains to the decision not to establish a standard definition of 'feminism' but, rather, to use the views of the women's movements in each country as the benchmark of state feminism. This decision is part of the research strategy of the larger Research Network on Gender Politics and the State (RNGS) project. Through their close collaboration, researchers in this project have incorporated concepts in the state feminism framework that will permit comparison across time and across countries with a limited amount of 'conceptual stretching', that is, extending concepts where they do not apply (Sartori 1970). Feminism, specifically which criteria will determine whether leaders, attitudes, goals, strategies, and policies can be classified as 'feminist', is an especially difficult concept to apply comparatively. There are no agreed-upon standards to determine, for example, whether a policy providing for women's health is as feminist as a demand for women's self-determination. As a substitute for providing a definition of feminism that will work in every context, we have opted for classifying leaders, frames, and policies in terms of the specific demands of the women's movements in each country at the time of the various debates. Readers of preceding chapters will be familiar with authors' conclusions that a particular policy 'coincides with women's movement demands' or a particular women's policy agency has a feminist leader or has adopted a gendered frame of the abortion issue that 'coincides with the frame of the women's movement'.

The question with respect to comparing women's movements is the extent to which it is possible to characterize the movement over the period of the debate as having a single goal or whether the movement—or movements—are splintered and in conflict. Thus the section titled 'Women's movements' explores the composition of women's movements as described in the chapters and their relationship to the abortion issue in the period from the 1960s to the late 1990s. There is information about the fate of the autonomous, socialist, and institutionalized components of various movements and the extent to which they are unified generally and specifically in support of a common goal for abortion law.

The fourth section, titled 'Women's Movements and the State: the Case for State Feminism', presents the analysis of the state feminism framework and hypotheses. The data for this analysis come from the 28 debates in the study which took place when women's policy agencies were in place.[1] These hypotheses are examined in the following order:

H1. Women's movements in democratic states have tended to be successful in increasing both substantive representation as demonstrated by policy content and descriptive representation as demonstrated by women's participation in policy-making processes, that is, *dual response.*

H2. Women's movements in democratic states have tended to be more successful where women's policy agencies have acted as *insiders* in the policy-making process, that is, have gendered policy debates in ways that coincide with women's movement goals.

H3. Women's policy agencies with greater resources and institutional capacity, defined by scope, type, and placement, have been more effective than agencies with fewer resources and less capacity in providing linkages between women's movements and policy-makers.

H4. Variations in women's movement characteristics and/or policy environments explain variations in both women's policy agency effectiveness and movement success in increasing women's representation.

H5. If women's policy agencies are necessary and effective linkages between movements and state responses, then variations in movement resources and policy environments will have no independent relation to state responses.

Text along with tables summarize the findings from each chapter using the conceptual framework of state feminism (Fig. 13.1). As with any attempt at comparison, inevitably there has been some loss of detail and nuance as the various cases were sorted into categories. Thus, it is important to keep in mind that these comparisons are based on decisions about the primary or most typical features gleaned from the descriptions of aspects of these 28 policy debates, rather than a full inclusion of all patterns found in the detailed chapters that precede this conclusion.[2]

The last section of this chapter has two parts: a review of nation state patterns of state feminism and abortion politics and a summary of the findings and their potential contribution to the construction of a theory of state feminism

❖ ABORTION POLITICS

All the countries studied in this book entered the twentieth century with laws that made abortion a crime with few exceptions. In the early 1900s, policy-makers in France and the Netherlands acted to make their laws even more restrictive. After that, the issue retreated from the public agenda. Leaders in democracies saw little need or provocation to concern themselves with the plight of women facing unwanted pregnancies. Those in fascist governments incorporated abortion policy into their grand eugenic schemes. Only in Catalonia, in Spain, were there efforts to implement reforms. These were squashed, however, by the victory of the authoritarian Franco regime.

While Social Democrats in Austria tried in vain in the 1920s and again in the 1950s to bring the question of reproductive rights into the public arena, it was not until the 1960s that the veil of public policy-makers' ignorance of the status and effects of these inherited nineteenth century criminal codes was lifted. Beginning with coalitions of doctors and lawyers in Great Britain, Canada, and the US seeking relief from threats of prosecutions, demands for liberalization rolled through the democracies of Western Europe: Germany, Austria, the Netherlands, then France, Belgium, Italy, and, finally, Spain. The issue came to the agenda in Ireland as well, but the demands were to strengthen the restrictions, not relax them.

Although abortion reform was taken up in similar fashion in all but one of the countries studied here, there were differences in the abilities of policy-makers to fashion a policy that settled the conflicts that unsettled many conventional political arrangements. If there were a race among these countries in finding such a solution, the Netherlands would win first prize, with Spain and Austria coming in close behind. The battle lasted longer in Belgium, Canada, Germany, Great Britain, and France but political settlements of the early 1990s show promise of widespread support. The abortion issue has rattled policy-makers in Italy just once since the early 1980s. Only in Ireland and the US do policy-makers still have to make their way through the minefield of a policy question which deeply divides the political parties, social movements, and the public.

The legislature is the institution that has made the most important decisions regarding abortion law. In every country, with the exception of Great Britain, this arena includes the political executive: the prime minister and cabinet. The parliament and government, including the ministries, were the major players in Belgium, France, Spain, and the Netherlands. In Canada, Germany, and the US the legislature shared power with the constitutional courts while in Austria the dominant Social Democratic Party was a major venue for abortion reform. In Ireland, and to a lesser extent Italy, important decisions have been taken through popular referendums.

At one time or another in every country abortion can be considered an emotive-symbolic issue that provokes conflicts over basic moral and religious values. As such, it can play havoc with regular arrangements among the political parties. This was definitely the case in Belgium, the Netherlands, and to a lesser extent West and unified Germany, where coalitions between Christian Democrats and liberal and/or socialist parties were disrupted along a religious divide that threatened the stability of the cabinet. Attitudes about reform have divided parties in Austria, Spain, Canada, and the US as well, usually with the left-wing parties in favour of reform and the right defending pro-life interests. The parties, left and right, are much less unified on one side or the other in France, Ireland, and Italy. In Great Britain, the issue was officially non-partisan, and while eventually the Labour Party formally endorsed abortion rights for women, the Conservative Party has refused to assist anti-abortion interests.

Eight of the first debates selected by researchers followed one of three routes to the public agenda. In Austria, Germany, and Italy, abortion came out of obscurity to the public arena as part of general and comprehensive reforms of authoritarian penal codes. Doctors practising abortion in defiance of restrictive laws provided a second route to public forums in Belgium, Canada, and the United States. The Social Democrat MPs in the Netherlands and the Socialist government in Spain provided a third avenue by introducing the first bills for reform.

Looking across all policy debates, we see that the most frequent catalyst for public attention to an abortion question came from anti-abortion rather than pro-abortion forces. Only in Ireland and Great Britain did the first debates studied here gain access in this way.[3] A more typical pattern (US2, US3, IT2, IT3, GB2, GB3, AU2, FR3, CA3) was that anti-abortion activists looked for opportunities to restrict reforms already enacted. The other avenues to public attention in the debates were through court cases (GR3, IR2, IR3), through requirements of previously enacted laws (FR1, SP2, NE3), or the unique instances of German unification and the regulation of mifegyne in Austria. In one case, the second debate in the Netherlands, the government kept control of the issue from one coalition negotiation to the next.

❖ GENDERING THE ABORTION ISSUE

Information about the frames or problem definitions of the abortion issue in debates as they unfolded is essential to understanding and comparing the influence of women's advocates both inside and outside the government. A major strategy of most women's movements has been to insert their frame or definition of abortion into the dominant discourse. This frame is usually a view that abortion policy is central to women's rights and that advancing women's rights and status must be the first priority in abortion law. Movement activists assumed, as did the researchers in this study, that by gendering the debate frame in a way that fits with movement goals the result would be procedural and policy success. Because the debate is 'about them', advocates for women would have an entree into policy-making systems. Similarly, if the dominant frame—the one that most policy-makers shared—was gendered, then the content of policy outcomes would address women's needs as defined in the debate. As discussed earlier, the state feminism framework is based on these assumptions. Let's see if the 32 debates in this study bear out these expectations.

Beginning with the first debates in each country, we examined the dominant frame of the issue when abortion first arrived on the public agenda. In seven of these debates, the status of the unborn fetus was central to the issue (BL1, GB1, IR1, IT1, NE1, SP1, US1). Doctors' rights were the focus of problem definitions in United States, France, and Canada. The state's integrity in the face of rising rates of illegal abortions also moved policy-makers to take up the issue in Germany, Great Britain, Italy, and the Netherlands. In only four debates were ideas about how abortion policy pertained to women even part of the initial dominant definitions: In France women's concerns were balanced with those of doctors, and in Italy and Great Britain with the state's need to regulate illegal abortions. Only in Austria, where women in the Social Democratic Party had for decades promoted abortion law reform, did the issue begin as a question of women's rights to self-determination.

By the end of the first debates, however, Austria was joined with Belgium, Great Britain, Ireland, Italy, and the US bringing gender into the dominant definition of the abortion issue. In four countries—Britain, Italy, US, and Belgium—along with Austria this gendering coincided at least in part with women's movement demands. In Great Britain and Italy psychological and social needs of women were balanced with concern about the fetus, while in Ireland the woman's life—not health or other circumstance—was the only interest that took precedence over that of the fetus. In the US the first debate yielded a policy definition that gave women's privacy to choose abortion a privileged position in any law-making scheme, whereas in Belgium the issue required policy-makers to determine who should make the abortion decision—women or doctors. In Germany too, the abortion issue acquired gendered aspects as a result of the first debate, but women were not portrayed in feminist or women's rights terms but as weak and needy, facing distress and conflict over problem pregnancies. The abortion issue was gendered between the first and second debates in the Netherlands and by the end of the second debates in Canada, France, and Spain. In all countries gendering coincided with women's movement frames. A typical pattern was to juxtapose women's rights to autonomy and equality against the life of the unborn. In all these cases, women's rights seemed to have the privileged position in the frame.

Does gendering last? Yes, for the most part. Once the frame of the issue was established to pertain in whole or in part to women's rights and needs, then the issue remained gendered in subsequent debates. In Austria and Belgium, the gendered frame was strengthened through the second and third debates. Similarly, in Ireland, although a limited view of women's rights in the abortion debates remains, the rights of women have expanded to include the right to travel to other countries to obtain abortions and, in extreme crisis, even with the government's help. The rights of women have been central, even dominant, in the recent British debates, which have countered continued efforts by anti-abortion groups to place the fetus at the centre of concern. In Italy and US, while the debates remain gendered, 1990s debates have not been as successful as the first debates in the 1970s. The gendered frame has narrowed in scope, focusing in both countries on women's health issues against fetal rights rather than the more feminist idea of women's broad right to self-determination and choice.

For the three countries where gender was not included in the frame until the second debate studied, the later gender references were also quite limited in comparison with earlier successes. In France, Canada, and the Netherlands, feminists were placed in the position of having to defend a dominant gendered frame against demands from anti-abortionists to raise the status of the fetus in the debate. In all three cases they adopted a strategy of narrowing the gendered ideas to focus on access in France and Canada, and in the Netherlands, on regular ungendered medical practice, to retain policy gains.

Now to the question of the effect gendering the debate in specific terms has on opening up participation in the policy-making process to women, as assumed in the state feminism framework. To examine this question we looked at the participation variable in debates following the initial successful gendering of the debate. In other words, once the issue was 'about women', were women included in the policy-making process the next time the issue came to the agenda? In every case with one exception—US2—they were, as long as the issue remained gendered. In Austria, Belgium, Great Britain, Ireland, Canada, France, the Netherlands, and even Germany, women managed to participate in a more or less regular fashion in the policy-making process in all debates that followed the initial gendering. This participation took a variety of combinations of the following forms: prominent women in political parties and as party spokespersons; women members of parliament and ministers; women appointed to investigating committees; women's movement, pro-choice, and anti-abortion lobbying organizations; groups presenting evidence to investigating committees; public demonstrations; consultations with women's policy agencies and through corporate channels. In contrast, when gender was removed from the dominant frame in the third debate in Italy, women activists were shut out of the policy-making process. In US3, the debate began and remained ungendered, focusing on the fetus versus medical practice, through what might have resulted in a statutory ban on late-term abortions were it not for the a women's policy agency used by the president to regender the issue. The immediate result of the regendering was an invitation from congressional committees for women to present evidence at subsequent hearings. The only case where there was a gendered debate but women did not participate was the second debate in the United States over the Hyde Amendment, which restricted funding. Women were shut out of a gendered debate because it took place in a completely closed policy arena.

The second question about the effect of gendering policy debates pertains to the impact on policy content. Again the results support the assumptions of the state feminism framework. When a particular set of gender ideas became part of the dominant frame of the debate, policy content put those ideas into law (see Table 13.2). In most cases, however, gendering did not incorporate all the demands of feminists within women's movements; thus policy content, while coinciding with movement goals, did not achieve all of the movements' goals. Group I includes four countries—Austria, Belgium, Great Britain, and Ireland—where the issue was gendered in terms that coincided with movement goals in the first debate and was sustained through the later debates. In these countries, the policy content followed in similar terms. Only in Austria, however, did the feminist frame of women's self-determination become part of a law that provides abortion without limits in the first trimester. Ireland's limited attention to women's right to life coincided with the concerns of a weak and defensive movement which refused to be engaged in actively promoting a feminist agenda, opting instead for a low profile on the issue. In Great Britain the law is more liberal in practice than on the books; nevertheless, it does take into account the social needs of women, which was the initial gendered frame of the debate. The frame of the debate in Belgium was so conflict-ridden that it took several years before a bill that coincided with gender ideas was put into effect.

Group II includes Italy and the US, where gendered frames in the first debates led to policy but where over the subsequent debates the frame was narrowed. The ideas that made it to the policy arena were more limited in Italy than in the US, focusing on women's health in contrast to the right of privacy and choice. Consequently, Italian abortion law is based on an indications or conditions approach, and abortion remains criminal in opposition to many feminists' goals of self-determination. In the US abortion law remains out of the criminal codes but the official definition of the issue in debates has narrowed to focus more directly on women's health rather than privacy. The constitutional guidelines as set forth by the Supreme Court do place women's liberty in a central place but, in competition with the States' powers to protect fetal life, this liberty has become more fragile.

In the countries in Group III, where the abortion issue was gendered to coincide with movement goals as a result of the second, not the first, debate studied, movements have maintained these gender references but in a narrowed form. In all—Canada, France, the Netherlands, and Spain—the state enacted policy that reflected these gendered ideas. In Canada, criminal abortion laws were declared unconstitutional based on the rights of women to personal security under the Constitution. In France women received funding for abortions from the government to advance their rights. Under the abortion reform in the Netherlands, women alone determine whether their situations are enough of an emergency to require abortion services. In Spain, after the idea that abortion was a matter of women's rights entered the official frame of the debate, the Ministry of Health eliminated many restrictions on access to abortion. All these laws remain in force.

Only Germany is in Group IV, where gendered debates did not produce policy that coincided with movement goals. All three debates were gendered to promote women's 'need for assistance, not punishment', but the needy women portrayed in this frame were very different from the independent women deserving of self-determination and reproductive rights portrayed by various activists in the women's movement. Despite two attempts by the legislature to choose a periodic model rather than an indications model, the Constitutional

Table 13.2. Gendered debates and policy content

Country	Debate 1	Debate 2	Debate 3
GROUP I: GENDERED THREE DEBATES; SUSTAINED OVER THREE DEBATES; COINCIDED WITH WOMEN'S MOVEMENT GOALS			
Austria *Women's self-determination*	Party bill: abortion without limits in first trimester after consultation. Became law in 1974	Defeat counter-movement to re-criminalize	Mifegyne approved; debate on legal abortion not reopened
Belgium *Woman makes decision*	No change in existing law; alternatives set forth providing for abortion under either medical or also socio-psychological conditions	Defeat of bill to suspend abortion prosecutions; continued criminalization	Abortion in first twelve weeks for woman in crisis; self-determination of crisis state along with physician
Great Britain *Social needs of women*	Successfully defend Abortion Act which provides for abortion for health of woman, family, fetus; wide discretion to doctors	Successfully defended	Upper limit of 24 weeks exception for physical/mental health of mother or handicapped child.
Ireland *Women's life is equal to life of fetus*	Constitutional amend-ment, right to life of woman equal with unborn	Right to travel and freedom of information approved	Parliamentary committee outlines options for abortion law from absolute ban to crisis pregnancy help
GROUP II: GENDERED THREE DEBATES; SCOPE DECLINING; COINCIDE WITH MOVEMENT GOALS MORE LIMITED WAY			
Italy *Women's health and psycho-social integrity*	Criminal except for physical/mental health, socio-economic family circumstances, fetal anomalies and malformations	Defeat of anti-abortion referendum	Defeat of anti-abortion amendments through Constitutional Court ruling
United States *Women's right to privacy in choosing abortion*	Abortion legal in first two trimesters without condition	No federal funds for abortion except for danger to mother's life	Defeat of Partial Birth Abortion Ban Act

Table 13.2. continued

GROUP III: GENDERED TWO OF THREE DEBATES; MAINTAINED GENDERING; SCOPE NARROWED; COINCIDED WITH MOVEMENT GOALS			
Canada *Woman's right to choose*	Decriminalized abortion for life/health of mother. Therapeutic Abortion Committee system	Abortion law declared unconstitutional based on rights of women to security in person	Bill to recriminalize abortion defeated in Senate
France *Women's reproductive rights*	Reaffirmation of legal abortion in first trimester without condition but with administrative hurdles	Funding of abortion from general budget	Public health code includes special offence of hindering access to abortions
The Netherlands *Women make own decisions about abortion*	Failure of limited abortion reform bill	Enactment of abortion for women in 'emergency situation' determined by women	Network of hospitals provide abortion on demand
Spain *Abortion important to women's rights*	Abortion on eugenic, medical, or ethical grounds	Access made easier by eliminating restrictions imposed by Minister of Health	
GROUP IV: GENDERED THREE DEBATES, NOT COINCIDING WITH MOVEMENT GOALS			
Germany *Women's need for assistance, not punishment*	Periodic model adopted: first twelve weeks with counselling	Decriminalized abortion in first twelve weeks with mandatory counselling	Unlawful but not punishable in first twelve weeks with counselling, medical, and rape indications.

Court ordered that abortion remain criminalized. Whether periodic or criminalized, the laws reflect the conventional portrayal of needy women by establishing mandatory counselling—usually to talk the woman out of an abortion—prior to allowing abortion as the most important aspect of abortion law reforms.

❖ WOMEN'S MOVEMENTS

This section examines similarities and differences in movement composition and demands pertaining to abortion. The state feminism framework solved the difficulties of finding a comparative definition of feminism by opting to use the country-based movements as the benchmark for whether the state—through

❖ DOROTHY MCBRIDE STETSON

its women's policy agencies—acted in a feminist way. Although this approach gives a straightforward measure of aspects of movement impact and women's policy agency activities, evidence from these chapters shows that the movement—or, in some countries, movements—are often heterogeneous and internally divided. Here we look at the components of the movements at the beginning of the policy debates, with special attention to their cohesiveness around a set of demands for specific frames and policies on abortion. Then we will examine any changes in the women's movements by the time of the most recent debates.

Evidence of women's movement characteristics at the time of the first debates on abortion shows that autonomous radical feminist groups were emerging and/or growing in all countries. These radical groups were tiny in some countries—Spain, Ireland—and quite vigorous in others—Italy, US, Great Britain. Once visible, however, in all countries they encountered women's rights activists already organized. In Austria, France, Italy, and the Netherlands, these 'older' branches of the movements were in left-wing unions and political parties. In Canada, Germany, Ireland, Spain, and the US, these were not affiliated with parties but were other types of organizations working to advance women's status. In Great Britain and Belgium, three types of branches—party, autonomous, and other organizations—were active in the early 1970s.

Relations among the various wings and branches of the movements ranged from tense to outright conflictual. In Austria, the autonomous 'out' groups and the insiders of the Social Democratic Party were in synergy: ultimately they needed each other. In France at the time of the first debate, there was open conflict among the leading radical feminist groups. In Great Britain as well, the socialist and the radical feminists were in a bitter battle over both goals and strategies. When the abortion issue did arrive at the public agenda, it became a top priority for women's movements in all but Ireland and Canada. In Austria, the Netherlands, Spain, and the US, this agreement brought the feuding wings together. They still remained divided over strategies—public demonstrations and protest versus cooperation and compromise—and goals—holding out for publicly funded abortion on demand versus accepting moderate liberalizing reforms.

In the Netherlands and Spain, the major abortion debates were settled by the mid-1980s. Since there was a relatively short time span between first and last debates, there were few changes in the women's movements. In the other countries, however, by the time of the third debates the autonomous wings of the women's movements had declined or disappeared. In Austria, Belgium, Canada, Great Britain, Italy, and the US, movement groups had presence in major political parties, legislatures, bureaucracies, and other interest groups, and thus had become integrated in a regular way with policy-making institutions. With the exception of Italy, the movements remained unified on abortion

280

rights as a top priority. In Ireland, the movement had consolidated but did not have the institutionalized presence found in other countries. In France and Germany all wings of the movement were in decline in the 1990s. While the French feminists could still unify when abortion rights were threatened, German activists were divided more than ever. Even the Constitutional Court's ruling that the rights of the unborn were paramount was not enough to unify them around a campaign for abortion rights for women.

When the activists in women's movements have been unified in support of women's abortion rights, they have still rarely spoken with one voice in present-ing their frames and specific policy demands; and in several debates the wings have presented alternative views. Yet each author in this book has had to classify each debate according to whether the gendered frames and the policy content coincided with women's movement demands, and given the requirements of the comparative method, they have had to make a judgement: either yes or no, no *maybes* allowed. When gendering and policy content coincided with the demands of one part of the movement we agreed to classify this as yes. The fact is, however, that none of the abortion issue frames or policies coincided com-*pletely* with all demands and goals of women's movements in any country. Throughout the analysis that follows here, we are well aware that in none of the movements, although often successful in gaining procedural and policy responses from the state, have all activists been completely satisfied, nor has any women's policy agency been able to intercede to overcome all the opposition to their goals.

❖ Women's Movements and the State: The Case for State Feminism

The major purposes of this cross-national study of abortion politics and women's movements have been: (1) to determine and explain variations in the success of women's movement in opening up democratic policy processes on abortion policy to women's representation: in other words, democratizing democracies in advanced industrial economies; and (2) to determine whether the state itself, by establishing specialist women's policy agencies, intervened effectively to achieve this success. This section examines findings in this study in relation to five hypotheses stated in Chapter 1 and in the introduction to Chapter 13. Sorting and classifying qualitative data shows trends in the findings and indicates to what extent these trends confirm or fail to confirm the hypotheses.[4] In this section, therefore, we depart from a country comparison as the primary focus to a debates comparison, while still pointing out trends in the various countries across these debates.

The core question in this study, in fact the very definition of 'state feminism', pertains to the role of women's policy agencies as insiders, allies, or symbols in

❖ Dorothy McBride Stetson

women's movement efforts to have an impact on policy-making processes and outcomes in democratic states. In the analytical framework of state feminism, the women's policy agency activities comprise an *intervening variable* between movement impact and explanations for variations according to movement resources and policy environments. Examining these hypotheses provides evidence of women's policy agencies and agency characteristics operating as intervening variables, and the extent to which agencies are necessary linkages between the movements and the state responses in the area of abortion policy and politics.

The first proposition examines the variations in the success of women's movements in 28 abortion debates. The movement impact typology used in this study comprises two measures of women's representation: descriptive, or procedural access through women's participation in policy-making processes, and substantive, or policy content through changes in the outcomes of the processes. There are four possible measures of movement impact: *dual response*, which is providing both substantive and descriptive representation; *co-optation*, descriptive representation only; *pre-emption*, substantive representation only; and *no response*.

H1. Women's movements in democratic states have tended to be successful in increasing both substantive representation as demonstrated by policy content and descriptive representation as demonstrated by women's participation in policy-making processes, that is, dual response.

The abortion debates in this study support this first hypothesis. In a majority (16) of the 28 debates, the women's movements were successful in opening up the process to women's participation and obtaining policy outcomes that coincided with movement demands (see Table 13.3). A majority of debates in a majority of countries yielded dual responses. The movements in Austria and Great Britain were successful across the range of debates from the1970s to the 1990s. The movements were successful in two of three debates in Canada, France, and the United States. In Ireland, the Netherlands, Spain, and Belgium only one debate was fully successful for the movements. The least successful movement was in Germany, which did not achieve dual response in any debate including the first without women's policy agencies.

The movements were partially successful in ten more debates gaining either descriptive representation—co-optation—through participation of women and women's movement activists in the debates over abortion or substantive representation—pre-emption—through policies favourable to movement goals. Italy's third debate ended in only partial success, although the first two debates which took place before the establishment of women's policy agencies had achieved dual response. Only two, or 7 per cent, of the debates were completely unsuccessful for the movements. Both of these debates—US2 and FR1—occurred in the 1970s.

Table 13.3. Women's movements and state responses in 28 abortion policy debates

Country	Dual response	Co-optation	Pre-emption	No response
Austria	AU1, AU2, AU3	o	o	o
Belgium	BL3	BL1, BL2	o	o
Canada	CA2, CA3	o	CA1	o
France	FR2, FR3	o	o	FR1
Germany	o	GR2, GR3	o[a]	o
Great Britain	GB1, GB2, GB3	o	o	o
Ireland	IR1	IR2, IR3	o	o
Italy	o[b]	o	IT3	o
Netherlands	NE3	o	NE2	o[c]
Spain	SP3	o	SP1	o
United States	US1, US3	o	o	US2
Total	16	6	4	2

[a] GR1 with no women's policy agency was Pre-emption
[b] IT1 and IT2 with no women's policy agencies were Dual response
[c] NE1 with no women's policy agency was No response

There was a trend toward greater success over the time period of the debates. In six countries movements had partial or no success in early debates (BL1, BL2, CA1, NE2, US2, SP1) but achieved complete success in later debates. Only in Ireland and Italy were movements less successful in later debates (IT3, IR2, IR3) than in earlier ones. In Germany, with no complete success in any abortion debate, the women's movement opened up the policy process to participation in the later debates (GR2, GR3) although they were unsuccessful in obtaining a policy outcome that at all coincided with movement goals.

To measure the role of the agencies in achieving movement success, we use the typology that includes measures of the extent to which the position of the agency in the abortion debate coincided with women's movement goals and the ability of the agency actors to insert this gendered perspective into the dominant frame of the debate. As we have seen, the gendering of the debate is an important step in gaining substantive representation in policy content. Agencies that accomplish both are called *insiders*, whereas taking a women's movement position but not affecting the debate places the agency as *marginal*. Agencies that gender the debate but in ways that do not coincide withe movement goals are *non-feminist*, while an agency that does neither is classified as *symbolic*.

H2. Women's movements in democratic states have tended to be more successful where women's policy agencies have acted as insiders in the policy-making process, that is, have gendered policy debates in ways that coincide with women's movement goals.

❖ DOROTHY MCBRIDE STETSON

In ten debates, women's policy agencies were insiders (see Table 13.4). The findings support the contention that such insider agencies produce dual responses in abortion policy-making. All ten of the insider agencies had this effect. Further, in a majority of the debates where movements were successful—ten out of 16—this success was accomplished through insider agencies. There is no case where the agency was fully engaged on the issue and the movement was unsuccessful. In a majority (16) of the 28 debates the agencies were either insiders or marginal allies, and twelve of these resulted in movement success. The findings also show, however, that women's policy agencies were only a little less likely to be symbolic or non feminist (twelve) than insiders or marginal (16) on the abortion issue; just one was non-feminist—FR1. The eleven symbolic agencies did not prevent movements from being successful in four debates. However, without agency input the movement was more likely to achieve descriptive representation (co-optation) rather than substantive (pre-emption). When the agencies are marginal, that is, sympathetic to movement goals but outside the policy arena, the movement impact varied including two instances of dual response, three of pre-emption, and one with no response to the movement. These findings suggest a question that the next hypotheses addresses: what kinds of agencies can intervene successfully on behalf of women's movements, and which kinds are marginalized or excluded altogether?

Our research design suggested that agencies with greater resources and institutional capacity would tend to be more successful. By *capacity* we examine the scope, type of organization whether political or administrative, proximity to political power, whether abortion was inside or outside the mandate of the agency and whether the leadership was feminist or not. All agencies in this study were cross-sectional in scope so we can eliminate this factor as an explanation for these variations.

Table 13.4. Women's policy agencies and movement impact

	Insider	Marginal	Symbolic	Non-feminist
Dual response	Ten debates: AU1, AU2, AU3, FR2, FR3, GB1, GB3, NE3, SP2, US3	Two debates: CA3, US1	Four debates: BL3, CA2, GB2, IR2	
Co-optation			Six debates: BL1, BL2, GR2, GR3, IR1, IR3	
Pre-emption		Three debates: CA1, SP1, IT3	One debate: NE2	
No response		One debate: US2		One debate: FR1
Total	Ten debates	Six debates	Eleven debates	One debate

H3. Women's policy agencies with greater resources and institutional capacity defined by type, proximity, and mandate have been more effective than agencies with fewer resources and less capacity in providing linkages between women's movements and policy-makers.

The agencies as a whole tend to be political (60 per cent), remote from power (56 per cent), with low resources (67 per cent) (see Table 13.5). Abortion is more likely to be included in their mandates than not (62 per cent) and 81 per cent had feminist leadership. The data do not provide strong support for the hypothesis, however. There are some important differences between the characteristics of insider agencies and those of marginal ones. Insiders are political rather than administrative while the marginal are equally both. They are closer to power, but not any more blessed with resources as a group and both have feminist leaders. The major difference between insider and marginal agencies is the extent to which the abortion issue was part of the agencies' mandates: 90 per cent to 33 per cent. In comparing insider with symbolic agencies, the differences in these characteristics are in the same direction, but not large enough to support the hypothesis. As we expected, it will be necessary to look at these agencies and their role in the larger context of characteristics of the movements in relation to the policy environments.

H4. Variations in women's movement characteristics and/or policy environments explain variations in both women's policy agency effectiveness and movement success in increasing women's representation.

We will examine this hypothesis as two independent propositions, showing the relationship of movement characteristics and policy environments first to agency effectiveness and then to movement success. The research design proposed that the stage of the women's movement at the time of the debate, whether emerging, growing, in consolidation, or in decline, along with the closeness to left-wing parties, priority of the abortion issue on the movement's agenda, the cohesiveness of the movement around the abortion demands, and the strength of the counter-movement would explain differences in state feminism. Specifically, we expected that the agencies would be most effective in assisting movements which were in stages of growth, close to the left, unified around abortion as a high priority and facing a weak counter-movement.

A movement can have all these characteristics, and its advocates inside the state may still face rough going in a policy environment that shuts them out. Thus we expected that movements and women's policy agencies would have more impact on the state in policy debates that take place in open rather than closed policy sub-systems when left-wing parties are in power.

The most important feature of the women's movement for insider women's policy agencies seems to be their closeness to the left (see Table 13.6). Agencies were more likely to have a symbolic role when the movement was moderately or not at all close to left-wing parties and unions. This goes along with the finding

❖ DOROTHY MCBRIDE STETSON

Table 13.5. Characteristics of women's policy agencies

	Advisory or admin.	Political	Near power	Remote from power	Mid-high resources	Low resources	Abortion in mandate	Abortion not mandate	Feminist leader	Non-feminist leader
Insider	3	7	6	4	3	7	9	1	9	1
Marginal	3	3	1	5	2	4	2	4	5	1
Symbolic	5	6	5	6	4	7	6	5	8	3
Total	11	16	12	15	9	18	17	10	22	5

Table 13.6. Women's movement characteristics and women's policy agency activities

	Emerge/ growth	Consoli- dation	Decline	Close to left	Not close to left	High priority	Not high priority	Unified	Not unified	Strong counter- movement	No strong counter- movement
Insider	3	5	2	8	2	9	1	9	1	5	5
Marginal	3	3	0	5	1	4	2	4	2	1	5
Symbolic	5	3	3	2	9	6	5	7	4	10	1
Non-fem.	0	0	1	1	0	1	0	0	1	1	0
Total	11	11	5	15	12	19	8	20	7	16	11

Table 13.7 Policy environments and women's policy agency activities

	Open	Moderately closed	Closed	Left in power	Left shares power	Left not in power
Insider	2	4	4	5	2	3
Marginal	0	3	3	2	2	2
Symbolic	1	3	2	0	2	5
Total	3	10	9	7	6	11

that agencies are more effective when the left is in power or shares power (8 of 10 cases). We did not find any symbolic agencies in debates when the left was fully in power; agencies when the left is out of power have a 50/50 chance of being symbolic (5 of 10 cases) (see Table 13.7). A unified movement with abortion as a high priority was nearly always present when an agency became an insider in a debate, with less frequency with marginal or symbolic agencies. A strong counter-movement seems to accompany symbolic agencies (10 of 11 cases), whereas the insiders face such strong societal opposition half the time and marginal even less frequently. The stage of the women's movement at the time of the debate shows no clear relationship to the effectiveness of women's policy agencies. Half of the insider agencies have interceded on behalf of consolidated movements and half when the movements are in either growth or decline. Similarly, the policy sub-system, whether open or closed, shows no relation to agency effectiveness. This may be due to the fact that some agencies, based on their location in the government and proximity to power are already situated inside closed policy sub-systems when the debates come to the agenda.

The characteristics of the women's movements are more closely associated with movement success than the policy environments (see Tables 13.8 and 13.9). Movements that had abortion as a high priority (14 of 16), were unified in their demands (15 of 16), and close to the left-wing parties (11 of 16) were more likely to achieve a dual response from the state, even in the face of strong counter-movements (9 of 16). There are some tendencies found in variations in the policy environments. If the left were in power or shared power this helped (10 of 16). The policy sub-system could be open or closed, but openness was more conducive to either a dual response or co-optation of women into the process whereas the closed process, while not prohibiting a dual response, was more likely to result in pre-emption or no response. As with the women's policy agencies, nearly every state response has occurred at every stage of the movements.

So far we have seen that more women's policy agencies (16) have been classified as either insiders or marginal—assisting women's movements in their efforts to affect policy content and procedure on abortion issues—rather than symbolic (11) or non-feminist (1). Twelve of these debates with insider or marginal agencies have dual responses from the state. The final question for analysis

Table 13.8. Women's movement characteristics and movement impact

	Emerge/ growth	Consoli- dation	Decline	Close to left	Not close to left	High priority	Not high priority	Unified	Not unified	Strong counter- movement	No strong counter- movement
Dual	6	7	3	11	5	14	2	15	1	9	7
Co-opt.	2	2	2	0	6	2	4	2	4	4	2
Pre-emp.	2	2	0	3	1	2	2	2	2	2	2
No resp	2	0	1	1	1	2	0	1	1	2	0
Total	11	11	6	15	13	20	8	20	8	17	11

Table 13.9. Policy environments and movement impact

	Open	Moderately closed	Closed	Left in power	Left shares power	Left not in power
Dual response	4	8	4	6	4	6
Co-optation	2	3	1	0	2	4
Pre-emption	0	1	3	2	0	2
No response	0	1	1	1	0	1
Total	6	13	9	9	6	13

is to assess whether these agencies were necessary links between the movements and the state.

H5. If women's policy agencies are necessary and effective linkages between movements and state responses, then variations in movement resources and policy environments will have no independent relationship to state responses.

We will examine this question in two ways. First, we present the cases sorted in two sets of tables. Table 13.10 shows those independent variables that have an association with women's movement impact measured according to whether or not the state gave a dual response. Table 13.11 treats women's policy agency activities—insider/marginal or symbolic/non-feminist—as an intervening variable to see whether the associations found in Table 13.10 disappear or hold up in Table 13.11. After we compare these tables, the second approach to examining the question will describe the shared women's movement and policy environment characteristics associated with particular patterns of state feminism: insider/dual response; marginal/dual response; symbolic/co-optation; symbolic/dual response; and marginal/ pre-emption.

Table 13.10 includes only those characteristics of movements and the policy environments that suggest an association with the dependent variable, movement impact. Table 13.11 shows these same variables controlling for the potential intervening variable women's policy agency activities. If the agencies' activities were necessary for women's movement success, then the direction of relationships found between the independent and dependent variables in Table 13.10 will disappear when arrayed according to the type of agency activities: insider/marginal or symbolic/non-feminist.

In Table 13.10 movements appear to be more successful when they are close to

Table 13.10. Characteristics of women's movements and policy environments associated with women's movement success/dual response

		Dual response (%)		
		yes	no	Total (N)
Close to the left	*yes*	73	27	100 (15)
	no	38	62	100 (13)
Priority of abortion	*high*	70	30	100 (20)
	not high	25	75	100 (8)
Unified on issue	*yes*	75	25	100 (20)
	no	13	87	100 (8)
Policy sub-system	*open or moderately closed*	63	27	100 (19)
	closed	44	56	100 (9)
Left in power	*shared or in power*	67	33	100 (15)
	out of power	46	54	100 (13)

✢ DOROTHY MCBRIDE STETSON

the left or when the left is in power When controlled for the intervening variable in Table 13.11, however, the association disappears for insider/marginal agencies. This supports the hypothesis that insider/marginal agencies may be necessary to movement success because they can overcome the absence of the favourable conditions derived from the support of left-wing parties and still achieve dual response. A contrasting proposition—that with symbolic or non-feminist agencies movements have difficulty overcoming their distance from the left or barriers in the policy environment—is only partially supported. Symbolic agencies offer no help in overcoming the loss of the movement's influence when the left is not in power. However, when the movement is close to the left it can still prevail despite the inaction of the state's women's policy agency.

Table 13.10 shows a very strong association between state response and movements that placed a high priority on the abortion issue, were unified on the issue, and, to a lesser extent, faced an open or moderately closed policy sub-system. With respect to the movement characteristics—unity and priority of issue—associations strengthened when controlled for agency activities, leading to the conclusion that agencies tended not to be necessary to success under these conditions. Insider/marginal agencies were a boost to movements that were unified around abortion as a high priority issue but they do not appear to be necessary for movement success. With the proviso that the number of cases is small, the results in Table 13.11 suggest that agencies could be important in

Table 13.11. Effects of women's movement characteristics and policy environments on women's movement success controlling for women's policy agency activities

		Women's policy agency activities					
		Insider/marginal Dual response (%)			Symbolic/non-feminist Dual response (%)		
		Yes	No	Total(N)	Yes	No	Total (N)
Close to left	Yes	82	18	100 (11)	67	33	100 (3)
	No	75	25	100 (4)	22	78	100 (9)
Priority of abortion	High	91	9	100 (12)	38	62	100 (8)
	Not high	33	67	100 (3)	20	80	100 (5)
Unified on issue	Yes	85	15	100 (12)	50	50	100 (8)
	No	50	50	100 (3)	0	100	100 (5)
Policy sub-system	Open/moderately closed	89	11	100 (9)	40	60	100 (10)
	Closed	67	33	100 (6)	0	100	100 (3)
Left in power	Shared or in power	80	20	100 (10)	33	67	100 (5)
	Out of power	80	20	100 (5)	25	75	100 (8)

CONCLUSION ❖

helping movements overcome barriers presented by closed decision making systems. With insider or marginal agencies, the state gave a dual response in two-thirds of the debates taking place in a closed policy system; without activist agencies, movements were always unsuccessful.

The second way of exploring whether or not woman's policy agencies are necessary to movement success is to look more carefully at each pattern of state feminism found in this study. In this comparison, we look at exceptional cases to find instances where agencies intervened and changed the outcome. There are five patterns that include two or more debates: insider/dual response (10); marginal/dual response (2); symbolic/dual response (4); symbolic/co-optation (6); marginal/pre-emption (3). Here are descriptions of the shared characteristics among these cases for each pattern with explanations for the exceptional cases.

The insider/dual response pattern occurred when the women's movements placed abortion as a high priority and were unified around their efforts to effect policy outcomes. In eight debates, the movements were close to the left when the left was in power. This state feminist success was achieved in closed, moderately closed, and open policy sub-systems, facing both strong and weaker counter-movements. These results reinforce the significance of the left-wing parties in assisting both the movements and the agencies in influencing abortion policy. Still there are those insider/dual response cases which occurred in a less friendly partisan environment. Were the women's policy agencies—the state's agents—able to bring about success anyway?

The exceptions to these similarities (NE3, GB1, GB3) occurred in only two countries, the Netherlands and Great Britain. NE3 was a debate that took place in the bureaucracy, a closed environment outside the usual arenas for abortion politics. However, the women's policy agency—the DCE—was placed inside that bureaucracy and had feminist leadership. This allowed it to have access and to be a conduit for women's movement demands. The fact that the left was not in power or that the movement was not cohesive and did not place this debate as a particularly high priority did not matter, given the characteristics of the women's policy agency. Two debates in Great Britain are also exceptions. GB1 and GB3 took place in a very open policy environment without the government whip, so it did not matter which party was in power. In the first debate in the early 1970s, the movement had not yet developed its strong ties with the Labour Party, so it was classified as moderately close rather than close to the left. The case can be made that in GB1, GB3, and NE3 the insider women's policy agencies were essential to movement success given the fact that the left was out of power and the movements faced very strong counter-movements. In all the other cases of insider/dual response, the left-wing parties were either in power alone or shared power in coalition governments. As we have seen, left-wing governments tended to be welcoming to activism by women's policy agencies with varying characteristics, and it is difficult to say whether the movements could have achieved similar successes on their own in such policy environments.

There are only two cases of marginal/dual response debates: CA3 and US1. In both, movements faced moderately closed policy environments. Otherwise there are few similarities in the movement characteristics and policy environments that might suggest any general conclusions about this pattern. It is interesting, however, that the agencies are similar: politically appointed bodies advisory to heads of departments. In Canada, there was a Minister for the Status of Women, but it was a member of a conservative government in 1989–91. Similarly, in the US, the advisory council was appointed by a Republican secretary. Moreover, in the US, the agency was far removed from the arena where the debate took place: the US Supreme Court.

The symbolic/dual response pattern was found in four debates. All women's movements faced strong counter-movements, but they were unified and for three of the four abortion was a top priority. Only two were quite close to the left but only one benefited from a left-wing government. What very likely explains movements' success in the absence of any assistance from the women's policy agency is the fact that none of them had to contend with a completely closed policy sub-system. Two were open and two were moderately closed. These symbolic agencies were either isolated in the cabinet (BL3), lacked feminist leadership (CA2), or had no mandate for the abortion issue (IR2). GB2 is something of a puzzle here, however, because in this debate the women's policy agency could have taken up the abortion issue and at least played a marginal role, but it chose not to do so.

There are six debates where the symbolic agencies watched the movement reach only minimal procedural success through co-optation. They are similar in that the movement was not close to the left during any of these debates, nor was the left in power. If we recall that eight insider agencies associated with movement success took part in debates when the movement was close to the left and the left shared power, this pattern reinforces the importance of the left-wing party status and relationship to the women's movement in explaining state feminism. Other characteristics are important: in two of the three symbolic/co-optation cases, the movement was not cohesive, abortion was not a high priority, the policy sub-systems were closed, and the counter-movement was strong. How then, one might ask, did the movement achieve any success at all in the absence of a helpful women's policy agency?

Co-optation involves participation of women in the policy debates, without achieving policy content that coincides with women's movement goals. It would make sense that in these cases the movement was able to break through to participate because of more open policy sub-systems, and this holds true for five of the six cases. In the case of BL1, the first debate in Belgium, the system was closed, but the arena was important: an investigating commission. Half of the commission's members were women and several were advocates for women's rights. Thus women were inside the process already. But why were these agencies not more active on behalf of the movement? Again, the party in power is telling: in all of these cases the centre or right was in power, and these parties appointed people to these agencies who opposed movement goals on abortion or they tended to discourage agency leaders from taking feminist stands on abortion in the process. These six cases of symbolic/co-optation took place in three countries: Belgium, Germany, and Ireland. The cultural environment in these countries was more discouraging for the movement activists and femocrats alike on the issue than in the other countries in this study.

Finally, there are three cases of marginal/pre-emption, where the agencies advocated movement goals, but were not heard by policy-makers. And while the policy outcome in these debates did not contradict movement goals, women were not admitted as participants in the policy-making process. The movement was close to the left in all three cases, and the left was in power in two. However, in contrast to the characteristics associated with insider success, the movements tended not to be cohesive in these debates, nor did they place abortion as a top priority. The policy sub-system was closed in two debates as well. The exception was SP1 where the movement was unified, placed abortion as a high priority, and the policy system was only moderately closed. In fact, the characteristics of Spain's first debate are quite similar to many of the insider/dual response cases. What limited the effectiveness of the women's policy agency—the Institute for Women—was that it had been created during the beginning of the debate and was in the process of organizing itself. It was thus probably not well-enough established to move on its agenda in an active way with the socialist government and in the parliament.

❖ NATION-STATE PATTERNS

One of the important methodological features of this study of state feminism in abortion politics was the decision to use the policy debate, rather than the nation-state, as the unit of analysis. This approach allowed researchers to look at patterns of movement activism and state response on the issue over time, within countries, and cross-nationally. As indicated in the introduction, whether or not there are nation-state trends would be a finding of the study. Having shown the various patterns of women's movement success and state feminism, this final section considers whether or not the result of this comparative analysis supports the use of policy debates rather than nation states for the study of movement impact.

In only three countries has the impact of women's movements on the state been consistent over the three debates. Policy-makers in Austria and Great Britain consistently responded positively to women's movements substantive and procedural demands for abortion processes and policies that took them into account. The Italian state, on the other hand, was persistent in keeping women and women's movements out of the policy process while at the same time maintaining an abortion policy that pre-empted their demands.

In six of the other countries the state responded in the same way to the movements in two of the three debates studied. However, there was no longitudinal trend. The Belgian state co-opted feminist women in the first two debates leading finally to a dual response in the third. Governments in Canada and France responded to the movement demands in the second and third debates with dual responses. Germany moved from pre-emption in the first to co-optation in the last two debates without ever providing a full movement success. In Ireland, the state allowed women to participate in all three debates but satisfied their policy demands only in part in the second debate granting women the right to travel abroad for abortion services. The US movement was more successful overall than that in Ireland, but its success was not steady, and it was brought up short immediately after a spectacular success in the debate over *Roe v. Wade* by an abrupt no response in the second debate over funding.

If there is a nation-state pattern in the Netherlands, it is one of gradual success for the Dutch women's movement. In three debates, the movement went from no response, to pre-emption, to dual response with the implementation of the law to effect abortion on demand. Spain too, in the two debates studied here, had a similar move from pre-emption to dual response and, similarly, obtained that success during the process of implementation of an abortion reform enacted without women's participation.

The findings with respect to the activities of women's policy agencies and state feminism show a similar mixed pattern when arranged by nation-state. There are three countries where agency activities could be said to conform a national pattern on the abortion issue. Only in Austria, however, is that pattern state feminist where the agencies—one was a quasi-state party body—were insiders gaining dual response in policy debates stretching from the 1970s to the 1990s. Belgium and Ireland show country patterns of inaction by their agencies on the abortion issue which were symbolic throughout the study. The Belgian commissions and council had mandates on the abortion issue but generally opted not to take part in the abortion debates; while those in Ireland, where state authorities in general are reluctant to take any initiative on the highly charged issue, had no mandate for abortion. Germany had no agency in the first debate studied but the agencies since then also followed the symbolic pattern. Like Ireland, their mandate on abortion was tenuous and, in addition, their political bosses installed non-feminists in these agencies and kept them remote from the crucial and divisive debates on abortion law in the 1990s.

Both France and Great Britain had insider agencies in two of the three debates and thus show a trend toward state feminism on the abortion issue. The

French machinery has been more institutionalized with greater resources and more continuity that agencies in Britain. French agencies have risen as high as ministerial cabinet rank, and an administrative structure reaching into the regions continues to provide information and monitor public issues. In Great Britain the only institutionalized structure is the Equal Opportunities Commission, which enforces the Sex Discrimination Act of 1975 and focuses on work and educational issues. The Women's National Commission, a conduit for opinion from women's organizations to the executive, has had few resources and little structure. Other offices tend to be closely associated with parties such as the shadow ministry for women in the Labour Party, whose leadership was active for only a few years with most of the energy and resources coming from its leader, Jo Richardson.

The US and Canada were similar to each other in that they had weaker marginal agencies in two of the three debates. Canada's array of women's policy machinery was more institutionalized that that in the US, but with the conservatives in power during crucial parliamentary debates they were at a disadvantage. In both Canada and the US, some debates took place in the Courts. The legal arena provided few avenues for agencies inside political or administrative institutions to gain access to the policy debates despite taking stands supportive of the women's movements on the issues at stake. Finally, as with the findings about movement success, the second and third debates in the Netherlands and the two debates in Spain showed a different role for the women's policy agencies, moving from symbolic/pre-emption and marginal/pre-emption respectively, to a full insider/dual response in the final debate. These results demonstrate the significance of insider agencies in the ministries in expanding women's access to both power and abortion services.

❖ SUMMARY OF FINDINGS: TOWARD A THEORY OF STATE FEMINISM

Finally, we summarize the contributions of the findings in this study of abortion politics in advanced industrial democracies toward a theory of state feminism. First of all, the framework and the methods have provided reliable evidence to examine the state feminism hypotheses. Selecting the individual debate as the unit of analysis rather than the nation-state has allowed longitudinal and cross-national comparisons. There is enough variation in patterns within countries to warrant departing from the nation-state analysis in setting up the research design and treating these nation-state patterns as a research finding rather than an assumption. The assumptions that were made in the research design—that gendering of issue frames in debates leads to gendered policy outcomes and participation—have been supported by the data. The definition of feminism in terms of the specific goals of women's movements

❖ DOROTHY MCBRIDE STETSON

during each debate has prevented conceptual stretching, but it has been necessary to generalize about movements at the expense of a full rendering of their diversity throughout the period under study.

The examination of the hypotheses posed at the beginning of this study has yielded meaningful results in explaining state feminism. It is clear that, through their women's policy agencies, states have offered institutional resources that help achieve feminist goals as presented by women's movements. When the movements are close to left-wing parties and those parties are in power, the conditions are especially favourable to state feminism. But these conditions are not sufficient; it is also important that the women's movements be unified around their demands and place the issue as a high priority on their agendas. The case for state feminism is further supported by the finding that when these favourable partisan conditions are not present, insider women's policy agencies with feminist leaders, depending on where they are placed in relation to the policy-making arenas, can still intervene to gain procedural and substantive policy responses to movement demands even in the face of strong counter-movements.

Activist insider or marginal state agencies are not essential for women's movements to have an impact on the policy-making process under all circumstances. Strong movements can be successful when state agencies are nothing more than symbolic decorations and the left is out of power. But without activist agencies, movements must depend on the policy sub-systems being either open or moderately closed, rather than closed, especially when the left is out of power to have an impact. Even then, they are likely to achieve only partial success by gaining access to policy arenas but not feminist policy outcomes.

❖ NOTES

1 These debates include all except the first debates in the Netherlands and Germany (NE1, GR1) and the first two debates in Italy (IT1, IT2).

2 These conclusions are in turn based upon decisions each researcher has made in examining the primary data to provide information according to the conceptual framework of state feminism that guides this comprehensive research project.

3 The debates covered in the chapters on Great Britain and France did not include the initial liberalization in the Abortion Act of 1967 and the loi Veil in 1975. For all three debates in Great Britain it was anti-abortion activists who raised the issue in an attempt to restrict the 1967 act. In France the debates took three different routes to the agenda: based on previous law, Socialist Party initiative, and anti-abortion campaigns.

4 The larger RNGS study (see Chapter 1, n. 2), when completed, will yield information on policy debates in five issue areas in 15 countries. The number of debates that result will permit quantitative/statistical testing of these hypotheses.

❖ Bibliography

❖ GOVERNMENT DOCUMENTS

❖ Austria

Frauenbericht (1985). *Bericht über die Situation der Frauen in Österreich*. Vienna: Bundeskanzleramt.

—— (1995). *Bericht über die Situation der Frauen in Österreich*. Vienna: Bundesministerium für Frauenangelegenheiten/Bundeskanzleramt.

❖ Belgium

Belgisch Staatsblad (1990). 05.04.1990, 6379–81.

Consultatieve Commissie voor de Status van de Vrouw (n.d). *Activiteitenverslag van de consultatieve commissie voor de status van de vrouw van 1976 tot 1982*. Brussels.

Kamer van Volksvertegenwoordigers, G. Z. (1981–2), *Parlementaire Handelingen*, 3.03.1982. Brussels.

—— (1989–90), *Parlementaire Handelingen*, 27–29.03. Brussels.

—— (1989–90), *Parlementaire Stukken*, 1025–1. Brussels.

Ministerie van Buitenlandse Zaken, Buitenlandse handel en Ontwikkelingssamenwerking (1981). *Werelconferentie van het decennium van de Verenigde Naties voor de Vrouw. Synthese van het Wereldaktieprogramma Kopenhagen 14-30 juli 1980*. Brussels.

Ministerie van Volksgezondheid en Leefmilieu, Emancipatieraad (1987). *Jaarverslag 1986–87*. Brussels.

Senaat, B.Z. (1988). *Parlementaire Stukken*, 246–6; 2473; 247–5; 247-2; 247–6; 247–8. Brussels.

Senaat, G.Z. (1976–7), *Parlementaire Stukken*, 954. Brussels.

—— (1989–90), *Parlementaire Handelingen*, 24-27.10.1989; 3-6.11.1989. Brussels.

❖ Canada

Brodsky, Gwen and Day, Shelagh (1989). *Canadian Charter Equality Rights for Women: One Step Forward or Two Steps Back?* Ottawa: Canadian Advisory Council on the Status of Women.

Canadian Advisory Council on the Status of Women (1990). 'Brief Submitted to the Legislative Committee on Bill C-43 by the Canadian Advisory Council on the Status of Women'. Ottawa: Canadian Advisory Council on the Status of Women (March).

Martin, Sheilah (1989). 'Women's Reproductive Health, the Canadian Charter of Rights and Freedoms, and the Canada Health Act' (background paper). Ottawa: Canadian Advisory Council on the Status of Women.

❖ *France*

Journal Officiel (1975). 18 January.
—— (1979). 29 December.
—— (1980). 1 January.
MDDF (Ministère Déléguée des Droits de la Femme) (1984). *La Contraception: Un Droit Fundamental*. Paris: MDDF.
Questions Écrites (1978–9; 1982–3; 1991–3). Paris: Assemblée Nationale.
SEDFVQ (Secrétariat d'État aux Droits des Femmes et à la Vie Quotidienne) (1991). Press Communiqué, 21 June. Paris.

❖ *Germany*

Bundesgesetzblatt Jahrgang (1995). 'Schwangeren-und Familienhilfeänderungsgesetz vom 21. August 1995', 1/44: 1050–7.
Bundesverfassungsgericht (1993). *Im Namen des Volkes in den Verfahren wegen verfassungsrechtlicher Prüfung der Vorschriften des §218b*. Karlsruhe: Bundesverfassungsgericht.
Deutscher Bundestag (1992). *Schutz des ungeborenen Lebens: Anhörung des Sonderausschusses 'Schutz des ungebornene Lebens'*. Bonn: Deutscher Bundestag.
Jahresbericht der Bundesregierung 1979 (1979). Bonn: Presse- und Informationsamt der Bundesregierung.
Merkel, Angela (1991a). Press release, 9 August (No. 67). Bonn: Bundesministerium für Frauen und Jugend.
—— (1991b). 'Rede in der 1. Lesung zur Neuregelung des Schwangerschaftsabbruchs im Deutschen Bundestag am 26. September 1991'. Press release 26 September (No. 77). Bonn: Bundesministerium für Frauen und Jugend.
Nolte, Claudia (1995). Speech to German Bundestag, 10 February. Reprinted in Bundesministerium für Familie, Senioren, Frauen und Jungend. *Pressemitteilung: Informationsdienst* No. 1. May.
Rönsch, Hannelore (1991a). Press release, 15 July. Bonn: CDU-Bundesgeschäftsstelle.
—— (1991b). 'Die politische Bedeutung der Gesetzlichen Regelung des Lebenschutzes.' Speech given at Konrad-Adenaur-Stiftung Fachtagung, 25–6 April.
Vertrag (1990). *Vertrag zwischen der Bundesrepublik Deutschland und der Deutschen Demokratischen Republik–Einigungsvertrag (Zweiter Staatsvertrag)*. 6 September.

❖ *Great Britain*

House of Commons (1975). *Special Reports and Minutes of Evidence of the Select Committee on the Abortion (Amendment) Bill*. Session 1974–75. 10 November. London: HMSO.

Parliamentary Debates (Hansard) House of Commons Official Report. (1970, 1974, 1975, 1987–88, 1990).
Parliamentary Papers (1974). *Report of the Committee Working on the Abortion Act* (Lane Committee).
Women's National Commission (1970–4). *Bulletin*.

❖ Ireland

All-Party Oireachtas Committee on the Constitution (2000). *Fifth Progress Report: Abortion*. Dublin: Stationery Office (November).
Dail Reports (1997). Parliamentary Debates: Official Report; Vol.482. Dublin: Stationery Office.
Green Paper on Abortion (1999). Dublin: Government Publications, Stationery Office.
Mahon, E., Conlon, C., and Dillon, L. (1998). *Women and Crisis Pregnancy in Ireland*. Dublin: Stationery Office.

❖ Italy

Commissione Pari Opportunità (1998). Elettrici ed Elette. Storia, testimonianze e riflessioni a cinquat'anni dal voto alle donne. Rome: Istituto Poligrafico e Zecca dello Stato.
Corte Costituzionale Italiana (1976). 'Sentenza della Corte Costituzionale Italiana, n.27, 18-2-1975'. L'aborto nelle sentenze, Milan: Giuffrè.
ISTAT (Istituto Nazionale di Statistica) (2000). *L'abortività volontaria in Italia: tendenze e nuovi comportamenti degli anni '90. Rome:* ISTAT.

❖ The Netherlands

Handelingen Eerste Kamer, 1967–1981.
Handelingen Tweede Kamer, 1967–1985.
Staatsblad, 1981. 1 May.

❖ Spain

DSCD (*Diario de Sesiones del Congreso de los Diputados*) (1983*a*). Madrid: Plenary Session 25 May.
—— (1983*b*). Madrid: Plenary Session 4 October.
—— (1983*c*). Madrid: Plenary Session 5 October.
—— (1983*d*). Madrid: Plenary Session 6 October.
—— (1983*e*). *Comisión de Justicia e Interior*. Madrid. 7 September.
—— (1985*a*). Madrid: Plenary Session. 28 May.
—— (1985*b*). *Comisión de Justicia e Interior*. Madrid.14 May.
DSS (*Diario de Sesiones del Senado*) (1983). Madrid. Plenary Session 30 November.
—— (1985). Madrid: Plenary Session 25 June.
—— (1985). 'Informe del Instituto de la Mujer sobre Aplicación de la Ley de Interrupción Voluntaria del Embarazo (Septiembre 1985)'. Unpublished internal documents.

DSS (1986*a*). 'Borrador de Orden Ministerial Sustitutoria de la de 31 de Julio de 1985 sobre la Práctica del Aborto en Centros o Establecimientos Sanitarios'. Unpublished internal documents.

Instituto de la Mujer (1986*b*). 'Comentarios al Proyecto de Real Decreto sobre la Práctica del Aborto en Centros o Establecimientos Sanitarios (31 Octubre 1986)'. Unpublished internal document.

—— (1986*c*). El Institute de la Mujer 1983–1986. Madrid: Institute de la Mujer.

—— (1986*d*). 'Informe del Instituto de la Mujer en Relación al Documento Remitido por el Ministerio de Sanidad sobre Desarrollo de la Ley de Interrupción Voluntaria del Embarazo (Agosto de 1986)'. Unpublished internal documents.

—— (1986*e*). 'Informe sobre la Ampliación de la Ley Orgánica 9/85 Realizado por el Instituto de la Mujer (Abril de 1986)'. Unpublished internal documents.

—— (1986*f*). 'Memoria Explicativa de la Necesidad de Sustitución de la Orden Ministerial de 31 de Julio de 1985, sobre la Práctica del Aborto en Centros o Establecimientos Sanitarios'. Unpublished internal documents.

—— (1986*g*). 'Segundo Informe sobre el Proyecto de Real Decreto sobre la Práctica del Aborto en Centros o Establecimientos Sanitarios (14 Noviembre 1986)'. Unpublished internal document.

—— (1986*a*). 'Informe del Ministerio de Sanidad y Consumo sobre Desarrollo de la Ley de Interrupción Voluntaria del Embarazo (Julio de 1986). Aborto: Síntesis de Análisis y Propuestas de Desarrollo'. Madrid. Unpublished internal documents.

Ministerio de Sanidad y Consumo (1986*b*). 'Proyecto de Real Decreto sobre la Práctica del Aborto en Centros o Establecimientos Sanitarios'. Madrid. Unpublished internal document.

❖ *United States*

Congressional Quarterly (1995, 1996, 1997).

Department of Health, Education and Welfare (1974). *The Rights and Responsibilities of Women*. Recommendations of the Secretary's Advisory Committee on the Rights and Responsibilities of Women 1973, 1974. Washington, DC.

House of Representatives (1990*a*). *Federal Council on Women Act*. Hearing before the Legislation and National Security Subcommittee of the Committee on Government Operations, 24 July.

—— (1990*b*). *Freedom of Choice Act of 1989*. Hearings before the Subcommittee on Civil and Constitutional Rights of the Committee on the Judiciary, 2–3 October.

—— (1995). *Partial Birth Abortion Ban Act of 1995*. Hearings before the Subcommittee on the Constitution of the Committee on the Judiciary, 15 June.

—— (1996) *Origins and Scope of Roe v. Wade*. Hearing before the Subcommittee on the Constitution of the Committee on the Judiciary, 22 April.

House and Senate (1997). *Partial-Birth Abortion: The Truth*. Joint Hearing before the Senate Committee on the Judiciary and the Subcommittee on the Constitution of the House Committee on the Judiciary, 11 March.

National Commission (1976). '... *To Form a More Perfect Union ...' Justice for American*

Women. Report of the National Commission on the Observance of International Women's Year. Washington, DC.
—— (1978). *The Spirit of Houston: The First National Women's Conference*. Washington, DC: National Commission on the Observance of International Women's Year.
Senate (1990) *Freedom of Choice Act of 1989*. Hearings before the Committee on Labor and Human Resources, 27 March, 23 May.
Congressional Record (1975; 1976; 1977).

❖ GENERAL

4 maart Comité. (1977). *Abortus vrij. De vrouw beslis (sine loco)*.
Abele, Frances (1992). *How Ottawa Spends 1991–92*. Ottawa: Carleton University Press.
Abortus (1977). *Analyse van de twee verslagen door de Staatscommissie voor de Ethische Problemen ingediend bij de Eerste-Minister op 15 juni 1976*. Zele: DAP Reinaert Uitgaven.
Acker, Joan (1995). 'Feminist Goals and Organizing Processes', in Myra Marx Ferree and Patricia Yancey Martin (eds), *Feminist Organisations: Harvest of the New Women's Movement*. Philadelphia: Temple University Press.
Actualités Sociales Hebdomaires (1996). 'La Cour de Cassation Rejette les Arguments des Militants anti-IVG'. 6 December.
Adamson, Nancy, Briskin, Linda, and Macphail, Margaret (1988). *Feminist Organizing for Change: The Contemporary Women's Movement in Canada*. Toronto: Oxford University Press.
Adler, Laure (1993). *Les Femmes Politiques*. Paris: Editions du Seuil.
Agence France Presse (1991). 'Création d'un groupe de travail interministériel pour faire face aux "commandos anti-IVG"'. 17 September.
Allison, Maggie (1994). 'The Right to Choose: Abortion in France'. *Parliamentary Affairs*, 47/2: 222–38.
Altbach, Edith Hoshino (1984). 'The New German Women's Movement', in E. H. Altbach, J. Clausen, D. Schultz, and N. Stephan (eds), *German Feminism: Readings in Politics and Literature*. Albany: State University of New York Press.
Anderson, James E. (1994). *Public Policymaking: An Introduction*. Boston: Houghton Mifflin Company.
Andrew, Caroline and Rodgers, Sanda (eds) (1997). *Women and the Canadian State*. Montreal: McGill-Queen's University Press.
Antonyshyn, Patricia B. Lee, and Merrill, Alex (1988). 'Marching for Women's Lives: the Campaign for Free-Standing Abortion Clinics in Ontario', in Frank Cunningham *et al.* (eds), *Social Movements, Social Change: The Politics and Practice of Organizing* (Socialist Studies iv). Toronto: Between the Lines.
Appleton, Andrew and Mazur, Amy G. (1993). 'Transformation or Modernization: The Rhetoric and Reality of Gender and Party Politics in France', in J. Lovenduski and P. Norris (eds), *Gender and Party Politics*. London: Sage Publications.
Arscott, Jane (1998). '"More Women": The RCSW and Political Representation, 1970', in Manon Tremblay and Caroline Andrew (eds), *Women and Political Representation in Canada*. Ottawa: University of Ottawa Press.

Associazione 'Choisir' (1974). *Un caso di aborto: il processo Chevalier.* Turin: Einaudi.

Associazione Orlando (1999). Appello: 'Che nessuna interferenza legislativa sia accettata in materia di scelta procreativa'. Bologna: Centro di Documentazione delle Donne, 30 May.

Balbo, Laura *et al.* (1991). *Complessità sociale e identità.* Milan: Angeli.

Baranski, Zygmunt and Vinall, Shirley W. (eds) (1991). *Women in Italy: Essays on Gender, Culture and History.* London: Macmillan.

Barazzetti, Donatella and Leccardi, Carmen (2000). 'Nel segno dell'ambivalenza. Donne e riproduzione in Calabria', in A. Oppo, S. Picone Stella, and A. Signorelli (eds), *Maternità, Identità, scelte. I percorsi di emancipazione femminile nel Mezzogiorno.* Naples: Liguori.

Barbagli, Marco and Saraceno, Chiara (1997). *Lo stato della famiglia in Italia.* Bologna: il Mulino.

Barreiro, Belén (1998). 'Democracia y Conflicto Moral: la Política del Aborto en Italia y España' (Ph.D. thesis). Madrid: Centro de Estudios Avanzados en Ciencias Sociales del Instituto Juan March de Estudios e Investigaciones.

Bashevkin, Sylvia (1998). *Women on the Defensive: Living through Conservative Times.* Toronto: University of Toronto Press.

Bataille, Claire (1982). 'Remboursement de l'avortement: le changement a reculons'. *Cahiers du Féminisme,* 21/November–December: 6–10.

Beccalli, Bianca (1984). 'The Modern Women's Movement in Italy', in M. Threlfall (ed.), *Mapping the Women's Movement: Feminist Politics and Social Transformation in the North.* London, New York: Verso.

Beckmann, Rainer (ed.) (1991). *Abtreibung in der Diskussion: Fünfzig Behauptungen und ihre Widerlegung.* Krefeld: Sinus.

Begin, Monique (1997). 'The Canadian Government and the Commission's Report', in C. Andrew and S. Rodgers (eds), *Women and the Canadian State.* Montreal: McGill-Queen's University Press.

Berger, Henri (ed.) (1975). *L'Avortement: Histoire d'un débat.* Paris: Flammarion.

Berliner Morgenpost (1991). 6 September.

Bimbi, Franca and Del Re, Alisa (eds) (1997). *Genere e democrazia: la cittadinanza delle donne a cinquant'anni dal voto.* Turin: Rosenberg and Sellier.

Bird, Caroline (1979). *What Women Want.* New York: Simon and Schuster.

Boccia, Maria Luisa (1993). 'Cancelliamo l'aborto dal codice penale'. *Democrazia e Diritto,* 2: 237–41.

—— (1995). 'Il danno del diritto'. *Critica marxista,* 3: 34–40.

Bono, Paola and Kemp, Sandra (eds) (1991). *Italian Feminist Thought: A Reader.* Oxford: Basil Blackwell.

Boseley, Sarah (2000). 'Abortion Guidelines Hailed by Campaigners: Royal College Calls for Operation within Three Weeks of Referral'. *Guardian,* 13 March: 76.

Bourne, Paula (1993). 'Women, Law and the Justice System', in R. Pierson, M. Cohen, P. Bourne, and P. Masters (eds), *Canadian Women's Issues, Volume I: Strong Voices.* Toronto: James Lorimer and Company.

Brandstaller, Trautl (1981). *Frauen in Österreich. Bilanz und Ausblick.* Vienna: Bundeskanzleramt.

Breen, Katie (1992). 'Veronique Neiertz: Danger, libertés menacées'. *Marie Claire*, 476/April: 125–6.

Brodie, Ian (1992). 'The Court Challenges Program', in F. L. Morton (ed.), *Law, Politics, and the Judicial Process in Canada* (2nd ed). Calgary: University of Calgary Press.

Brodie, Janine (1992). 'Choice and No Choice in the House', in J. Brodie, S. Gavigan, and J. Jenson (eds), *The Politics of Abortion*. Toronto: Oxford University Press.

——, Gavigan, Shelley, and Jenson, Jane (1992). *The Politics of Abortion*. Toronto: Oxford University Press.

Burt, Sandra (1998). 'The Canadian Advisory Council on the Status of Women: Possibilities and Limitations', in M. Tremblay and C. Andrew (eds), *Women and Political Representation in Canada*. Ottawa: University of Ottawa Press.

Busnelli, Francesco Donato (1988). 'Lo statuto del concepito'. *Democrazia e diritto*, 24: 213–22.

Bustelo, Carlota (1979). *La Alternativa Feminista: Conferencia pronunciada por Carlota Bustelo en el Club Siglo XXI el Día 3 de Mayo de 1979*. Madrid: Partido Socialista Obrero Español.

—— (1986). 'La mujer Española en Europa: un Nuevo Alcance en la Igualdad de Oportunidades', in Club Siglo XXI (ed.), *España en Europa: el Reto (la CEE en el Club Siglo XXI)*. Barcelona: Plaza and Janés.

—— (1987). 'Hacia la Igualdad'. *Transporte, Comunicación y Mar*, 19:14–15.

—— (1988). 'Evoluzione dei Comportamenti e del Ruolo della Donna Spagnola nell'Ultimo Decennio', in Alberto Caracciolo (ed.), *Democrazia e Sviluppo nella Spagna Post-Franchista: I Problemi della Transizione*. Milan: Franco Angeli.

CADAC (Coordination Nationale pour le Droit à l'Avortement et à la Contraception) (1991). 'Avortement contraception: un droit menacé ; une mobilisation nécessaire'. *Enjeux et Débats*, 11/30 November: 3.

Caldwell, Lesley (1986). 'Feminism and Abortion Politics in Italy', in J. Lovenduski and J. Outshoorn (eds), *The Politics of Abortion*. London: Sage.

—— (1991). *Italian Family Matters: Women, Politics and Legal Reforms*. London: Macmillan.

Calloni, Marina (1997). 'Zur kulturellerelativität europäischer Abtreibungsgesetze', in M. Kettner (ed.), *Beratung als Zwang. Schwangerschaftsberatung, genetische Aufklärung und die Grenze der kommunikativen Vernunft*. Frankfurt a. M: Campus.

—— (2002). *Il Guisto, il Bene e le Differenze. Il conflitto pubblico-privato dell' aborto*. Rome: Donzelli.

Campbell, Kim (1996). *Time and Chance: The Political Memoirs of Canada's First Woman Prime Minister*. Toronto: Random House.

Caprile, Giovanni (ed.) (1981). *Il Papa e il diritto alla vita. Il magistero di Paolo VI e di Giovanni Paolo II sull'aborto*. Rome: Ed. La Parola.

CARAL (Canadian Abortion Rights Action League) (1990). 'Brief to the Legislative Committee on Bill C-43'. Ottawa: CARAL (January).

—— (1998). 'Abortion in Canada Today: The Situation Province-by-Province' (Background Paper). Ottawa: CARAL.

Casini, Carlo and Quarenghi, Vittoria (1981). *La ricomposizione dell'area cattolica dopo il Referendum sull'aborto*. Milan: Editoriale LCA.

Cavarero, Adriana (1990). *Nonostante Platone. Figure femminili nella filosofia antica.* Rome: Editori Riuniti.

Celis, Karen (1996). 'Abortus in België. 1880–1940'. In *Belgisch Tijdschrift voor Nieuwste Geschiedenis*, 26/3–4: 201–40.

—— (1997). 'Wij waren de eersten. IJveren voor de liberalisering van voorbehoedmiddelen en abortus (1945–1980)', in D. De Weerdt (ed.), *De Dochters van Marianne. 75 jaar Socialistische Vooruitziende Vrouwen.* Ghent: AMSAB.

Cesbron, Paul (1997). *L'Interruption de Grossesse depuis la loi Veil: Bilan and Perspectives.* Paris: Flammarion – Médecine-Sciences.

CFDT (Confédération Française et Démocratique du Travail) (1982). 'IVG: Projet de loi pour le remboursement'. *Syndicalisme Hebdo*: 9 December.

Chamberlayne, Prue (1995). 'Gender and the Private Sphere: A Touchstone of Misunderstanding between Eastern and Western Germany'. *Social Politics*, 2/1: 25–36.

Chiaromonte, Franca, Negrini, Grazia, Muraro, Luisa, Tidei, Rossana, Lamberti, Raffaella, Paciotti, Elena, Campari, Maria Grazia, Paolozzi, Letizia, Bocchetti, Alessandra, Dioguardi, Daniela, Giardina, Maddalena, Cigarini, Lia, Ceresa, Ivana, Putino, Angela, Borrello, Giovanna, and Cavarero, Adriana (1989). 'Una proposta per cancellare la parola aborto dal codice penale'. *Noi Donne*, 1993/3: 90–2.

Chinese, Maria Grazie, Lonzi, Carla, Lonzi, Marta, and Jaquinta, Anna (1977). *È già politica.* Milan: Scritti di Rivolta Femminista.

Claeys, Vicky (1985). *Het Belgische abortusverhaal. Een overzicht van de geschiedenis op het vlak van ethiek, wetgeving en praktijk.* Brussels: Federatie CGSO.

Cobb, Roger and Elder, Charles D. (1983). *Participation in American Politics: The Dynamics of Agenda-Setting.* Baltimore: Johns Hopkins University Press.

Cohan, Alvin (1986). 'Abortion as a Marginal Issue: The Use of Peripheral Mechanisms in Britain and the United States', in J. Lovenduski and J. Outshoorn (eds), *The New Politics of Abortion.* London: Sage.

Cohen, Marjorie Griffin (1993). 'The Canadian Women's Movement', in R. Pierson, M. Cohen, P. Bourne, and P. Masters (eds), *Canadian Women's Issues, Volume I: Strong Voices.* Toronto: James Lorimer and Company.

Collectif Féministe Contre La Répression et Coordination des Groupes Femmes Paris (1979). *La Pergola: Qui Sont Les Coupables?* Paris. Collected in *Agence Femmes Information: Avortement (dossier de presse, 1975–1981).*

Collier, David (1991). 'New Perspectives on the Comparative Method', in D. A. Rustow and K. P. Erickson (eds), *Comparative Political Dynamics: Global Research Perspectives.* New York: Harper Collins.

—— and Mahon, James E. (1993). 'Conceptual "Stretching" Revisited: Adapting Categories in Comparative Analysis'. *American Political Science Review*, 87: 845–55.

Collins, Anne (1985). *The Big Evasion: Abortion, the Issue That Won't Go Away.* Toronto: Lester and Orpen Dennys.

Commission of the Evangelical Church in Germany (1972). 'Denkschrift zu Fragen der Sexualethik', in Friedrich-Christian Schroeder (ed.), *Abtreibung: Reform des §218.* Berlin: Walter de Gruyter.

Condit, Celeste Michelle (1990). *Decoding Abortion Rhetoric: Communicating Social Change.* Urbana: University of Illinois Press.

Congregazione per la Dottrina della Fede (1974). 'Dichiarazione sull'aborto procurato'. *Enchiridion Vaticanum 5. Documenti ufficiali della Santa Sede 1974–76.* Bologna: Edizioni Dehoniane.

—— (1987). *Istruzione su il rispetto della vita umana nascente e la dignità della procreazione,* Milan: Edizioni Paoline.

Conradt, David P. (1993). *The German Polity* (5th edn). New York: Longman.

Coote, Anna and Campbell, Beatrix (1982). *Sweet Freedom: The Struggle for Women's Liberation.* Oxford: Basil Blackwell.

Costa-Lascoux, Jacqueline (1992). 'La donna, la procreazione e la bioetica', in G. Duby and M. Perrot (eds), *Storia delle donne in Occidente. Il Novecento.* Rome-Bari: Laterza.

Costain, Anne N. (1982). 'Representing Women: The Transition from Social Movement to Interest Group', in Ellen Boneparth (ed.), *Women, Power and Policy.* New York : Pergamon Press.

Coughlan, Michael J. (1990). *The Vatican, the Law and the Human Embryo.* London: Macmillan.

Craig, Barbara Hinkson and O'Brien, David M. (1993). *Abortion and American Politics.* Chatham, N.J.: Chatham House Publishers.

Cunningham, Frank, Findlay, Sue, Kadar, Marlene, Lennon, Alan, and Silva, Ed (eds) (1988). *Social Movements, Social Change: The Politics and Practice of Organizing* (Socialist Studies iv). Toronto: Between the Lines Press.

Czarnowski, Gabriele (1994). 'Abortion as Political Conflict in Unified Germany'. *Parliamentary Affairs,* 47/2: 252–67.

Dahlerup, Drude (1987). 'Confusing Concepts—Confusing Reality: A Theoretical Discussion of the Patriarchal State', in A. S. Sassoon (ed.), *Women and the State: The Shifting Boundaries of Public and Private.* London: Unwin Hyman.

Dalton, Russell J. (1993). *Politics in Germany* (2nd edn). New York: Harper Collins.

Damiani, Cristina and Graziosi, Marina (1981). *Studi sull'aborto. Posizioni e documenti del movimento delle donne.* Milan: Cooperativa Edizioni Ottanta.

De Clercq, Bertrand (1977). 'De discussies rond een legalisering van opzettelijke abortus'. *Res Publica,* 19/2: 305–22.

De Keyser, Karin and De Meuter, Sofia (1993). 'Juridische aspecten van de Wet Zwangerschapsafbreking'. *Res Publica,* 32/4: 179–210.

Delgado, M. and Livi-Bacci, M. (1992). 'Fertility in Italy and Spain: the Lowest in the World.' *Family Planning Perspectives,* 24/4: 162–71.

D'Elia, Cecilia (1996). 'Prospettive dell'aborto in Italia'. *Democrazia e Diritto,* 1: 127–38.

Democrazia e Diritto (1993). 'Diritto sessuato'. Special issue, No. 2.

—— (1996). 'La legge e il corpo'. Special issue, No. 1.

De Musso, Flora and Pasotti, Rita (1989). *A proposito dell'aborto (1971–1989)* (Rassegna stampa). Milan: Archivio della Libreria delle Donne.

DeSanto, Tony (1989). 'Pro-lifers irked by PM's Stand'. *Catholic Register,* 5 August.

Deutscher Frauenärzte (1972). 'Stellungnahme deutscher Frauenärzte zum Problem der Schwangerschaftsunterbrechung', in Friedrich-Christian Schroeder (ed.), *Abtreibung: Reform des §218.* Berlin: Walter de Gruyter.

deValk, Alphonse (1974). *Morality and Law in Canadian Politics: The Abortion Controversy.* Montreal: Palm.

De Winter, Lieven (1992). 'The Belgian Legislator' (Ph.D. thesis). European University Institute Florence, Department of Political and Social Sciences.

Dijkstra, T. and Swiebel, J. (1982). 'De overheid en het vrouwenvraagstuk: emancipatiebeleid als mode en taboe', in S. L. Sevenhuijsen *et al.* (eds), *Socialisties-Feministiese Teksten 7*. Amsterdam: Feministische Uitgeverij Sara.

Diotima (1987). *Il pensiero della differenza sessuale*. Milan: La Tartaruga.

—— (1995). *Oltre l'uguaglianza*. Naples: Liguori.

—— (1997). *Il pensiero della differenza sessuale*. Milan: La Tartaruga.

D'Orazio, Emilio (ed.) (1989). 'Aborto: una disamina filosofica, giuridica e medica della legge 194 e delle sue prospettive' (Tavola rotonda con interventi di C. Flamigni, M. Marigo, M. Mori). *Notizie di Politeia*, 5/14: 4–16.

Dulude, Louise (1975). 'Abortion in Canada: Background Notes on the Proposed Amendments to the Criminal Code'. Ottawa: Canadian Advisory Council on the Status of Women.

Dunlop, Marilyn (1990). 'Doctors to Oppose New Abortion Law'. *Toronto Star*, 17 January.

Dunphy, Catherine (1996). *Morgentaler: A Difficult Hero*. Toronto: Random House of Canada.

Dunsmuir, Mollie (1997). 'Abortion: Constitutional and Legal Developments' (*Current Issue Review Publication* 89-10E). Ottawa: Parliamentary Research Branch Library of Parliament..

Durán, María A. and Gallego, María T. (1986). 'The Women's Movement in Spain and the New Spanish Democracy', in Drude Dahlerup (ed.), *The New Women's Movement: Feminism and Political Power in Europe and the USA*. London: Sage.

Edelman, Murray (1985). *The Symbolic Uses of Politics*. Urbana: University of Illinois Press.

Edlinger, Gertrude (1981). 'Dokumentation der politischen Geschichte zur Reform des §144 STB'. *Studien zur Reform des Österreichischen Strafgesetzes, Band II*. Vienna: Ludwig-Boltzmann Institut.

Eisenstein, Hester (1990). 'Femocrats, Official Feminism and the Uses of Power', in S. Watson (ed.), *Playing the State: Australian Feminist Interventions*. London: Verso.

El País (2000). 19 February.

Enigl, Marianne and Perthold, Susanne (eds) (1993). *Der weibliche Körper als Schlachtfeld. Neue Beiträge zur Abtreibungsdiskussion*. Vienna: Promedia.

Enschede, C. J. (1966). 'Abortus op medische indicatie en strafrecht'. *Nederlands Tijdschrift voor Geneeskunde*, 110: 1349–53.

ER Advies (1983). *Advies Afbreking Zwangerschap*. The Hague: Emancipatieraed.

Ergas, Yasmine (1986). *Nella maglie della politica. Femminismo, istituzioni e politiche sociali nell'Italia degli anni '70*. Milan: F. Angeli.

—— (1992). 'La costituzione del soggetto femminile: il femminismo negli anni '60/'70', in G. Duby and M. Perrot (eds), *Storia delle donne in Occidente. Il Novecento*. Rome-Bari: Laterza.

Escario, Pilar, Alberdi, Inés, and López-Accotto, Ana I. (1996). *Lo Personal es Político: el Movimiento Feminista en la Transición*. Madrid: Instituto de la Mujer.

Faccio, Adele (1975a). *Le mie ragioni. Conversazioni con 70 donne*. Milan: Feltrinelli.

—— (1975b). *Il reato di massa*. Milano: SugarCo.

Fasching, Waltraud (1988). 'Für die ersatzlose Streichung des §144', in B. Geiger and H. Hacker (eds), *Individualität und Kollektivität in frauenbewegten Zusammenhängen. Exemplarische Untersuchung zur autonomen in Österreich 1972–1988*. Vienna: Jubilämsfond der Österreichischen Nationalbank.

Ferrajoli, Luigi (1976). 'Aborto, Morale e Diritto Penale'. *Prassi e Teoria*, 3: 397–418.

—— (1996). 'La differenza sessuale e le garanzie dell'uguaglianza'. *Democrazia e Diritto*, 2: 49–73.

Ferree, Myra Marx (1987). 'Equality and Autonomy: Feminist Politics in the United States and West Germany', in M. F. Katzenstein and C. M. Mueller (eds), *The Women's Movements of the United States and Western Europe*. Philadelphia: Temple University Press.

—— (1995a). 'Making Equality: The Women's Affairs Offices in the Federal Republic of Germany', in D. M. Stetson and A G. Mazur (eds), *Comparative State Feminism*. Thousand Oaks, CA: Sage.

—— (1995b). 'Patriarchies and Feminisms: The Two Women's Movements of Post-unification Germany'. *Social Politics*, 2/1: 11–24.

—— and Martin, Patricia Yancey (eds) (1995). *Feminist Organisations: Harvest of the New Women's Movement*. Philadelphia: Temple University Press.

FFBIZ e.V. (Frauenforschungs-, -bildungs- und -informationszentrum) (1991). 'Frauen Begehren Selbstbestimmung' 120 Jahre Kampf dem §218*. Berlin: FFBIZ e.V.

Findlay, Sue (1987). 'Facing the State: The Politics of the Women's Movement Reconsidered', in H. Maroney and M. Luxton (eds), *Feminism and Political Economy: Women's Work, Women's Struggles*. Toronto: Methuen.

—— (1998). 'Representation and the Struggle for Women's Equality: Issues for Feminist Practice', in M. Tremblay and C. Andrew (eds), *Women and Political Representation in Canada*. Ottawa: University of Ottawa Press.

Fiori, A. and Sgreccia, Elio (eds) (1975). *Aborto: riflessioni di studiosi cattolici*. Milan: Vita e Pensiero.

—— (1976). *Obiezione di coscienza*. Milan: Vita e Pensiero.

Il Foglio del Paese delle Donne (1999). 'Fuori dalla Legge', 24 February.

Folguera, Pilar (1988). 'De la Transición Política a la Democracia: La Evolución del Feminismo en España durante el Período 1975–1988', in P. Folguera (ed.), *El Feminismo en España: Dos Siglos de Historia*. Madrid: Fundación Pablo Iglesias.

Frabotta, Biancamaria (ed.) (1975). *Femminismo e lotta di classe in Italia (1970–1973)*. Rome: Savelli.

—— (1976). *La politica del femminismo*. Rome: Savelli.

Fraisse, Geneviève (1995). *Muse de la Raison: Démocratie et exclusion des femmes en France*. Paris: Gallimard.

Francescato, Donatella and Prezza, Miretta (ed.) (1979). *Le condizioni della sessualità femminile. Maternità, aborto, consultorio*. Bari: De Donato.

Francome, Colin (1984). *Abortion Freedom: A Worldwide Movement*. London: George Allen and Unwin.

Frauen gegen den §218—Bundesweit Koordination (1991). *Vorsicht 'Lebenschützer!' Die Macht der organisierten Abtreibungsgegner*. Hamburg: Konkret Literatur.

Freeman, Jo (1975). *The Politics of Women's Liberation: A Case Study of an Emerging Social Movement and its Relation to the Policy Process.* New York: Longman.

Fried, Marlene Gerber (ed.) (1990). *From Abortion to Reproductive Freedom: Transforming a Movement.* Boston: South End Press.

Frischer, Dominique (1997). *La Revanche des Misogynes.* Paris: Albin Michel.

Fröschl, Erich and Zoitl, Helge (eds) (1986). *Der österreichische Weg 1970–1985. Fünfzehn Jahre die Österreich verändert haben.* Vienna: Dr Karl Renner Insititut.

Galli, G. (1978). *L'interruzione volontaria della gravidanza.* Milan: Giuffrè.

Gamson, William A. (1975). *The Strategy of Social Protest.* Homewood, Il: Dorsey Press.

Garrow, David J. (1994). *Liberty and Sexuality: The Right to Privacy and the Making of Roe v. Wade.* New York: Macmillan.

Gavigan, Shelley (1992). 'Beyond *Morgentaler*: The Legal Regulation of Reproduction', J. Brodie, S. Gavigan, and J. Jenson (eds), *The Politics of Abortion.* Toronto: Oxford University Press.

Gelb, Joyce (1989). *Feminism and Politics: A Comparative Perspective.* Berkeley: University of California Press.

Geller-Schwartz, Linda (1995). 'An Array of Agencies: Feminism and State Institutions in Canada', in D. M. Stetson and A. G. Mazur (eds), *Comparative State Feminism.* Thousand Oaks, CA: Sage Publications.

German Bishops Conference ([1970] 1972). 'Stellungnahme der Deutschen Bischofkonferenz zur Strafrechtsreform', in Friedrich-Christian Schroeder (ed.), *Abtreibung: Reform des §218,* Berlin: Walter de Gruyter.

Ginsborg, Paul (1998). *Storia d'Italia 1943–1996. Famiglia, Società, Stato.* Turin: Einaudi.

Giovanni Paolo II (1993). *Veritatis Splendor.* Milan: Edizioni Paoline.

—— (1995). *Evaneglium Vitae. Valore e inviolabilità della vita umana.* Casale Monferrato: Piemme.

Girvin, Brian (1986). 'Social Change and Moral Politics: The Irish Constitutional Referendum 1983'. *Political Studies,* 34: 61–81.

Githens, Marianne and Stetson, Dorothy McBride (eds) (1996). *Abortion Politics: Public Policy in Cross-Cultural Perspective.* New York: Routledge.

Giugni, Marco (1995). 'Outcomes of New Social Movements', in H. Kriesi, R. Koopmans, J. Duyvendak, and M. Giugni (eds), *New Social Movements in Western Europe: A Comparative Analysis.* Minneapolis: University of Minnesota Press.

Globe and Mail (1990). 'Abortion Law Would Force Women to Lie, CMA Says'. 7 February.

Goetz, Klaus H. (1996). 'The Federal Constitutional Court', in G. Smith, W. E. Paterson, and S. Padgett (eds), *Developments in German Politics 2.* Duke, NC: Duke University Press.

Goggin, M. L. (ed.) (1993). *Understanding the New Politics of Abortion.* Newbury Park, CA: Sage Publications.

Golias Magazine (1995). 'Les Associations anti-avortement'. March/April: 51–8.

Gößler-Leirer, Irmtraud and Edlinger, Gertrude (1982). *Recht und Menschlichkeit. Eine Dokumentation zur Änderung des §144.* Vienna: Zentralsekretariat der SPÖ.

Gozzini, Mario (1978). *Contro l'aborto fra gli 'abortisti'.* Tonino: Gribaudi.

Grmek, M. (ed.) (1996). *Storia del pensiero medico occidentale.* Rome-Bari: Laterza.

Gruppo Democratico Cristiano alla Camera dei Deputati (1977). *Libro bianco sull'aborto. Cronaca di un dramma della coscienza italiana*. Milan: Rusconi.

Gruppo di Lavoro sui Problemi Etici posti dalla Scienza (1996). 'L'interruzione volontaria della gravidanza. Documento', *Protestantesimo*, 51: 337–42.

Gruppo Femminista per una Medicina della Donna (1976). *Aborto libero? Il metodo Karman e la sperimentazione sulle donne*. Milan: La Salamandra.

Guadagnini, Marila (1987). 'Una rappresentanza limitata: le donne nel Parlamento italiano dal 1948 ad oggi'. *Quaderni di Sociologia*, 4: 190–210.

—— (1997). *Il sistema politico italiano: temi per una discussione*. Turin: Il segnalibro.

Hadley, Janet (1996). *Abortion: Between Freedom and Necessity*. Philadelphia: Temple University Press.

Halimi, Gisele (1973). *La Cause des Femmes*. Paris: Bernard Grasset.

Harding, Sandra (1986). *The Science Question in Feminism*. Ithaca, NY: Cornell University Press.

Harsch, Donna (1997). 'Society, the State, and Abortion in East Germany, 1950–1972'. *American Historical Review*, 102/1: 53–84.

Hassoun, D. (1997). 'Histoire de la légalisation de la contraception et de l'avortement en France', in Paul Cesbron (ed.), *L'Interruption de grossesse depuis la loi Veil: Bilan et Perspectives*. Paris: Flammarion–Médecine-Sciences.

Hemmings, Susan (1979). 'Abortion Demo Special'. *Spare Rib*, December: 20–5.

Henshawe, S., Singh, S., and Haas, T. (1999). 'The Incidence of Abortion Worldwide'. *International Family Planning Perspectives*, 25/Supplement: S30–8.

Hernes, Helga M. (1987). *Welfare State and Woman Power: Essays in State Feminism*. Oslo: Universitetsforlaget.

Hesketh T. (1990). *The Second Partitioning of Ireland: The Abortion Referendum of 1983*. Dublin: Brandsma Books.

Heywood, Paul (1995). *The Government and Politics of Spain*. London: Macmillan.

Hindell, Keith and Simms, Madeleine (1970). *Abortion Law Reformed*. London: Peter Owen.

Hogan, G. and Whyte, G. (1994). *The Irish Constitution*. J. M. Kelly (3rd edn). Dublin: Butterworths.

Hondeghem, Annie and Nelen, Sarah (2000). 'Een beleid op weg. Situering van het Gelijke-Kansenbeleid in België'. *Tijdschrift voor Genderstudies*, 1: 36–48.

Hooghe, Marc (1990). 'De politieke strijd rond abortus 1971–1990'. *Jaarboek seksualiteit, relaties, Geboortenregeling*. Ghent: CGSO.

—— (1994). 'De organisatiestructuur van de Vlaamse vrouwenbeweging. Autonomie en integratie in een gesloten politieke cultuur'. *Sociologische Gids*, 41/2: 144–61.

Hornsby-Smith, Michael and Whelan, C. (1996). 'Religious and Moral Values', in C. Whelan (ed.), *Values and Social Change in Ireland*. Dublin: Gill and Macmillan.

Hug, C. (1999). *The Politics of Sexual Morality in Ireland*. Basingstoke: Macmillan

Inglehart, Ronald (1990). *Culture Shift in Advanced Industrial Society*. Princeton: Princeton University Press.

Ingrao, Chiara and Peretti, Isabella (1998). *Dai diritti delle donne alle politiche di mainstreaming*. Rome: Unità Didattica-Corso di formazione a distanza, BAICRE.

Irish Times (1996). 23 April.

Irish Times (1997a). 19 November.

Irish Times (1997b). 21 November.

Irish Times (1997c). 24 November.

Irish Times (1997d). 29 November.

Irish Times (1997e). 1 December.

Jahn, Gerhard ([1971] 1972). Speech to the Schwäbischen Gesellschaft, 7 October. In Friedrich-Christian Schroeder (ed.), *Abtreibung: Reform des §218*. Berlin: Walter de Gruyter.

Jenson, Jane (1989). 'Ce n'est pas un hasard: The Varieties of French Feminism', in J. Howorth and G. Ross (eds), *Contemporary France, Volume. 3: A Review of Interdisciplinary Studies*. London: Pinter Publishers.

—— (1992). 'Getting to *Morgentaler*: From One Representation to Another', in J. Brodie, S. Gavigan, and J. Jenson (eds), *The Politics of Abortion*. Toronto: Oxford University Press.

—— (1997). 'Competing Representations: The Politics of Abortion in Canada', in C. Andrew and S. Rodgers (eds), *Women and the Canadian State*. Montreal: McGill-Queen's University Press.

—— and Sineau, Mariette (1995). *Mitterrand et les Françaises: un rendez-vous manqué*. Paris: Presses de la Fondation Nationale des Sciences Politiques.

Jourdan, Clara (1993). '194: un cattivo compromesso'. *Democrazia e Diritto*, 2: 231–6.

Kamenitsa, Lynn (1993). 'Social Movement Marginalization in the Democratic Transition: The Case of the East German Women's Movement' (Ph.D. thesis). Indiana University.

—— (1997). 'East German Feminists in the New German Democracy: Opportunities, Obstacles and Adaptation'. *Women and Politics*, 17/3: 41–68.

—— (1998). 'The Complexity of Decline: Explaining the Marginalization of the East German Women's Movement'. *Mobilization: An International Journal*, 3/2: 245–63.

Kaplan, Gisela (1992). *Contemporary Western European Feminism*. London: UCL Press and Allen and Unwin.

Katholischen Arbeitsgemeinschaft für Krankenpflege in Deutschland (1972). 'Stellungnahme zur Änderung des §218 des Strafgesetzbuches', in Friedrich-Christian Schroeder (ed.), *Abtreibung: Reform des §218*. Berlin: Walter de Gruyter.

Katholische Nachrichten Dienst (1995). *Inland*, 28 March.

Kelber, Mim (1994). *Women and Government: New Ways to Political Power*. Westport, CT: Praeger.

Kellough, Gail (1996). *Aborting Law: An Exploration of the Politics of Motherhood and Medicine*. Toronto: University of Toronto Press.

Kenawi, Samirah (1995). *Frauengruppen in der DDR der 8oer Jahre*. Berlin: Grauzone.

Ketting, E. (1978). *Van misdrijf tot hulpverlening. Een analyse van de maatschappelijke betekenis van abortus provocatus in Nederland*, Alphen a.d. Rijn: Samson.

Kiechle, Brigitte (1991). *Selbstbestimmung statt Fremdbestimmung: zur aktuellen Auseinandersetzung um den §218*. Frankfurt a. M.: isp-Verlag.

King, Gary, Keohane, Robert O., and Verba, Sidney (1994). *Designing Social Inquiry: Scientific Inference in Qualitative Research*. Princeton: Princeton University Press.

Kingdon, John W. (1995). *Agendas, Alternatives and Public Policies* (2nd edn). New York: HarperCollins.

Kirejczyk, M. (1996). *Met technologie gezegend. Gender en de omstreden invoering van in vitro fertilisatie in de Nederlandse gezondheidszorg.* Utrecht: Jan van Arkel.

Klein-Schonnefeld, Sabine (1994). 'Germany', in B. Rolston and A. Eggert (eds), *Abortion in the New Europe: A Comparative Handbook.* Westport, CT: Greenwood.

Kolinsky, Eva (1988). 'The West German Greens—A Women's Party?'. *Parliamentary Affairs*, 41/1: 129–48.

Komitee Selbstbestimmung der Frau (ed.) (1980). *Zur Abtreibungssituation in Österreich.* Vienna: Eigenverlag.

Köpl, Regina (1983). 'Frauenpolitik der SPÖ. Reformpolitik im Spannungsfeld bürger-lich-patriarchaler Hegemonie und sozialdemokratischer Partizipationsstrategie' (Ph.D. thesis). Vienna University.

—— (1984). 'SPÖ-Frauenpolitik am Beispiel der Entkriminalisierung des Schwanger-schaftsabbruches'. *Österreichische Zeitschrift für Politikwissenschaft*, 1984/4: 457–65.

Kuhl, Mara (1998). 'Belgische overheidsstructuren voor vrouwenbeleid' (unpublished postgraduate thesis). Centre for Women's Studies, University of Antwerp.

Kurland, Philip B. and Casper, Gerhard (eds) (1990). *Landmark Briefs and Arguments of the Supreme Court of the United States: Constitutional Law, Roe v. Wade (1973).* Frederick, MD: University Publications of America.

Lapis (1998). *Sezione aurea di una rivista.* Rome: il Manifesto.

Lehner, Karin (1985). 'Sozialdemokratische Reformbestrebungen zum §144 in der ersten Republik unter besonderer Berücksichtigung der bevölkerungspolitischen Intentionen' (unpublished thesis). Gruwi-Fakultät, Vienna University.

Le Matin (1979). 2 November.

Le Matin (1982*a*). 5 March.

Le Matin (1982*b*). 17 October.

Le Matin (1982*c*). 21 October.

Le Monde (1982*a*). 5 April.

Le Monde (1982*b*). 5 August.

Le Monde (1982*c*). 6 August.

Le Monde (1982*d*). 12 December.

Le Monde (1982*e*). 19 December.

Le Monde (1991). 20 May.

Le Monde (1992*a*). 19 January.

Le Monde (1992*b*). 12 June.

Le Monde (1992*c*). 7 December.

Le Nouvel Observateur (1971). 5 April.

Lesselier, Claudie and Venner, Fiammetta (1997). *L'Extrême Droite et Les Femmes: Enjeux et Actualité.* Villeurbanne: Editions Golias.

Lewis, Jane (ed.) (1993). *Women and Social Policies in Europe: Work, Family and the State.* Aldershot: Edward Elgar.

Lijphart, Arend (1971). 'Comparative Politics and Comparative Method'. *American Political Science Review*, 65: 682–93.

Lijphart, Arend (1989). *Patterns of Majoritarian and Consensus Government in Twenty One Countries*. New Haven: Yale University Press.

Linz, Juan J. (1993). 'Religión y Política en España', in Rafael Díaz-Salazar and Salvador Giner (eds), *Religión y Sociedad en España*. Madrid: Centro de Investigaciones Sociológicas.

Litchfield, Michael and Kentish, Susan (1974). *Babies for Burning*. London: Serpentine Press.

Liverani, Pier Giorgio (1979). *Aborto anno uno. Fatti e misfatti della legge 194*. Milan: Ares.

Lombardi Vallauri, Luigi (1976). *Abortismo libertario e sadismo*. Milan: Scotti Comuzzi.

Lonzi, Carla (1974). *Sputiamo su Hegel. La donna clitoridea e la donna vaginale*. Milan: Scritti di Rivolta Femminile.

Lotta Femminista (1972). 'L'offensiva'. *Quaderni di Lotta Femminista*,1. Turin: Musolini.

Lovenduski, Joni (1986a). *Women and European Politics: Contemporary Feminism and Public Policy*. Amherst: University of Massachusetts Press.

—— (1986b). 'Parliament, Pressure Groups, Networks and the Women's Movement: The Politics of Abortion Law Reform in Britain (1967–83)', in J. Lovenduski and J. Outshoorn (eds), *The New Politics of Abortion*. London: Sage.

—— (1995). 'An Emerging Advocate: The Equal Opportunities Commission in Great Britain', in D. M. Stetson and A. G. Mazur (eds), *Comparative State Feminism*. Thousand Oaks, CA: Sage Publications.

—— and Outshoorn, Joyce (eds) (1986). *The New Politics of Abortion*. Beverly Hills-London: Sage Publications.

—— and Randall, Vicky (1993). *Contemporary Feminist Politics: Women and Power in Britain*. Oxford: Oxford University Press.

Lowi, T. J. (1963). 'American Business, Public Policy, Case Studies and Political Theory'. *World Politics*, 16: 677–715.

Luker, K. (1984). *Abortion and the Politics of Motherhood*. London: University of California Press.

McAdam, D., McCarthy, J. D., and Zald, M. N. (1996). 'Introduction: Opportunities, Mobilizing Structures, and Framing Processes: Towards a Synthetic, Comparative Perspective on Social Movements', in D. McAdam, J. D. McCarthy, and M. N. Zald, *Comparative Perspectives on Social Movements*. New York: Cambridge University Press.

McCarthy, John and Zald, Mayer (eds) (1979). *The Dynamics of Social Movements: Resource Mobilization*. Cambridge, MA: Winthrop.

McCormick, Peter (1994). *Canada's Courts*. Toronto: James Lorimer and Co.

McDonnell, Kathleen (1984). *Not an Easy Choice: A Feminist Re-Examines Abortion*. Toronto: Women's Press.

McLaren, Christie (1990). 'MD's and the New Abortion Law', *Globe and Mail*, 19 June.

Magli, Ida (1995). *Sulla dignità della donna. La violenza sulle donne, il pensiero di Wojtyla*. Parma: Guanda.

Mahon, E. (1987). 'Women's Rights and Catholicism in Ireland'. *New Left Review*,166/November–December: 53–78.

—— (1994). 'Ireland: A Private Patriarchy'. *Environment and Planning*, 26: 1277–96.

—— (1995). 'Ireland's Policy Machinery: The Ministry for Women's Affairs and the Joint Oireachtas Committee on Women's Rights', in D. M. Stetson and A. G. Mazur (eds), *Comparative State Feminism*. Thousand Oaks, CA: Sage Publications.

—— (1996). 'Women's Rights and Catholicism in Ireland', in M. Threlfall (ed.), *Mapping the Women's Movement*. London and New York: Verso.

—— and Conlon, C. (1996). *Legal Abortions Carried Out in England on Women Normally Resident in the Republic Of Ireland*. (*Appendix 21*)Report of the Constitution Review Group, Dublin: Stationery Office.

——, —— and Dillow, L. (1998) *Women and Crisis Pregnancy in Ireland*. Dublin: Stationery Office.

Malcolmson, Patrick and Myers, Richard (1996). *The Canadian* Peterborough, Ontario: Broadview Press.

Maleck-Lewy, Eva (1994). *Und wenn ich nun Schwanger bin? Frauen zwischen Selbstbestimmung und Bevormundung*. Berlin: Aufbau Taschenbuch.

—— (1995). 'Between Self-determination and State Supervision: Women and the Abortion Law in Post-unification Germany'. *Social Politics: International Studies in Gender, State, and Society*, 2/1: 62–75.

—— and Ferree, Myra Marx (1996). 'Talking about Women and Wombs: Discourse about Abortion and Reproductive Rights in the GDR During and After the "Wende"'. Paper presented at the Conference on Gender and Reproductive Politics in Eastern Europe. Ciocco, Italy.

Mandel, Michael (1994.) *The Charter of Rights and the Legalization of Politics in Canada* (revised edn). Toronto: Thompson Educational Publishing.

Marín, José A. (1996). *Aborto y Constitución*. Jaén: Universidad de Jaén.

Maroney, Heather Jon and Luxton, Meg (eds) (1987). *Feminism and Political Economy: Women's Work, Women's Struggles*. Toronto: Methuen.

Marques-Pereira, Bérengère (1989). *L'avortement en Belgique. De la clandestinité au débat politique*. Brussels: Éditions de l'Université de Bruxelles.

Marsh, David and Chambers, Joanna (1981). *Abortion Politics*. London: Junction Books.

Martini, Paolo and Dell'Osso, Giuseppe (1979). *Aborto: aspetti medico-legali della nuova disciplina*. Milan: Giuffrè.

Mattern, Michael G. (1991). 'German Abortion Law: The Unwanted Child of Reunification'. *Loyola of Los Angeles International and Comparative Law Journal*, 13: 643–94.

Mazur, Amy (1995). 'Strong State and Symbolic Reform: The Ministère des Droits de la Femme in France', in D. M. Stetson and A. G. Mazur (eds), *Comparative State Feminism*. Thousand Oaks, CA: Sage Publications.

—— (ed.) (2001). *State Feminism, Women's Movements, and Job Training Policy in the Global Economy: Making Democracies Work*. New York: Routledge.

—— and Parry, Janine (1998). 'Choosing Not to Choose in Comparative Policy Research Design: the Case of the Research Network on Gender, Politics and the State'. *Journal of Policy Studies*, 26/3: 384–95.

Meier, Marion and Oubaid, Monika (1987). *Mütter—die besseren Frauen*. Braunschweig: Gerd J. Holtzmeyer.

Melchiori, Paola (1995). *Crinali. Le zone oscure del femminismo*. Milan: La Tartaruga.

Melich, Tanya (1998). *The Republican War Against Women* (updated edn). New York: Bantam Books.

Memoria (1987). 'Il movimento femminista negli anni '70', 19–20/1–2.

—— (1989). 'Genere e soggetto. Strategie del femminismo fra Europa e America', special issue, 25/1.

Merz, Jon F., Jackson, Catherine A., and Klerman, Jacob A. (1995). 'A Review of Abortion Policy: Legality, Medicaid Funding, and Parental Involvement, 1967–1994'. *Women's Rights Law Reporter*, 17/1: 1–61.

Mesner, Maria (1993). 'Die Auseinandersetzung um den Schwangerschaftsabbruch in Österreich. Zur politischen Kultur der Zweiten Republik' (unpublished dissertation). GEWI-Fakultät, Vienna University.

MFPF (Mouvement Français pour le Planning Familial) (1982). *Contraception et Avortement: le droit des femmes*. Paris: MFPF.

—— (1982). *Avortement: Toujours pas de remboursement!* Paris: MFPF.

—— (1982). *D'une Revolte à une Lutte: 25 Ans d'histoire du Planning Familial*. Paris: Editions Tierce.

—— (1983). Communiqué de Presse, 24 February.

Milan Women's Bookstore Collective (1990). *Sexual Difference: A Theory of Social-Symbolic Practice*. Bloomington: Indiana University Press. Translation of Libreria delle Donne di Milano (1987). *Non credere di avere dei diritti*. Turin: Rosenberg and Sellier.

Millns, Susan and Sheldon, Sally (1998). 'Abortion', in P. Cowley (ed.), *Conscience and Parliament*. London: Cass.

Mitteldeutscher Express (1994). 21 January.

Mohr, James C. (1978). Abortion in America: The Origins and Evolution of National Policy, 1800-1900. New York: Oxford University Press.

Morris, Barbara and Norton, Noelle (1998). 'Building Communities from the White House: Clinton's Office of Women's Initiatives and Outreach.' Paper presented at the annual conference of the American Political Science Association, Boston, August.

Morton, F. L. (1992a). Pro-Choice vs. Pro-Life: Abortion and the Courts in Canada. Norman: University of Oklahoma Press.

—— (ed.) (1992b). Law, Politics and the Judicial Process in Canada (2nd edn) Calgary: University of Calgary Press.

—— and Knopff, Rainer (2000). The Charter Revolution and the Court Party. Peterborough, Ont: Broadview Press.

Morton, Mildred (1998). 'The Morgentaler Judgment: How the Decisions Differ' (Backgrounder, Publication BP-174E). Ottawa: Research Division, Library of Parliament.

Mossuz-Lavau, Janine (1991). Les lois de l'amour: Les politiques de la sexualité en France (1950–1990). Paris: Editions Payot.

—— and Sineau, Mariette (1981). 'France', in J. Lovenduski and J. Hills (eds), The Politics of the Second Electorate: Women and Public Participation. London: Routledge and Kegan Paul.

Movimento di Liberazione della Donna–Partito Radicale (1975). Contro l'aborto di classe (ed. M. Teodori). Rome: Savelli.

Mujeres (1983). o

—— (1984a). 1

315

——— (1984b). 2

——— (1984c). 4

Müller, Wolfgang C. (1996a). 'Political Parties', in V. Lauber (ed.), Contemporary Austrian Politics. Boulder, CO: Westview Press.

——— (1996b). 'Political Institutions', in V. Lauber (ed.), Contemporary Austrian Politics. Boulder, CO: Westview Press.

Muraro, Luisa (1991). L'ordine simbolico della madre. Rome: Editori Riuniti.

Muth, Ulrich (1994). Die Diskussion über eine Reform des strafrechtlichen Abtreibungsverbots in der Bundesrepublik Deutschland bis zum 15. Strafrechtsänderungsgesetz vom 18.05.1976. Munich: Verlag v. Florentz.

NAC (National Action Committee on the Status of Women) (1990). 'Submission to the Parliamentary Committee on Bill C-43'. Toronto: NAC (7 February).

Nash, Mary (1986). 'Ordenamiento Jurídico y Realidad Social del Aborto en España: Una Aproximación Histórica', in M. C. García-Nieto (ed.), Ordenamiento Jurídico y Realidad Social de las Mujeres: Siglos XVI a XX. Madrid: Universidad Autónoma de Madrid.

New York Times (1977). 13 July.

Newton, Michael T. and Donaghy, Peter J. (1997). Institutions of Modern Spain: A Political and Economic Guide. Cambridge: Cambridge University Press.

Noi Donne (1995). 'La prima parola e l'ultima', ed. Serena Tinari. Rome.

O'Connor, Karen (1980). Women's Organizations' Use of the Courts. Lexington, MA: Lexington Books.

——— (1996). No Neutral Ground. Boulder, CO: Westview Press.

O'Neil, Maureen and Sutherland, Sharon (1997). 'The Machinery of Women's Policy: Implementing the RCSW', in C. Andrew and S. Rodgers (eds), Women and the Canadian State. Montreal: McGill-Queen's University Press.

Oroff, Ann Shola (1993). 'Gender and the Social Rights of Citizenship: The Comparative Analysis of Gender Relations and Welfare States'. American Sociological Review, 58: 303–28.

Outshoorn, Joyce (1986a). De politieke strijd rondom de abortuswetgeving in Nederland 1964–1984. Den Haag: VUGA.

——— (1986b). 'The Rules of the Game: Abortion Politics in The Netherlands', in J. Lovenduski and J. Outshoorn, The New Politics of Abortion. London/Beverly Hills: Sage Publications.

——— (1994). 'Between Movement and Government: "Femocrats" in the Netherlands', in H. Kriesi (ed.), Schweizerisches Jahrbuch fur Politische Wissenschaft, 34. Bern: Haupt.

——— (1995). 'Administrative Accommodation in the Netherlands: The Case of the Department for the Coordination of Equality Policy', in D. M. Stetson and A. G. Mazur, Comparative State Feminism. Thousand Oaks/London/Delhi: Sage Publications.

——— (1996a). 'The Meaning of "Woman" in Abortion Policy: A Comparative Approach'. Paper presented at the conference of the American Political Science Association, San Francisco, August.

——— (1996b). 'The Stability of Compromise: Abortion Politics in Western Europe', in

Marianne Githens and Dorothy McBride Stetson (eds), Abortion Politics: Public Policy in Cross-cultural Perspective. New York and London: Routledge.

Outshoorn, Joyce (1998). 'Furthering the Cause: Femocrat Strategies in National Government', in J. Bussemaker and R. Voet (eds), Gender, Participation and Citizenship in the Netherlands. Aldershot: Ashgate.

—— (2000). 'Abortion in the Netherlands: The Successful Pacification of a Controversial Issue', in H. Krabbendam and H. M. ten Napel (eds), Regulating Morality: A Comparison of the Role of the State in Mastering the Mores in the Netherlands and the United States. Antwerp/Apeldoorn: Maklu.

Pal, Leslie (1992). 'How Ottawa Dithers: The Conservatives and Abortion Policy', in F. Abele (ed.), How Ottawa Spends 1991–1992. Ottawa: Carleton University Press.

Palini, Anselmo (1977). L'aborto nella discussione teologica cattolica. Brescia: Queriniana.

—— (1992). 'Aborto: un dibattito da non chiudere'. Vita e Pensiero, 1: 600–8.

Palo, Gianangelo (ed.) (1977). L'aborto nella discussione teologica cattolica. Brescia: Queriniana.

Paltiel, Frieda (1997). 'State Initiatives: Impetus and Effects', in C. Andrew and S. Rodgers (eds), Women and the Canadian State. Montreal: McGill-Queen's University Press.

Paolo VI (1968). Humanae Vitae. Lettera enciclica, Turin: Ed. Paoline.

Paolozzi, Letizia and Leiss, Alberto (1999). Un paese sottosopra. Milan: Pratiche.

Parti Socialiste (1979). Proposition de loi du PS [avortement]. Paris: Parti Socialiste.

Passeri, Grazia and Pergameno, Silvio (1981). Referendum: quali, come. Roma: Quaderni Radicali.

Pateman, Carol (1988). The Sexual Contract. Stanford: Stanford University Press.

Pattis, Eva (1995). Aborto Perdita e Rinnovamento. Un paradosso nella ricerca dell'identità femminile. Como: Ed. RED.

Pelinka, Anton (1998). Austria: Out of the Shadow of the Past. Boulder, CO: Westview Press

Peretti, Isabella and Socrate, Daniela (1988). 'L'aborto fra norma e coscienza'. Democrazia e Diritto, 24/3–4: 223–48.

Phillips, Anne (1991). Engendering Democracy. University Park: University of Pennsylvania Press.

—— (1995). The Politics of Presence. Oxford: Oxford University Press.

Picard, Andre (1990). 'Quebec Clinics Pledge Defiance of Law if Criminal Penalties for Abortion Revived'. Globe and Mail, 29 May.

Pieroni Bortolotti, Francesca (1963). Alle origini del movimento femminile in Italia. Turin: Einaudi.

—— (1978). 'Movimento femmnista e movimento operaio'. Critica Marxista, 16/5: 79–109.

Pierson, Ruth R. (1993a). 'The Politics of the Body', in R. Pierson, M. Cohen, P. Bourne, and P. Masters (eds), Canadian Women's Issues, Volume I: Strong Voices. Toronto: James Lorimer and Company.

—— (1993b). 'The Mainstream Women's Movement and the Politics of Difference', in R. Pierson, M. Cohen, P. Bourne, and P. Masters (eds), Canadian Women's Issues, Volume I: Strong Voices. Toronto: James Lorimer and Company.

—— (1993c). 'The Canadian Women's Movement', in R. Pierson, M. Cohen, P. Bourne, and P. Masters (eds), *Canadian Women's Issues, Volume I: Strong Voices*. Toronto: James Lorimer and Company.

——, Cohen, Marjorie Griffin, Bourne, Paula, and Masters, Philinda (eds) (1993). *Canadian Women's Issues, Volume I: Strong Voices*. Toronto: James Lorimer and Company.

Pinl, Claudia (1989). 'Das Ende des "Heiligen Grals": "Neuer Feminismus" in der Bundestagfraktion der Grünen'. *Beiträge zur feministischen Theorie und Praxis*, 12/24: 133–44.

Pipes, Mary (1986). *Understanding Abortion*. London: Women's Press.

Pirovano, Piero (1981). *Per la vita oltre il referendum. Nascita e storia di un movimento*. Milan: Edizioni amici per la vita.

Pitch, Tamar (1998). *Un diritto per due*. Milano: Il Saggiatore.

Pitkin, Hanna Fenichel (1967). *The Concept of Representation*. Berkeley: University of California Press.

Pohoryles, Ronald (1981). 'Determinanten und Resultate der österreichischen Strafrechtsreform in den siebziger Jahren'. *Österreichische Zeitschrift für Politikwissenschaft*, 1981/1: 39–50. Vienna: Verlag für Gesellschaftskritik.

Potts, Malcolm, Diggory, Peter, and Peel, John (1977). *Abortion*. Cambridge: Cambridge University Press.

Pro-choice Alliance (1990). *Abortion–Who Decides? Towards a Woman's Choice on Abortion*. Lewes: Pro-choice Alliance (pamphlet).

Przeworski, Adam (1991). *Democracy and the Market: Political and Economic Reforms in Eastern Europe and Latin America*. Cambridge: Cambridge University Press.

Pursch, Günter (ed.) (1992). *§218, die Entscheidung: das Wortprotokoll des Deutschen Bundestages vom 25. Juni 1992*. Frankfurt: Ullstein.

Quotidien du Médecins (1982). 'Avortement—Non Remboursements'. 14 September: 31.

Ravera, Camilla (1979). *Breve storia del movimento femminile in Italia*. Rome: Editori Riuniti.

Razack, Sherene (1991). *Canadian Feminism and the Law: The Women's Legal Education and Action Fund and the Pursuit of Equality*. Toronto: Second Story Press.

Reid, M. (1992). 'Abortion Law in Ireland after the Maastrict Referendum', in A. Smyth (ed.), *The Abortion Papers*. Dublin: Attic Press.

Richardson, Jo (1990). 'Human Fertilisation and Embryology Bill'. *Newsletter of the Shadow Ministry for Women*. London: Labour Party.

Rivolta Femminile (1971). *Sessualità femminile e aborto*. July.

Rochon, Thomas R. and Mazmanian, Daniel A. (1993). 'Social Movements and the Policy Process'. *Annals of the American Academy of Political and Social Science*, 528: 75–87.

Rodotà, Stefano (ed.) (1993). *Questioni di bioetica*. Rome-Bari: Laterza.

—— (1995). *Tecnologie e diritti*. Bologna: Il Mulino.

Rolston, Bill and Eggert, Anna (eds) (1994). *Abortion in the New Europe: A Comparative Handbook*. Westport: Greenwood.

Rosenberg, Dorothy (1996). 'Distant Relations: Class, "Race," and National Origin in the German Women's Movement'. *Women's Studies International Forum*, 19/1–2: 145–54.

318

Rosenfeld, Rachel A. and Ward, Kathryn B. (1996). 'Evolution of the Contemporary U.S. Women's Movement'. *Research in Social Movements, Conflict and Change*, 19. Greenwich, CT: JAI Press.

Rossanda, Rossana (1978). *Le altre. Conversazioni a Radiotre sui rapporti tra donne e politica, libertà, fraternità, uguaglianza, democrazia, fascismo, resistenza, stato, partito, rivoluzione, femminismo.* Milan: Bompiani.

Rossi-Doria, Anna (1996). *Diventare cittadine*. Firenze: Giunti.

Roudy, Yvette (1991). 'L'avortement, quinze ans après'. *Le Figaro*, 5 July.

Rowbotham, Sheila (1989). *The Past is Before Us: Feminism in Action since the 1960s.* Boston: Beacon Press.

Sabbadini, Linda Laura (1998). 'Rilievi statistici sulla fecondità in Italia'. Paper presented at the workshop on *Ragioniamo di maternità*, Rome, 28 May.

Safran, William (1995). *The French Polity* (4th edn). White Plains, NY: Longman Group.

Sainsbury, Diane (ed.) (1994). *Gendering Welfare States*. London: Sage.

Salemi, Rosellina (1989). *Sulla pelle delle donne. Mangiagalli: aborti medici politici. Una vicenda che ha lacerato il Paese.* Milan: Rizzoli.

Sanna, Francesco (ed.) (1989). *L'aborto in Italia. Dati e organizzazioni dei servizi a dieci ani dalla legge.* Rome: Ed. Lavoro.

Sardi, Paolo (1975). *L'aborto ieri e oggi.* Brescia: Paideia.

Sartori, Giovanni (1970). 'Concept Misformation in Comparative Politics'. *American Political Science Review*, 74: 1033–53.

Sauer, Birgit (1995). '"Doing Gender": Das Parlament als Ort der Geschlecterkonstruktion', in A. Burkhardt, W. Dieckmann, K. P. Fritzsche, and R. Rytlewski (eds), *Sprache des Parlaments und Semiotik der Demokratie.* Berlin: Walter de Gruyter.

Sawer, Marian (1990). *Sisters in Suits: Women and Public Policy in Australia.* Sydney: Allen and Unwin.

—— (1993). 'Reclaiming Social Liberalism: The Women's Movement and the State'. *Journal of Australian Studies*, 37: 1–21.

Scanlon, Geraldine (1990). 'El Movimiento Feminista en España, 1900–1985: Logros y Dificultades', in J. Astelarra (ed.), *Participación Política de las Mujeres.* Madrid: Centro de Investigaciones Sociológicas and Siglo XXI.

Schattschneider, E. E (1960). *The Semi-sovereign People: A Realist's View of Democracy in America.* New York: Holt, Rinehart and Winston.

Schneider, Anne and Ingram, Helen (1993). 'Social Construction of Target Populations: Implications for Politics and Policy'. *American Political Science Review*, 87: 334–47.

Scheppele, Kim Lane (1996). 'Constitutionalizing Abortion', in M. Githens and D. M. Stetson (eds), *Abortion Politics: Public Policy in Cross Cultural Perspective.* New York: Routledge.

Schroeder, Friedrich-Christian (ed.) (1972). *Abtreibung: Reform des §218.* Berlin: Walter de Gruyter.

Schwarzer, Alice (1990). 'Jetzt eine neue Frauenbewegung'. *Emma*, 4: 4–6.

Science and Technology Group (1991). 'In the Wake of the Alton Bill: Science, Technology and Reproductive Politics', in S. Franklin, C. Lury, and J. Stacey (eds), *Off-Center: Feminism and Cultural Studies.* London: Harper Collins Academic.

Sgreggia, Elio S. (1974). 'L'insegnamento dei Padri della Chiesa in tema d'aborto'. *Medicina e Morale*, 3: 398–417.

Sheldon, Sally (1997). *Beyond Control: Medical Power and Abortion Law*. London: Pluto Press.

Simms, Madeleine (1994). 'Britain', in B. Rolston and A. Eggert (eds), *Abortion in the New Europe: A Comparative Handbook*. Westport, CT: Greenwood Press.

Simonds, Wendy (1995). 'Feminism on the Job: Confronting Opposition in Abortion Work', in M. M. Ferree and P. Y. Martin (eds), *Feminist Organisations: Harvest of the New Women´s Movement*. Philadelphia: Temple University Press.

Smit, J. (1966). 'Met u, over u, zonder u'. *De Nieuwe Stem*, 21: 719–21.

—— (1984). 'De politieke beperkingen van het goede hart', in J. Smit (ed.), *Er is een land waar vrouwen willen wonen. Teksten 1967–1981*. Amsterdam: Sara.

Smith, T. A. (1975). *The Comparative Policy Process*. Santa Barbara, CA: Clio Books.

Snow, David A. and Benford, Robert D. (1992). 'Master Frames and Cycles of Protest', in A. D. Morris and C. M. Mueller (eds), *Frontiers in Social Movement Theory*. New Haven: Yale University Press.

Social Democratic Party of Germany (1974). *Das Argument §218*. Bonn: Vorstand der SPD.

Socialistische Vrouwen (n.d.). *Abortus uit het strafrecht: een lange weg*. Brussels.

Sottosopra (1983). *Più donne che uomini*, 4 October.

—— (1996). *È accaduto non per caso*. Milan: Libreria delle Donne.

Spagnoletti, Rosanna (ed.) (1978). *I movimenti femministi in Italia*. Roma: Savelli.

Spalter-Roth, Roberta and Schreiber, Ronnie (1995). 'Outsider Issues and Insider Tactics: Strategic Tensions in the Women's Policy Network during the 1980s', in M. M. Ferree and P. Y. Martin (eds), *Feminist Organizations*. Philadelphia: Temple University Press.

Staggenborg, Suzanne (1991). *The Pro-Choice Movement: Organization and Activism in the Abortion Conflict*. New York: Oxford University Press.

Steinberg, Deborah L. (1991). 'Adversarial Politics: The Legal Construction of Abortion', in S. Franklin, C. Lury, and J. Stacey (eds), *Off-Center: Feminism and Cultural Studies*. London: Harper Collins Academic.

Stetson, Dorothy McBride (1987). *Women's Rights in France*. Westport, CT: Greenwood Press.

—— (1997). *Women's Rights in the U.S.A.: Policy Conflict and Gender Roles*. New York: Garland.

—— and Mazur, Amy G. (eds) (1995). *Comparative State Feminism*. Thousand Oaks: Sage Publications.

—— (2000). 'Women's Movements and the State: Job-Training Policy in France and the U.S'. *Political Research Quarterly*, 53/3: 597–623.

Stone, Deborah (1997). *Policy Paradox: The Art of Political Decision Making*. New York: Norton.

Soper, J. Christopher (1994). 'Political Structures and Interest Group Activism: A Comparison of the British and American Pro-Life Movements'. *The Social Science Journal*, 31/3: 319–34.

Studlar, Donley, and Tatalovich, Raymond (1996). 'Abortion Policy in the United States and Canada: Do Institutions Matter?', in M. Githens and D. M. Stetson (eds), *Abortion Politics: Public Policy in Cross-Cultural Perspective*. New York: Routledge.

Sunday Times (1975). 30 March.

Sundman, Kerstin (1999). *Between the Home and the Institutions: The Feminist Movement in Madrid, Spain*. Gothenburg, Sweden: Acta Universitatis Gothoburgensis.

Talos, Emmerich (1996). 'Corporatism: The Austrian Model', in V. Lauber (ed.), *Contemporary Austrian Politics*. Boulder, CO: Westview Press.

Tarrow, Sidney (1989). *Struggling to Reform: Social Movements and Policy Change during Cycles of Protest* (Western Societies Program, Occasional Paper No. 21). Ithaca, NY: Cornell University.

Tatafiore, Roberta, and Tozzi, Silvia (eds) (1989). *Noi Donne*, special issue No. 5.

Tatalovich, Raymond (1997). *The Politics of Abortion in the United States and Canada: A Comparative Study*. Armonk, NY: M. E. Sharpe.

Tettamanzi, Dionigi (1975). *La comunità cristiana e l'aborto*. Rome: Edizioni Paoline.

Threlfall, Monica (1985). 'The Women's Movement in Spain'. *New Left Review*, 151: 44–73.

—— (1996). 'Feminist Politics and Social Change in Spain', in M. Threlfall (ed.), *Mapping the Women's Movement: Feminist Politics and Social Transformation in the North*. London and New York: Verso.

—— (1998). 'State Feminism or Party Feminism?: Feminist Politics and the Spanish Institute of Women'. *The European Journal of Women's Studies*, 5/1: 69–93.

Traverso, Carlo Emilio (1977). *La tutela costituzionale della persona umana prima della nascita*. Milan: Giuffrè.

Tremblay, Manon and Andrew, Caroline (eds) (1998). *Women and Political Representation in Canada*. Ottawa: University of Ottawa Press.

Trujillo, Gracia (1999). 'El Movimiento Feminista como Actor Político en España: El Caso de la Aprobación de la Ley de Despenalización del Aborto de 1985'. Paper presented at the meeting of the Spanish Association of Political Science and Public Administration, Grenada, 30 September–2 October.

UNIFEM: http://undp.org/unifem

Unione Giuristi Cattolici Italiani (1975). *Difesa del diritto alla nascita*. Rome: Giuffrè.

United Nations (1992). *Women in Politics and Decision-Making in the late Twentieth Century*. Dordrecht: Martinus Nijhoff.

Vairo, Gaetano (1979). 'Lo stato di necessità nell'aborto'. *Rivista di polizia*, 1: 3–24.

Valentini, Chiara (1997). *Le donne fanno paura*. Milan: il Saggiatore.

Valiente, Celia (1995). 'The Power of Persuasion: The *Instituto de la Mujer* in Spain', in D. M. Stetson and A. G. Mazur (eds), *Comparative State Feminism*. Thousand Oaks, CA: Sage Publications.

—— (1997). 'State Feminism and Gender Equality Policies: The Case of Spain (1983–95)', in F. Gardiner (ed.), *Sex Equality Policy in Western Europe*. London and New York: Routledge.

Vallance, Elizabeth (1979). *Women in the House: A Study of Women Members of Parliament*. London: The Athlone Press.

Van De Lanotte, Johan, Bracke, Siegfried and Goedertier, Geert (1998). *België voor Beginners: Wegwijs in het Belgisch Labyrint*. Brugge: Die Keure.

Vander Stichele, Caroline (1983). 'Het abortusprobleem in de feministische pers: confrontatie met de moraaltheologische reflectie' (unpublished licentiate's thesis). Katholic University of Louvain, Department of Theology.

Van Mechelen, Renée (1979). *Uit eigen beweging. Balans van de vrouwenbeweging in Vlaanderen, 1970–1978.* Louvain: Kritak.

—— (1996). *De meerderheid. Een minderheid. De vrouwenbeweging in Vlaanderen: feiten, herinneringen en bedenkingen omtrent de tweede golf.* Louvain: Van Halewyck.

Vanmeenen, Elsy (1991). 'De betekenis van de Feministisch-socialistische koördinatie in de vrouwenbeweging in de strijd om abortus uit het strafrecht te halen (1976–1982)' (unpublished licentiate's paper). Department of History, Free University of Brussels.

Van Molle, Leen and Gubin, Eliane (1998). *Vrouw en politiek in België.* Tielt: Lannoo.

Venner, Fiammetta (1995). *L'Opposition à L'Avortement: du lobby au commando.* Paris: Berg International Éditeurs.

Verrycken, Mariette (1977). 'De werkzaamheden van de staatscommissie voor ethische problemen'. *Res Publica,* 19/2: 285–303.

Vickers, Jill, Rankin, Pauline, and Appelle, Christine (1993). *Politics as if Women Mattered: A Political Analysis of the National Action Committee on the Status of Women.* Toronto: University of Toronto Press.

Viennau, David (1989). 'Abortion: Commons Deadlocked, Survey Says'. *Montreal Gazette,* 22 July.

Vinckx, Els (1991). 'De katholieke zuil in Vlaanderen t.a.v. de abortusproblematiek (1955–1974)' (licentiate's thesis). Department of History, Free University of Brussels.

Walker, G. (1990). 'The Conceptual Politics of Struggle: Wife Battering, the Women's Movement and the State'. *Studies in Political Economy,* 33: 63–90.

Weinziel, Erika (1986). 'Kirche seit 1970', in E. Fröschl and H. Zoitl (eds), *Der österreichische Weg1970–1985. Fünfzehn Jahre, die Österreich verändert haben.* Vienna: Europa Verlag.

Wiarda, Howard (1993). *Introduction to Comparative Politics: Concepts and Processes.* Belmont, CA: Wadsworth.

Wilding, Norman and Laundy, Philip (1972). *An Encyclopedia of Parliament* (4th edn). London: Cassell.

Wilsford, David (1991). *Doctors and the State: The Politics of Health Care in France and the United States.* Durham, NC: Duke University Press.

Wilson, Jane (1989). 'Doctor Calls Bill "An Insult"'. *Ottawa Citizen,* 4 November.

Wimmer-Puchinger, Beate (1988). *Frauen im Schwangerschaftskonflikt –Beratungsangebote.* Vienna: Ludwig Bolzmann Institut für Schwangerenbetreuung und Geburtenregelung.

Witte, Els (1990). 'Twintig jaar strijd rond de abortuswetgeving in België (1970–1990)'. *Res Publica,* 32/4: 427–87.

—— (1993). 'De liberalisering van de abortuswetgeving in België', in M. Scheys (ed.), *Rapporten en Perspectieven omtrent Vrouwenstudies. Deel4: Abortus.* Brussels.

Women Watch 2001. http://www.un.org/womenwatch

Women's Legal Education and Action Fund (LEAF) (1990). 'Submission to the Legislative Committee of Parliament on Bill C-43'. 30 January.

Women's Legal Education and Action Fund (LEAF) (1996). *Equality and the Charter: Ten Years of Feminist Advocacy Before the Supreme Court of Canada.* Toronto: Emond Montgomery Publications.

Zald, Mayer N. (1996). 'Culture, Ideology, and Strategic Framing', in D. McAdam, J. D. McCarthy, and M. N. Zald (eds), *Comparative Perspectives on Social Movements: Political Opportunities, Mobilizing Structures, and Cultural Framings.* Cambridge: Cambridge University Press.

Zarri, Adriana (1981). *I guardiani del sabato. Riflessioni sulla chiesa italiana dopo il referendum sull'aborto.* Rome: COM-Nuovi Tempi.

Zincone, Giovanna (1992). *Da sudditi a cittadini.* Bologna: il Mulino.

❖ Index

Printed in the United States
107829LV00001B/71/A

9 780199 242665